Together in music

Together in music

Coordination, expression, participation

Edited by

Renee Timmers
Freya Bailes
Helena Daffern

OXFORD
UNIVERSITY PRESS

UNIVERSITY PRESS

Great Clarendon Street, Oxford, OX2 6DP,
United Kingdom

Oxford University Press is a department of the University of Oxford.
It furthers the University's objective of excellence in research, scholarship,
and education by publishing worldwide. Oxford is a registered trade mark of
Oxford University Press in the UK and in certain other countries

First Edition published in 2022

Impression: 1

Published in the United States of America by Oxford University Press
198 Madison Avenue, New York, NY 10016, United States of America

British Library Cataloguing in Publication Data

Data available

Library of Congress Control Number: 2021935955

ISBN 978–0–19–886076–1

DOI: 10.1093/oso/9780198860761.001.0001

Printed and bound by
CPI Group (UK) Ltd, Croydon, CR0 4YY

Dedicated to Kia Ng for his enthusiasm and inspiration to bring together music and science to investigate ensemble performance

Contents

PART 2. EXPRESSION, COMMUNICATION, AND INTERACTION

PART 3. PARTICIPATION, DEVELOPMENT, AND WELLBEING

Contributors

Freya Bailes, Associate Professor in Music Psychology, School of Music, University of Leeds, Leeds, UK

Dawn Bennett, Assistant Provost and Director of the Transformation CoLab with Bond University, Robina, Queensland, Australia

Frédéric Bevilacqua, Head of the Sound Music Movement Interaction, IRCAM, CNRS-Sorbonne Université, Paris, France

Laura Bishop, Postdoctoral Research Fellow, RITMO, University of Oslo, Oslo, Norway

Mary T. Black, Visiting Research Fellow, School of Music, University of Leeds, Leeds, UK

Alana Blackburn, Senior Lecturer in Music, School of Humanities, Arts and Social Sciences, University of New England, Armidale, Australia

Michael Bonshor, Course Director, Music Psychology in Education, Performance and Wellbeing, Department of Music, University of Sheffield, Sheffield, UK

Dermot Breslin, Senior Lecturer in Organisational Behaviour, Management School, University of Sheffield, Sheffield, UK

Florian Buchheit, Research Assistant, Swiss Center for Affective Science, University of Geneva, Geneva, Switzerland

Karen Burland, Professor of Applied Music Psychology, School of Music, University of Leeds, Leeds, UK

David A. Camlin, Lecturer in Music Education, Royal College of Music, London, UK

Carlos Cancino-Chacón, Assistant Professor at the Institute of Computational Perception, Johannes Kepler University Linz, Linz, Austria

Carlo Chiorri, Associate Professor in Psychometrics, Department of Educational Sciences, University of Genoa, Genoa, Italy

Eric F. Clarke, Heather Professor of Music, Faculty of Music, University of Oxford, Oxford, UK

Sara D'Amario, Postdoctoral Research Associate, Department of Music Acoustics, University of Music and Performing Arts, Vienna, Austria

Helena Daffern, Associate Professor in Audio and Music Technology, Department of Electronic Engineering, University of York, York, UK

Jane W. Davidson, Professor of Creative and Performing Arts, Faculty of Fine Arts and Music, University of Melbourne, Melbourne, Australia

Katie Edwards, Research Assistant, Department of Neuropsychology, University of Michigan, Ann Arbor, MI, USA

Helen J. English, Associate Professor of Music, School of Creative Industries, University of Newcastle, Newcastle City Precinct, Australia

Çağrı Erdem, PhD Fellow, RITMO Centre for Interdisciplinary Studies in Rhythm, Time, and Motion, Department of Musicology, University of Oslo, Oslo, Norway

Daniel Galbreath, Scholarship and Communications Coordinator, Wyoming Community Foundation, Laramie, Wyoming, USA

Sandra Garrido, Senior Lecturer, School of Psychology and MARCS Institute for Brain, Behaviour and Development, Western Sydney University, Sydney, Australia

Satinder Gill, Research Affiliate, Centre for Music and Science, University of Cambridge, Cambridge, UK

Jane Ginsborg, Professor of Music Psychology, Centre for Music Performance Research, Royal Northern College of Music, Manchester, UK

Donald Glowinski, Lecturer and Senior Researcher, Department of Psychology and Educational Sciences, Swiss Center for Affective Sciences, University of Geneva, Geneva, Switzerland

Werner Goebl, Professor of Music Acoustics and Performance Science, Department of Music Acoustics—Wiener Klangstil (IWK), University of Music and Performing Arts Vienna, Vienna, Austria

Didier Grandjean, Professor, Department of Psychology and Educational Sciences, Swiss Center for Affective Sciences, University of Geneva, Geneva, Switzerland

Angelina Gutiérrez, Associate Professor of Music, Theological Studies, English Studies and Education, Saint Scholastica's College, Manila, Philippines

Elizabeth Haddon, Senior Lecturer in Music, Department of Music, University of York, York, UK

Alexander Refsum Jensenius, Professor of Music Technology, RITMO Centre for Interdisciplinary Studies in Rhythm, Time and Motion, Department of Musicology, University of Oslo, Oslo, Norway

Kathryn King, Doctoral Researcher, Faculty of Music, University of Oxford, Oxford, UK

Ryan Kirkbride, Doctoral Researcher, School of Music, University of Leeds, Leeds, UK

Gunter Kreutz, Professor of Systematic Musicology, Faculty of Linguistics and Cultural Studies, Carl von Ossietzky University Oldenburg, Oldenburg, Germany

Catherine Laws, Professor of Music, Department of Music, University of York, York, UK

Cecile Levacher, Independent Psychologist, Former Research Assistant, Department of Psychology and Educational Sciences, Swiss Center for Affective Sciences, University of Geneva, Geneva, Switzerland

Jennifer MacRitchie, Senior Research Fellow in Health and Wellbeing, School of Humanities and Communication Arts, MARCS Institute for Brain, Behaviour and Development, Western Sydney University, Sydney, Australia

Su Yin Mak, Professor of Music Theory, Department of Music, The Chinese University of Hong Kong, Hong Kong

Chiara Malagoli, Postdoctoral Researcher, Department of Education Science, University of Genoa, Genoa, Italy

Benjamin Matuszewski, Researcher at IRCAM (Institute for Research and Coordination in Acoustics/Music, Paris), and Doctoral Researcher, Centre de Recherche Informatique et Création Musicale, Paris 8 University, Paris, France

J. Murphy McCaleb, Senior Lecturer of Music, School of the Arts, York St. John University, York, UK

Juliana Moonette Manrique, Assistant Professor, School of Music, Saint Scholastica's College, Manila, Philippines

Wendy K. Moy, Assistant Professor of Music Education, College of Visual and Performing Arts and School of Education, Syracuse University, Syracuse, NY, USA

Hiroko Nishida, Associate Professor, Faculty of Design, Kyushu University, Fukuoka, Japan

Chiara Noera, Adjunct Researcher, Swiss Center for Affective Sciences, University of Geneva, Geneva, Switzerland

Naomi Norton, Associate Lecturer in Music Education, Department of Music, University of York, York, UK

Emily Payne, Lecturer in Music, School of Music, University of Leeds, Leeds, UK

Nicola Pennill, Postdoctoral Researcher, Royal Northern College of Music, Manchester, UK

Cayenna Ponchione-Bailey, Leverhulme Early Career Research Fellow, Department of Music, University of Sheffield, Sheffield, UK

Irene Pujol Torras, Music Therapist, London, UK

Tal-Chen Rabinowitch, Assistant Professor, School of Creative Arts Therapies, University of Haifa, Haifa, Israel

Evgenia Roussou, Doctoral Researcher, School of The Arts, University of Hull, Hull, UK

James Saunders, Professor of Music, Open Scores Lab, Bath School of Music and Performing Arts, Bath Spa University, Bath, UK

Simon Schaerlaeken, Postdoctoral Researcher, Neurology, School of Medicine, University of California, San Francisco, CA, USA

Andrea Schiavio, Senior Researcher, Centre for Systematic Musicology, University of Graz, Graz, Austria

Christoph Seibert, Professor of Music Informatics, Institute for Music Informatics and Musicology, University of Music Karlsruhe, Karlsruhe, Germany

Christopher Terepin, Doctoral Researcher, Department of Music, King's College London, London, UK

Gavin Thatcher, Lecturer in Theatre, Theatre Department, Brunel University London, London, UK

Philip Thomas, Professor of Performance, School of Music, Humanities and Media, University of Huddersfield, Huddersfield, UK

Renee Timmers, Professor of Psychology of Music, Department of Music, University of Sheffield, Sheffield, UK

James Williams, Senior Lecturer in Therapeutic Arts, School of Arts, College of Arts, Humanities, and Education, University of Derby, Derby, UK

Stuart Wood, Independent Scholar, UK

Daisuke Yokomori, Associate Professor, Faculty of Languages and Cultures, Kyushu University, Kyushu, Japan

Introduction to "Together in music: coordination, expression, participation"

Renee Timmers, Freya Bailes, and Helena Daffern

Introduction

We are delighted to introduce this volume to you on "Together in music: Coordination, expression, participation." This book is the outcome of a three-year research network that investigated non-verbal expressive communication in ensemble performance and in which context the conference "Together in music: Expression, communication, and performance" was organized. It contains contributions related to the three central projects of the network—PhD work on ensemble performance and communication of Sara D'Amario, Ryan Kirkbride, and Nicola Pennill, and contributions from authors who presented at the Together in Music conference. Several additional chapters were invited for completion and coherence of the book from both established and new writers. We are proud to be able to bring together a collection of chapters that showcase the most recent developments in this area of research since many chapters are written by early career researchers, with some presenting and discussing the main research findings of their PhD work. The location of the conference and network has created some unavoidable emphasis on writers and perspectives from the UK. Also, there is an emphasis on Western classical and popular music. Nevertheless, the book has an international dimension with contributions from authors based in a total of 13 countries.

Musical ensembles as creative groups

Recent years have seen a rise in interest, from a diversity of fields, in the musical ensemble as an exemplary form of "creative group behavior" and "joint action" (e.g. Clarke & Doffman, 2017; Glowinski et al., 2013). In the former characterization, ensembles are understood and investigated as high-functioning small-group organizations that have implicit and explicit coordinative structures in place to collaboratively work on a (musical) outcome (Tovstiga et al., 2005; Tuckman, 1965). Furthermore, rehearsals and performances of musical ensembles exemplify fruitful contexts for emergent creative and distributed behavior (Sawyer, 2006), where novel musical interpretations are negotiated and discovered through improvisatory interaction between people, their environments, and instruments. This line of research builds on findings and theories from organizational studies and combines these with insights from social and ecological psychology.

Renee Timmers, Freya Bailes, and Helena Daffern, *Introduction to "Together in music: coordination, expression, participation"*
In: Together in music. Edited by: Renee Timmers, Freya Bailes, and Helena Daffern, Oxford University Press. © Oxford University Press 2022. DOI: 10.1093/oso/9780198860761.001.0001

Ensemble performance as joint action

The second characterization zooms in more closely on the act of making music together: music-making is a shared activity that requires people to closely coordinate their actions in time and space in ways that generate a sonorous outcome. This outcome and interaction are endlessly variable, depending on the music performed, and the affordances of music relate both to the musical results and to the in-the-moment, shared action. This line of research has its basis in cognitive psychology, with its increased emphasis on ways in which human cognition is shaped through interaction with others and the physical, as well as socio-cultural, environment (Clarke, 2005; Sebanz et al., 2006; Thompson & Varela, 2001).

Ensemble music participation to enhance wellbeing

Additionally, this volume investigates musical ensembles from a third perspective, namely as a cultural activity enabling individual and social wellbeing and development through various routes (MacDonald et al., 2013). As a creative practice, participation in music is associated with a spectrum of social and personal benefits. This may relate to offering a sense of belonging and identity, supporting physical and mental health, strengthening social bonds and community, and contributing to experiences of life satisfaction. The emotional and social power of music is becoming better recognized and is leading to an increased number of applications of music in a variety of contexts, linking healthcare and the community (e.g. Ansdell & DeNora, 2016). Group music-making is at the heart of applications of music for wellbeing, and indeed is often experienced as a rewarding and beneficial activity. Research in this area is assessing evidence for the beneficial effects of musical participation and aims to identify the various factors involved in empowering or otherwise benefitting people individually or as a collective through music, and how this may vary depending on context.

Levels of investigation, readership, and types of contributions

Given this surge of interest in musical ensembles, this volume has taken up the ambitious challenge to bring together these different perspectives on group music-making in one volume. As research is conducted across different research disciplines, including management, psychology, empirical musicology, ethnomusicology, acoustics, computer science, and medical sciences, there is a need to bring strands together to facilitate exchange and promote dialogue and synthesis. Few books have been specifically dedicated to ensemble music performance before, and this book addresses the need for a collection that enables an increased insight into musical ensembles from different analytical levels. The volume starts from the meso-level when considering ensembles as creative groups or teams (Part 1) and investigating how musical groups organize or interact at a social and organizational level. It then zooms in to consider musical coordination and interaction at a micro-level (Part 2), when considering group music-making as forms of joint action. Finally, a macro-level perspective is taken in Part 3, examining health and wellbeing affordances associated with the socio-musical forms of organization and the acoustical, expressive, and emotional joint behaviors. Each part offers its own innovations and addresses particular research challenges: innovations in research methodologies and technologies are important for each part, but particularly so for the advancement of research explored in Part 2, which measures complex behaviors in fine detail. Theory building and establishment of ecologically, as well as scientifically, valid evidence are crucial for research on health and wellbeing, as developed in Part 3, while Part 1 benefits from an increasing body of research in organizational studies that considers forms of organization and the dynamics of organization, including processes of decision-making, communication, behavioral interaction patterns, and contextual constraints and facilitators of group dynamics.

Each part of the book contains two types of contributions. The first set of chapters in a part provides reviews of research on a particular topic or issue, while the remaining chapters present and discuss the method and outcomes of particular case studies of group music-making. Large-scale studies of ensemble music-making are still relatively rare, due to the often data-intense nature of music performance studies (Glowinski et al., 2013; Palmer, 1997; Wing et al., 2014) and sometimes the limited number of resources and funding available to researchers in this area (Bullen et al., 2004; Gibson & Hazelkorn, 2017). As a consequence, this field features a plurality of small-scale studies, which often employ a variety of research methods and address partially overlapping, but often also quite distinct objectives. With this book, we aimed to transform this limitation into an advantage and give room to this range of case studies, which together offer rich insight into quite a few different musical contexts and issues. By combining case study chapters with review chapters, a context and framing of the case studies are offered, as well as room for dialogue between theory and synthesized knowledge, as explained in the review chapters and the particular findings set out by the case studies.

As the volume is organized into three parts, one of the challenges for the book, as well as future research, is to examine cross-connections between the parts and to probe more closely how micro- and meso-level behaviors are related to each other and feed into the macro-level perspective and vice versa. Where applicable, relationships with other chapters within and across parts have been indicated throughout the book. Musical interaction has too often been investigated primarily at a particular spatiotemporal level, while we believe that meaningful group interaction is established at the intersection of those levels (Arrow et al., 2000): coordination happens at particular levels (such as synchronization and communication) and across levels. This cross-level interaction is emphasized by ecological, complex systems, and ethnographic accounts of music, and is a returning argument made by several authors in this volume. The concluding chapter explores cross-connections between parts of the book and reflects on this multi-level perspective on group music-making.

Most chapters are oriented toward Western classical or popular music-making and are set in Western democracies, with only a few exceptions, which we acknowledge is a limitation of the book. Nevertheless, we expect the work to have relevance beyond specific genres and cultures by addressing questions that cross musical boundaries, although findings and outcomes are likely to vary depending on the musical context. Specifically, we hope the book is insightful and of use to a variety of music practitioners (teachers, coaches, performing musicians, conductors, managers), higher-education students, and researchers with an interest in music, arts, behavior, organization, cognition, and wellbeing, and to have relevance and possibly an impact outside of the academic world. With this in mind, we would like to encourage readers to dip into the book and engage with the reviews and case studies of the different parts. Readers may seek to further develop knowledge and understanding of this fascinating human activity, or they may aim to refine and promote technical applications to investigate or enable joint music-making. We hope that these enquiries will help to introduce new perspectives to refine thinking and reflection on music practice and research, whether for a specific purpose such as education, music therapy, or community music, or for knowledge development towards an interdisciplinary understanding of ensemble music-making.

Book preview

As a guide, the review chapters in Part 1 consider emergence and self-organization in ensembles (Chapter 1), influencing group behavior as part of musical composition (Chapter 2), factors shaping the organizational dynamics of community ensembles (Chapter 3), perspectives on, and different types of agency in, ensembles (Chapter 4), and methods to investigate ensemble organization and communication (Chapter 5). The case studies in Part 1 report empirical research that explores different forms of leadership and organization in musical ensembles (Chapters 7 and 8), examine collaboration and communication in performance duos (Chapters 11 and 12), social, personal, and musical affordances of being part of a chorus in the context of a queer community choir (Chapter 10) and an English Parish Church (Chapter 6), as well as the relevance of identity for the success and dynamics of musical ensembles (Chapter 9).

The review chapters of Part 2 consider embodied perspectives on ensemble synchronization and micro-level coordination (Chapter 13), the use of gestures and movement to support joint music-making (Chapter 14), developments in the use of technology and acoustic or movement measurements to investigate music-making in larger ensembles (Chapter 15), to investigate ensemble singing (Chapter 16), and to investigate timing and synchronization in particular (Chapter 17), including directions for future research. The case study chapters of this part investigate indeterminacy and group dynamics in contemporary music performance (Chapter 18), methods to visualize relations between musicians during a performance (Chapter 19), technology to support joint live coding of music (Chapter 20), the use of metaphors and multisensory concepts by conductors to enhance ensemble performance (Chapter 21), a historical case study and comparison of synchronization and timing (Chapter 22), and the role of visual gaze and body movements for ensemble coordination as well as social motivation (Chapter 23).

Finally, the review chapters of Part 3 offer a general introduction to ensembles for wellbeing (Chapter 24), considerations of ensemble musicians' health and wellbeing (Chapter 25), relationships between synchronization, communication, and wellbeing (Chapter 26), the role of amateur ensemble participation for personal development outside work (Chapter 27) and for personal and social empowerment (Chapter 28), and the use of ensembles (or assemblages) in music therapy (Chapter 29). The final chapters report case studies that include a consideration of ensemble participation across different age ranges, from late adulthood (Chapter 30) to a longitudinal study of youth orchestra participation (Chapter 31). Uses of ensembles for joint instrumental learning are presented in Chapter 32. Two case study chapters focus on collaborative workshops, first exploring the potential of collaborative notation to enable creative interaction and communication (Chapter 33), then using interactive exercises to facilitate singers' awareness of their vocal physicality (Chapter 34). Last, but certainly not least, a case study of ensemble singing for wellbeing and social inclusion in the Philippines (Chapter 35) is described.

Conclusion

As mentioned, we are proud to be able to bring together such a range of studies, and are immensely grateful to the three superb PhD students, as well as our network collaborators—Catherine Laws, Luke Windsor, and Guy Brown, who made the network collaboration a very enjoyable success—and to the contributors to this book whose work is central and crucial to all it has to offer. The book is dedicated to Kia Ng, who was part of the initiative for the network, but tragically could not be part of it.

Acknowledgements

The network was made possible by funding from the White Rose Consortium for Arts & Humanities. We would like to thank the reviewers for their constructive and helpful feedback on chapters: Laura Bishop, Mary Black, Alana Blackburn, Karen Burland, David Camlin, Eric Clarke, Sara D'Amario, Helen English, Daniel Galbreath, Donald Glowinski, Elizabeth Haddon, Kelly Jakubowski, Alexander Refsum Jensenius, Elaine King, Ryan Kirkbride, Michaela Korte, Gunter Kreutz, Catherine Laws, Jennifer MacRitchie, Murphy McCaleb, Wendy Moy, Emily Payne, Nicola Pennill, Cayenna Ponchione-Bailey, Sarah Price, Andrea Schiavio, Sten Ternström, Gavin Thatcher, James Williams, Stuart Wood, and Caroline Waddington-Jones.

References

Ansdell, G., & DeNora, T. (2016). *Musical pathways in recovery: Community music therapy and mental wellbeing*. Routledge.

Arrow, H., McGrath, J. E., & Berdahl, J. L. (2000). *Small groups as complex systems: Formation, coordination, development, and adaptation*. Sage Publications.

Bullen, E., Robb, S., & Kenway, J. (2004). "Creative destruction": Knowledge economy policy and the future of the arts and humanities in the academy. *Journal of Education Policy, 19*(1), 3–22.

Clarke, E. F. (2005). *Ways of listening: An ecological approach to the perception of musical meaning*. Oxford University Press.

Clarke, E. F., & Doffman, M. (Eds.). (2017). *Distributed creativity: Collaboration and improvisation in contemporary music*. Oxford University Press.

Gibson, A. G., & Hazelkorn, E. (2017). Arts and humanities research, redefining public benefit, and research prioritization in Ireland. *Research Evaluation, 26*(3), 199–210.

Glowinski, D., Mancini, M., Cowie, R., Camurri, A., Chiorri, C., & Doherty, C. (2013). The movements made by performers in a skilled quartet: A distinctive pattern, and the function that it serves. *Frontiers in Psychology, 4*(841), 1–9. https://doi.org/10.3389/fpsyg.2013.00841

MacDonald, R., Kreutz, G., & Mitchell, L. (Eds.). (2013). *Music, health, and wellbeing*. Oxford University Press.

Palmer, C. (1997). Music performance. *Annual Review of Psychology, 48*(1), 115–38.

Sawyer, R. K. (2006). Group creativity: Musical performance and collaboration. *Psychology of Music, 34*(2), 148–65.

Sebanz, N., Bekkering, H., & Knoblich, G. (2006). Joint action: Bodies and minds moving together. *Trends in Cognitive Sciences, 10*(2), 70–6.

Thompson, E., & Varela, F. J. (2001). Radical embodiment: Neural dynamics and consciousness. *Trends in Cognitive Sciences, 5*(10), 418–25.

Tovstiga, G., Odenthal, S., & Goerner, S. (2005). Sense making and learning in complex organisations: The string quartet revisited. *International Journal of Management Concepts and Philosophy, 1*(3), 215–31.

Tuckman, B. (1965). Developmental sequence in small groups. *Psychological Bulletin, 63*(6), 384–99.

Wing, A. M., Endo, S., Bradbury, A., & Vorberg, D. (2014). Optimal feedback correction in string quartet synchronization. *Journal of the Royal Society Interface, 11*(93), 20131125. https://doi.org/10.1098/rsif.2013.1125

PART 1

COORDINATION AND ENSEMBLE ORGANIZATION

1

Music ensembles as self-organized groups

Nicola Pennill and Dermot Breslin

Introduction

Musical ensembles have many unique features relating to their context and culture, and yet, in similar ways to other groups of people working together, they are shaped by social interactions. Therefore, theoretical and empirical work in this area can contribute to wider research on group dynamics and vice versa. Ensembles exist in diverse forms, from large orchestras with a conductor to small, self-directed groups. For the purposes of this chapter, we focus on rehearsals and working practices of small groups with no conductor, in which there are clear parallels to teams and groups in other workplace situations. Given restrictions in the scope of prior research on this topic, our main focus is on vocal and instrumental ensembles in the Western classical and jazz tradition. We take the perspective that small ensembles may be regarded as a type of team working towards creative outputs with high levels of interdependence between members, which adapts and changes as it works toward shared goals. This perspective can be generalized to other creative, self-organized groups that, in their search for operational effectiveness and goal attainment, are faced with challenges of working together and the need to foster flexibility and freedom within a stable and efficient group environment.

The literature on group and team organization provides many departure points for investigation of the complex coordination and interpersonal dynamics of ensembles as working groups. This chapter will explore current themes from organizational studies research in relation to music ensembles. First, organizational characteristics of music ensembles are presented as a number of tensions, in which it is argued that ensembles play a delicate balancing act between competing forces of stability versus change, collectivity versus individuality, and maturity versus emergence. Second, and in light of these tensions, key structural and temporal dimensions of ensembles as organizations are examined. The unique ways in which these tensions are managed in ensembles through structure and time have implications for the management of teams in wider organizations and for research on organizational studies.

Organizational characteristics of music ensembles

Organization in chamber music ensembles has parallels with work in other dynamic and complex workplace settings, including the need for shared goals, collaborative processes, and high levels of interdependence between members (Arrow et al., 2000; Glowinski et al., 2016). Group processes can be examined through a number of lenses, including those relating to

Nicola Pennill and Dermot Breslin, *Music ensembles as self-organized groups* In: *Together in music*. Edited by: Renee Timmers, Freya Bailes, and Helena Daffern, Oxford University Press. © Oxford University Press 2022. DOI: 10.1093/oso/9780198860761.003.0001

social, cultural, and contextual factors which present a number of tensions for groups. These are explored in the following section.

Stability versus change

Balancing paradoxical tensions of stability and change allows ensembles to learn from previous experience, and continue to adapt to changing environmental stimuli. Stability is needed for effective operation, while change provides a way of adapting to new circumstances and accommodating experiences (Grote et al., 2018; Tsoukas & Chia, 2002). Dynamic organizations manage these tensions in various ways, both implicitly and explicitly, creating energy and momentum (through change), while also remaining stable enough to be efficient and coherent, as they coordinate activities and achieve alignment. Mechanisms that give rise to stability include those which foster collaboration and integration through social bonding, or accountability through assignment of roles or cultural expectations. In their study of rehearsal of contemporary dancers, Harrison and Rouse (2014) explored coordination through study of interaction patterns between dancers in a small ensemble, and proposed a model of "elastic coordination" that relates closely to the context of music ensemble practice. They found cycles of both divergent and convergent behaviors, as during a series of rehearsals, the group moved through periods of "integration," as ideas came together, and of "de-integration" as they moved apart. While the former acts to coordinate group actions, the latter allows individuals the freedom to explore new opportunities. These tensions in the creative process provided a source of energy and impetus to the process and were regarded as integral to the dynamics of the group, and achievement of its goals.

Collectivity versus individuality

By definition, a group comprises individual members, and balancing the needs of the group with those of the individual is a fundamental requirement of group work. Ensembles may be viewed as a type of "expert" team, in which members have specific technical contributions and defined roles (Fiore & Salas, 2006; Muethel & Hoegl, 2013), and a degree of homogenous knowledge which allows members to understand the contributions of others (Cooke et al., 2000). Parallels arise, too, with research on coordination in sports teams, which share a focus on "performance" outcomes and teamwork (Bourbousson et al., 2010; Camerino et al., 2012; Chelladurai, 1990). What these contexts have in common is the need to function in a high-performance, dynamic environment and to manage the tensions between individual and collective imperatives.

Collective creative processes are shaped by social, cognitive, and motivational factors (Paulus & Brown, 2007). Together, these act to draw individual-level contributions into the collective milieu. Music ensembles often work with loose agendas, retaining some ambiguity about processes or outcomes in order to accommodate the free expression of ideas, leveraging the power of real-time collaboration (Sawyer, 2006; Sawyer & Dezutter, 2009). Work with problem-solving teams suggests that creative solutions to complex problems arise from processes of "interactive flow," as individuals offer contributions to shared outcomes (van Oortmerssen et al., 2015). In jazz ensembles, Clarke et al. (2013) identified the micro-dynamics of hidden creative processes, such as how musicians resolve tensions around fixed and improvised elements, enabling creativity and individuality, while simultaneously acting to integrate and coordinate these individual efforts within the collective effort.

Maturity versus emergence

As they enact cycles of preparation and performance, ensembles behave as emergent, dynamic entities, which can adapt and evolve, rather than static, "mature" organizations which seek to institutionalize views and behaviors. It may be argued that well-established groups exhibit a degree of stasis, having worked together over a period of time and developed shared norms and routines. However, even in such cases of apparent maturity in group relations, ensembles continue to emerge and develop as they renew performances through preparation processes (Pennill, 2019).

Music ensemble performance can be viewed as inherently emergent (Badino et al., 2014; Bishop, 2018; Borgo, 2005; Moran, 2014; Tovstiga et al., 2005). In their landmark text, Arrow et al. (2000) define small groups as complex adaptive systems (CAS), arguing that the emergence of interaction and dynamic behavior of teams is fundamental to their performance and evolution, and hence to their meaningful study. Other studies have since adopted approaches which consider teams as CAS (for a review, see Ramos-Villagrasa et al., 2018). In the CAS view, members of teams are viewed as "agents" which conform to non-linear system dynamic theory (Eidelson, 1997), exhibiting chaotic behavior which, through their interactions and processes of adaptation, become an organized whole (Campbell et al., 2011; Lewin, 1993).

Studies of music groups as complex systems include research in jazz, choirs, and chamber groups. Jazz musician and researcher David Borgo describes jazz performance as a system with "neither too much, nor too little order" (Borgo, 2005, p. 4). Making the case for a systems-based understanding of improvised music performance, he highlights its real-time nature, reliance on audience reception, the social or cultural context, and its inseparability from other networks. Müller et al. (2018) measured breathing, heart rate, and vocal and movement measures in a large choir. Coupling and synchronization between members showed that coordination operated at the level of the whole choir and between individual members. As the authors described it, "the network dynamics of each individual singer are likely to be influenced by a complex coordination or the function of the choir as a whole" (p. 16). From an exploration of sense-making in a professional string quartet, Tovstiga et al. (2005, p. 224) advanced a "field of interaction" model. In this, they view the quartet as a complex, dichotomous system in which the group coordinates through individual and collective action, through both implicit and explicit modes of communication. These examples support the argument for ensembles as emergent, complex systems. As complex systems mature, they continue to exhibit characteristics of emergence, as a small change in local interactions can rapidly lead to new macro-level patterns of behavior (Breslin, 2014). Ensembles as complex systems hence simultaneously straddle processes of maturity and (re)birth.

The three tensions described in this chapter are summarized in Table 1.1. Contextual environment may interact with these tensions, as described by Grote et al. (2018) in their study of team adaptative coordination. Groups may experience high or low stability or demands for flexibility, depending on which interpersonal coordination and shared leadership is adjusted in each of four possible quadrants (high/low stability; high/low flexibility). They found that

Table 1.1 Structural and temporal processes in ensembles as organizations

Tensions	Structural processes	Temporal processes
Stability and change	Ensembles both adhere to shared norms and adopt minimal structures which facilitate continual adaptation.	Ensembles move through recurring episodes of action and transition.
Collectivity versus individuality	Through a distribution of leadership, ensembles self-organize, simultaneously allowing individual freedom and, through constant dialogue and exchange, integration into the collective.	Individual contributions are integrated into the collective effort and consensus is built through real-time interaction flow.
Maturity versus emergence	Through role switching and expressive deviations, ensembles disrupt the status quo and role structure associated with group maturity.	Developed groups can experience episodes of rapid, punctuated change and rebirth as they pass through key tipping or transition points.

structural coordination mechanisms (such as conventions and plans) were more suited to demands of high stability, whereas interpersonal coordination mechanisms (such as sharing leadership and mutual adjustment by individuals) were more suited to conditions requiring high flexibility (p. 132).

Dimensions of ensembles as organizations

The tensions described so far provide possible ways to place music ensembles within a wider organizational framework. Next, we examine them through the dimensions of structure and time. These structural and temporal processes shape how ensembles resolve competing tensions, manage their musical tasks, and progress towards their goals.

Structural processes and self-organization

In the absence of hierarchy, groups adopt measures for self-organization to achieve and maintain structure (Attaran & Nguyen, 2002). Studies in music have explored how this is expressed in practice. Gilboa and Tal-Shmotkin (2012) examined the ways in which string quartets resemble self-managed teams (SMTs), using an assessment tool originally devised for business teams. They concluded that the characteristics of the quartets closely resembled those of other non-music teams. In jazz groups, Barrett (1998) outlined a number of ways ensembles seek to establish structure. First, members need to challenge taken-for-granted habits to ensure that the group allows new forms to emerge over time; many veteran jazz musicians deliberately seek to create disruptions by putting themselves in unfamiliar musical situations. Second, jazz musicians see deviations or errors as opportunities for the process of adaptation and learning. Third, and crucially, successful jazz ensembles adopt minimal structures that allow for maximum flexibility. In ensembles, these can include what have been referred to as credos, or visions (Weick, 1998), which can provide guidance to individuals without stipulating specific courses of behavior. Fourth, improvising jazz musicians can be viewed as a complex adaptive system (see "maturity and emergence"), as musicians improvise on the "border of chaos" (Borgo, 2005). Fifth, jazz ensembles become members in a community of practice (Brown & Duguid, 1991), as they "hang out." This immersion within the group process allows them to have an in-depth understanding of their ways of operating, and to anticipate the actions of others. Sixth, jazz ensembles tend to alternate between soloing and supporting. This switching of roles allows individuals to see the group process through a different lens, and furthermore allows the group to remain responsive to changes (Bigley & Roberts, 2001). Finally, jazz ensembles distribute both tasks and leadership. Individuals are in constant dialogue and exchange with one another, as they react to the situation at hand.

Such shared, distributed or "system" leadership may be regarded as a natural consequence of emergence, and has been well documented over a number of decades. In this paradigm, leadership is viewed as a set of activities shared between team members (Pearce & Conger, 2002), rather than imposed by a single "leader." Tovstiga et al. (2005) found that string quartet players adopted the role of leader on an "as needed" basis, while in a professional eight-piece vocal ensemble, Lim (2013) described a "horizontal" model of leadership, in which the group chose not to appoint an artistic director, but rather to share management roles around the group. Shared leadership was also explored in music groups by Bathurst and Ladkin (2012), who found that leadership tasks were diverse, including understanding the technical demands of instruments, creating a setting whereby ensemble members could see and hear each other effectively, establishing tempo, for example by using preparatory breaths, addressing problems as they arise, and establishing a blended sound. Together, these aspects resulted in an emergent form of leadership, in which all players contributed, and in which the group was able to make collective decisions in response to unfolding events. Leadership has been shown to emerge (and disappear) amongst individual team members over time (Emery et al., 2013). A longitudinal study of social networking in virtual software development teams found that interaction patterns evolved over time from a central hub model to a more decentralized structure (Long & Siau, 2007). The decision-making and communication were found to become shared between a group of key members, rather than concentrated in the central hub, as knowledge of (and demand for) key skills became better understood by the network. Such distribution of leadership inhibits hierarchical forces and reflects localized and ever-changing dynamics, which shape interactions in the ensemble as it evolves and develops over time.

Temporal processes

Time is a key factor underpinning group function (McGrath, 1990; McGrath et al., 1984). How groups form and develop over time has been much studied, and time is increasingly incorporated as a key component of group research. For example, time as a factor in group organization has led to the development of frameworks within which to understand team performance, including ways that group activity can be viewed as phases or episodes of activity (Ancona et al., 2001; Gersick, 1988, 1989; Li & Roe, 2012; Marks et al., 2001; Mathieu et al., 2014).

Changes in rehearsal processes and behavior have been studied over time in music ensembles. Within single rehearsals, shifts in relationship quality have been observed around the middle of rehearsals of duo partnerships, from shorter to longer bursts of interaction between members, and more sustained work on musical passages (with less verbal exchange) in later stages (King, 2016). Time constraints have been shown to affect behavior during ensemble rehearsal, whereby shorter time frames relied more on individual performer skill (Kokotsaki, 2007). Over a series of rehearsals, Blank and Davidson (2007) found that the frequency and duration of rehearsals increased as performance approached, and in a study of a series of 13 rehearsals of a duo partnership, differences were found in the types of tasks employed over time (Ginsborg et al., 2006).

In the organization studies literature, a number of models of team development and performance have been advanced. One of the most well-known is the stage model first proposed by Tuckman in the 1960s, which predicts that groups pass through sequential phases of "forming," "storming," "norming," and "performing" (Tuckman, 1965; Tuckman & Jensen, 1977). Researchers have adopted this model to support studies of group behavior in musical contexts (e.g. Blom & Encarnacao, 2012; Creech & Hallam, 2017). While this and other linear models of team development continue to have wide relevance to groups, there are other, dynamic models that may better reflect the nuances of complex behavior in ensembles, such as sudden shifts in behavior resulting from critical points in performance preparation.

Perspectives on the way groups pace and organize their activities represent an important departure from the step-wise, phased models that predict progressive stages in groups of all types. The punctuated equilibrium model of team development (Gersick, 1988, 1989) acknowledges that environmental factors affect progress, including the timeline of delivery. It predicts a change in behavior at the calendar midpoint, in which the team's internal pacing responds to increasing urgency. It has formed the basis of research that explores wider implications of temporal pacing and transitions in teams, and is proposed as a "group task progress model," rather than as a "group development model." Gersick's model has also been described as indicating a "tipping point" in which there is a shift from inertia to change (Zellmer-Bruhn et al., 2003). A key difference between this and the Tuckman model is that change can be "revolutionary" and rapid in response to key events, including the calendar midpoint, as well as "evolutionary" and gradual. The temporal model for team development advanced by Marks et al. (2001) suggests that multitasking, adaptive teams move through recurring episodes of action and transition. The authors describe this as the "rhythm of team task accomplishment" (p. 361). This differs from Tuckman's model in that episodes may run sequentially, simultaneously, and even recursively over time. This adaptive quality means that groups retain the ability to reform and rejuvenate their ways of interacting. Small changes in local rules of interaction can thus allow the group to alternate between business-as-usual and punctuated change (Breslin, 2014).

These frameworks offer examples where research perspectives other than the well-trodden linear model can provide new ways to look at how groups progress over time. As an example of this, longitudinal research in newly formed vocal ensembles suggested non-linear, dynamic development of music groups as they prepared for performance over a three-month period (Pennill, 2019). Data from interview, observation, and verbal interactions captured during a series of rehearsals revealed underlying structures, with discontinuous phases and predictable "transition" points. The phases were conceptualized as an initial "exploration" phase which featured social bonding and task understanding, a "transition" phase characterized by disruption and change, and a final "integration" phase as coordination was re-established for an approaching performance (Pennill, 2019). These phases were associated with changing communication styles and interpersonal dynamics, as the groups worked within a fixed time frame of performance preparation.

Conclusion

This chapter examined organizational characteristics of self-organized small group music ensembles employing key themes from organizational studies. It contributes to the study of ensemble rehearsal and performance by exploring tensions experienced in group performance and rehearsal, while highlighting structural and temporal processes at play in resolving them, in particular how the dualities of stability versus change, collectivity versus individuality, and maturity versus emergence can provide a lens through which to study and interpret ensemble interactions.

Consideration of how these elements are manifested in ensemble settings and expressed in terms of the structure and timeline of performance preparation can provide new tools with which researchers can investigate the musical "team". They raise a number of questions for future research. For example, how does the demand for balancing tensions shift in the changing conditions which arise as performance approaches? What is the optimum balance of each tension for successful performance? How can the demands of rehearsal and the transitions experienced by ensembles contribute to wider study of phase transitions in work groups? Instruments and methods used in team research can be used by researchers to pursue these questions and some of these are considered elsewhere in this volume.

For practicing musicians and educators, these perspectives offer ways to reflect on group dynamics, as well as musical processes in the rehearsal room. By taking account of the internal and external forces impacting interpersonal interactions, musicians can be more fully prepared to respond appropriately to keep the group on track, balancing rules and structure with more flexible approaches.

Acknowledgments

Nicola Pennill's PhD research was funded by the White Rose College of Arts and Humanities.

References

Ancona, D., Okhuysen, G. A., & Perlow, L. A. (2001). Taking time to integrate temporal research. *Academy of Management Review*, 26(4), 512–29.

Arrow, H., McGrath, J. E., & Berdahl, J. L. (2000). *Small groups as complex systems: Formation, coordination, development, and adaptation*. Sage.

Attaran, M., & Nguyen, T. T. (2000). Creating the right structural fit for self-directed teams. *Team Performance Management, 6*, 5–33.

Badino, L., D'Ausilio, A., Glowinski, D., Camurri, A., & Fadiga, L. (2014). Sensorimotor communication in professional quartets. *Neuropsychologia, 55*, 98–104.

Barrett, F. (1998). Creativity and improvisation in jazz and organizations: Implications for organizational learning. *Organization Science, 9*(5), 605–22.

Bathurst, R., & Ladkin, D. (2012). Performing leadership: Observations from the world of music. *Administrative Sciences, 2*(1), 99–119.

Bigley, G. A., & Roberts, K. H. (2001). The incident command system: High-reliability organizing for complex and volatile task environments. *The Academy of Management Journal, 44*(6), 1281–99.

Bishop, L. (2018). Collaborative musical creativity: How ensembles coordinate spontaneity. *Frontiers in Psychology, 9*(1285), 1–17.

Blank, M., & Davidson, J. (2007). An exploration of the effects of musical and social factors in piano duo collaborations. *Psychology of Music, 35*(2), 231–48.

Blom, D., & Encarnacao, J. (2012). Student-chosen criteria for peer assessment of tertiary rock groups in rehearsal and performance: What's important? *British Journal of Music Education, 29*(1), 25–43.

Borgo, D. (2006). *Sync or swarm: Improvising music in a complex age.* Continuum.

Bourbousson, J., Seve, C., & McGarry, T. (2010). Space-time coordination dynamics in basketball: Part 1. Intra- and inter-couplings among player dyads. *Journal of Sports Sciences, 28*(3), 339–47.

Breslin, D. (2014). Calm in the storm: Simulating the management of organisational co-evolution. *Futures, 57*, 62–77.

Brown, J. S., & Duguid, P. (1991). Organizational learning and communities-of-practice: Toward a unified view of working, learning, and innovation. *Organization Science, 2*(1), 40–57.

Camerino, O. F., Chaverri, J., Anguera, M. T., & Jonsson, G. K. (2012). Dynamics of the game in soccer: Detection of T-patterns. *European Journal of Sport Science, 12*(3), 216–24.

Campbell, J., Flynn, J. D., & Hay, J. (2011). The group development process seen through the lens of complexity theory. *International Scientific Journal of Methods and Models of Complexity, 6*(1), 1–33.

Chelladurai, P. (1990). Leadership in sports: A review. *International Journal of Sport Psychology, 21*, 328–54.

Clarke, E., Doffman, M., & Lim, L. (2013). Distributed creativity and ecological dynamics: A case study of Liza Lim's "Tongue of the Invisible." *Music and Letters, 94*(4), 628–63.

Cooke, N. J., Salas, E., Cannon-Bowers, J. A., & Stout, R. J. (2000). Measuring team knowledge. *Human Factors, 42*(1), 151–73.

Creech, A., & Hallam, S. (2017). Facilitating learning in small groups. In J. Rink, H. Gaunt, & A. Williamon (Eds.), *Musicians in the making: Pathways to creative performance* (Vol. 1, pp. 57–76). Oxford University Press.

Eidelson, R. J. (1997). Complex adaptive systems in the behavioral and social sciences. *Review of General Psychology, 1*(1), 42–71.

Emery, C., Calvard, T. S., & Pierce, M. E. (2013). Leadership as an emergent group process: A social network study of personality and leadership. *Group Processes & Intergroup Relations, 16*(1), 28–45.

Fiore, S. M., & Salas, E. (2006). Team cognition and expert teams: Developing insights from cross-disciplinary analysis of exceptional teams. *International Journal of Sport and Exercise Psychology, 4*(4), 369–75.

Gersick, C. J. G. (1988). Time and transition in work teams: Toward a new model of group development. *Academy of Management Journal, 31*(1), 9–41.

Gersick, C. J. G. (1989). Marking time: Predictable transitions in task groups. *Academy of Management Journal, 32*(2), 274–309.

Gilboa, A., & Tal-Shmotkin, M. (2012). String quartets as self-managed teams: An interdisciplinary perspective. *Psychology of Music, 40*(1), 19–41.

Ginsborg, J., Chaffin, R., & Nicholson, G. (2006). Shared performance cues in singing and conducting: A content analysis of talk during practice. *Psychology of Music, 34*(2), 167–94.

Glowinski, D., Bracco, F., Chiorri, C., & Grandjean, D. (2016). Music ensemble as a resilient system. Managing the unexpected through group interaction. *Frontiers in Psychology, 7*(1548), 1–7.

Grote, G., Kolbe, M., & Waller, M. J. (2018). The dual nature of adaptive coordination in teams: Balancing demands for flexibility and stability. *Organizational Psychology Review, 8*(2–3), 125–48.

Harrison, S. H., & Rouse, E. D. (2014). Let's dance! Elastic coordination in creative group work: A qualitative study of modern dancers. *Academy of Management Journal, 57*(5), 1256–83.

King, E. (2016). Social familiarity: Styles of interaction in chamber ensemble rehearsal. In H. Prior & E. King (Eds.), *Music and familiarity: Listening, musicology and performance* (pp. 253–70). Routledge.

Kokotsaki, D. (2007). Understanding the ensemble pianist: A theoretical framework. *Psychology of Music, 35*(4), 641–68.

Lewin, R. (1993). *Complexity—life at the edge of chaos.* J. M. Dent.

Li, J., & Roe, R. A. (2012). Introducing an intrateam longitudinal approach to the study of team process dynamics. *European Journal of Work Organizational Psychology, 21*(5), 718–48.

Lim, M. C. (2013). In pursuit of harmony: The social and organisational factors in a professional vocal ensemble. *Psychology of Music, 42*, 307–24.

Long, Y., & Siau, K. (2007). Social network structures in open source software development teams. *Journal of Database Management, 18*(2), 25–40.

Marks, M. A., Mathieu, J. E., & Zaccaro, S. J. (2001). A temporally based framework and taxonomy of team processes. *Academy of Management Review, 26*(3), 356–76.

Mathieu, J. E., Tannenbaum, S., Donsbach, J., & Alliger, G. (2014). A review and integration of team composition models: Moving toward a dynamic and temporal framework. *Journal of Management, 40*(1), 130–60.

McGrath, J. E. (1990). Time matters in groups. In J. Galegher, R. E. Kraut, & C. Egido (Eds.), *Intellectual teamwork: Social and technological foundations of cooperative work* (pp. 23–61). Lawrence Erlbaum.

McGrath, J. E., Kelly, J. R., & Machatka, D. E. (1984). The social psychology of time: Entrainment of behavior in social and organizational settings. *Applied Social Psychology Annual, 5*, 21–44.

Moran, N. (2014). Social implications arise in embodied music cognition research which can counter musicological "individualism." *Frontiers in Psychology, 5*, 676. https://doi.org/10.3389/fpsyg.2014.00676

Muethel, M., & Hoegl, M. (2013). Shared leadership effectiveness in independent professional teams. *European Management Journal, 31*(4), 423–32.

Müller, V., Delius, J. A. M., & Lindenberger, U. (2018). Complex networks emerging during choir singing. *Annals of the New York Academy of Sciences*, *14311*(1), 85–101.

Paulus, P. B., & Brown, V. R. (2007). Toward more creative and innovative group idea generation: A cognitive-social-motivational perspective of brainstorming. *Social and Personality Psychology Compass*, *1*, 248–65

Pearce, C. L., & Conger, J. A. (2002). *Shared leadership: Reframing the hows and whys of leadership*. Sage.

Pennill, N. (2019). *Ensembles working towards performance: Emerging coordination and interactions in self-organised groups* [Doctoral dissertation]. University of Sheffield.

Ramos-Villagrasa, P. J., Marques-Quinteiro, P., Navarro, J., & Rico, R. (2018). Teams as complex adaptive systems: Reviewing 17 years of research. *Small Group Research*, *49*(2), 135–76.

Sawyer, R. K. (2006). Group creativity: musical performance and collaboration. *Psychology of Music*, *34*(2), 148–65.

Sawyer, R. K., & Dezutter, S. (2009). Distributed creativity: How collective creations emerge from collaboration. *Psychology of Aesthetics, Creativity, and the Arts*, *3*(2), 81–92.

Tovstiga, G., Odenthal, S., & Goerner, S. (2005). Sense making and learning in complex organisations: The string quartet revisited. *International Journal of Management Concepts and Philosophy*, *1*(3), 215–31.

Tsoukas, H., & Chia, R. (2002). On organizational becoming: Rethinking organizational change. *Organization Science*, *13*(5), 567–82.

Tuckman, B. (1965). Developmental sequence in small groups. *Psychological Bulletin*, *63*(6), 384.

Tuckman, B., & Jensen, M. A. C. (1977). Stages of small-group development revisited. *Group Organization Studies*, *2*(4), 419–27.

van Oortmerssen, L. A., van Woerkum, C. M., & Aarts, N. (2015). When interaction flows: An exploration of collective creative processes on a collaborative governance board. *Group Organization Management*, *40*(4), 500–28.

Weick, K. E. (1998). Improvisation as a mindset for organizational analysis. *Organization Science*, *9*(5), 543–55.

Zellmer-Bruhn, M., Waller, M. J., & Ancona, D. (2003). The effect of temporal entrainment on the ability of teams to change their routines. *Research on Managing Groups and Teams*, *6*, 135–58.

2

Group behaviors as music

James Saunders

Introduction

Musicians form complex interpersonal relationships both with each other when playing to-gether and with an audience. Such relationships are often by-products of the necessities and conventions of musical performance, for example through the role of non-verbal interac-tion in ensemble performance (Glowinski et al., 2015; see Chapters 1, 14, and 23), but they also offer opportunities to control musical material and the interaction between players and audiences. In some recent work, composers are exploring ways to use social behavior as a compositional strategy, taking a process-driven approach using decision-making, cueing, and negotiation of interpersonal relationships. Such work uses group behaviors to suggest methods for harnessing specific motivations of players, bringing art and life closer together by "mapping the two onto each other by using people as a medium" (Bishop, 2012, p. 127), facilitating "the process of engaging with the world and oneself through play" (Sicart, 2014, p. 84). Models drawn from social psychology, heuristics, and decision theory can be usefully applied to suggest the ways in which composers initiate these processes and how performers respond to them. This has the potential to make direct reference to social processes that are recognizable from daily life, consequently creating tangible points of contact between art and the everyday, projecting values that emerge from the behaviors, and creating the possibility of empathic responses from observers.

This chapter sets out a framework for thinking about group behaviors in music, drawing on research in social psychology and game studies to explore how different aspects of group behaviors can be explicitly explored in musical compositions. In doing so, I trace the ap-proach I have taken in some recent work and consider the strategies evident in work by others. I focus on the agency of participants in realizing the work, how practicable decision-making strategies might be developed by participants, and the impact of these considerations on the values translated through the work.

Group behaviors and decision-making

Social psychology research has investigated group behaviors as complex interpersonal pro-cesses, explaining and predicting the relationship between people when interacting in groups (Hogg & Vaughan, 2018, pp. 44–7). Social cognition theory, in particular, characterizes some of the drivers of group behaviors. Fiske and Taylor (2017, p. 16) define the *motivated tactician* as "a fully engaged thinker with multiple cognitive strategies available, who (consciously or unconsciously) chooses among them based on goals, motives, and needs." More recently, this

James Saunders, *Group behaviors as music* In: *Together in music*. Edited by: Renee Timmers, Freya Bailes, and Helena Daffern, Oxford University Press. © Oxford University Press 2022. DOI: 10.1093/oso/9780198860761.003.0002

characterization has shifted to that of *activated actors* who operate in social environments that "rapidly cue perceivers" social concepts, without awareness, and almost inevitably cue associated "cognitions, evaluations, affect, motivation, and behaviour" (Fiske & Taylor, 2017, p. 16). In particular, Fiske and Taylor (2017, p. 16) note that this perspective "emphasises fast reactions, variously viewed as implicit, spontaneous, or automatic indicators of responses unconstrained by perceiver volition." In musical performance, such situations suggest an alternative to the "presentation of an identity, a musical persona, in a defined social context" (Auslander, 2006, p. 119). While any staged activity might be characterized by participants projecting an identity (Auslander, 2006), by creating situations where more instinctive actions are required, there is the possibility of revealing aspects of the participants' everyday characters and behaviors.

This speed of response is significant and lends itself to the use of heuristics, a useful decision-making strategy that "ignores part of the information, with the goal of making decisions more quickly, frugally, and/or accurately than more complex methods" (Gigerenzer & Gaissmaier, 2011, p. 454). Heuristics are suited to environments where some relevant information is unknown. In contexts where a score communicates a set of rules or constraints on action to create a space where participants can act, group behaviors can be mediated through decision-making framed consciously or intuitively through heuristics.

The implication of embedding heuristics in a basic set of rules, algorithms, or instructions is effective in music where a dynamic process enacted by participants takes precedence over more fixed material and structuring, and a more predictable outcome. Broadly, a set of rules creates a decision space (Saunders, 2015, 2020), the result of which, when articulated by participants, produces the behavioral–musical result and suggests certain characteristics and values embedded in the rule structure (Flanagan & Nissenbaum, 2014). Such *behavioral–musical* systems focus on how rules present a framework that governs interaction, how decisions are enacted through the ways players make choices, and how values are suggested by the outcome of these decisions. These systems build on Cook's notion of music-as-script "choreographing a series of real-time, social interactions between players: a series of mutual acts of listening and communal gestures that enact a particular vision of human society" (2001, para. 15). Rather than enacting such a vision, however, they present processes through which many different versions of human society may emerge and where the social behavior of people becomes the material being interrogated by processes within the composition.

Group dynamics and processes

The processes at the heart of group behaviors are driven by *group dynamics*, which Forsyth (2014, p. 18) defines as "the influential interpersonal processes that occur in and between groups over time." He proposes five separate processes that influence the behavior of groups: formative, influence, performance, conflict, and contextual processes:

- *Formative processes* are "the personal and situational forces that prompt people to join groups or remain apart from them, as well as the part interpersonal attraction plays in creating stable relationships among group members" (p. 18). They focus on the transition from individual to collective behaviors and the ways in which group members balance personal and group needs, goals, and identities.

- *Influence processes* "organize the group's procedures, interaction patterns, and inter-member relations" (p. 18) through the wide spectrum of interpersonal forces that operate between group members. They include the balance between conformity and dissent, the role of social influence, the impact of specific roles and leadership, and the way group membership may alter individual opinions and actions.
- *Performance processes* "facilitate and inhibit people's performance in groups" (p. 19) when undertaking tasks. They focus on the productiveness of a team, as well as individual and collective motivation, and the way groups make decisions.
- *Conflict processes* frame the tensions that "undermine the cohesiveness of the group and cause specific relationships within the group to weaken or break altogether" (p. 19). They are driven by aspects of competition, power struggles, resource allocation, disagreement, and problematic interpersonal relationships.
- *Contextual processes* consider how the "social and environmental context" (p. 19) affects the group dynamics, especially where groups operate in terms of the physical location and the situation or purpose for which they are formed.

It is worth noting the connection between this framework and that presented by Michael Nyman in relation to experimental music, in which he identifies individual and group decision-making through *people processes* and *contextual processes*. People processes "allow the performers to move through given or suggested material, each at [their] own speed," while contextual processes "are concerned with actions dependent on unpredictable conditions and on variables which arise from within the musical continuity" (Nyman, 1999, p. 6). Both of these processes are entangled with Forsyth's framework.

Each of the five processes Forsyth proposes can be used to develop compositional strategies that underpin behavioral-music compositions. Formative and contextual processes may provide a situational influence on the way a piece operates in terms of the preparation and site of a realization. Influence, performance, and conflict processes may operate more directly within a realization as it occurs. In order to consider group behaviors as a compositional strategy, a means to translate these dynamic processes from social psychology to music is necessary. Using Forsyth's processes as a framework, the examples below demonstrate ways in which composers have used group dynamics to create behavioral-music pieces.

Formative processes

Group formation in music is, to an extent, predetermined by the context of performance. Individuals might come together through organizational structures (e.g. ensembles, crowds, friendship), events (e.g. concerts, rehearsals, protests), and places (e.g. stadiums, public spaces, concert halls). They may have worked together previously, either as a whole or as a partial group, or have never met. Convention or circumstances might determine the operation of a group, such as through an ensemble's institutional hierarchies or two soloists working together for the first time. Many pieces do not prescribe these processes, situating them instead within the normal operation of the people realizing the piece, or leaving them unspecified.

Some composers, however, use formative processes to make explicit an attitude to group working. Alexis Porfiriadis stages a formative process as a fundamental component of all his ensemble pieces. He precedes each piece with a standardized text which sets out a specific approach to formation, stating, for example, in *For four people* (2018) that performers

> are invited to make a group realization of the composition using any amount of this material. The order of procedures and their respective timings should be decided collectively prior to the performance. All decisions about how to structure and perform the piece should be made collectively (not by one individual), through a process of conversation and rehearsal.

In practice, the group must decide how to proceed. This immediately tasks them with determining how the transition from individual to collective behaviors should be managed. By not stating how to achieve this, Porfiriadis sets up a formative process that informs later stages of the realization. He notes that this "decision to let the performers use the material provided to construct collectively their performance relies on social and political reasons" in order to "make a statement of collaboration and collective responsibility between the performers of my scores" (2016).

Formative processes can also occur within a piece as it is realized. In my piece *everybody do this* (Saunders, 2014), players within a large ensemble each give spoken instructions in different categories (such as noises, pitches, devices, and recordings) that direct the actions of other players. They do this using a *lingua franca* that simplifies the kinds of interaction possible, with keywords and numbers cueing specific responses (for example, the cue "noise 8" requires everyone to make the noise they have labelled "8"). The players may all give instructions and must respond to instructions given by others as best they can. In realizing the piece, individual players have autonomy within these constraints. They have complete freedom as to the type and frequency of instructions they give. This creates agency within a common frame of reference. It generally results in a playful—and occasionally slightly more sinister—interaction between people. It foregrounds subgroup formation. Players form temporary alliances or rivalries where cues are coordinated or exchanged in a competitive way, possibly hijacking or steering the wider group, depending on personal preferences. These relationships are fluid and transitory, forming and disbanding continuously during the piece.

Formative processes such as these manage the transition from individual to collective behaviors, whether groups are created through a formal process or more dynamically as a result of member decisions. In musical situations, where hierarchies and modes of interaction may be institutionalized or assumed, compositions which address group formation have the potential to comment on the structure of social space.

Influence processes

Many indeterminate pieces use influence processes via the formalization of procedures and interactions through rules. Such pieces may use social influence, where majority or minority subgroups exert power on the whole group, questioning how individuals might assert their independence or conform, depending on the strength, immediacy, and size of the group (Latané, 1981). Influence might be reciprocal or weighted towards one or more individuals or subgroups.

In Laura Steenberge's *Some Folk Songs* (2010) for two voices, initially one singer leads by singing an agreed text to any melody that "comes off the top of the head." The second singer tries to sing the same text and melody as close to unison as possible. Designating the first singer as the leader creates a clear influence through a defined procedure. Although the second player may exert a smaller amount of influence, such as through inaccuracies which affect the first player's subsequent melody, this situation is weighted in terms of the power relationship (albeit in a fairly relaxed and congenial manner).

A greater degree of reciprocality is present in Charlie Sdraulig's *between* (2012–13) for flute and violin, where the two players continuously respond to changes in parameters of each other's sound. The contingent nature of each player's actions creates a careful equilibrium that is constantly tested by inflection. Sdraulig (2013, p. 10) comments that the players' perception shapes the piece in retrospect such that

> A change in a sound or a variable only impacts upon the piece when it is perceived to have occurred. Sonic information is constantly perceived and filtered through the system for interaction before a player responds by making or modifying their sound. One player's actions then influence the other. The piece is a perpetual loop of perceiving and action in response to what is perceived. The performers are entirely dependent on one another. Almost every element of the piece is contingent on another element.

In larger groups of people, social influence might be more nebulous and changeable. John Zorn's *Cobra* (1984) presents a pool of cues that the improvisers may request from a prompter, who then articulates these through giving downbeats that initiate the requested change. Players may break free of this situation and temporarily take over the group through "guerrilla operations." The improvising musicians are controlled by the cues they are given and also are able to request cues to give. The prompter selects the cues to give from the available player requests but is also able to initiate cues directly. The types of cue Zorn uses define relationships between players, time, and material. Zorn highlights the importance of decision-making by the players and prompter as part of this interaction, and the impact on social behavior and influence. He notes

> I basically create a small society and everybody finds their own position in that society. It really becomes like a psycho drama. People are given power and it's very interesting to see which people like to run away from it, who are very docile and just do what they are told, others try very hard to get more control and more power. So it's very much like the political arena in a certain kind of sense. (documented in Bailey, 1993, p. 78)

Influence processes, in particular, mediate the power relationships between group members. In compositions which use these processes, rules may determine the group's procedures and consequently shape their interaction patterns and intermember relations.

Performance processes

Where activities are focused more on reaching goals, whether imposed or self-determined, the ability of groups to perform effectively becomes significant. In many compositions, there may not be an explicit goal presented, other than the successful completion of the tasks and achieving the implicit aesthetic result (Saunders, 2020). In contrast, some compositions may use strategies for creating purpose, either through explicitly stating the purpose or presenting a situation where players must determine a purpose. Mary Flanagan and Helen Nissenbaum (2014, pp. 105–6) frame these decision spaces in games as either *coercive* or *cooperative*. In coercive spaces, designers "may achieve certain behaviors through force (or tight constraints)." In cooperative spaces, they "may encourage certain behaviors while still allowing players to exercise choice" by "drawing on known motivators or rewards (such as points, penalties, and levels), feedback (sensory cues with direct pleasant or unpleasant associations), and cues with certain meanings (such as a doorway, green or red light, the sound of an explosion, and so on)." These two forces are also present in rule-based music.

My piece *all voices are heard* (Saunders, 2015) models consensus decision-making. The aim is to achieve consensus, defined here as all players playing the same sound sequence in unison such that they are in agreement as to its uniformity. Players use performance processes to determine the best strategy to achieve group consensus in a future state of the piece. The piece asks players simultaneously to play a sequence of sounds chosen from a limited set of sources to which all have access (such as a common list of words, set of objects, or group of pitches). This event repeats, with players using a heuristic each time to either (1) play the same material as that which they played previously, (2) play material that matches what another player played previously, (3) play something new, or (4) remain silent. So for example, one player might decide that they want all other players to conform to their sound and prioritize option (1). Conversely, another player might always try to conform to the majority sound, aiming to reinforce that to achieve consensus and prioritize option (2). In both cases, the players are trying to achieve the same aim, but their strategies differ and are evidenced by the decisions they make. In *all voices are heard*, players' decisions must therefore consider both the stated aim of the process and the likely responses of the other players, facilitating or inhibiting the progress of other players and impacting on the group's productiveness.

A more implicit balance between coercion and cooperation is present in Cassandra Miller's vocal piece *rounding* (2017). Singers individually listen to a source recording on headphones and record themselves singing along to it while carrying out a body-scan meditation. They then come together as a group and undertake the same process in parallel, this time each using their own recordings as a source. This group session is recorded and forms the basis of the next iteration of individual recordings. This cycle of individual and group recordings continues until a public performance where the final group realization is presented. The intermingling of individual and group responses to the task results in a complex iterating sequence, the efficacy of which relies on the necessary interdependence of group members. Individual singers' recordings are influenced by the previous group recording, which in turn is constructed from earlier individual recordings. Group performance is mediated by individual responses and idiosyncrasies, enabling convergence towards a group voice to emerge.

The capacity for a group to reach a specified goal can be traced through performance processes such as these, considering individual and collective motivation, and the way groups make decisions. In these processes, the resultant music can be experienced as a sonification of dynamic interaction between people and their progress towards a goal.

Conflict processes

Conflict can both inhibit the performance of a group by undermining relationships and energize it through the potential benefit of competition. In behavioral-music compositions, conflict might arise, for example, from limiting the available resources available to players, setting goals that are impossible to achieve for all group members, or the artificial imposition of hierarchies.

In David Pocknee's *Economics* (2010/2017), the sound each player makes is modified in four different parameters (pitch, dynamics, speed, and duration) by players placing money on charts in front of the other players. The amount of money present alters a parameter in a specific way, for example "if 5 Euro Cents are placed in your Dynamics: Louder circle, then you must play louder." Players use their own money, including any currently on their own chart, to moderate changes to other players' sounds. They may not take money from others. The score also states that "Players can ask the audience for money. This is a form of public subsidy." The piece sets up a dynamic set of power relationships between the players, and between the players and audience, facilitated by financial transactions. Pocknee (2017, Fig. C.4) notes that in a 2010 performance

> the audience organically got involved in the piece and started competing with each other and the performers, placing their credit cards, car keys, wallets etc. in the circles on the performer's scores. In the audio recording you can even hear the Zoom recorder being picked up and used as currency.

Here conflict is staged as a compositional process, with players exerting direct control over each other through competition and transaction.

Making impossible demands on players is another way to create conflict, through limiting resources and opportunities within a prescribed task. I take this approach in *reaching an acceptable and stable solution* (Saunders, 2018a), in which the aim is for players to find a distribution of resources such that they can all play the available sounds at specified times. The group has a shared resource of ten sound-producing objects that are within reach. Players independently assign each of the available objects to a number in their scores, which indicates when the object is to be used. Selections of objects by one player may cause difficulties for another player, and the requirement is made harder by having more players and/or fewer objects, such that in some situations, it might not be possible to complete the task accurately. The players must balance the use of a shared resource in order to make a specified sequence of different sounds while helping or hindering others to do the same. Player allocations of sounds conflict with each other, so that by the end of the piece, it is challenging for players to use the necessary objects at the right time as other players are likely to be using them. The piece plays with conflict but also encourages compromise, problem-solving, and courtesy.

Conflict processes are among the most extreme ways to explore group behaviors, given their reliance on intra-group oppositions, whether hostile or benign. Pieces which use conflict as a mode of interaction expose tensions between people when undertaking specified tasks, potentially leading to the breakdown of the group and an inability to reach an agreed conclusion.

Contextual processes

The context in which pieces are conceived and realized may also have an impact on the way groups operate. The environmental context may impose physical constraints on the way players interact, while the social context may place limits and demands on individual choices. In both situations, the relationship between the players and the specific context in which they work is a significant factor in determining how a piece unfolds.

In John Lely's *Symphony No 4: The Great Outdoors* (2009), a group of players with portable percussion instruments begin in close proximity to a conductor, then "gradually disperse over the course of a performance." They walk away from the conductor, occasionally articulating a synchronized event which "occurs on a cue from the conductor, and consists of all players sounding their instruments in visual unison." As they disperse, spatial displacement may cause the synchronization of the sounds to vary, depending on the listener's relative position. Similarly, in one of the variations suggested by Pauline Oliveros in her *Sonic Meditation VII* (1971), a group of players strike stones together while seated in a circle, before gradually moving "anywhere in the environment" while keeping "in audible contact with at least one other person." Here the dispersal controls group cohesion, using aural perception to maintain ties between players. In both pieces, the spatial context has a significant impact on the group ecology, such that "the place shapes the group rather than the group shaping the place" (Forsyth, 2014, p. 481).

Context is also significant in environments where players respond to complex sequences of cues and instructions, where the possibility for failure is high. In my piece *you are required to split your attention between multiple sources of information* (Saunders, 2018b) for string quartet and large ensemble, the players are presented with a stream of pre-recorded auditory cues to which they must respond with specified sounds. The cues regularly switch between different types and are directed at different subgroups and individuals within the two ensembles, requiring the players to think and act very quickly. The level of *cognitive load* impacts on the way players remember associations between cues and responses, and affects decision-making and action in a networked situation. In the piece, moments of ordered information are disrupted by less predictable cue sequences and regular changes of cue type. The cues include samples of real-world sounds which induce a range of different responses, as well as text-to-speech computer voices giving verbal cues. The density, speed, and patterning of these cues cause different amounts of cognitive load on the players, altering their response times and, with it, the texture of the resulting music. Mousavi et al. (1995, p. 332) suggest that this *split-attention effect* has an impact on cognitive load by requiring subjects to integrate multiple information sources mentally "before they can be understood, [otherwise] learning may be inhibited." In the piece, all the cues and responses are aural, requiring players to negotiate the stream of information in one mode. The increased cognitive load affects the speed of response by players and the variations in time required to complete sound-producing actions on the different instruments, producing an unpredictable trail of sounds after each cue.

The different kinds of social and environmental contexts in which pieces such as these operate constrain the ways in which players interact. Context is a significant global influence on group behaviors through determining the relationship between players, and between players and their working environment.

Conclusion

The examples presented above demonstrate some ways in which group dynamics may be deployed to manipulate and test group behaviors in a musical context. Through using disparate mechanisms such as cueing, formalized hierarchies, cognitive load, goal attainment, environmental constraints, and social influence, scores may determine modes of interaction that translate specific values inherent in their rule systems (Flanagan & Nissenbaum, 2014). Frameworks such as Forsyth's group dynamics processes suggest ways in which group behaviors might be developed as musical processes, set within the context of modes of interaction examined in social psychology more widely. John Zorn (2004) summarizes the appeal for taking this approach, suggesting that

> What you get on the stage, then, is not just someone reading music but a drama. You get a human drama. You get life itself, which is what the ultimate musical experience is: it's life. Musicians relating to each other, through music.

At a time where communities are being separated, divisions are emphasized, and autocratic government is prevalent, work that explores how people might work together and reflect on social interaction has the potential to encourage positive social change.

References

Auslander, P. (2006). Musical personae. *TDR/The Drama Review, 50*(1), 100–19.

Bailey, D. (1993). *Improvisation: Its nature and practice in music.* Perseus Books Group.

Bishop, C. (2012). *Artificial hells: Participatory art and the politics of spectatorship.* Verso Books.

Cook, N. (2001). Between process and product: Music and/as performance. *Music Theory Online, 7*(2). www.mtosmt.org/issues/mto.01.7.2/mto.01.7.2.cook.html

Fiske, S. T., & Taylor, S. E. (2017). *Social cognition: From brains to culture* (3rd ed.). Sage.

Flanagan, M., & Nissenbaum, H. F. (2014). *Values at play in digital games.* MIT Press.

Forsyth, D. R. (2014). *Group dynamics* (6th ed.). Wadsworth/Cengage Learning.

Gigerenzer, G., & Gaissmaier, W. (2011). Heuristic decision making [SSRN Scholarly Paper]. *Social Science Research Network.* http://papers.ssrn.com/abstract=1722019

Glowinski, D., Dardard, F., Gnecco, G., Piana, S., & Camurri, A. (2015). Expressive non-verbal interaction in a string quartet: An analysis through head movements. *Journal on Multimodal User Interfaces, 9*(1), 55–68.

Hogg, M. A., & Vaughan, G. M. (2018). *Social psychology* (8th ed.). Pearson.

Latané, B. (1981). The psychology of social impact. *American Psychologist, 36*(4), 343–56.

Mousavi, S. Y., Low, R., & Sweller, J. (1995). Reducing cognitive load by mixing auditory and visual presentation modes. *Journal of Educational Psychology, 87*(2), 319–34.

Nyman, M. (1999). *Experimental music: Cage and beyond.* Cambridge University Press.

Pocknee, D. (2017). *How to compose a PhD thesis in music composition* [Doctoral dissertation]. University of Huddersfield.

Porfiriadis, A. (2016). Artist statement. Alexisporfiriadis.Blogspot.Com. http://alexisporfiriadis. blogspot.com/p/about.html

Saunders, J. (2015). Heuristic models for decision making in rule-based compositions. In J. Ginsborg, A. Lamont, M. Phillips, & S. Bramley (Eds.), *Proceedings of the Ninth Triennial Conference of the European Society for the Cognitive Sciences of Music* (ESCOM) (pp. 715–19). Royal Northern College of Music, August 17–22, 2015. http://escom.org/proceedings/ESCOM9_Manchester_2015_Abstracts_Proceedings.pdf

Saunders, J. (2020). What's the point? Balancing purpose and play in rule-based compositions. In P. Thomas, & E. Payne (Eds.), *Performing indeterminacy*. Cambridge University Press.

Sdraulig, C. (2013). *Interaction in line, breath and process*. https://static1.squarespace.com/static/5d63bf2d3fe4d500012964f7/t/5d673a87cdd58a000116b4d7/1567046290487/Interaction+in+line%2C+breath+and+process.pdf

Sicart, M. (2014). *Play matters*. MIT Press.

Zorn, J. (2004). The game pieces. In C. Cox, & D. Warner (Eds.), *Audio culture: Readings in modern music* (pp. 196–200). Continuum.

Scores

Lely, J. (2009). *Symphony No 4: The Great Outdoors* [score].

Miller, C. (2017). *rounding* [score]. In J. Weeks (2018). *Partsongs*. CoMA, 84–6.

Oliveros, P. (1971). *Sonic Meditations I–XXV* [score]. Smith Publications.

Pocknee, D. (2010/2017). *Economics* [score]. Available at: http://davidpocknee.ricercata.org/compositions/e030_economics-2017/david-pocknee_economics-2017_2017-06-28b.pdf (Accessed: August 23, 2020).

Porfiriadis, A. (2018). *For four people* [score]. Available at: http://intuitivemusic.dk/iima/ap_for_four_people.pdf (Accessed: August 23, 2020).

Saunders, J. (2014). *everybody do this* [score]. Available at: https://doi.org/10.17870/bathspa.9771770.v1 (Accessed: August 23, 2020).

Saunders, J. (2015). *all voices are heard* [score]. Available at: http://researchspace.bathspa.ac.uk/6763/1/all%20voices%20are%20heard.pdf (Accessed: August 23, 2020).

Saunders, J. (2018a). *reaching an acceptable and stable solution* [score]. Available at: http://researchspace.bathspa.ac.uk/13178/1/reaching%20an%20acceptable%20and%20stable%20solution%20NEW.pdf (Accessed: August 23, 2020).

Saunders, J. (2018b). *you are required to split your attention between multiple sources of information* [score]. Available at: http://researchspace.bathspa.ac.uk/11548/1/you%20are%20required%20to%20split%20your%20attention%20between%20multiple%20sources%20of%20information.pdf (Accessed: August 23, 2020).

Sdraulig, C. (2013). *between* [score]. Available at: https://static1.squarespace.com/static/5d63bf2d3fe4d500012964f7/t/5d65c87fb85c0e0001978f5b/1566951577267/between.pdf (Accessed: August 23, 2020).

Steenberge, L. (2010). *Some Folk Songs* [score and audio]. Available at: https://laurasteenbergeportfolio.com/compositions/some-folk-songs/ (Accessed: August 23, 2020).

Recordings

Pocknee, D. (2010/2017). *Economics* [video]. Available at: https://youtu.be/01SEFV2uiFA (Accessed: August 23, 2020).

Saunders, J. (2014). *everybody do this* [videos]. Available at: http://www.james-saunders.com/things-2/ (Accessed: August 23, 2020).

Saunders, J. (2015). *all voices are heard* [videos]. Available at: http://www.james-saunders.com/all-voices-are-heard-2015/ (Accessed: August 23, 2020).

Saunders, J. (2018a). *reaching an acceptable and stable solution* [video]. Available at: http://www.james-saunders.com/reaching-an-acceptable-and-stable-solution-2018/   (Accessed: August 23, 2020).

Saunders, J. (2018b). *you are required to split your attention between multiple sources of information* [video]. Available at: https://youtu.be/9aRB1jrWmWc (Accessed: August 23, 2020).

Sdraulig, C. (2013). *between* [video]. Available at: https://vimeo.com/122186504 (Accessed: August 23, 2020).

Zorn, J. (1984). *Cobra* [video]. Available at: https://youtu.be/yp-oZbmsQVw (Accessed: August 23, 2020).

3

Organizational dynamics in community ensembles

David A. Camlin

Introduction

Looking into organizational dynamics in community ensembles, this chapter addresses the following questions:

1. How do musical, social, and paramusical factors shape participation in community music ensembles?
2. How do participants progress from peripheral or non-participation to full participation in such ensembles?
3. What factors both facilitate and impede such participation, and how might these tensions be addressed?

These questions are explored from a broadly constructionist perspective, recognizing that in understanding the kinds of sociocultural practices under discussion, "truth, or meaning, comes into existence in and out of our engagement with the realities in our world" (Crotty, 1998, p. 8). In other words, the meaning of participation in community music ensembles is something which is constantly negotiated and renegotiated between those involved.

A number of theoretical perspectives are introduced as "lenses" through which to view the resulting discussion. These include a consideration of the inherent tensions involved in performing both "works" and "relationships" as a holistic practice (Camlin, 2016, 2018; Camlin et al., 2020), as well as the value of a "situated" understanding of sociocultural practice (Lave & Wenger, 1991; Wenger, 1999), and how this can lead to the formation of "rational communities" (Biesta, 2006; Lingis, 1994) of practice which both include and exclude participants in the formation of group identity (see also Chapters 13 and 27). The chapter draws on contemporary theories of cultural participation (Crossick & Kaszynska, 2016; Gross et al., 2017; Hunter et al., 2016), as well as more psychological theories (Apter, 2007; Berne, 1973) for understanding some of the different ways in which participants come to view the group and their place in it. These different theoretical perspectives are summarized in Fig. 3.1.

The resulting discussion draws on the author's practical experience of leading community ensembles to illustrate some of the associated complexities, before considering some implications for practice, as well as opportunities for future research.

David A. Camlin, *Organizational dynamics in community ensembles* In: *Together in music*. Edited by: Renee Timmers, Freya Bailes, and Helena Daffern, Oxford University Press. © Oxford University Press 2022. DOI: 10.1093/oso/9780198860761.003.0003

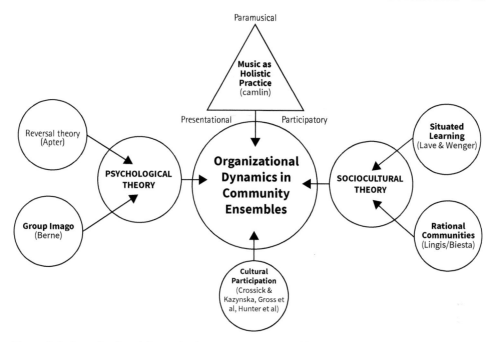

Figure 3.1 Organizational dynamics in community ensembles—theoretical framework.

Theoretical framework

Music as a holistic practice

Musical performances tend to be characterized as either presentational or participatory (Turino, 2008). Music is either something which is performed for a listening audience, what we might term the performance of musical "works," or else it is something which is enjoined as part of the fabric of social life, or the performing of human "relationships" (Camlin, 2018, 2019; Camlin et al., 2020). Of course, the reality is more complex and nuanced than this two-dimensional conceptualization allows. Compared to a professional ensemble, community ensembles may appear to emphasize the participatory/relational dimension, but it should not be assumed that a simple dichotomy exists between these two dimensions of musical experience (see also Chapter 8). Community ensembles certainly want to sound good, especially when performing to a public audience. Similarly, even a professional orchestra is still liter-ally *performing* the relationships between its members when it performs, because "attuning" to the other players in order to collectively realize particular sonorous effects requires high levels of interpersonal awareness, entrainment, and synchronization (see also Chapters 17, 19, and 26).

Increasingly, attention is given not just to musical outcomes and experiences, but also to what we might refer to as a "third" dimension of musical experience, the "paramusical" (Stige et al., 2013, p. 298) outcomes and benefits arising from participation, such as positive impacts on participants' health and wellbeing (MacDonald et al., 2013). The success of any commu-nity ensemble is therefore measured against a complex interplay between these musical, so-cial, and paramusical dimensions, as this comment from a participant in a previous study (Camlin et al., 2020) highlights:

I just love the feeling of being connected with the group of singers that I experience each time. I want more of that in my life. I feel better able to cope with whatever life throws at me; better resourced and more confident. No matter how I'm feeling when I arrive at one of these gatherings, after a very short time of being with and singing with the choir I have a big smile on my face that reflects my wonderful internal sense of belonging and rootedness, joy and connectedness. (Participant 01)

Situated learning

The extent to which any combination of these dimensions is more—or less—present within the practices of a community ensemble is both highly situated and highly variable. To take the example of group singing, a village choir in a rural community may be set up with the intention of being somewhere for local residents to relax with each other, have fun and, connect with others in their community through music (social), while a choral society in the nearby town may have a more explicit focus on realizing particular musical "works" (musical) and a "wellbeing" choir attached to the local hospital or general practice (GP) surgery may have the amelioration of mental health symptoms as its primary focus (paramusical). However, in each of these examples, the other two dimensions are not absent altogether, merely emphasized in different ways. All musical groups—to a greater or lesser extent—want to have fun, sound good, and feel good, both during and after a musical experience.

To understand the organizational dynamics of community ensembles, it is therefore helpful to view them through the theoretical lens of "situated learning" (Lave & Wenger, 1991; Wenger, 1999). Lave and Wenger's model highlights the great variety of sociocultural contexts and "communities of practitioners" (1991, p. 29) which support participation. While the *practices* of community ensembles may vary—because of these sociocultural and musical differences—the *process* of membership of such groups is not so different. If "the mastery of knowledge and skill requires newcomers to move toward full participation in the sociocultural practices of a community," then ensemble membership is about finding a group of others who share similar values and beliefs regarding music and its performance and who engage in practices that express those values and beliefs, as this participant's comment suggests:

When I discovered [the choir] it was like finding my tribe again and being able to do it every week. [The choir] has been invaluable for me to integrate into a new area so that I feel I belong here and can make a place for myself here. (Participant 02)

Often, the search for a suitable community ensemble is about rejecting the ones which are "not really my kind of thing" as much as it is about stumbling into something that feels like the perfect fit for one's needs:

I tried [one choir] but it was too formal for me and there were only 3 other tenors – all men. I then joined [another choir] and I went to that for a year until it folded due to lack of funding. I couldn't find another one within easy reach so [I] haven't sung [in a choir] for the past two and a half years until last week. (Participant 03)

There are no hard and fast rules about which values may be emphasized within a particular community ensemble, although for participants to move towards full participation, a match is necessary between objectives and values. In general, the more emphasis there is on public performance, the more likely that the culture and values of the group will be about achieving the highest standard of technical execution in service to the musical "works" being performed. Similarly, the more emphasis there is on the relational aspects of musical performance, the more likely that the group's culture and values will be about having fun without feeling judged on the quality of sound produced. Paradoxically, of course, the realization of the latter can support the former; when people perform music without anxiety, they are more likely to perform well.

Rational communities

These underpinning values serve to both include and exclude individuals, depending on the extent to which their own values correspond with those of the group. Hence, one of the functions of organizational dynamics within community ensembles is to communicate tacit information about these underpinning values, which in turn help to promote group cohesion (see also Chapter 9).

> To ask "What community?" is also to ask "What kind of practice?", "What kind of people are deemed capable of engaging in it?", "What kinds of attitudes, beliefs, and actions does it exist to sustain?", and "What kinds of attitudes, beliefs, and actions are necessary to sustain and nourish it?" (Bowman, 2009, p. 109)

Over time, a group's practices may become "reified" (Wenger, 1999, pp. 58–68) or coalesce into a "rational community" (Biesta, 2006, pp. 56–7) whose members may simply believe that their practices are what any rational person (like themselves) would engage in. The tacit and often ritualized nature of some of these dynamics can be hard to fathom for "newcomers" to any particular community of practice. Discovering a group whose values and practices mirror your own beliefs about how to be musical can be intensely validating, while encountering a group with quite different values and practices can be destabilizing and uncomfortable: "granting legitimate participation to newcomers with their own viewpoints introduces into any community of practice all the tensions of the continuity-displacement contradiction" (Lave & Wenger, 1991, p. 116). At worst, this kind of displacement can be experienced by prospective group members as a kind of "symbolic violence" (Schubert, 2012), where their aspirations about group membership are dashed, and their personal identity consequently challenged.

Barriers to participation

Barriers to participation are complex, because of the situated nature of participation. As previously noted, perhaps the greatest barrier to participation is the lack of a sufficiently broad range of communities of musical practice with which to choose to engage. Even in more urban areas, participants may have to travel a reasonable distance to engage with a "community of practice" which resonates most strongly with their own values and interests. In a rural area, the relative lack of opportunities and the more significant distance between such opportunities can be even more inhibiting.

The audition is perhaps the most obvious example of a barrier to participation, as it will deter some participants from even considering membership, and it will prevent others from becoming members. However, for some communities of practice, the audition is an important tool for explicitly communicating the underpinning values of the group, namely its emphasis on public performance and the realization of musical "works," and the consequent technical skills of its members to manipulate sound in particular ways to support these values. The audition process might also be one means through which an established group identifies new members who will disrupt the group dynamic the least, by dint of their complementary skills, expertise, and experience.

Questions of "access" and "inclusion" highlight the fact that many organized communities of musical practice appear to emerge from within quite privileged socioeconomic situations (Crossick & Kaszynska, 2016, pp. 29–33). This might be because the costs of maintaining the community are quite high, e.g. hiring a venue, paying a musician to direct the work, purchasing resources, organizing registers and communications, and managing financial transactions. It might also be that music participation is a signifier or "doxa" of social status, i.e. part of "a set of core values and discourses which a field articulates as its fundamental principles and which tend to be viewed as inherently true and necessary" (Burnard & Trulsson, 2015), and which may therefore serve to reinforce social stratification. The question of "who" participates in such activities may be as much about sociocultural background as it is about economics, or even music: "Nothing more clearly affirms one's 'class', nothing more infallibly classifies, than tastes in music" (Bourdieu, 1979, p. 18).

Protective frames and safe danger

Becoming proficient at making music involves developing a range of skills and attitudes which support musical expression, e.g. controlling one's voice/instrument, developing aural skills, adjusting tone, following and reading notation, blending with others (see chapters of Part 2). Developing such capabilities therefore requires the automation of a corresponding range of neural schema (Levitin, 2008, p. 217). For the newcomer to musical activity, developing this neural automaticity takes time and repetition to become proficient, and is best achieved through a process of "multiple coding," i.e. building up multiple neural traces which activate the same schema across visual, auditory, and motor cortices in the brain (Levitin, 2008, pp. 164–5). Supporting newcomers to develop their musicality therefore requires some sensitivity around how these neural schema might develop, and also recognizing that each person is different when it comes to such development. For some, following musical notation may be familiar and comfortable, while for others, it may be completely foreign, like attempting to decipher an alien language. A similar effect may be experienced when learning by ear or improvising.

If developing this musical proficiency is about developing participants' "cultural capabilities" to "co-create versions of culture" (Gross et al., 2017) in order to perform both "works" and "relationships," then participants require some guarantee of musical and psychological safety within which to develop these expressions of their "everyday creativity" (Hunter et al.,

2016). There is inevitably a period of "liminality" as newcomers move from non-participation through the periphery towards full participation, and being able to enter such liminal spaces without fear of criticism, embarrassment, or shame is important in participants' ongoing development. The conditions of "safe danger" (Camlin et al., 2020) or "safety without safety," i.e. "to take risks, whether emotional, psychological, technical, or physical" (Higgins, 2008, p. 391), while feeling safe in doing so—might be seen to be established through what Apter (2007) refers to as a "protective frame" (pp. 50–3), i.e. a way of structuring activity which enables participants to experience what otherwise may feel overwhelming, threatening, or too difficult to accomplish, for example improvising in a group before doing so individually.

Group imago

As this discussion suggests, the "generative process of producing their own future" (Lave & Wenger, 1991, p. 57) can be a complex negotiation for musical "communities of practice" of sometimes competing agendas. Different elements within the group seek to assert what they believe to be its core values through the expression of particular behaviors and attitudes. Paradoxically, "this combination of discontinuity and continuity creates a dynamic equilibrium that can be construed as stable and as the same practice" (Wenger, 1999, p. 94).

To understand the complex ways in which community ensembles navigate such tensions of continuity and discontinuity, we therefore turn to Eric Berne's classic theory of "Group imago" (Berne, 1973), which suggests four stages of membership which are experienced by a group's members, including the leader. "Group imago: describes "any mental picture, conscious, preconscious or unconscious, of what a group is or should be like" (Berne, 1973, p. 244), and can be considered alongside other classic theories of group process like Tuckman's "stages" of group development (Tuckman, 1965; Tuckman & Jensen, 1977). However, in emphasizing a dynamic theory of individual experience, it helps to illuminate some of the tensions under discussion (and also discussed in Chapter 1). An illustration of Berne's theory is represented in Fig. 3.2.

The first stage of a group imago is "provisional," i.e. "an image of what the group is going to be like for [a new member] and what they may hope to get out of it" (Berne, 1973, p. 161). It becomes an "adapted" group imago once they meet the rest of the group, based on "appraisals of the other people, usually made by observing them during rituals and activities" (p. 163). It only becomes an "operative" group imago once the new member is more integrated within the group and has a sense of "their own place in the leader's group imago" (p. 164). The fourth and final stage of the process is an "adjusted" group imago, where the group member "relinquishes some of their own proclivities in favor of the group cohesion" (p. 244).

In any group, the different mental images that group members have of the group and where they fit within it affect not just their own experience, but that of the group identity as well. The addition of a new member to an existing group—which may have already learned how to "perform" with a collectively "adjusted" group imago that capitalizes on the capabilities of all of its members—can be destabilizing as the group needs to relearn how to incorporate the newcomer without unduly affecting the group's performative ability. To prevent this instability, some groups become effectively "closed" groups which do not accept new members, except under particular circumstances, for example when recruiting new members to a particular section.

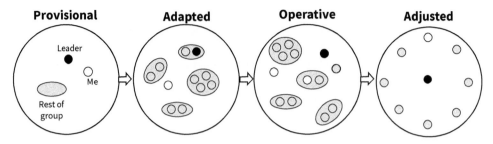

Figure 3.2 Group imago.
Reproduced from Berne, E. (1973). The structure and dynamics of organizations and groups. Ballantine Books.

Discussion

To illustrate some of the above issues, I consider how they might be seen to manifest within a number of non-auditioned "Natural Voice" (Natural Voice Network, n.d.) community choirs in the UK, which I lead as part of my professional practice as a musician. I do not suggest that these reflections are representative of a more general experience of community music ensembles, merely that borrowing from my experience as choir leader helps me to discuss some possible practical implications of the above theoretical perspectives, including facilitating and challenging factors for participation. This approach also helps to address a recent recommendation to "ensure that singing group leaders are given a voice along with the participants' views, to obtain input from those 'on the ground'" (Dingle et al., 2019, p. 10).

Types of participants

Leader
The leader and musical director of a community choir has perhaps the greatest influence on participants' experience of the group's dynamics, at least partly because their group imago is likely to be the most influential in shaping the group's culture and values, through musical arrangement and repertoire selection, as well as through behavior, values, and attitudes. Either they are appointed as leaders because their culture and values are expected to influence the group's evolution and practice, or—as in my case—they have founded the group in the first place. In relation to the theoretical framework introduced, situated leadership responsibilities might include:

- Attending *holistically* to the musical quality and also to the way that relationships are formed and sustained within the group, as well as being aware of how the "paramusical" benefits of participation can enhance both;
- Creating opportunities within *protective frames* for participants to move from the periphery to the centre of the group's practice, which might involve the (implicit or explicit) delegation of sectional responsibility, or facilitating individual expressivity through structured improvisation in groups of reducing size, i.e. whole group > small group > pairs > solo;

- Being aware of when a strong group cohesion can form a *rational community* of practice which can be daunting for newcomers to encounter. Therefore, personally welcoming new members and supporting them to "adapt" their "provisional" image of the group by ensuring they are introduced to others in their section, and the group, through "Getting to Know You" activities;
- Recognizing potential *barriers to participation* and addressing them wherever possible, for example through welcoming all voices and experiences without audition or judgement, and ensuring voices are sufficiently "warmed up" before singing. Ironically, such activities might call on participants to release tension in their bodies and voices through expressive sounds and movements which might seem quite strange to a newcomer, so sensitivity is required to judge what is appropriate;
- Structuring activity to facilitate the automation of neural schema which support participants' evolving musicality, i.e. using "multiple coding" (Levitin, 2008, pp. 164–5) and "chunking" (p. 217) as pedagogical strategies to support automation, listening carefully to the resulting musical expression, and making further adjustments as necessary;
- Supporting members to develop an "operative" *group imago* by personal communications with individuals to reassure them that their experience of the group is important, and reinforcing core values about the "humanizing" and inclusive nature of group singing;
- Recognizing that each time the group membership changes, so too does the group's functional imago; and attending to these discontinuities, especially when key figures within the group cease participation, and how the remaining individuals re-establish an "adjusted" group imago without them.

Newcomers

For newcomers to a choir, moving through the four stages of group imago is a sensitive process; hence, "a new-comer's tasks are short and simple, the costs of error are small, [with] little responsibility for the activities as a whole" (Lave & Wenger, 1991, p. 110). Having access to the leader from the outset—in person and by phone/e-mail—is important to be able to make an informed assessment about the group and whether it is likely to correspond well with their own values and aspirations for membership. Being able to participate more peripherally (Lave & Wenger, 1991)—either through one-off "taster" sessions or by trying out a number of different choirs before committing to one, or just being able to sit at the back of the rehearsal—can help prospective members to "adapt" their "provisional" imago to something more realistic. Physically starting at—or moving to—the periphery of a choir's seating arrangement, from where they can make more of a judgement not just about their own participation, but also about that of the other members, affords newcomers some degree of physical and psychological safety while they "adjust" their provisional mental image of the group to the reality which confronts them.

Old-timers

Conversely, for the "old-timers" in the choir, they often demonstrate their proximity to the center of practice (Lave & Wenger, 1991) by contributing more actively to the group's culture and collective "adjusted" group imago, through participation in a range of activities, which might include:

- Arriving early to help the leader set up the room;
- Organizing water for other participants to drink before and during the rehearsal;
- Approaching newcomers to welcome them to the group and acting as a role model during their initiation, sitting next to them, and supporting their participation in sensitive ways, such as helping them navigate a musical score;
- Operating as section leaders, either informally or in a more formally agreed way with the leader;
- Adopting a range of different section leadership styles, either leading from the front, from within, or from behind the section as circumstances dictate;
- Assuming organizational responsibilities and management functions, including in some instances setting up committees to structure the everyday running of the choir.

Implications for practice

Recognizing the complex and situated ways in which community music ensembles cohere and evolve is important in sustaining a healthy and inclusive practice. As groups change and evolve, so too must the leadership approaches which sustain them. As participants grow in confidence and skill, they need new challenges to sustain their interest, which can realign a group's culture and purpose towards exciting new territories. In turn, this can lead to external perceptions of the group as a kind of "elite," making it less accessible to newcomers, and so a balance between music's different dimensions (presentational, participatory, paramusical) needs to be continually brokered and (re)negotiated.

Future research

There are also a number of complex questions surrounding the organizational dynamics of community music ensembles which require further understanding. Chief among these are the complex issues surrounding access and inclusion. While current research is clear about the great variety of benefits associated with participation in group singing, what is less clear is the extent to which these supposed benefits are a result of the activity, or actually a prerequisite for participation in it. For example, does singing make you happier? Or do happier people tend to want to sing more? Presumably most community ensembles would like to think of their practices as accessible and inclusive, but there is little research undertaken on how such practices may actually hinder participation, i.e. because of the way in which *rational communities* of music or "reified" musical practices may impede or discourage participation. The experience of non-participation is less well understood, as research is more often conducted with those who have already chosen to participate, rather than with those who choose not to.

Therefore, as well as the "need to know more about the negative physical and psychological experiences" (Dingle et al., 2019, p. 10) associated with participation in community ensembles, and the need for "more research testing theoretical models and adopting robust methodologies" (p. 10), future research also needs to focus on the experience of non-participation—especially the ways in which organizational dynamics in community ensembles might hinder participation—in order to better understand the limits of participation and the ways in which community ensembles might develop more inclusive and accessible practices.

Conclusion

Organizational dynamics within community music ensembles are a complex area to explore, addressing the *holistic* tensions involved in performing both musical "works" and human "relationships." *Situated* approaches to understanding practice are essential, because of the wide range of diverse practices involved. A consideration of organizational dynamics can help to unearth some of this complexity, as it illustrates the different ways that group organizational structures can both impede participation through the emergence over time of "elite" *rational communities*, as well as facilitate participation through supportive psychological measures, e.g. *protective frames* and the concept of *safe danger*. Understanding the mental models of participation—such as *group imago*—which underpin the membership of community ensembles helps to reveal more of this complexity, but it remains a partial view. The experience of non-participation needs to be foregrounded in future research in order to develop a fuller picture of the issue and highlight ways to maximize participation.

References

Apter, M. J. (2007). *Reversal theory: The dynamics of motivation, emotion and personality* (New ed.). Oneworld Publications.

Berne, E. (1973). *The structure and dynamics of organizations and groups*. Ballantine Books.

Biesta, G. J. J. (2006). *Beyond learning: Democratic education for a human future*. Paradigm Publishers.

Bourdieu, P. (1979). *Distinction*. Routledge.

Bowman, W. (2009). The community in music. *International Journal of Community Music, 2*(2/3), 109–28.

Burnard, P., & Trulsson, Y. H. (2015). *Bourdieu and the sociology of music education* (Revised ed.). Routledge.

Camlin, D. A. (July, 2016). *Music in three dimensions*. [Paper presentation]. International Society for Music Education Conference.

Camlin, D. A. (February, 2018). *Assessing quality in socially engaged musical performances*. [Paper presentation]. Reflective Conservatoire.

Camlin, D. A. (June 19, 2019). *Recovering our humanity: What's love (and music) got to do with it?* [Paper presentation]. International Fjord Summer School 2019. https://www.uib.no/en/rs/grieg/122694/exploring-artistic-pedagogic-and-therapeutic-practices-interdisciplinary-knowledges

Camlin, D. A., Daffern, H., & Zeserson, K. (2020). *Group singing as a resource for the development of healthy publics. Humanities and Social Sciences Communications*. https://doi.org/10.1057/s41599-020-00549-0

Crossick, G., & Kaszynska, P. (2016). *Understanding the value of arts and culture: The AHRC cultural value report*. Arts & Humanities Research Council. http://www.ahrc.ac.uk/documents/publications/cultural-value-project-final-report/

Crotty, M. J. (1998). *The foundations of social research: Meaning and perspective in the research process*. Sage.

Dingle, G., Clift, S., Finn, S., Gilbert, R., Groarke, J., Irons, J. Y., Bartoli, A., Lamont, A., Launay, J., Martin, E., Moss, H., Sanfilippo, K. R., Shipton, M., Stewart, L., Talbot, S., Tarrant, M., Tip, L., & Williams, E. (2019). An agenda for best practice research on group singing, health, and wellbeing. *Music and Science, 2*, 1–15. https://doi.org/10.1177/2059204319861719

Gross, J., Wilson, N., & Bull, A. (2017). *Towards cultural democracy*. Kings College. https://www.kcl.ac.uk/cultural/resources/reports/towards-cultural-democracy-2017-kcl.pdf

Higgins, L. (2008). *Safety without safety—Participation, the workshop, and the welcome.* [Paper presentation]. *Community Music Activity.*

Hunter, J., Micklem, D., & 64 Million Artists. (2016). *Everyday creativity.* 64 Million Artists. http://64millionartists.com/everyday-creativity-2/

Lave, J., & Wenger, E. (1991). *Situated learning: Legitimate peripheral participation.* Cambridge University Press.

Levitin, D. J. (2008). *This is your brain on music: Understanding a human obsession.* Atlantic Books.

Lingis, A. (1994). *The community of those who have nothing in common.* Indiana University Press.

MacDonald, R., Kreutz, G., & Mitchell, L. (Eds.). (2013). *Music, health, and wellbeing.* Oxford University Press.

Natural Voice Network. (n.d.). *Natural Voice Network.* http://www.naturalvoice.net/

Schubert, J. D. (2012). Suffering/symbolic violence. In M. Grenfell (Ed.), *Pierre Bourdieu: Key concepts* (pp. 179–194). Routledge.

Stige, B., Ansdell, G., Elefant, C., & Pavlicevic, M. (2013). *Where music helps: Community music therapy in action and reflection.* Ashgate.

Tuckman, B. (1965). Developmental sequence in small groups. *Psychological Bulletin, 63*(6), 384–99.

Tuckman, B. W., & Jensen, M. A. C. (1977). Stages of small-group development revisited. *Group & Organization Management, 2*(4), 419–27.

Turino, T. (2008). *Music as social life: The politics of participation.* University of Chicago Press.

Wenger, E. (1999). *Communities of practice: Learning, meaning, and identity* (New Ed). Cambridge University Press.

4

Agency in ensemble interaction and rehearsal communication

Su Yin Mak, Hiroko Nishida, and Daisuke Yokomori

Introduction

Agency refers to the capacity to act and act upon, to initiate and carry out actions either for their own sakes or to influence and affect others. The concept is often invoked in music studies, but the nature and types of actions and agents are understood differently in various disciplines. In this chapter, we begin with an overview of current perspectives on musical agency and trace their implications for research on ensemble music-making. Next, using conversational segments drawn from two case studies as illustrations, we consider agential roles and ascriptions that are not accounted for in current paradigms. In closing, we explore the theoretical implications of our findings and propose a new critical perspective.

Sociocultural and metaphorical perspectives of musical agency

The extant research on musical agency may be categorized under two perspectives: the sociocultural and the metaphorical. According to the former, agents are always human, and their actions involve music-making and/or forms of engagement with musical experiences as a means of interaction with the world. Small (1998), for example, coined the novel term "musicking" to emphasize that music is an activity (verb) rather than an abstract, autonomous object (noun). Turino's study of music as social life likewise views musical participation and experience as expressions of personal and collective agencies (Turino, 2008). Music educators have also written extensively about the role of agency in music learning, as summarized in Wiggins (2015). The alternative epistemology, commonly found in music theory and music psychology, assigns agency to musical works or their components. It is well known that both lay listeners and professional musicians habitually construe the dynamic processes of music in terms of gestures and events, and since actions necessarily imply actors, agential descriptions are pervasive in discourse about music throughout the ages. We speak, for example, of "yearning" or "striving" melodies, "rushing" or "plodding" rhythms, and harmonic "progressions," "expectations," or "arrivals;" standard terminology for compositional devices in Western classical music is also rich in agential implications (e.g. "suspensions," "lament" basses, "deceptive" cadences).

This latter explanation of musical agency is epitomized by Lakoff and Johnson's influential "conceptual metaphor" paradigm (1980). The cognitive process involves conceptual

Su Yin Mak, Hiroko Nishida, and Daisuke Yokomori, *Agency in ensemble interaction and rehearsal communication* In: *Together in music*. Edited by: Renee Timmers, Freya Bailes, and Helena Daffern, Oxford University Press. © Oxford University Press 2022.
DOI: 10.1093/oso/9780198860761.003.0004

mapping, based on analogical reasoning and inferences, by which a target domain (here music) is understood in terms of the entities, properties, and relations of a source domain drawn from generic human perceptions and actions. Purposive agency is thereby attributable not only to composers, performers, and listeners, but also to sonic phenomena imagined as simulacra of human agents. Indeed, it could be argued that all characterizations of intra-opus musical agency as "imaginary" (Graybill, 2011; Maus, 1988), "fictional" (Klorman, 2016; Monahan, 2013), or "virtual" (Hatten, 2018) are essentially metaphorical in conception, regardless of whether Lakoff and Johnson's paradigm is explicitly evoked.

Paradoxically, however, the human actions that musical gestures seemingly simulate are not necessarily correlated to the physical actions of real-world performers: a striving melody might well be produced by the downward bow motion of a violinist, who would also remain firmly seated while executing a rushing rhythm. This has meant that, when musical agency is considered in the context of performance, scholars working from sociocultural and metaphorical perspectives would focus on different types of actions and agents, even when a similar research methodology is applied. Here we refer to two empirical studies that investigate the kinesthetic aspects of music-making in ensembles by way of audiovisual documentation of performances and rehearsals and subsequent analysis of the performers' visible physical gestures. Davidson and Good's observational study of a student string quartet (2002) focuses on the communicative and social functions of the players' gestures and considers how their interpersonal dynamics affect moment-to-moment musical coordination; the topic of intra-opus agency does not arise at all. King and Ginsborg's study of interactions in ensemble rehearsal (2011), by contrast, additionally investigates how performers' gestures and glances correlate with features of the music being performed. In characterizing these correlations as "expressive," King and Ginsborg imply that performers draw upon mental representations of the work's metaphorical agency while playing and that their physical actions are external indicators of such representations. Graybill's notion of facilitative agency (2018), which describes how performers generate a cognitive infrastructure in support of their performance by means of audiation (or the ability to generate auditory imagery in the absence of a sounding stimuli), is likewise implicitly metaphorical in conception.

Recent music-theoretical models of musical agency

In music theory, research efforts have largely focused on score-based, composer-centric accounts of metaphorical agency in Western classical music. Edward T. Cone's *The Composer's Voice* (1974) is one of the earliest studies to propose a taxonomy for intra-opus agents and the conventions that govern their interactions. For example, Cone identifies a triad of personas for vocal music: (1) a vocal persona created by the singer's melody, akin to the protagonist depicted in the text; (2) a virtual instrumental persona implied by the accompaniment, which represents the effects of the outer world on the vocal persona and/or the subconscious reaction of the vocal persona to external reality; and (3) a complete musical persona, inferred from the interaction of instrumental and vocal personas, that denotes the composer's voice.

Cone's notion of implicit agents controlled by a unitary central subjectivity has prompted theoretical extensions in subsequent research. One oft-cited model that partly takes the work of Cone as a point of departure is Seth Monahan's meta-study of musical action and agency in music-analytical writing (2013). Monahan (2013) defines as agential "psychodramatic or anthropomorphic ascriptions of sentience, volition and deeds to musical works, their internal elements, and fictionalized versions of their composers" (p. 321) and posits a fourfold taxonomy of fictional agent classes arranged in a hierarchical network from low to high: (1) the individuated element: "any discrete component of the musical fabric that can be construed as having autonomy and volition ... [such as] individual themes, motives, gestures, keys, chords, topics, and even pitch classes;" (2) the work persona: "a unitary, continuous consciousness" that represents "the work itself, personified;" (3) the fictional composer: "the person postulated by the analyst as the controlling, intending author of the musical text ... based on, but not coextensive with, the actual, historical composer;" and (4) the analyst, or interpreter of the musical text (p. 333). He then defines the "relational logic" of the four agent classes as a nested hierarchy: "Any fictional agency called forth in an analysis may also be understood by the reader as an action of any or all of the higher-ranking (but not lower-ranking) agent classes" (pp. 327–34).

Robert Hatten's theory of virtual agency (2018) offers a different account of listeners' inferences of agency in music. He defines virtual agency as music's "capacity to simulate the actions, emotions, and reactions of a human agent" (p. 1) and proposes an alternative fourfold hierarchy of agent levels: "in order from most basic to most complex, these levels proceed from (1) unspecified virtual actants to (2) virtual human agents to (3) their ongoing actorial roles in lyric, dramatic, and/or narrative trajectories and, finally, to (4) their transformation as parts of a larger, singular consciousness or subjectivity that is negotiated by each individual listener" (p. 17). For Hatten, the ascription of agency begins when the listener perceives purposive action in music, but the nature of the actant is initially unclear. Next, the listener may embody the actions, thereby producing virtual agents with human (as opposed to mechanical) characteristics. Interactions among the virtual agents, such as conflict or dialogue, may in turn suggest a lyric, dramatic, and/or narrative trajectory for the musical work. Finally, the various virtual agents within the ongoing trajectory may fuse into a singular subjectivity as the listener interiorizes the perceived agencies into currents of thought and feeling.

Of present interest is the extent to which Hatten's and Monahan's theories may be extended to accommodate performance. Although Monahan (2013, p. 348) proposes the concept of avatar for the alternative guises that each of his four agency types can assume and includes "fictionalized performers" and "ad hoc fictional characters" among his avatars for individuated elements, these avatars are virtual rather than real-world agents. Indeed, Monahan acknowledges that his model of agency cannot account for the considerable agential complexities that the act of performance introduces, as performers and composers can simultaneously assume the roles of agent and patient to each other:

> To the extent that a pianist is executing tasks prescribed by Beethoven, we can regard him or her as the composer's action; we will project mental states onto Beethoven as a response to the performer's realization of "the score," strictly defined. But the myriad expressive inflections that are not "the score, strictly defined" allow us to regard Beethoven as the pianist's action, in that his or her performance may implicate a specific understanding of the work's creator. (p. 362)

Accordingly, performance-specific and work-specific features would merge into one another and the relational hierarchy he proposes would break down.

Hatten (2018) devotes a chapter in his book to the interactions between work and performer agencies:

> The performer may inject actual agency into the work, either enhancing or deflecting attention from the implied virtual agencies, or the performer may attempt to remain "invisible," as a transparent source—merely a transducer of the virtual agencies implied by the work. (p. 239)

His focus, however, is primarily hermeneutic. While the agential input of performers in the construction of musical meaning receives acknowledgement, aspects of performance that do not mimic the imagined gestures and actions encoded into the score are largely bypassed.

A third recent theory of agency that does engage with the internal mental representations upon which the performer draws while playing is Edward Klorman's theory of multiple agency, developed in his book *Mozart's Music of Friends* (2016). Klorman's model presents the musical score as an encoded exchange analogous to a theatrical script, with fictional instrumental personas appearing as dramatic characters, their instrumental parts as scripted dialogue, and the real-world performers as actors who perform these roles on stage. The concept of "multiple agency" conflates the real-world player and the fictional instrumental character into a combined persona; for example, "the cello" would refer to the combined persona of the real-world cellist, the fictional cello persona, and the cello part as utterances of that persona (p. 134).

Exploring agency in ensemble performance

Our study, which is part of a larger research project on conceptual and rhetorical metaphors in the discourse of professional string quartet rehearsal, integrates sociocultural and metaphorical approaches to investigate the interactions between work and performer agencies in ensemble music-making.[1] Over two nine-month periods, we observed and documented the rehearsal practice of the Hong Kong-based Romer String Quartet and the Japan-based Quartet Excelsior, yielding roughly 45 hours of video recordings. The following section reports our findings and explores their theoretical implications, using conversational segments from both case studies as illustrations.

Agential ambiguity and ascriptive fluidity: What is "it?"

In our two case studies, we found that the performers manifest their agencies both physically and metaphorically during ensemble interaction and communication, and that these intersect with perceived intra-opus agencies in fluid and dynamic ways. The following excerpt (Table 4.1) is taken from a rehearsal session of the Quartet Excelsior.[2]

---

[1] The larger research project expands an earlier ethnographic-documentary study by the first author (Mak, 2016) and is funded by the Research Grants Council of Hong Kong (GRF CUHK 14610418). Excerpts 1 and 2 in the following discussion were previously cited in a conference paper by the present authors (Mak et al., 2018).

[2] In this chapter, we reference all quotations from our empirical data with the instrumental role of the player, the name of the ensemble, and the date of the rehearsal session. The rehearsals were conducted in Cantonese (Romer) and Japanese (Excelsior), but here we present the conversational excerpts in English translation.

Table 4.1 Agential representations in ensemble rehearsal (Excelsior, March 15, 2017)

	Utterances	Analytical annotation
Vc:	How should I put it … should it be, like, sentimental?	Agent = the music ("it")
Va:	Yes, yes.	
Vc:	Right? I mean, as though …	
Vn1:	As though one is lovesick …	Agent = ad hoc imaginary persona (Monahan's avatar)
Vc:	Something like, "Ahhh, I am in despair!"	Agent = the performer (metaphorical action)
Va:	So … as though drunk?	Ambiguous agency
Vc:	Well, … it's Schubert, after all … I don't know …	Agent = the music ("it"). Composer's name appears as adjectival description of style rather than as agent.
Vn2:	Um … like a film?	Ambiguous agency
Vc:	Yes, but not quite … I guess there are some parts that are beautiful, but …	
	I mean, playing something like this, more *piano* [Demonstrates on instrument]	Agent = the performer (physical action)
Vc:	I mean … hmm … how should I put it? The overall condition, yes, the condition, could be a bit more … how should I put it?	
Va:	You mean, the shape?	
Vc:	Yes, yes, yes. Tone color as well.	Agent = the performer
	[Demonstrates on instrument. Vn1 and Vn2 join in.]	(physical action)
Vc:	If it's *pianissimo*, it would be something like this.	
Va:	I think it's better to keep it simple, with the feeling of an accompaniment.	
Vn2:	Like a guitar or something.	
Vn1:	[Nods] Yes, to create the atmosphere only.	

The cellist begins with an adjectival description of emotion, ascribing agency to the music but without specifying a specific element as the agent (should "*it*" be sentimental). The first violinist elaborates the idea through suggesting an imaginary persona ("as though lovesick"), who is then explicitly enacted by the cellist ("Ahhh, *I'm* in despair!"). The violist's response to this exchange is interesting because of its agential ambiguity. It is unclear from the utterance whether she means that the music, represented by an imaginary persona, is "drunk with love" or that the players themselves should play in a "drunken" manner. When the second violinist offers the alternative metaphor "like a film," it is similarly uncertain whether she is referring to the music or the players. However, when the cellist responds by demonstrating how the passage should be executed, his physical action unmistakably identifies him as the agent.

The players' constant shifts between speaking and playing, between metaphorical and physical expressions of agency, and between assigning agency to the music and themselves suggest a merging of work and performers' agencies, as modelled by Klorman's concept of multiple agent (2016) and Monahan's notion of avatar (2013); the enactment of an imaginary lovesick persona also accords with the dramatic basis of their theories. Yet it is noteworthy that the agential elements within the musical work are never explicitly identified. The players only refer to the music as "it," a vague designation which does not align with any individuated element or instrumental part; nor does "it" imply the unifying, continuous subjectivity of an overall work persona or the all-knowing hermeneutic authority of Monahan's "analyst." Moreover, the imaginary persona is an ad hoc representation that is not consistently sustained. When the rehearsal conversation turns towards the discussion of performance execution, attention to the musical work's perceived agency is replaced by technical, non-metaphorical considerations ("*pianissimo*," "tone color," "like an accompaniment").

It is also significant that the composer (whether historical or fictional) does not appear as an agent. Traditions of analysis and criticism for Western classical music have tended to assume that the score is a complete and self-contained record of the composer's creative intentions and that the performer is a vehicle for their reproduction. Although recent musical scholarship has moved away from this narrow ideology of *Werktreue*, the agency of performers is still very much seen as dictated by the agency of the composer. Zbikowski (2018, para. 11) argues, for example, that it is "the distribution of the composer's agency through the secondary agency of the score that makes it possible for the performer, many years after the death of the composer, to be the patient correlated with the composer's agent."

Yet in the rehearsal segment cited in Table 4.1, the composer's name is only used adjectivally as a descriptor for style: the cellist says, "it's Schubert," not "it's what Schubert *wrote*." In the rest of our data, we have found that composers' names typically function as intertextual references, cited in the same manner as style periods, genres, or other musical works and performers. Such usage eliminates the composer's authorial role and represents the musical work's metaphorical agency as both autonomous and sporadic, evoked only when an interpretative need arises. By contrast, the performers consistently refer to themselves in the first person, either as an individual "I" or as a collective "we," and they address each other directly in the second person when negotiating interpretative opinions. This suggests that, within the players' moment-to-moment perception of musical agency, they see themselves as bona fide agents rather than as actors performing the composer-scripted roles of their idealized, generic selves.

Physical and metaphorical manifestations of performers' agency

In addition to sound-producing motor movements, the performers' physical agency may also manifest itself in the form of co-speech gestures that serve a metaphorical function, as Table 4.2 illustrates.

In this conversation, the violist has trouble finding the right word for expressing his meaning, so the two violinists use a flexed-biceps gesture to clarify (see Fig. 4.1). Interestingly, the violist then responds by evoking an ad hoc imaginary persona ("Hercules"), and the first violinist confirms by way of an intertextual reference ("*Scheherazade*"). From this and other

Table 4.2 Interaction of physical and metaphorical agencies (Romer, February 15, 2015)

	Utterances	Analytical annotation
Va:	I guess we need that broadness, but not that strongness — is "strongness" even a word?	Agent = the performer (metaphorical description)
Vn1:	Yes, we don't want this. [Vn1 and Vn2 make flexed-biceps gesture]	Gestural visualization of metaphor
Va:	You mean, not Hercules.	Agent = ad hoc imaginary persona
Vn1:	No, not Hercules but *Scheherazade*.	Intertextual reference

Figure 4.1 Flexed-biceps gesture (Romer, February 15, 2015)

examples from our data corpus, we hypothesize that speech, musicking, and physical gestures serve as complementary means of conceptualizing and expressing metaphorical agency in the players' discourse.

Interactions between work and performers' agencies

We suggested earlier that the players' constant shifting between assigning agency to the music and themselves in their rehearsal conversations might be read, à la Klorman (2016) and Monahan (2013), in terms of the merging of work and performers' agencies. We would now like to re-examine this claim with reference to other short excerpts from our data.

There are numerous instances in the rehearsal sessions of both ensembles where the performers engage in actions not explicitly or even implicitly licensed by the score. The following remark is typical: "When the three of us see you run off, we don't follow you, right? We don't try to bring you back?" (Va, Romer, September 19, 2014). Here the violist clearly sees himself and other ensemble members as agents responsible for the metaphorical actions of "running," "following," and "bringing back," but these actions refer to an aspect of performance—namely, a problem in ensemble coordination—rather than any intra-opus element.

Table 4.3 Interchangeability of agential roles (Romer, February 15, 2015)

Speaker	Utterances	Analytical annotation
Vn2 [to Vn1]:	They are all 16th notes, I'm sure you'll find your beat … hahaha, you can slowly get on the train. You'll feel it, when the harmony changes …	Agent = performer
Va:	Then it says bingo, you have arrived … what I imagine is, we play along for 10 bars or so and then it tells us what to do.	Agent = intra-opus musical element (the harmony)
Vn1:	Then we don't have to play so long.	Agent = performer

Other instances of metaphorical usage similarly suggest distinct agencies for the musical work and the performer. Consider the following utterance taken from a later portion of the same rehearsal: "I think you are inside a house and hear someone approaching from afar … This means a storm, but I have to pretend to be calm" (Va, Romer, September 19, 2014). The violist imagines the musical structure as a house, the performer to be situated within, and an unspecified anthropomorphized intra-opus agent ("someone") to be approaching from afar. The storm metaphor that follows, however, is phenomenal rather than agential; it erases the intra-opus agency suggested earlier and instead focuses exclusively on the violist's own reaction. In the utterance "I will add a short … like, a comma, here," taken from an Excelsior rehearsal, the player similarly acts upon, rather than reacts to, the music through the metaphor of punctuation (Vn1, Excelsior, August 3, 2016).

We have also found that intra-opus musical elements and performers can function both as agents and as actions of each other, as Table 4.3 illustrates. In this excerpt, the second violinist clearly casts the first violinist ("you") as the agent in her opening "train" metaphor. Agency switches to the musical work when the violist imagines an intra-musical element ("the harmony") talking to the ensemble, and then *back* to the performers ("we") when the first violinist responds.

Theoretical implications

The interchangeability of agential roles in ensemble interaction and communication suggests that the traditional view of the string quartet (and, by extension, ensemble music) as stylized conversation, with each instrument imagined as a speaker, might be reconceived as a circular network that includes three types of dialogue: (1) interactions between metaphorical intra-opus musical elements; (2) discussions and exchanges between real-world performers; and (3) a continuous metaphorical dialogue between the musical work and the performer (see Fig. 4.2).

There are similarities between our model and Klorman's theory of multiple agency (2016) in that both partly efface the distinction between real and metaphorical realms and suggest that performers may metonymically identify with the music they perform. There is, however, also an important difference: the components within our network of relationships are unequal, and the figure of the composer is also absent. We assign greater structural weight to the metaphorical dialogue between the musical work and the performers because the act

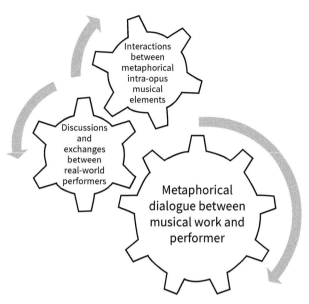

Figure 4.2 Network of agential dialogues in ensemble interaction and communication

of interpretation, of performers "owning" a work in the standard repertoire through their unique creative input, is fundamental to the performance practice of Western classical music. Moreover, since this metaphorical dialogue is itself initiated by the performer, we further propose that work agency may be read as secondary to the agency of the performer. Instead of seeing performers as conduits for metaphorical agencies prescribed by the score, we suggest that musical works may serve as vehicles for performers' expressions of their own agencies. This claim reverses the semiotic hierarchy that score-based, composer-centric ideologies often assume.

Conclusion

In closing, we offer the following refinement of the conceptual metaphor paradigm we presented at the start of this chapter. Whereas Lakoff and Johnson's model construes music as a single target domain, we view the musical text and the act of music-making as two distinctive, but related, target domains which can both be potentially mapped directly onto the source domain of human perceptions and actions, and which can also interact with each other in the creative act of performance.

Acknowledgments

We are grateful to the Romer String Quartet and the Quartet Excelsior for participating in our research, and to the Chinese University of Hong Kong, the Inamori Foundation, and the Research Grants Council of Hong Kong for providing funding support. We also thank Yukino Tagawa for her help in preparing Fig. 4.1.

References

Cone, E. T. (1974). *The composer's voice*. University of California Press.

Davidson, J. W., & Good, J. (2002). Social and musical co-ordination between members of a string quartet: An exploratory study. *Psychology of Music, 30*, 186–201.

Graybill, R. (2011). Whose gestures? Chamber music and the construction of permanent agents. In A. Gritten, & E. King (Eds.), *New perspectives on music and gesture* (pp. 221–41). Ashgate.

Graybill, R. (2018). Facilitative agency in performance. *Music Theory Online, 24*(3). https://doi.org/10.30535/mto.24.3.9

Hatten, R. (2018). *A theory of virtual agency for Western art music*. Indiana University Press.

King, E., & Ginsborg. J. (2011). Gestures and glances: Interactions in ensemble rehearsal. In A. Gritten, & E. King (Eds.), *New perspectives on music and gesture* (pp. 177–201). Ashgate.

Klorman, E. (2016). *Mozart's music of friends: Social interplay in the chamber works*. Cambridge University Press.

Lakoff, G., & Johnson, M. (1980). *Metaphors we live by*. University of Chicago Press.

Mak, S. Y. (2016). String theory: An ethnographic study of a professional quartet in Hong Kong. *Intégral, 30*, 53–65.

Mak, S. Y., Nishida, H., & Yokomori, D. (2018). Metaphorical cognition in the discourse of professional string quartet rehearsal. In R. Parncutt, & S. Sattmann (Eds.), *Proceedings of ICMPC15/ESCOM10* (pp. 261–6). Centre for Systematic Musicology, University of Graz.

Maus, F. E. (1988). Music as drama. *Music Theory Spectrum, 10*, 56–73.

Monahan, S. (2013). Action and agency revisited. *Journal of Music Theory, 57*(2), 321–71.

Small, C. (1998). *Musicking: The meanings of performing and listening*. Wesleyan University Press.

Turino, T. (2008). *Music as social life: The politics of participation*. University of Chicago Press.

Wiggins, J. (2015). Musical agency. In G. E. McPherson (Ed.), *The child as musician: A handbook of musical development* (2nd ed.). Oxford Scholarship Online. https://doi.org/10.1093/acprof:oso/9780198744443.001.0001

Zbikowski, L. (2018). Performing agency: A response. *Music Theory Online, 24*(3). https://doi.org/10.30535/mto.24.3.11

5

Investigating emergent coordination in small music groups

Nicola Pennill and Jane W. Davidson

Introduction

Music ensemble participation fundamentally involves people working together. The way this emerges and is organized is partly dependent on size: small groups negotiate their interpersonal dynamics in a manner very different to large ensembles. In a conducted ensemble, the individual's opinion is generally of lower status than a player in a small ensemble who holds their own musical line and often contributes in equal measure to the ensemble decisions and performance. This chapter focuses on ensembles of people in duos, trios, quartets, and quintets of various instrumental and vocal combinations. It aims to summarize the overarching approaches to investigating these collaborations in the study of Western music, focusing on coordination as it relates to social interaction, and the organization and alignment of members' ideas. This is a relatively new field of study. As recently as 1997, Jane Davidson (p. 55) observed that "in research terms, the social communication aspects of rehearsal and performance have been largely ignored." Researchers have since adopted a range of methods to explore the small ensemble as a collective, in which individuals interact verbally and non-verbally to negotiate a coordinated joint performance.

Given our emphasis on social interaction, we start by summarising selected research which uses mainly qualitative methods based on observation in the field. One of the challenges facing researchers in investigating ensembles is to find ways to ensure ecological validity, and methods which capture experiences of musicians therefore have particular value. We then consider how these observations can be coded and analyzed, and integrated with other methods. We consider the implications of an emergence perspective, which incorporates time as a factor, and offer an example of a longitudinal, mixed methods study. Finally, we consider possible future routes to investigation, and opportunities to combine approaches in response to directions of current research.

Observation of behaviors in the field

Ways in which coordination within an ensemble arises from interactions between group members have been examined extensively through observation of gestures, behaviors, and verbal discourse (see also Chapters 1, 4, 12, and 14). Such investigations often involve scrutinizing how an ensemble comes together in rehearsal to develop and then execute musical works for performance. Given the wide range of possible contexts and contributing factors

Nicola Pennill and Jane W. Davidson, *Investigating emergent coordination in small music groups* In: *Together in music.*
Edited by: Renee Timmers, Freya Bailes, and Helena Daffern, Oxford University Press. © Oxford University Press 2022.
DOI: 10.1093/oso/9780198860761.003.0005

(for example, familiarity, experience, repertoire choices), in-depth case studies are commonly used, often in conjunction with interviews to capture group member perspectives.

A particular challenge arising in observation case studies is to capture data in a way that retains a natural setting, allowing social and musical interactions to unfold. Williamon and Davidson (2002) followed a naturalistic process after inviting two pianists to come together to develop a program of duets for performance. The researchers traced how the players gained expressive and communicative assurance as they grew in familiarization with one another and made decisions about technical and expressive aspects of the music. In order to minimize researcher interference, a video camera was set up in the rehearsal room and the musicians were left alone to work. Subsequently, the researchers were able to undertake a detailed analysis of the video material collected. The researchers supplemented these data sources by preparing questions for the performers to answer after the final performance. Exploration of the data led to qualitative assessments of all forms of interaction—spoken, non-verbal gestures, eye contact, and the interview data. The researchers also undertook systematic observations to calculate the frequency and form of non-verbal gestures and eye contact. This approach, in its combination of qualitative and quantitative data analyses, revealed how the two excellent sight-readers used rehearsals to consolidate their timing, phrasing, and sense of musical style. It also showed how coordinated non-verbal gestures and eye-contact emerged, increasing in frequency over time. The interviews offered some explanations for why specific behaviors emerged.

Davidson and Good (2002) worked with a student string quartet to explore how they collaborated in a final rehearsal and performance. While the researchers explored non-verbal and musical concerns in ways similar to those described in the aforementioned study, detailed analysis of the verbal exchanges revealed a complex longstanding and underpinning web of interpersonal relationships that were shaping the interactive behavior between the four players. The researchers focused on these psychosocial aspects in some detail. By allowing the quartet players to review the rehearsal and performance videos and make free comments on what they observed, deep interpersonal histories and interaction styles emerged. Without these sources of information, some of the rehearsal room behaviors and resulting performance effects would not have been appropriately interpreted.

Drawing on approaches adopted in Davidson's work and taking methods from ethnomusicology, Bayley (2011) worked principally as an ethnographer to study how composer Michael Finnissy worked with the Kreutzer Quartet in a rehearsal of his Second String Quartet. She worked to acquire an on-the-scene immersion in the rehearsal environment, collecting diverse types of data through observation, conversation, and textual study, and made audio recordings of the rehearsal to supplement her fieldnotes. She reported that this type of detailed observation and engagement with the composer and performers enabled her to capture the norms and values of the group that would have otherwise been missed or constrained had she not been in the rehearsal room. In her analyses, she quantified how much time was spent on different activities during the rehearsal and also showed how different aspects of interaction took place at different times during the rehearsal; for example, talk about notation took place in the first half of the rehearsal. She was critical of the limitations of this type of quantification, noting that interpersonal interactions are multiple and overlapping and that calculating elements of the interactions overly reduced the rich complexity of the rehearsal. To maximize the potential of her data on interactivity, she focused additionally on the language employed during the rehearsal and observed this changed from concerns with the notation through to achieving an interpretation which enabled the players to shape the piece for performance.

The value of reflective naturalistic studies is further exemplified in a study by Geeves et al. (2014) which focuses on a moment in performance for musicians performing *The Wheel of Frank Confession Tour* (WOFCT). In this example, a cabaret ensemble adopted a loosely structured approach to performer participation, leading to improvised elements in performance. In the moment selected, the coordination of the quartet is under threat as the leader improvises and changes the last chorus of a song that had been previously rehearsed and performs suddenly in a different manner. The article examines the mechanisms in operation— trust, improvisatory strategies, eye contact, and gesture—as the other three musicians follow the leading performer and smoothly transition into unprecedented performance territory to secure a successful conclusion to the song.

Analyzing and coding behaviors

As noted in the example from Bayley (2011), quantitative measures are often combined with qualitative data. However, in the study of social dynamics, methods which enable researchers to quantify observation data are widely used, for example to measure the frequency of particular behavior types (see also Chapter 14). One way in which behaviors can be measured is by translating and coding observation data, and describing it through the syntax of a coding scheme. Depending on the focus of the study, a pre-existing scheme may be used, or a new one created. Creating a new scheme has the advantage of being tightly targeted to the research aims but requires validation and testing. Many researchers choose to select from existing schemes, as in the approach taken by King and Ginsborg (2011) as they assessed gestures employed during singing/playing episodes in ensemble rehearsal. Non-verbal communication between singer and pianist duos was categorized as either a *state* (an action with a duration, such as pulsing with a hand across several bars or gazing at a co-performer during a bar/phrase) or a *point* (an action with no specific duration, such as glancing at a playing partner or making a gesture to coincide with a downbeat). These categories were drawn from previous research (Cassell, 1998; Ekman & Friesen, 1969), and using the software *Observer XT* (Noldus Information Technology), the researchers were able to create a log of rehearsal events. Recording both "state" categories (duration and percentage of rehearsal time) and "point" categories (as rate of occurrence per minute of rehearsal time) enabled comparisons of the proportion of time engaged in actions/gestures by individual performers in different rehearsals.

A different approach to measurement was taken in a series of case studies of performers, in which Chaffin and colleagues identified starts, stops, and repetitions in rehearsals, combined with analysis of verbal commentaries, to investigate how performers attended to musical features to guide unfolding performances and memorization (Chaffin & Imreh, 2002; Chaffin, Lisboa, et al., 2010). Recording performance cues and methods in this way was subsequently adapted as a set of "musical dimensions" by Ginsborg and others to record and quantify rehearsal behaviors in ensemble settings (Ginsborg and King, 2012; Ginsborg et al., 2006; see Chapter 12).

In their review of measurement of social interaction in music ensembles, Volpe et al. (2016) highlighted the predominance of case study research. As a useful complement to this, survey and questionnaire studies have provided a further form of quantitative data, which takes a broader perspective to a given phenomenon. In the field of ensemble organization and group dynamics, a number of studies have used questionnaire methods, including investigations of piano duos (Blank & Davidson, 2007), wind quintets (Ford & Davidson, 2003), and string quartets (Gilboa & Tal-Shmotkin, 2012; Murnighan & Conlon, 1991).

Integrating observations with other measures

The ability to integrate measurement tools within an ecological setting presents exciting opportunities for research. A number of specialist centers have facilities to capture multimodal aspects of ensemble performance, enabling the exploration of relationships between, for example, cognitive strategies, movements, and performance outcomes. Examples of these are the analysis of ensemble leadership as interpreted through body sway (Badino et al., 2014) or head movements (Glowinski et al., 2015). A review of the range and types of measurement used in such studies is given in Volpe et al. (2016). While studies of synchronization and brain function in ensembles are beyond the scope of this chapter, below we offer an example of how direct measurement was used in conjunction with observation to investigate performance outcomes in a vocal quintet.

Expressive choices and sharing of musical ideas by ensembles can be traced through observation and coding of verbal discussion, which can be combined with other measures of performance to examine how these ideas are implemented. In our example, coded verbal interactions were analyzed alongside physical measurement of tuning via individual audio recordings from head-mounted microphones, and electrolaryngograph signals in a newly formed vocal quintet. In a series of rehearsals over a four-month period, the group spent progressively less time discussing tuning, while achieving a greater consistency in intonation (D'Amario et al., 2018). Other examples of ensemble research considering different timescales from a longitudinal perspective include observations of communication modes within a single rehearsal (e.g. Williamon & Davidson, 2002), collaboration processes of a composer and performer working together over a series of three workshops (Clarke et al., 2016), and diary studies of members of student ensembles preparing over two terms of study (Ginsborg, 2017). Longitudinal studies such as these allow repeated observations of the same variables over a short or long period of time, highlighting developmental processes, including phases of relative change and stability, as discussed next (see also Chapter 1).

Emergence as a lens for music ensemble enquiry

Methods that incorporate time as a factor can contribute to research on ensemble social interactions by considering the nature of change and transformation, and the "emergence" of new states. An emergent view of group working assumes a transformation of individual skills and knowledge, shaped by the group context, into collective phenomena (Goldspink & Kay, 2010). We can readily think about such emergence when we read Vikram Seth's novel *An Equal Music* (1999) which not only exposes individual imperfections, but also shows that when members of a string quartet collaborate and face the difficulties of coming together in music, change occurs and those individuals become something much more significant than the sum of their individual parts.

With relatively few long-term studies specifically related to music ensemble development over time, there is a further opportunity to draw on the established field of enquiry into group development from social sciences research, especially those which explore group development and evolution over time (Breslin, 2016; Bush et al., 2017; Mathieu et al., 2014). Interdisciplinary perspectives such as these provide a departure point to consider further methods of investigation. We next offer one such example which has adapted a method used in team behavior research to investigate ensemble interactions over time.

Investigating emerging verbal interactions in ensembles

A recent mixed methods study of two newly formed vocal ensembles used a combination of group interaction analysis (quantitative) and interview and observation data (qualitative) to explore how the process of performance preparation evolved over time. The quantitative analysis was based on methods used in group interaction research, although not before used in music. In the longitudinal case study, Pennill (2019) used the THEME* software algorithm (Patternvision, Ltd.) as the analysis tool to identify evolving patterns of behavior as these new ensembles formed and worked together over a three-month period. Designed for the purpose of temporal pattern ("T-pattern") detection (Magnusson, 2000, 2018), THEME* has been applied in a range of settings, including research on small-group collaborations, sports, medicine, animal behavior, and at many levels of biological and interpersonal organization (for a review, see Casarrubea et al., 2015). T-patterns are recurrent behavior patterns which are very hard, or impossible, to detect by direct observation. This analysis method is a powerful tool to reveal patterned behaviors which are happening in naturalistic settings such as ensemble rehearsals. In Pennill's study, rehearsals were video-recorded in the field (Case 1) and in a laboratory setting (Case 2) (Pennill, 2019). Verbal interactions were captured, and the rehearsal utterances were time-stamped and coded using the Behavior Analysis scheme (Farley et al., 2018). Interview and observation data analysis enabled exploration of participant experiences.

T-pattern analysis showed that patterns of verbal interactions were evident from the very first encounters onwards. As rehearsals progressed, the patterns increased in complexity, with more group members and types of behaviors represented in the patterns. Drawing on research in work teams, this finding is consistent with the development of implicit coordination in the groups, where implicit coordination is proposed as the means by which team members anticipate and dynamically adjust behaviors without recourse to direct communication, and hence improve effectiveness (Rico et al., 2008). In the following illustrative example, a sequence of repeated behaviors is revealed during one rehearsal, as members of the ensemble establish patterns of communication (see Fig. 5.1). A repeated sequence occurred three times within a 30-minute period of rehearsal, which happened in parallel with, and was embedded within, explicit social and music talk. Verbal utterances from individual group members (S1, S2, S3, and S5) and behavior codes assigned from video transcripts are indicated by dots, and the recurring sequences which repeat within the time interval are shown as vertical lines. The singers were unaware that as a precursor to a singing episode, there was a series of five verbal contributions from members of the same type and order. Analysis over

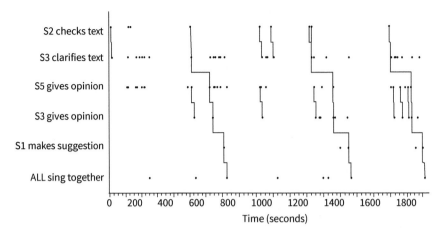

Figure 5.1 Example of pattern diagram from THEME®.

Reproduced from Pennill, N. (2019). Ensembles working towards performance: Emerging coordination and interactions in self-organised groups. [Doctoral dissertation]. The University of Sheffield.

the series of rehearsals and across the two groups revealed that emergence of interactions was triggered by changing internal and external factors, including approaching deadlines and increasing social familiarity.

Conclusion

The researcher investigating ensemble coordination and social dynamics has a range of tools at their disposal. As we have seen, finding a balance between maintaining ecological validity and direct measurement remains an ongoing challenge. However, depending on the chosen focus, combining methods in creative ways provides new and exciting research opportunities.

The studies discussed in this chapter offer a range of observation techniques, research findings, and theoretical postulations. Methods are borrowed from social psychology and organizational management to code verbal and non-verbal behaviors, social relationships, and task- as well as social-oriented processes. Combining these investigations with analysis of musical coordination in timing or tuning offers rich insight into interaction processes at social and musical levels. As data sets are inevitably large, case study approaches have been the most common type of research in this area. One potential common theme is that of emergence and self-organization in musical ensembles (Pennill, 2019), specifically when small groups are concerned (see also Chapter 13). Pennill's example was given as a study that combined methods within an emergence paradigm to explore ensemble development in newly formed groups. The mixed approach enabled a holistic view of music ensembles as dynamic and interconnected: patterned behaviors emerged early on and shaped future interactions, while being shaped by contextual constraints.

These perspectives and methods have shone a light on many of the elements of ensemble interaction, and in a range of real-life and controlled contexts. However, there remain gaps and opportunities for new methods to enable further contributions to be made. The study of the ensemble as an emergent, communicative entity requires further investment and exploration (Cross, 2014), as relatively few studies conducted to date are longitudinal in design and so are not sufficient to fully capture dynamic, emergent ensemble interactions. Furthermore, the active research field of social sciences offers directions and methods to be further exploited, as also exemplified in chapters throughout this book (see, for example, Chapters 2, 7, 8, and 19). Finally, to enhance observational power and generalizability, the use of computational methods to analyze and interpret observation data offers potential for development, including the emerging field of social signal processing to capture behavioral cues such as blinks, smiles, and frowns (Vinciarelli et al., 2009).

Moving forwards, inevitably, there are a number of remaining research challenges to be addressed in the study of ensembles and social interaction. Among these are ways to improve generalizability of findings and address cross-genre and cross-cultural differences, and to consider impact potential which is wider than the scope of music. There is a growing body of research that reveals interest in the ensemble as a site for distributed cognitive processes and a crucible for understanding in-the-moment human interaction. However, as Bayley (2011) explained in her quartet study, the various approaches need to embrace all aspects of process without diminishing the complexity or sense of change in and through interpersonal and musical processes.

Acknowledgments

Nicola Pennill's PhD research was funded by the White Rose College of Arts and Humanities.

References

Badino, L., D'Ausilio, A., Glowinski, D., Camurri, A., & Fadiga, L. (2014). Sensorimotor communication in professional quartets. *Neuropsychologia*, *55*, 98–104.

Bayley, A. (2011). Ethnographic research into contemporary string quartet rehearsal. *Ethnomusicology Forum*, *20*(3), 385–411.

Blank, M., & Davidson, J. (2007). An exploration of the effects of musical and social factors in piano duo collaborations. *Psychology of Music*, *35*(2), 231–48.

Breslin, D. (2016). What evolves in organizational co-evolution? *Journal of Management Governance*, *20*(1), 45–67.

Bush, J. T., Lepine, J. A., & Newton, D. W. (2017). Teams in transition: An integrative review and synthesis of research on team task transitions and propositions for future research. *Human Resource Management Review*, *28*(4), 423–33.

Casarrubea, M., Jonsson, G. K., Faulisi, F., Sorbera, F., Di Giovanni, G., Benigno, A., Crescimanno, G., & Magnusson, M. (2015). T-pattern analysis for the study of temporal structure of animal and human behavior: A comprehensive review. *Journal of Neuroscience Methods*, *239*, 34–46.

Cassell, J. (1998). A framework for gesture generation and interpretation. In R. Cipolla (Ed.), *Computer vision in human-machine interaction* (pp. 248–65). Cambridge University Press.

Chaffin, R., & Imreh, G. (2002). Practicing perfection: Piano performance as expert memory. *Psychological Science*, *13*(4), 342–9.

Chaffin, R., Lisboa, T., Logan, T., & Begosh, K. T. (2010). Preparing for memorized cello performance: The role of performance cues. *Psychology of Music*, *38*(1), 3–30.

Clarke, E., Doffman, M., & Timmers, R. (2016). Creativity, collaboration and development in Jeremy Thurlow's Ouija for Peter Sheppard Skærved. *Journal of the Royal Musical Association*, *141*(1), 113–65.

Cross, I. (2014). Music and communication in music psychology. *Psychology of Music*, *42*(6), 809–19.

D'Amario, S., Howard, D. M., Daffern, H., & Pennill, N. (2018). A longitudinal study of intonation in an a cappella singing quintet. *Journal of Voice*, *34*(1), 159.e13–E27.

Davidson, J. (1997). The social in music performance. In D. J. Hargreaves & A. C. North (Eds.), *The social psychology of music* (pp. 209–28). Oxford University Press.

Davidson, J., & Good, J. M. M. (2002). Social and musical co-ordination between members of a string quartet: An exploratory study. *Psychology of Music*, *30*(2), 186–201.

Ekman, P., & Friesen, W. V. (1969). The repertoire of nonverbal behavior: Categories, origins, usage, and coding. *Semiotica*, *1*(1), 49–98.

Farley, S., Evison, R., Rackham, N., Nicolson, R., & Dawson, J. (2018). The Behavior Analysis coding system. In E. Brauner, M. Boos, & M. Kolbe (Eds.), *The Cambridge handbook of group interaction analysis* (pp. 584–93). Cambridge University Press.

Ford, L., & Davidson, J. (2003). An investigation of members' roles in wind quintets. *Psychology of Music*, *31*(1), 53–74.

Geeves, A. M., McIlwain, D. J., & Sutton, J. (2014). The performative pleasure of imprecision: a diachronic study of entrainment in music performance. *Frontiers in Human Neuroscience*, *8* (863), 1–15.

Gilboa, A., & Tal-Shmotkin, M. (2012). String quartets as self-managed teams: An interdisciplinary perspective. *Psychology of Music*, *40*(1), 19–41.

Ginsborg, J. (2017). Small ensembles in rehearsal. In J. Rink, H. Gaunt, & A. Williamon (Eds.), *Musicians in the making: Pathways to creative performance* (pp. 164–185). Oxford University Press.

Ginsborg, J., Chaffin, R., & Nicholson, G. (2006). Shared performance cues in singing and conducting: A content analysis of talk during practice. *Psychology of Music*, *34*(2), 167–94.

Ginsborg, J., & King, E. (2012). Rehearsal talk: Familiarity and expertise in singer-pianist duos. *Musicae Scientiae*, *16*(2), 148–67.

Glowinski, D., Dardard, F., Gnecco, G., Piana, S., & Camurri, A. (2015). Expressive non-verbal interaction in a string quartet: An analysis through head movements. *Journal of Multimodal User Interfaces*, *9*(1), 55–68.

Goldspink, C., & Kay, R. (2010). Emergence in organizations: The reflexive turn. *Emergence: Complexity & Organization*, *12*(3), 47–63.

King, E., & Ginsborg, J. (2011). Gestures and glances: Interactions in ensemble rehearsal. In A. Gritten, & E. King (Eds.), *New perspectives on music and gesture* (pp. 177–201). Ashgate.

Magnusson, M. S. (2000). Discovering hidden time patterns in behaviour: T-patterns and their detection. *Behavior Research Methods, Instruments, & Computers*, *32*(1), 93–110.

Magnusson, M. S. (2018). Temporal patterns in interactions. In E. Brauner, M. Boos, & M. Kolbe (Eds.), *The Cambridge handbook of group interaction analysis* (pp. 323–53). Cambridge University Press.

Mathieu, J. E., Tannenbaum, S., Donsbach, J., & Alliger, G. (2014). A review and integration of team composition models: Moving toward a dynamic and temporal framework. *Journal of Management*, *40*(1), 130–60.

Murnighan, J. K., & Conlon, D. E. (1991). The dynamics of intense work groups: A study of British string quartets. *Administrative Science Quarterly, 36*, 165–86.

Pennill, N. (2019). *Ensembles working towards performance: Emerging coordination and interactions in self-organised groups* [Doctoral dissertation]. University of Sheffield.

Rico, R., Sanchez-Manzanares, M., Gil, F., & Gibson, C. (2008). Team implicit coordination processes: A team knowledge-based approach. *Academy of Management Review, 33*(1), 163–84.

Seth, V. (1999). *An equal music*. Penguin.

Vinciarelli, A., Pantic, M., & Bourlard, H. (2009). Social signal processing: Survey of an emerging domain. *Image and Vision Computing, 27*(12), 1743–59.

Volpe, G., D'Ausilio, A., Badino, L., Camurri, A., & Fadiga, L. (2016). Measuring social interaction in music ensembles. *Philosophical Transactions of the Royal Society B: Biological Sciences, 371*(1693). https://doi.org/10.1098/rstb.2015.0377

Williamon, A., & Davidson, J. (2002). Exploring co-performer communication. *Musicæ Scientiæ, 6*(1), 53–72.

6

The ministry of sound

Musical mediations in an English parish church

Kathryn King

Introduction

Not all musical ensembles exist to make music. One million people attend an Anglican parish church service in England each week (Botting, 2018) and in doing so, almost all will become part of an ensemble that does not rehearse, has no fixed membership, and requires no audition or musical training to join: the parish congregation. This chapter draws on a study of one such congregation to highlight how music mediates its social interactions and its socialities mediate music, to simultaneously promote and problematize the practice of both.

The study, which contributed to a graduate project investigating experiences of Anglican music, was undertaken at St Mary's, a Victorian church in a semi-rural parish in southern England, using ethnographic approaches and survey methods.[1] St Mary's favors traditional liturgies and music, and its congregation, consistent with the Church of England's long-standing position that communal singing is the "ideal" in parish worship (Church of England, 1922, pp. 4–5; 1992), joins the large SATB (soprano, alto, tenor, bass) choir in singing hymns and psalms. They use mainly simple, well-known Anglican musical settings from nineteenth- and early twentieth-century hymnals, and are accompanied by an organist, who also leads the weekly choir practice. This genre of church music—in contrast to the elaborate polyphony that characterizes English cathedral services, and the expressive creativity of some contemporary worship styles—is often portrayed as unaffecting: a bland, "half-hearted" sonic "wallpaper" of little consequence to the congregation, both in the literature (e.g. Stringer, 2016, pp. 176–181) and by observers:

> It's what I refer to as "the washing over" ... I don't think [the congregation] even notice the musical content ... It's very much a duty really ... It's the [liturgy] that's important to people, they don't mention the music at all. (St Mary's choir member)

This study, however, found compelling evidence that behind the appearance of quiet reserve, the congregation was engaged in, and affected by, the church's music in a web of profound and profoundly different ways. This chapter highlights two.

---

[1] All names are pseudonyms, and identifying details have been changed.

Kathryn King, *The ministry of sound* In: *Together in music.* Edited by: Renee Timmers, Freya Bailes, and Helena Daffern, Oxford University Press. © Oxford University Press 2022. DOI: 10.1093/oso/9780198860761.003.0006

Music and community consonance: Forming and performing the ensemble

Émile Durkheim (2008) argued that the function of organized religion is to create a sense of community. Shared religious doctrine and practice are not, however, necessarily sufficient to unify a group, as the history of the Christian church and the literature on congregational conflict demonstrate (Edgell, 1999; Tucker, 2009). Nor does communal worship inevitably result in collectivism (Adnams, 2016, p. 196). At St Mary's, however, congregants' sense of shared identity was a striking feature, permeating their interview narratives (which presupposed a consensus among co-congregants) and everyday speech (routinely in the first-person plural):

> We sing well. We enjoy singing well ... (Tom, congregant)
> We make our musical decisions for a reason. (Ellie, organist)
> We do not want tambourines and guitars! (Barbara, congregant)

Music can be a powerful force for affiliation (Clarke et al., 2015), and at St Mary's, music was implicated in the formation and performance of the church community in several interrelated ways.

First, the church's music was a central determinant of its membership. In a questionnaire survey, more than half of the congregation cited music as "an important factor" in deciding where to worship. A similar proportion "agreed strongly" that they enjoyed singing in church and wanted as many opportunities to sing together as possible. Several interviewees explained further that they began attending St Mary's specifically because of its traditional music, after their former churches adopted a contemporary musical style: "[My old church] didn't seem religious enough ... somehow I didn't enjoy it the same. I like to go to join in without all that other background, the arm waving ..." (Amanda, parishioner).

Second, the shared musical taste that drew many members to St Mary's promoted a sense of group identity, both by signaling members' mutual interest and "ingroup" status (Lonsdale & North, 2009) and through its close association with socio-demographic characteristics and other cultural preferences (Bourdieu, 1984; Savage, 2015), by bringing together individuals with similar backgrounds and shared interests. Survey data revealed a marked commonality in age, ethnicity, social background, cultural orientation, and the activities in which they engaged outside church.

Third, the act of music-making consolidated parishioners' sense of community. Collective music-making has been found in other contexts to act as an accelerator of social bonding (Pearce et al., 2015), and the extensive congregational singing engaged in at St Mary's was identified by almost all interviewees as fundamental to the social connectivity they felt and valued in the church. David, retired and living alone, described it as "of paramount importance." Daniel, another parishioner, explained:

> [Hymn-singing] can bring the whole worshipping community together. When it's a said service ... it's just between yourself and God ... [Singing] brings a community together in a way that, I hate to say it, even the Creed, said, doesn't ...

Fourth, bodily synchrony such as that involved in a St Mary's service—an hour-long ritual of musically cued standing, sitting, kneeling, and singing together in the rhythm required by the liturgy—is an effective instrument of empathy (Clarke et al., 2015). As Julia, a choir member put it, "It's very much involving. You have to keep your wits about you, or you find you're the only one standing up or the only one sitting down, or whatever." Schutz (1951, pp. 92–96) described this close listening and other-directed attention as a "mutual tuning-in" relationship, a "sharing of the other's flux of experiences in inner time, [a] living through a vivid present in common ... the experience of the 'We', which is at the foundation of all possible communication."

Congregational singing therefore brought together the individuals who became the ensemble and, through its performance, created the conditions for a sense of shared identity through common interests, for social bonding through embodied synchrony, and for an intimate cognitive connection through the empathy of collective endeavor.

Tension and dissent in the social and musical

Paradoxically, music was also, however, the source of social conflict in the ensemble, and social conflict played out through its music. One example of the latter came from Jack, an accomplished countertenor, who had recently given up his place in the choir of another church following the appointment of a new choral director there. Jack had "absolutely loved" the choir but felt uncomfortable working with the new director because of opinions he had expressed in a social situation outside church. Jack chose to leave the choir as a result. As he put it:

> ... the thing about music, and particularly music that is so close to the soul and the ego, you feel it much more, it isn't just something that you do like, oh, we've got different dustmen ... I just didn't want to sing with this person. I did try ... But that meant no choir really ...

To avoid the "mutual tuning-in" of a musical encounter with the new director, Jack left not only that church's choir, but also that church. The social tension had manifested in Jack's musical experience, prompting actions which altered the social composition and the musical sound of the two ensembles of which he was part.

There were also examples of the converse situation: musical conflicts impacting on in-ensemble interpersonal relationships. There was robust consensus among the congregation, for example, that high musical standards should be maintained—three quarters of survey respondents agreed or strongly agreed—consistent with a principle of the Church that everything in worship should, as an offering to God, be of the highest possible quality (Church of England, 1992, p. 67; Long, 1972, p. 35). However, when asked which was more important, participation or musical excellence, a disjuncture in views became apparent. Rachel and Joy's experience exemplified one perspective. Both had recently decided to stop singing in St Mary's choir, because after Ellie, a new organist, arrived, they began worrying about "getting the notes right." This meant that for them, the choir "wasn't enjoyable anymore:"

> JOY: Now, for me, it's more highbrow, because Ellie's more of a ... professional musician ...
> RACHEL: Ellie is on a different level.
> JOY: ... Ellie is the highest level ... It was great in the time when we had Simon [leading the choir] ... it was just a nice atmosphere, wasn't it? ... He wasn't just there for the music, was he? ... He never changed anything, you did the same anthems, the same hymns ... You just went and had a good sing.

By contrast, some of the newer choir members—several of whom had been attracted by Ellie's expertise—were frustrated by the absence of musical challenge and a perceived lack of aesthetic aspiration, as Ellie sought to accommodate some of the other members, for whom singing was above all a method of worship. Gerry, for example, a new choir member, sensed "a slight feeling" towards him from one of the longer-standing members of the choir, because "I sing in a kind of shaping off way, the proper way [laughing], the cathedral way. And he can hear me do that, but he never copies me ..." These musical tensions had social consequences, changing the culture of the choir and the atmosphere in the wider congregation, which one member described as divided along a line which is "not entirely about education ... or about class either, but it has elements of that sort of thing," and also their social composition, as long-time choir members gradually left on the grounds that the choir stalls are "a different place now."

These tensions are not unique to St Mary's. Debates about musical participation versus quality have been a feature of the Protestant Church throughout its history (Church of England, 1992). The class aspects of musical difference are well documented (Bennett et al., 2009; Savage, 2015), and that music manifests and mediates extra-musical conflict has been illustrated in church contexts (e.g. Nekola, 2009) and beyond (e.g. Born, 2003). What these examples show, however, is how the particular network of social and musical factors that coalesce at St Mary's can be active in reinforcing its congregation's social ties, while at the same time generating tension and sparking divisions that have opposite, but similarly powerful effects on its music and its people.

Conclusion

The above observations illuminate just two ways in which, within one case-study church, a dynamic assemblage of individuals is engaged through music in an active aesthetic and social process of cultural production. Negotiating matters of class, morality, aesthetics, and cultural distinction, and blurring the boundaries between social and musical interaction, the examples highlight the potentially profound impact of ensemble participation on the individuals and ensembles who engage in it, on the Church as a corporate body, and on the music they produce. It is possible here to give only a flavor of these negotiations; there are too many to enumerate in a brief chapter. The intention then is not to have provided a comprehensive account, but rather to suggest that even in the most apparently unassuming contexts, if people are making music together, an array of identities, meanings, affiliations, and divisions are also in the making (see also Chapter 3). In musical ensembles, as in other culturally constructed social relationships, "nothing never happens" (McQuown et al., 1971, p. 708).

References

Adnams, G. (2016). "Really worshipping" not "just singing." In M. Ingalls, C. Landau, & T. Wagner (Eds.), *Christian congregational music: Performance, identity and experience* (pp. 185–200). Routledge.

Bennett, T., Savage, M., Bortolaia Silva, E., & Gayo-Cal, M. (2009). *Culture, class, distinction.* Routledge.

Born, G. (2003). Music and the social. In N. Cook, H. Herbert, & R. Middleton (Eds.), *The cultural study of music: A critical introduction* (pp. 261–74). Routledge.

Botting, B. (2018). *Statistics for mission 2017*. The Church of England Research & Statistics. https://www.churchofengland.org/sites/default/files/2019-01/2017StatisticsForMission_0.pdf

Bourdieu, P. (1984). *Distinction: A social critique of the judgement of taste* (R. Nice, Trans.). Routledge.

Church of England. (1922). *Music in worship: The report of the Archbishops' Committee on Music in Church appointed in May, 1922*. Central Board of Finance of the Church of England, Society for Promoting Christian Knowledge (SPCK).

Church of England. General Synod. (1992). *In tune with heaven: The report of the Archbishops' Commission on Church Music*. Church House Publishing and Hodder & Stoughton.

Clarke, E., DeNora, T., & Vuoskoski, J. (2015). Music, empathy and cultural understanding. *Physics of Life Reviews, 15*, 61–88. https://doi.org/10.1016/j.plrev.2015.09.001

Durkheim, É. (2008). *The elementary forms of the religious life*. Dover Publications.

Edgell, P. (1999). *Congregations in conflict: Cultural models of local religious life*. Cambridge University Press.

Long, K. R. (1972). *The music of the English church*. Hodder & Stoughton.

Lonsdale, A. J., & North, A. C. (2009). Musical taste and ingroup favoritism. *Group Processes & Intergroup Relations, 12*(3), 319–27.

McQuown, N., Bateson, G., Birdwhistell, R., Brosin, H., & Hockett, C. (1971). *The natural history of an interview*. University of Chicago Library.

Nekola, A. (2009). *Between this world and the next: The musical "worship wars" and evangelical ideology in the United States, 1960–2005* [Doctoral dissertation]. University of Wisconsin-Madison. http://search.proquest.com/docview/305033619/

Pearce, E., Launay, J., & Dunbar, R. I. M. (2015). The ice-breaker effect: Singing mediates fast social bonding. *Royal Society Open Science, 2*(10), 150221. https://doi.org/10.1098/rsos.150221

Savage, M. (2015). *Social class in the 21st century*. Pelican.

Schutz, A. (1951). Making music together: A study in social relationships. *Social Research, 18*(1), 76–97.

Stringer, M. D. (2016). Worship, transcendence and danger: Reflections on Siegfried Kracauer's "The Hotel Lobby." In M. Ingalls, C. Landau, & T. Wagner (Eds.), *Christian congregational music: Performance, identity and experience* (pp. 169–84). Routledge.

Tucker, K. W. (2009). Music wars: A new conflict? *Liturgy, 24*(4), 3–9.

7
Playful production
Collaborative facilitation in a music ensemble context

Elizabeth Haddon and Catherine Laws

Introduction

This mini-case study of The Assembled explores the approach, rationale, and processes used to develop performances operating at the intersection of experimental music and devised theatre practices. The Assembled was formed by Catherine Laws in 2011 in the Department of Music, University of York, UK, with the aim of providing an ensemble context to explore processes of creating new, experimental performances through collaboration. The first part of the chapter discusses the aims of the ensemble; the second part considers interaction within the ensemble, informed by data from semi-structured interviews with group members conducted by the first author over a three-month period.[1]

Group ethos

The intention was for the group primarily to devise material collectively or work from open scores, finding and developing sounds, structures, and interactions that offer players considerable freedom in performance. There would be no specified instrumentation: the line-up would result from membership, not vice versa; one of the creative challenges was to work with whatever combination of instruments arose. Consequently, in addition to standard Western instruments and voices, the ensemble has included accordion, erhu, Javanese rebab, Northumbrian pipes, melodica, toy piano, Indian harmonium, Thai instruments, Nepalese sarangi, acoustic and electric guitars, and live electronics. The personnel have been international and diverse in their musical training and performing experience.

Importantly, all members were to play: there would be no conductor or external rehearsal leader. One or more member(s) might sometimes take more of a lead, instigating a project or providing initial compositional ideas, but from within the group, already a participant. In rehearsals, all members would contribute through processes of group experimentation, discussion, and review (including in-session group review of audio and video recordings of rehearsals).

Finally, attention would be paid to the relationship of the ensemble to the space of performance, its wider context, and hence to the audience. Importantly, this might involve physical movement or developing aspects of instrumental gesture. Players would consider themselves as bodies in a space and focus this awareness—how they play, their positioning relative to

---

[1] Ethical approval for the study was granted by the University of York Arts and Humanities Ethics Committee.

Elizabeth Haddon and Catherine Laws, *Playful production* In: *Together in music.* Edited by: Renee Timmers, Freya Bailes, and Helena Daffern, Oxford University Press 2022. DOI: 10.1093/oso/9780198860761.003.0007

each other and the audience, and any movement—in support of the musical aims, making this part of the content of the work.

Overall, some of the aims were—and continue to be—primarily aesthetic; others more pedagogic. Aspects of the underlying rationale and working practices relate to three established contexts: experimental music collectives, new music practices that foreground embodied aspects of performance, and devised theatre practices. These are detailed below, in order to contextualize the work.

Models for collective music-making

In some respects, The Assembled builds on the approaches of other experimental music collectives that have aimed to operate somewhat democratically, such as the UK's Scratch Orchestra, formed in 1969 and defined as "a large number of enthusiasts pooling their resources … and *assembling* [emphasis added] for action (music making, performance, edification)" (Cardew, 1974, p. 10). This group, one of many emerging in the 1960s and 1970s with democratic ideals and similar political concerns, produced performances of unconventional scores and notations, often indeterminate, along with forms of guided improvisation.

The democratic model, with ensemble interaction as a form of socio-musical practice, is significant for The Assembled. It is not assumed that hierarchies are necessarily problematic; indeed, in an educational context (and perhaps in any setting), there are always differences in status and power, both real and perceived. Leadership, of some kind—or *facilitation*, as discussed Perspectives from members: Facilitation—is often necessary, not just administratively, but also to initialize projects. However, the intention has been to develop group awareness of how and why hierarchies form, and their use in any particular project. The group has been drawn to composers explicitly interested in issues of individual agency and group interaction; examples include Christian Wolff, whose "contingent pieces" are concerned with "the mutual effects players have on each other in the real time of performance" (Saunders, 2009, p. 362; see also Chapter 18), and James Saunders, whose *Things To Do* series foregrounds group dynamics, whether between ensemble members or between the ensemble and audience (see also Chapter 2). However, The Assembled operates somewhat differently to most experimental music and improvisation ensembles: partly through the processes used to develop work—cycles of action and reaction, playing and reviewing—and through the focus on the physicality of performance and the relation to the space or context of performance.

A focus on embodiment is arguably more prevalent in recent experimental music (Gottschalk, 2016). Walshe (2016, para. 8) argues that many composers are "finally willing to accept that the bodies playing the music are part of the music, that they're present, they're valid and they inform our listening whether subconsciously or consciously." This wider concern with the physicality and mediation of performance resonates with The Assembled's careful consideration of matters of body, space, and context. However, the tendencies Walshe identifies emphasize, and often work *through*, the performer's body, but primarily from a composer-director perspective. The Assembled attempts to be more flexible with roles, involving all members in creative decisions. Moreover, the presentational, choreographic, or spatial performance elements stem from musical and interactional matters: they are usually ways of externalizing or emphasizing things that have developed, implicitly, in the musical materials and relationships.

The Assembled and devised theatre working practices

Overall, the work of The Assembled diverges from most other experimental music practice in its more extensive collaborative development. Broadly speaking, there have been three methods of operation:

- Working, initially, from an extant "score" (never fully notated, and always "open," whether graphic, verbal (with textual instructions), or semi-notated), sometimes used only as a starting point, realized in various ways before diverging, developing the ideas, transforming the starting points, and so on;
- Taking a non-musical starting point—a picture, text, or concept, for example—and exploring ways of "translating" it into music or otherwise responding to it;
- Workshopping a musical idea brought by one group member, e.g. guidelines for a group improvisation, a snippet of (open) score, a working process—anything that can generate some initial material. This is subsequently developed, sometimes primarily by that individual with input from the rest of the group, sometimes more fully collaboratively.

In combination, these approaches result in working processes close to those of devised theatre. This is a broad field: practitioners and critical commentaries routinely note the difficulties of definition, due to the variety of practices employed. However, most agree with Heddon and Milling (2005) that at the core lies a process of generating performance through collaboration, with the literary play text no longer central (though texts or scores might still be used or developed as part of the process). Mermikides and Smart (2010, p. 28) propose a definition focused on "a certain playful openness: to a range of stimuli; to creative risk and experimentation; to the views and inputs of a variety of participants, including performers; to change and development throughout the process even beyond the first performance." Likewise, they identify a typical process (noting that the phases of the work often overlap or repeat): generation of initial ideas; exploration and development of ideas; shaping of material into a structured piece; performance and production; and reflection (p. 22). These principles, and the cyclical, iterative processes, are close to the ways in which The Assembled operates, but with music as the main material.

Significantly, the nature and status of both rehearsal and performance are here somewhat different to those of conventional musical processes, due to the cycles of devising and group review; also because the process is at least as significant as the output. Therefore, The Assembled often offers work-in-progress showings, performs multiple versions of pieces that differ considerably in content, or finds other ways of inviting the audience inside the working processes.

Perspectives from members: Facilitation

This section focuses on selected themes from the thematic analysis of the semi-structured interviews with current and former members of The Assembled: working methods and group ethos. Players endorse the value of exploring processes via shared working practices and stated awareness of an environment in which each person can act as a facilitator. Higgins (2008, p. 330) observes that "facilitation is concerned with encouraging open dialogue among different individuals with differing perspectives." This suggests a commitment to enabling verbal constructs of meaning; a corresponding process of musical dialogue is also ongoing within The Assembled.

Group members identified aspects enabling open verbal and musical dialogue. These include the attitude of the group's founder, who, despite being the staff member with ultimate responsibility for the group, engages in active exploration of musical material as an equal player. A member observed that: "the fact that she's playing ... and that she's trying different sounds as well, learning, if you like, takes away the idea of her kind of wanting it to go in a certain way, or judging us as an ensemble participant." Instead of deploying unidirectional leadership to realize goals, explorative processes enable each player to voice ideas. Another player stated that facilitation "emphasizes a sense of bringing things together into the same space and allowing them to co-exist and then create or cross-pollinate." Players may be "nurturing each other in terms of creativity and sharing ideas," generating collective aims and responsibility for decisions, resulting in collaborative facilitation (see also Chapter 8). They observed that the sense of choice and focus on sound took them towards a greater presence in the moment, trust, and acceptance, facilitating collaborative engagement.

The different perspectives afforded by the unorthodox line-up positions each player as the expert authority on their instrument and create timbral and textural variety, differing techniques and playing styles, transference of these across instruments, and curiosity and respect for co-players. Musical starting points might derive from sonic concerns, in which members might collaboratively consider aspects of sound quality and explore means to transform and develop it. Any member might initiate exploration of ideas, feeling able to "contribute very thoroughly, from their own perspective;" while they could freely express ideas, not all ideas were taken up, largely because the creation of the group's music happened as a "collective effort," focusing on "overall collective interests." Although an idea might be expressed but not developed because "nobody ever coalesced around that idea," players would not view this negatively: "you're being listened to ... it doesn't really matter if your idea doesn't get taken on because you were able to express it ... not every contribution is going to fit." All ideas were therefore contributions to the process: "even if it was a quite far-out comment, people would listen." Players were concerned to ensure that the language used "doesn't restrict things," particularly in order to enable creativity following such abstract starting points as "what is the sound of white?," for example.

Members observed that rehearsal conversations "were not so much 'what should each individual do to make this work?'; it was more evaluating what we had done on a musical level, collectively." Comments were "addressed to the overall way that the composition or improvisation was actually working as a whole." This de-individualized focus seems to strengthen the collective, particularly as the exploration of material was viewed as "more like drama," not only through consideration of space and movement as essential to performance, but also through co-player awareness and developing a shared language to discuss the processes used for both free improvization and realizing stimulus-based material. A specific sound, movement, or quality might be described and labeled to enable players to subsequently recall and respond to improvisatory starting points or structural cues. Particularly when "stepping outside of the box or comfort zone" in generating new sounds, players would consider "performance-wise, how we can make the connection between this strange thing and what our practice currently is," thereby sharing vocabulary, discussing aims, context, and possible outcomes.

Shared vocabulary

Description and labeling were also applied to rehearsal recordings, used to enable reflection of rehearsal processes. Labeling might be "a bullet point list ... it'll be 'running section' or just something to jog your memory." Here, it appears that the language used and "the importance of consistency to describe certain things" have crucial implications for "what those words will trigger and mean for people to then do." This "shared vocabulary" operates not just as working discourse, delineating and distinguishing kinds of processes, but also acts as a longitudinal means of consolidating and strengthening the group: the vocabulary is "limited to what you've done, and you're drawing on things, maybe outside of the piece to then try to explain what is going on, and then it's unique to the group." This collaborative codification of sounds, movement, and process facilitates individual and group reflection.

Conclusion

Emerging from this brief study are three concepts underpinning collaborative facilitation within The Assembled: (1) the shaping of the ethos of the group through the approaches articulated above, developed in the working practices; (2) the expertise, curiosity, and reflective engagement of group members; and (3) the verbal interaction shaping exploratory musical processes, involving open questions, generation of ideas, description and labeling, shared vocabulary, and awareness of implications of choices made in verbal articulation of process and ideas. These operate within a context promoting the expression and consideration of individual views, resulting in collective facilitation of players' verbal, musical, and performative engagement. More detailed discussion is beyond the scope of this chapter, but there is potential for further investigation of the collaborative mechanisms at work, to explore challenges as well as successes, and to consider pedagogic value. Considering the nature of "playful production" via the lens of The Assembled suggests that the focus of "production" is more than purely sonic or dramatic: it encompasses the social, shapes attitudes towards individual responsibility and collaborative concern, and enhances the development of reflective capacity as well as innovative performance.

Acknowledgments

The authors would like to thank the members of The Assembled who contributed to this chapter.

References

Cardew, C. (Ed.). (1974). *Scratch music*. MIT Press.

Gottschalk, J. (2016). *Experimental music since 1970*. Bloomsbury.

Heddon, D., & Milling, J. (2005). *Devising performance: A critical history*. Palgrave Macmillan.

Higgins, L. (2008). The creative music workshop: Event, facilitation, gift. *International Journal of Music Education, 26*(4), 326–38.

Mermikides, A., & Smart, J. (Eds.). (2010). *Devising in process*. Palgrave Macmillan.

Saunders, J. (Ed.). (2009). *The Ashgate research companion to experimental music*. Ashgate.

Walshe, J. (2016). *The new discipline: A compositional manifesto*. Retrieved from http://www.borealisfestival.no/2016/the-new-discipline-a-compositional-manifesto-by-jennifer-walshe-2/

8
Teaching through ensemble performance

J. Murphy McCaleb

Introduction

Strategies for teaching ensemble performance in higher education (HE) historically draw on lecturers as conductors or mentors. Ostensibly mirroring leadership in Western classical ensembles, these traditions have solidified into a pedagogy which can easily remain unexamined through habit or presumed beneficence. Breaking with tradition and trying out new forms of pedagogy, coupled with new forms of leadership, may present opportunities to explore potentially more efficient and effective ways of working.

A potentially problematic perspective on teaching ensemble performance is a presumption that "successful performance, in which students execute their individual part accurately in the manner dictated to them, is […] evidence of successful learning" (Mantie, 2012, p. 118). This prioritization of product over process has been highlighted in research over the last decade on choral performance (Freer, 2011) and wind bands (Allsup & Benedict, 2008). Freer (2011) describes this as the performance–pedagogy paradox, proposing that leaders of pedagogic ensembles feel tension between presenting a high-quality performance, which conductors may strive for, and providing high-quality learning experiences, on which mentors may wish to focus. Although these outcomes are not necessarily mutually exclusive, he suggests that successfully achieving both is the exception rather than the norm—a perspective I share.

Traditional models of ensemble pedagogy mirror elements of transactional and transformational leadership, depending on which side of the performance–pedagogy paradox they are most subject to. Transactional leadership prioritizes goal achievement whereas transformational leadership focuses on group members' individual development (McCaleb, 2014). However, just as Freer proposes that the performance–pedagogy paradox can be resolved through balancing both goals, these two kinds of leadership may be balanced in a third path. Professional chamber ensembles exhibit qualities similar to the business model of alternating leadership, where members assume "*ad hoc* leadership positions […] by temporarily and freely [alternating] back to be observers, followers, and so forth" (Andert et al., 2011, p. 54; cf. McCaleb, 2014; see Chapter 1). This case study investigates how this style of flexible leadership might be applied within HE, where the lecturer rehearses and performs within student groups.

J. Murphy McCaleb, *Teaching through ensemble performance* In: *Together in music*. Edited by: Renee Timmers, Freya Bailes, and Helena Daffern, Oxford University Press. © Oxford University Press 2022. DOI: 10.1093/oso/9780198860761.003.0008

Method and pedagogical approach

In my work at York St John University, I have used observations of rehearsal videos and focus groups in the 2017/18 academic year to assess participatory ensemble teaching across all three years of an undergraduate music program. Working with 34 students across five groups, these ensembles included:

- Three jazz combos (Hancock Ensemble, 14 students; Bru, nine students; and Beck, eight students) where I played bass trombone;
- One soul band (12 students) where I played bass trombone and made transcriptions and arrangements; and
- One acoustic folk band (Storytellers, five students) where I played accordion and sang.

My involvement in each ensemble was based upon two key tenets. First, I am a musician, just as my students are. Thus, I operated in the ensembles in such a way as to be no more or less musically important than any of the students. To this end, none of the ensembles traditionally used a conductor, and I played instruments in them that are rarely used to lead. This mirrors Leonard Tan's description of democratic musical participation, where "every player has to participate actively and thoughtfully in order to render the whole greater than the sum of its parts; there can be no 'spectators'. No one does everything, but everyone does something" (2014, p. 66). Second, it was not necessarily my place to provide solutions in rehearsals. Rather, a maieutic approach was anticipated to encourage students to make decisions about the ensembles for themselves. Allowing students to play a larger leadership role (even temporarily) should allow them to "learn musical independence as they might learn civic participation, by *making musical decisions that matter*" (Shieh & Allsup, 2016, p. 33).

Focus groups led by myself at the end of each academic term provided insight into the students' experiences. I minimized my influence in the focus groups by speaking in broad enough terms to limit students second-guessing intended topics or answers, by avoiding providing personal opinions on any of the topics discussed and by not discussing this strand of my research with my students during this academic year. The students were aware that this research was on ensembles and how they might improve, but no other information was provided. Having transcribed, anonymized, and thematically coded these conversations, key topics emerged (cf. Vaughn & Turner, 2016). The appropriateness of this coding and emergent topics was verified by another member of university staff.

Findings and discussion

Decision-making in participatory ensemble teaching

Regular engagement with the decision-making that shapes an ensemble appears to benefit students' development as ensemble musicians. As noted within the focus groups at the end of the academic year, members of all ensembles thought they improved, both in terms of "coordination in performance, on a technical level" (P7, Soul Band) and how "the group got more confidence and more comfortable" (P15, Hancock Ensemble). In particular, students spontaneously commented in these focus groups how they would "listen out to everyone else playing and having [their] own ideas, […] therefore contributing to [the ensemble development]" (P5, Soul Band). Likewise, they spoke of how important they felt it was to have the opportunity to voice their opinions, which would help them lead their own ensembles in the future (P1, Soul Band and P18, Storytellers). As Shieh and Allsup (2016, p. 34) remark, decision-making is "understood as a capacity or power, one that is cultivated with, through, and beyond a lifetime of thoughtful engagements." Engaging with many musical decisions in rehearsals increased students' capacity for dealing with technical challenges, as well as boosting confidence and gaining artistic independence as individuals.

Equality

The democratization of the decision-making process was noticed by students throughout rehearsals and at the end of the project, with remarks in the focus groups including "everyone has an equal voice" (P4, Soul Band) and "we all have an opinion and we all are like an equal" (P18, Storytellers). This equality extended to myself, with one student saying "our feedback and […] concerns [were as] important as yours; […] you don't get that in other ensembles" (P25, Beck). However, this equality was not without conditions: "Everyone there had the chance to input their own opinion. […] If they didn't speak up, […] it's their fault [. . .]. The chance for ownership there all the time" (P15, Hancock Ensemble). Students viewed this democratization positively, with one remarking that they thought that it was "probably what's made this [group] more successful than if you did decide to just solely lead"—success, in this instance, being interpreted as the overall quality achieved in the performance (P8, Soul Band).

Midway through the project, some students indicated discontent with some of the decisions I had made on their behalf. In Soul Band, two members wanted more say on larger interpretative decisions that went into the arrangements being performed. One pointed out that if she had done the arrangement, she would have made it fit her current range on her instrument better (P9, Soul Band). Another suggested that harder harmonies should be evenly spread among the singers, allowing them to feel "like we had more control over what we were doing" (P8, Soul Band). As Shieh and Allsup (2016, p. 31) clarify, "an appropriate standard for fostering musical independence might well be the exhortation that *students make musical decisions that matter.*" Following these students' comments, I deliberately refrained from making arrangements for the remaining three ensembles, and elected not to choose any repertoire for Storytellers. In this group, these students remarked as to how I was more the "focused facilitator" (P20, Storytellers) and "stabilizers on a bike" (P22, Storytellers) than the key decision-maker.

The role of lecturers

My explicit aim to step back from leadership was observed as noteworthy by the students, even though it may not be uncommon in HE for lecturers to act as facilitators. Increased stepping back may come with a risk of lack of action and improvement. However, that does not appear to be the case. One student remarked that I was "the one that was drawing our attention to things. […] It was us as a group that decided what would happen and how we'd do it" (P15,

Hancock Ensemble). Placing responsibility on students this way was pivotal, as one remarked "there's a difference being told what you need to improve and recognizing it in yourself" (P25, Beck). One student said "You made us actually think about what was wrong ourselves" (P3, Soul Band), and another specifically pointed out that I "ask more questions rather than statements" (P7, Soul Band). Another student commented "you gave us the puzzle and we had to put it together" (P11, Hancock Ensemble). Students often compared this approach to leadership more as being a "focused facilitator" (P20, Storytellers) who played in the band as well (P26, Beck). While the students were not privy to the motivations underlying my strategy as an ensemble leader, they clearly noticed how it had deviated from tradition, commenting that I should have been "the leader," and yet I somehow was not (P22, Storytellers).

My efforts to stay out of the spotlight were particularly noticed by one student, who pointed out in a focus group that I was the only member of the Hancock Ensemble *not* to solo in the performance: "in the actual performance, you took a relatively [...] back seat approach, but in the rehearsals you were very much at the forefront" (P15, Hancock Ensemble). Stepping back in this way took some getting used to, both for me and the students. It was frustrating to recognize an easy solution to a rehearsal issue but not to act on it immediately, instead encouraging the students to identify and resolve the issue for themselves, a strategy which ran counter to students' expectations. Most praised how helpful this approach was, particularly in comparison to other ensembles. It was somewhat disheartening to hear how students were so used to hearing leaders "just going 'you're wrong' or 'let's just do it again,' or [saying] what's wrong in such a technical way that nobody could possibly understand" (P7, Soul Band) or how one student would be "afraid to speak, never mind say that I've done [something] wrong" (P28, Beck).

Power

One theme that emerged from my own observations and notes was that of the power imbalance between myself and my students. Regardless of how democratic an ensemble is, the lecturer still acts as gatekeeper and validator—encouraging behaviors, expectations, and standards, and validating decisions and measures of quality. At times, this imbalance was willingly accepted by the students, one of whom remarked that they were "relying more on [my] judgement, because I felt you were the one who was familiar with the genre, so I was trusting you a bit more" (P4, Hancock Ensemble). As the "validation of knowledge is inseparable from issues of power" (Mantie, 2012, p. 107), the power relationship between myself and my students likely has implications for students' learning. Attempts at leveling the playing field through participatory lecturing bear resemblance to a "truly active pedagogic encounter," "one in which there is concern and care between parties, [placing] teacher and learner in a horizontal space" (Allsup & Benedict, 2008, p. 166). In later work, Allsup (2012, p. 173) problematizes this horizontal space, writing that "the democratic classroom is indeed one where learners have a stake, a very large stake, in the outcome of their education; it is also a place [...] where power is shared and distributed. But having a stake in one's learning is not the same as knowing all that one needs to know to secure a desired end." There is scope for more in-depth inquiry into this topic in music pedagogy *writ large*. It may be that encouraging creative autonomy in students requires more situations where they have the space to be independent—with opportunities for feedback on what they do given that freedom.

Conclusion

Adopting participatory ensemble teaching in HE has had several key outcomes. First, there is potential for students to feel increased ownership over the ensembles in which they participate, encouraging achievement of higher-quality performances. Second, equality in decision-making processes can encourage students to act increasingly as reflective practitioners. Third, undertaking this project has highlighted the complicated power relationships (and imbalances) that are at play between lecturers and students—a social context which might impact students' democratic engagement in both their learning and ensemble musicking. I do not think that this approach to ensemble teaching is to be adopted in place of traditional transactional or transformational leadership styles, but to complement them, creating a broader spectrum of ensemble participation.

At this stage, it is difficult to tell what impact participatory ensemble teaching has on students' long-term musical development. Prioritizing students' development as reflective practitioners within ensembles over traditional approaches to ensemble teaching does not negate the performance–pedagogy paradox—if anything, it exacerbates this tension between expected learning and performance outcomes. However, this research project does illuminate how focusing more on students' learning than on the creation of high-quality performances might necessarily change the roles I and my students inhabit.

There is scope within HE music curricula to question the role of traditional teaching methods, particularly when those methods might minimize students' development as autonomous reflective practitioners. To borrow a call to action from Allsup and Benedict (2008, p. 170), "Like it or not, we [as teachers] are role models for our students. We need to ask ourselves, 'What is wrong with a particular educative model that perpetuates systems of domination and that serve less than transformative endpoints? Who does this model serve? And more importantly, who is not served?'" Ensemble teaching in HE can serve all of our students more effectively, but lecturers need to be willing to break from tradition to explore the ways in which we might do so.

Acknowledgments

I would like to thank Dr David Lancaster for his assistance verifying the coding of the focus groups.

References

Allsup, R. E. (2012). Music education and human flourishing: A meditation on democratic origins. *British Journal of Music Education, 29*(2), 171–9.

Allsup, R. E., & Benedict, C. (2008). The problems of band: An inquiry into the future of instrumental music education. *Philosophy of Music Education Review, 16*(2), 156–73.

Andert, D., Platt, A., & Alexakis, C. (2011). Alternative, grassroots, and rogue leadership: A case for alternating leaders in organizations. *Journal of Applied Business Research, 27*(2), 53–61.

Freer, P. K. (2011). The performance-pedagogy paradox in choral music teaching. *Philosophy of Music Education Review, 19*(2), 164–78.

Mantie, R. (2012). Striking up the band: Music education through a Foucaultian Lens. *Action, Criticism & Theory for Music Education, 11*(1), 99–123.

McCaleb, J. M. (2014). *Embodied knowledge in ensemble performance.* Routledge.

Shieh, E., & Allsup, R. E. (2016). Fostering musical independence. *Music Educators Journal, 102*(4), 30–5.

Tan, L. (2014). Towards a transcultural theory of democracy for instrumental music education. *Philosophy of Music Education Review, 22*(1), 61–77.

Vaughn, P., & Turner, C. (2016). Decoding via coding: Analyzing qualitative text data through thematic coding and survey methodologies. *Journal of Library Administration, 56*(1), 41–51.

9

The impact of group identity on the social dynamics and sustainability of chamber music ensembles

Alana Blackburn

Introduction

This chapter presents an analysis of important features that contribute to a chamber music ensemble's group identity, and highlights how these features assist in understanding ensemble social dynamics and sustainability. Two major themes emerge: the similar characteristics, goals, and objectives of ensemble members often based on repertoire choice and programming; and a shared sound or musical aesthetic developed through an interpretation of repertoire, instrumental combination, and the collective skills and knowledge of the musicians.

This case study draws from the findings of a larger research project (Blackburn, 2017) in which chamber musicians who had formed and participated in numerous ensembles were individually interviewed. The aims of the larger project were to explore individual and group identify formation, and group processes. The data were collected through individual semi-structured interviews with 30 professional chamber musicians, identified using pseudonyms, who represented 58 different ensembles. The interviews were transcribed verbatim and analyzed using thematic analysis. The process of data analysis was inductive, and five main themes were obtained; this case study focuses on the theme "group identity." The musicians were members of "unconventional" or "non-traditional" ensembles, those with unusual instrumentation, and those flexible in instrumentation and members. The focus on these types of ensembles adds to earlier studies of ensemble work, which have explored more standard ensembles such as the string quartet (Butterworth, 1990; Davidson & Good, 2002; Gilboa & Tal-Shmotkin, 2010; Murnighan & Conlon, 1991; Young & Colman, 1979).

The following sections explore the foundations of an ensemble's motivation, describe the challenges and obstacles these unconventional ensembles face when developing an audience, and look at a deeper level of group identity in terms of the working relationship between group members.

Setting shared goals, objectives, and vision

The participants were asked how they initially became involved with, or formed, their current and past chamber music ensembles. They presented quite varied responses, from playing

Alana Blackburn, *The impact of group identity on the social dynamics and sustainability of chamber music ensembles* In: *Together in music*. Edited by: Renee Timmers, Freya Bailes, and Helena Daffern, Oxford University Press. © Oxford University Press 2022.
DOI: 10.1093/oso/9780198860761.003.0009

with friends during university studies to more formal contractual agreements. The answers became more consistent when the musicians reflected on why particular ensembles survived over longer periods of time. This suggested a further line of enquiry into the personal and collective experiences of working in musical ensembles, and the values placed on such collaborations.

It was clear from the experience of the participants that ensembles that are successful in terms of longevity and audience following had developed a clear purpose for their ensemble—defining specific philosophies, goals, and strategies that they all shared. These ideologies and visions provided the basis for sustaining ensembles and contributed to a mutual rapport that evolved over time.

> I felt a musical affinity . . . socially I think we've got a similar value system, so that was another thing that drew us together . . . we had a great professional respect for each other. (Jessica)

The members of one of Jessica's ensembles together formed a group identity based on shared values and mutual professional respect. Although echoed by many of the participants, there were two examples of ensembles not succeeding because the goals were neither shared nor agreed upon:

> A group who had been around for a long time, for 20 years I suppose by the time that they had come to a point where they were struggling a bit to define their artistic raison d'être . . . they lost steam . . . the performer commitment was dwindling . . . that was the point they were at, they were so stuck in the past, everyone knew what the [ensemble] had been, but no one knew what it was going to be. And you can only stretch that line so thin, until it breaks. (Dennis)

> Artistically and musically to find a strong identity was actually difficult to sort of step beyond what they were doing so far . . . yeah, a good vision. Because the difficulty I think with this group was that it wasn't particularly bound to any genre or type of music. (Kylie)

These accounts of lived experience indicate that shared goals and vision clearly shape and impact the identity and individuality of an ensemble. The two comments above also illustrate the value of ensembles periodically rethinking and adapting their vision according to the changing environment.

Repertoire and programming

Many of the participants described their ensemble as an "early music ensemble" or "contemporary music ensemble," without considering the identity of the group beyond the type of repertoire they play. It was common to see that these unconventional ensembles that varied instrumentation from project to project had no standard repertoire available to them. They often arranged existing pieces or commissioned new works. Groups that aligned repertoire choice with the values of the ensemble found that the desire to perform new works gave purpose, developing a reputation for musical and aesthetic innovation. This desire was also a way to align and motivate group members. Alice, for example, explains:

> We perform repertoire that we think is important for people to hear that wouldn't hear it otherwise … just basically to bring works to audience … it was all about exposure to stuff that nobody else is doing … this makes us no money, it's always been a labor of love. (Alice)

Their decisions and purpose are based around particular repertoire that becomes an essential part of the objectives and uniqueness of the ensemble. This provides inspiration and motivation to continue doing what is seen as artistically important, highlighted by Alice's comment of "labor of love."

There are noticeable challenges presented to these unconventional ensembles in terms of programming and repertoire. By programming unheard or new works, ensembles that are quite eclectic in genre often find it hard to "sell" their program. Several participants indicated that venues are not familiar with what they are actually offering and building an audience can be difficult. To overcome these barriers, participants explained that they ensured each of the aspects unique to the ensemble aligned with a clear set of goals and aims, which related to building a distinct group identity. Over time, the reputation based on these distinct values is reported to have created trust and respect within their music communities, including the audience and other musicians.

Ensemble sound and musical aesthetic

The participants also described group "sound" or "aesthetic" as a form of identity. Based on the participants' comments, "sound" is defined in this context as a particular sonic quality based on the technical abilities of the players, the combination of instruments that make up a group, and the tonal color formed by the blending of these two elements (Blackburn, 2017). Group sound or aesthetic is something that is developed over time, can separate one group from another within a particular genre, and can become recognizable to an audience. Developing this sound establishes a close interpretative connection within the group musically, forming a creative social dynamic. It also heightens the awareness and collaboration players experience when working together for a long period of time.

For many new music groups, part of the identity of the ensemble was defined as pioneering. Contributing to the interpretation and aesthetics of modern performance is a motivation shared by many ensemble members of these groups. Groups become identified with innovation and experimentation. Group identity motivates and drives the ensemble; the collective input and shared philosophy help sustain the group, musically and socially, as indicated in this excerpt from Alan:

> Our contribution is to interpretation of particular aesthetics, or creation of techniques or approaches, and that's amazing. That's when you see the work you do just shoot directly into the flow of ideas that everyone shares in, and that's been incredibly empowering I think for the ethos of the group. (Alan)

The participants provided different interpretations of what constitutes a "group sound," depending on two different combinations of instruments. For homogenous ensembles, or ensembles that are made of the same instrument family, there was discussion of "blending," "balance," and "mixing" in terms of sound production. This ultimately led to a specific sound that was refined by the ensemble. Taking ownership of this sound becomes part of the identity of the group. To accelerate the process of developing an ensemble sound, one participant shared an experience of being in an ensemble where members were chosen because of similar educational backgrounds and skills. This ensured unity in the ensemble in terms of musical knowledge and interpretation, as well as a player's instrumental sound:

> You have followed the same course and the same path so you end up having a lot of common view of the music ... We need people who understand the kind of sound we like ... we can see who is learning this kind of sound that we look for and who is learning the intonations and the things that kind of make our work much faster and that lead to a good result. (Stella)

For ensembles that had mixed instrumentation, the participants spoke of the importance of the performers maintaining individuality while working on an ensemble sound. Mia says:

> What I like about our group is that everyone does have an individual sound. It's not just all a homogenous sort of mixed sound, and you can hear that. It sounds very personal. (Mia)

Group dynamics and sustainability

In order to create a sustainable ensemble in terms of professionalism and excellence, group understanding of what an ensemble *is* and producing a meaningful identity are important. For some participants, this meant answering philosophical questions such as "what is the group? Why are you here? What's your 'thing'?" (Dennis) or "what are you? What are you doing? What is your core?" (Robert). Once established, a professional working environment was set where individual "egos" and personal relationships are kept outside the rehearsal and performance space, allowing professional relationships and positive group dynamics to form.

> I always declare in the initial pitch, "this is the financial situation of the thing, don't do it because we're mates, you have to be really into these pieces ... if the general profile of the program is not artistically interesting to you, just say no and we'll go for a drink instead." (Bridgette)

> It's not a group of friends, it's an arts organization. It's not a, you know, "yay, it's great that we have fun time in rehearsal and we have great concerts", that's a side effect of actually doing what we're doing. (Jack)

The dynamics and sustainability of an ensemble depend on the working relationship within the rehearsal. When an ensemble is project-focused, different members come together, based on who is needed, and group dynamics are therefore re-evaluated. These project-led ensembles meet sporadically; therefore, the shared expectation of the ensemble is that each player draws on a high level of professionalism, expertise, and skill, ensuring they are personally prepared in terms of rehearsal and performance. For Alan, professionalism and expertise form part of the identity of his ensemble and are used to enhance its reputation. To him, this compares to the working method of more traditional ensembles that perform more regularly and have fixed personnel.

> It's part of the pressure of having an infrequent operation as far as performance goes. Where, you know, we're not playing on a regular basis like a string quartet is. So each instrumentalist has to be very steeped in what they're doing, very experienced. (Alan)

Alan also recognizes that audiences identify the ensemble as a highly skilled group performing complex repertoire at an expert level. Excellence is ensured by the artistic director's choice of players based on technical proficiency, establishing the group as *something of quality*. Alan also describes the motivation members have for the ensemble:

> It was a very strong energy from the group to continue, and that people would do what it takes; that we were gonna [sic] become the most amazing ensemble possible. (Alan)

Conclusion

The participants linked group identity closely with the collective aims and vision of a group (as also discussed in Chapter 4). They were able to easily and clearly define an ensemble in terms of performing a certain type of repertoire, and a particular aesthetic.

The participants in the study displayed awareness of the importance of developing a deeper sense of identity—to not only set their ensembles apart from others or to find a niche, but also to develop a shared identity and purpose as a means for motivating group members and to create a sustainable ensemble. In order to do this, the participants spoke of creating a mutual creative vision and philosophy through asking questions related to the ideology of the group, designing a list of goals, and specifying the purpose or vision of the ensemble. Participants found that, although a consistent vision and aesthetic concept needed to be clear throughout the lifetime of the ensemble, the vision also had to evolve and adapt to changing environmental factors and external influences.

Understanding the processes of forming group identity and the need for refocusing this identity over time highlights important social and functional features of professional unconventional chamber music ensembles. This information can benefit musicians through the forming stages of an ensemble by emphasizing the impact every component has on its identity, and how identity can shape the working environment and longevity of an ensemble.

References

Blackburn, A. (2017). *The modern classical chamber music ensemble: Exploring individual identities, management and group processes* [Doctoral dissertation]. University of New England.

Butterworth, T. (1990). Detroit String Quartet. In J. R. Hackman (Ed.), *Groups that work (and those that don't): Creating conditions for effective teamwork* (pp. 207–24). Jossey-Bass Inc.

Davidson, J., & Good, J. M. M. (2002). Social and musical co-ordination between members of a string quartet: An exploratory study. *Psychology of Music, 30*(2), 186–201.

Gilboa, A., & Tal-Shmotkin, M. (2010). String quartets as self-managed teams: An interdisciplinary perspective. *Psychology of Music, 40*(1), 19–41.

Murnighan, K. J., & Conlon, D. E. (1991). The dynamics of intense work groups: A study of British string quartets. *Administrative Science Quarterly, 36*(2), 165–86.

Young, V. M., & Colman, A. M. (1979). Some psychological processes in string quartets. *Psychology of Music, 7*(1), 12–18.

10

Come together

An ethnography of the Seattle Men's Chorus family

Wendy K. Moy

Introduction

The purpose of this ethnography was to examine the culture of the Seattle Men's Chorus (SMC), at over 300 members, North America's largest community chorus and the world's largest gay men's chorus. Particular attention was paid to the musical and social interactions of its members with the primary question: "What is the culture of the Seattle Men's Chorus?" There are lessons to be learned from the SMC's success by choruses whose very survival may depend on their ability to cultivate their culture to increase singing membership. To further an understanding of the SMC's culture, I examined their sets of relationships (Small, 1998) through the theoretical lens of social capital, a sociological theory about maximizing relationships (Putnam, 1995).

A small, growing body of literature examines community choirs through an ethnographic lens (Bartolome, 2010; Kennedy, 2009; Okigbo, 2010; Youngblood, 2013). Recurrent themes are the expression of identity through song and the sense of community that provides healing and social support (see Chapter 28). Through an interpretative case study, Langston (2005) examined the manifestation of social capital indicators and networks in a community chorus. He found that social capital was present through the indicators of trust, participation, networks and connections, learning, membership of faith-based organizations, contact with family and friends, shared norms and values, and the newly "discovered" indicator of fellowship. Brown et al. (2016) surveyed choral audiences regarding bonding and bridging capital. Their report concluded that choruses can cultivate connectedness through the design of their concerts and that high levels of social capital occur when the concert programming aligns with the backgrounds of the audience members.

The Seattle Men's Chorus

Established in 1979, the SMC is one of the founding choruses of the Gay and Lesbian Choruses Association (GALA).[1] At the time of this research, the vision of the SMC was "A world that accepts and values our gay and lesbian citizens." Additionally, the mission stated, "Seattle Men's Chorus and Seattle Women's Chorus entertain, enlighten, unify, and heal our audience and members, using the power of words and music to recognize the value of gay and straight people and their relationships" (Flying House Productions, 2013, p. i). Over the

---

[1] https://galachoruses.org/about/history

Wendy K. Moy, *Come together* In: *Together in music.* Edited by: Renee Timmers, Freya Bailes, and Helena Daffern, Oxford University Press.
© Oxford University Press 2022. DOI: 10.1093/oso/9780198860761.003.0010

years, the SMC branched out beyond Seattle churches and the symphony hall to perform in major international venues. They have collaborated with prominent guest artists and commissioned new works from composers such as Alice Parker and Jake Heggie.[2]

Methodology

Data collection involved the three pillars of ethnography: observation, interview, and analysis of the material culture. Multiple forms of data were collected in various locations from 2011 to 2013 (Moy, 2015). I observed the SMC during rehearsals, retreats, concerts, social breaks, post-rehearsal social functions, and the GALA Festival. I also observed their organizational culture at a board meeting, annual meeting, and chorus town hall meeting. I conducted interviews with the artistic director, assistant artistic director, accompanist, sign language interpreter, executive director, marketing director, chorus manager, board president, volunteers, and 20 singing members. In the same vein as Bartolome's study (2010), I use the real name of the chorus and its staff members' real names. To protect the privacy of the individual singers, I have used pseudonyms.

Open coding of fieldnotes, journals, and interviews was first employed and resulted in 400 codes that were gradually grouped into 31 categories. Inductively analyzed for patterns, these categories led to broad descriptive themes which became the focal point for focused coding. Descriptions formed concerning the culture of the chorus, and connections between codes emerged.

Two overarching themes emerged regarding the culture of the SMC. The first theme was the chorus as a chosen family (Weeks, 2000), providing a source of self-worth, friendship, and support. The second theme identified the servant leadership of Artistic Director Dennis Coleman as fostering this culture. In line with qualitative research (Creswell & Creswell, 2018), these themes were compared with existing literature/theory, with a particular emphasis on the concept of social capital.

SMC as chosen family

Source of self-worth

For Sean, attending an SMC show and later becoming a singing member brought about a sense of self-worth as a gay man. Upon coming out as gay, he felt a sense of loss when he became estranged from his family. Seeing the SMC confidently sing lyrics from the song *Michael's Letter to Mama* (Moy, 2015) helped him realize that he was not alone. Sean sent a thank you note following his attendance of an SMC concert:

> SMC seems to generate some kind of energy that reaches beyond measures of music to something greater. I was so proud to see you perform: handsome, gifted, generous, happy gay men. Seeing you sing made me proud that I, too, am openly and happily homosexual.

---

[2] https://www.seattlechoruses.org/learn/seattlemenschorus/

The concert was the impetus for Sean reaching out to his biological family, which led to reconciliation and healing after three decades of silence. Later, Sean's work relocated him to Hawaii, where he had a difficult time finding a chorus that provided the same community of support. While the SMC was not the impetus for his return to Seattle, it was a significant motivator. He reflected upon his first SMC rehearsal after leaving Hawaii, "I guess it's a little hard to put into words, the culture, because I walked into that room and it ... feels [sic] a little like home."

Source of friendship and support

SMC members have weathered many challenges together: deaths from human immunodeficiency virus (HIV)/acquired immune deficiency syndrome (AIDS)-related illness, homophobic persecution at work, disownment by and estrangement from family members, and rejection by their religious organizations. Through these life challenges, the SMC has been a source of friendship and support, especially in the case of Mark, a chorus member in his 60s who came out as gay to his wife and children later in life:

> I wake up Monday mornings excited that today is chorus. I wish when I woke up the rest of the week that it was [also] Mondays [sic] because I feel a part of a group, and I don't feel isolated anymore. I feel like I have family and I have a support system ... I know that I can say anything and not be judged, where in my old life I couldn't ...

Servant leadership of Artistic Director

The second theme that emerged was the servant leadership of the Artistic Director Coleman, who served from 1986 until he retired in 2016. He led with the philosophy that while preparing for a performance was important, members' needs were also a priority. Coleman took intentional steps to ensure that the membership included people who needed the SMC:

> There are some people that really need this experience ... their partner just died, they have no friends, they just moved to the city ... so we do our best to help those people and to make sure they can find a place ... And it's become their home and it's their life now. And it's like their church ...

While Coleman worked towards the goal of a good show, he also sought to create a positive rehearsal atmosphere, "You want to come. You have friends there. You look forward to seeing them. You know you're safe in terms of the conductor; you trust him to get you where you need to be." SMC members commented on Coleman's leadership style. Sean said, "He's never blamed us for anything. He will always say, 'That's my fault. That happened because I did this.' We know it's our fault. No one's kidding anyone. We know we did it. But that's the way he is ..." Additionally, the value of the family experience was equivalent to, or outweighed, the experience of traveling and performing. Sean continued:

> If Dennis said, "We're going to rehearse and then we're going to do the show in an alley behind Safeway [grocery store]," we'd all come ... It's just the experience of being to-gether and rehearsing and being with Dennis has its own value [so] that [performing for an audience is] just icing.

Coleman's leadership has dramatically impacted the lives of the SMC members. Ron shared, "For 30 years, he has made SMC his life and has made his [journey of personal] healing SMC's healing. He has been—there are very few people I could say this about—one of my personal heroes." More than an Artistic Director, Coleman oversaw the health of the SMC members much in the way that a pastor serves their congregation. In doing so, people who needed the most encouragement and support (even though they may not have recognized their need) were given the opportunity to be a part of the SMC family. By not focusing on growth, but rather meeting the members' needs, Coleman helped the SMC grow from a 22-member orga-nization to become the largest community chorus in North America.

Social capital in the SMC

The themes of family and servant leadership find resonance in research on social capital and the choral ensemble (Langston, 2005). Bonding social capital consists of horizontal ties within closed networks of people, such as family, close friends, neighbors, or work colleagues (Stone, 2003; Woolcock et al., 2004). Linking social capital emphasizes vertical ties between organizations, institutions, and/or people who possess differing degrees of power or influ-ence (Stone, 2003; Woolcock et al., 2004). Bridging social capital consists of ties that look outward across different demographics (Putnam, 2000; Woolcock et al., 2004) and fosters "broader identities and reciprocity" (Putnam, 2000, p. 23). All three forms were present in the SMC: bonding capital—member to member; linking capital—chorus to artistic director; and bridging capital—chorus to community. Bonding capital was indicated among the mem-bers through fellowship, networks, trust and reciprocity, and shared norms. Linking capital was indicated between the SMC and Coleman through shared norms and values, learning, trust and reciprocity, and fellowship. Bridging capital was seen between the audience and the SMC through the indicator of learning, a bidirectional process, which is significant in that it signals a connection between two groups with differing ideologies and philosophies.

These findings support Langston's (2005) that new communities form around groups with shared histories. If the chorus is a model for ideal relationships, as indicated by Small (1998), then the SMC has demonstrated success not only in their size, but also in their mission to en-tertain, enlighten, unify, and heal their audience and members. They have cultivated bonding capital among their singers and also reached across power and ideological differences to de-velop bridging and linking capital.

Discussion

While the findings of this qualitative inquiry may not be generalizable to all or most choral programs and community choruses, choral directors and artistic directors who lead en-sembles in similar contexts can assess their social capital and build strong, thriving choral communities through similar strategies employed by the SMC (Moy, 2015). The more that choral directors are aware of non-musical elements of a choir, the better they will be prepared to meet the needs of their chorus, thereby retaining and gaining members, and ultimately improving the musical quality of performances. It is rarely—if ever—sustainable to be merely focused on repertoire and recruitment; the act of making music in a choir is a social endeavor and must consider the social needs of both singers and audiences to ensure long-term sustainability for the choral art.

Future research focusing on the role of the SMC in the HIV/AIDS advocacy movement may reveal the impact that singing in a choral ensemble has on healing (see also Part 3), prevention/health issues, and the cultural stigma that accompanied HIV/AIDS. While this study focused on an American gay men's chorus, future research may take a similar approach with different types of choruses from around the world.

Conclusion

The SMC, serving as a chosen family, supports previous research that a community chorus can be a place of meaningful community, healing, and support (Bartolome, 2010; Kennedy, 2009; Okigbo, 2010; Youngblood, 2013). This study also supports findings that it is possible and imperative for choruses to cultivate social capital (Brown et al., 2016). Perhaps more importantly to the SMC members, the ensemble provides a support network as the American LGBTQ community continues to report significant personal discrimination and institutional discrimination (National Public Radio et al., 2017). This discrimination goes up to the governmental level as the Trump administration recently finalized a regulation that will eliminate the protection of non-discriminatory rights of transgender patients in healthcare provision (Sanger-Katz & Weiland, 2020). Despite, and perhaps because of, the current climate, the SMC continues to sing and work towards their (updated) vision of "A more harmonious world that celebrates the unique identities and talents of all people."[3]

References

Bartolome, S. J. (2010). *Girl choir culture: An ethnography of the Seattle girls' choir* [Doctoral dissertation]. University of Washington.

Brown, A., Fenton, S., Marinshaw, K., Ratzkin, R., Tran, J., & Menchaca, M. (2016). *Assessing the audience impact of choral music concerts*. Chorus America. https://www.chorusamerica.org/sites/default/files/resources/Assessing_the_Audience_Impact_of_Choral_Concerts-FINAL_0.pdf

Creswell, J. W., & Creswell, J. D. (2018). *Research design: Qualitative, quantitative, and mixed methods approaches*. Sage.

Flying House Productions. (2013). *Seattle Men's Chorus and Seattle Women's Chorus Member Handbook*. Seattle, WA: Author.

Kennedy, M. C. (2009). The gettin' higher choir: Exploring culture, teaching, and learning in a community chorus. *International Journal of Community Music, 2*, 183–200.

---

[3] https://www.seattlechoruses.org/about/

Langston, T. W. (2005). *Capitalizing on community music: A case study of the manifestation of social capital in a community choir* [Doctoral dissertation]. University of Tasmania.

Moy, W. K. (2015). *Come together: An ethnography of the Seattle Men's Chorus family* [Doctoral dissertation]. University of Washington.

National Public Radio, Robert Wood Johnson Foundation, & Harvard T. H. Chan School of Public Health. (2017). *Discrimination in America: Experiences and views of LGBTQ Americans.* https://www.rwjf.org/en/library/research/2017/10/discrimination-in-america--experiences-and-views.html

Okigbo, A. C. (2010). *Ingoma yomzabalzo—music of the struggles: Ethnography of a South African Zulu choral music and the HIV/AIDS struggle* [Doctoral dissertation]. Indiana University.

Putnam, R. D. (1995). Bowling alone: America's declining social capital. *Journal of Democracy, 6*(1), 65–78.

Putnam, R. D. (2000). *Bowling alone: The collapse and revival of American community.* Simon & Schuster.

Sanger-Katz, M., & Weiland, N. (August 12, 2020). *Trump administration erases transgender civil rights protections in health care.* New York Times. https://www.nytimes.com/2020/06/12/us/politics/trump-transgender-rights.html

Small, C. (1998). *Musicking: The meanings of performing and listening.* University Press of New England.

Stone, W. (2003). Bonding, bridging and linking with social capital. *Stronger Families Learning Exchange Bulletin, 4*, 13–16.

Weeks, J. (2000). *Making sexual history.* Polity Press.

Woolcock, M., Grootaert, C., Narayan, D., & Jones, V. N. (2004). Measuring social capital: An integrated questionnaire. *World Bank Working Papers, 1*(1), 1–53.

Youngblood, F. K. (2013). *Womansong: Healing in a communal musicking village* [Unpublished Master's thesis]. Florida State University.

11

Working practices of professional piano accompanists outlined through a conceptual framework

Evgenia Roussou

Introduction

A review of the literature on piano accompaniment and ensemble performance (Roussou, 2017) has revealed a growing understanding of the roles of piano accompanists, and a positive development in musico-functional and sociocultural attitudes towards them. This was observed both in terms of the acknowledgement of the skills required and the role of the accompanist in the duo soloist–accompanist medium. Instead of a negative sense of disregard, subservience and typecasting of the piano accompanist, a positive recognition of piano accompaniment as both an art and a science, were observed:

> … the scientific, the technical, the stylistic, the psychological, and the artistic elements must be put to work, be synthesised into the work of creative art that a recital of quality represents. Such a synthesis will be affected by a very simple process: by both artists' transmitting and receiving feelings, based on complete agreement about the poetic, musical, and spiritual content of a musical piece … (Adler, 1965, p. 238)

Providing support for this perspective and enhancing insight, outcomes of two empirical studies are reported in this chapter that investigated working practices of professional accompanists as observed from behavior during performance and rehearsal and the viewpoint of the musicians involved. These studies were part of a larger project, which included the formulation of a novel conceptual framework of professional piano accompaniment practice, outlining interacting factors that shape accompaniment practice (Roussou, 2017). In this chapter, the four central themes of this framework are reported.

Empirical studies

Using qualitative enquiry, professional musicians' expectations regarding piano accompanists were investigated, including their skills and roles in rehearsal and performance. Specifically, Study 1 investigated the viewpoints of musicians concerning the expectations, skills, and roles of piano accompanists using semi-structured interviews with 20 experienced professional performers: ten instrumental and vocal soloists, and ten pianists with extensive

Evgenia Roussou, *Working practices of professional piano accompanists outlined through a conceptual framework* In: *Together in music*. Edited by: Renee Timmers, Freya Bailes, and Helena Daffern, Oxford University Press. © Oxford University Press 2022. DOI: 10.1093/oso/9780198860761.003.0011

accompaniment experience (mean length of 33.3 years). Study 2 investigated practices of piano accompaniment, through analysis of commentary on rehearsals and performances, of three pairs of professional musicians: a flautist, a violinist, a singer, and three active professional accompanist practitioners (mean accompaniment experience length of 39.3 years). The foci of the observations were: (1) to explore how the expectations, skills, and roles which surfaced from Study 1 unfolded in practice (rehearsals and performances); and (2) to investigate how professional accompanists' "toolkits" are formed, molded, and applied in practice.

All data collected were analyzed using interpretative phenomenological analysis (Smith et al., 2009), and resulted in the emergence of 17 superordinate themes which were then categorized further into four overarching categories: *interaction, communication, support,* and *expectations and assumptions.* The working practices of professional piano accompanists as emerged from the two empirical studies are outlined under each thematic category below, and supported by selected quotes from the participants, where participants are indicated by numbers or letters if participating in Study 1 or 2, respectively.

Summary of thematic findings

Theme 1: Interaction

Interaction refers to the accompanist's actions in relation to the soloist's that contribute to the achievement of ensemble and musical coherence, and the application of musical receptiveness, musicality, and musical interpretation during both rehearsal and performance. These actions are planned and/or intuitive (Katz, 2009), and can be of musical, aural, visual, and social nature. Practices of musical interaction embrace the accompanist's: (1) flexibility, in adapting to different ways of executing a passage during rehearsals, being attuned to the soloist's musical thinking and perception; (2) sensitivity, in following and leading when the musical material demands it; and (3) alertness, in responding to the soloist's spontaneous interpretative moments during performance. Aurally, a piano accompanist reacts to the sound created, and listens and adapts their playing, creating a good balance responding to the unfolding musical cues. Visually, a piano accompanist interacts by responding to visual cues such as gestures, movements made with the soloist's instrument and body, and looking at the soloist, directly or with their peripheral vision. Practices of social interaction embrace the accompanist actively, expressing rapport by having a dynamic, flexible, and open-minded attitude, achieving a sense of positivity, offering new insights on interpretation, debating and discussing ideas, demonstrating the ability to choose the right words when giving constructive criticism, and sharing "chemistry," trust, respect, and a strong depth of togetherness with the soloist. Illustrations are reported in Box 11.1 of how pianists flexibly adapt to the circumstances through openness of interaction with the soloist.

Theme 2: Communication

Communication with the soloist is both verbal and non-verbal, being achieved through listening, sensing and responding, visually reacting to body movement and gestures, and discussing, debating, or compromising on ideas. The piano accompanist communicates with the

Box 11.1 Selected quotes illustrating interaction

Singer soloist: "when I started talking to [Pianist C] at the beginning and saying to him 'can you go faster' sort of thing, at the minute that he began to respond with me, I picked up, this guy isn't going to be offended at anything I say […] I'm not walking on hot coals, or broken glass or whatever, I haven't got to be careful, we can just work together and that's great" (cited in Roussou, 2017, p. 203)

Pianist 5: "it's an automatic thing, you just know you have to do it […] for example knowing where the soloist has gone and catching them when they have suddenly missed a whole line out during performance […] there are instinctive accompaniment things that you just do, which are connected with what you hear, how you process everything and how well you know the music" (cited in Roussou, 2017, p. 130)

Pianist 4: "if the soloist intends for a very good reason to take very fast speed in a third movement of a concerto, then he expects his accompanist to follow […]sometimes accompanists for audition, have to change on the day, ten times […] so an accompanist on the spot has to change the speed of the movements depending on the soloist, and respond to each personality within their own context, to help that personality to shine […] an open mind is needed here to be able to be flexible, to change your own interpretation in combination with the soloist" (cited in Roussou, 2017, p. 102)

---

soloist by: (1) playing rather than talking, sometimes solely through the music, being on the "same wavelength" as the soloist; (2) responding to the soloist's personality, respecting and taking on board the soloist's ideas, finding the balance between sharing ideas and making comments, and being flexible and prepared to compromise; and (3) sensing and detecting the soloist's intentions, understanding and feeling the soloist's movements and breathing/bowing in certain instances without looking, developing—through experience—a sixth sense which would allow them to pick up signals from the soloist and respond accordingly. Box 11.2 provides quotes of participants illustrating the various modes of communication that accompanists employ.

Theme 3: Support

The data illustrated the various ways in which the piano accompanist may demonstrate support towards the soloist, and what this entails in terms of practical, musical, perceptive, and social conduct. Expressing support embraces actions, which, depending on how they are interpreted and applied, could also be considered under the two overarching categories of interaction and communication above. The piano accompanist expresses support towards the soloist by conveying the feeling of approving, liking, and accepting the soloist, encouraging and inspiring a positive and relaxing working environment, and demonstrating empathy

Box 11.2 Selected quotes illustrating communication

Violin soloist: "we spent quite a lot of time today in the rehearsal talking about tempos" (cited in Roussou, 2017, p. 200)

Pianist B: "communication was good, because she was looking at me quite a lot, and I was looking at her quite a lot […] at the vital moments we were both attuned to what we were trying to do [interpreting her intentions via] gestures with the flute and head" (cited in Roussou, 2017, p. 177)

Pianist 2: "it comes almost as a second nature, a sixth sense, that you can pick it up, and this comes from experience I think, over the years" (cited in Roussou, 2017, p. 152)

Box 11.3 Selected quotes illustrating support

Soloist 3: "an accompanist is a cushion, so they are there to support but they're also there to give, to be flexible, to expand to detract as much as, or as little as they need, to fit around the soloist" (cited in Roussou, 2017, p. 94)

Pianist 3: "once, you are in the flow of things, then, it's a matter [of] continually checking and monitoring a thousand times a second exactly what's going on, between the two parts" (cited in Roussou, 2017, p. 123)

Pianist 9: "you've got to know how to keep going; if you are accompanying a singer [and] they jump, you've got to know how to jump with them" (cited in Roussou, 2017, p. 128)

(King & Roussou, 2017) towards the soloist. They consider the soloist's level of experience, helping them to find confidence in themselves, coaching them when necessary, and making them feel safe and secure. During performance, the accompanist perceives the soloist's mood, provides comfort, support, and encouragement, and keeps calm so as to put a nervous soloist at ease, inspiring confidence in the soloist that they will cover any mishaps during performance, and anticipating and covering possible errors on the soloist's behalf by instantaneously reacting and tactfully adjusting their playing to accommodate an error. The quotes from participants given in Box 11.3 illustrate the relevance of support provided by accompanists, in particular, while playing.

Theme 4: Expectations and assumptions

This category embraces essential attributes of piano accompaniment with respect to setting the necessary conditions for successful rehearsal and performance. This includes being aware of the logistics of an engagement, assuring assumptions and practicalities of rehearsing and performing in a duo are being met, such as the level of their personal preparation prior to rehearsing, and the pianist's practical and technical skills, such as sight-reading, and piano technique and dexterity. Attributes essential to the piano accompanist's toolkit include: (1) being an experienced performer, a good musician, and an accomplished pianist with excellent technique; (2) being familiar with the repertoire and having a broad knowledge of the soloist's instrument, and languages and diction for singers; (3) being able to play with others and interact within an ensemble, being easy to work with, and evoking enjoyment; (4) knowing how to rehearse and having good time management skills; and (5) possessing a wide range of practical skills, including sight-reading, score-reading, harmonization, transposition, and improvisation. The quotes in Box 11.4 illustrate the high expectations that pianists have of themselves as accompanists, as well as their constructive input towards the rehearsal process.

Application of the four thematic categories in practice

Taking a hypothetical incident of skipping (beats/bars/lines, repeat signs, and so on) by the soloist during performance as an example, an application of these four thematic categories

Box 11.4 Selected quotes illustrating expectations and assumptions

---

Pianist 7: "I think they should arrive expecting somebody who is going to be supportive and encouraging, able to play the accompaniment without any technical or musical problems […] the job of the accompanist I think should be to make the soloist sound as good as possible" (cited in Roussou, 2017, p. 103)

Pianist 1: "for an accompanist it's about being open minded enough to, use that time [rehearsal] in the most constructive way possible, so there's a bit of planning and preparation involved in, the things I am going to need to rehearse with the person, and also, the willingness to rehearse what the other person wants to rehearse" (cited in Roussou, 2017, p. 126)

---

of skills combined in practice by a piano accompanist is illustrated below (see also Roussou, 2017, p. 227).

During a live performance, the accompanist—being familiar with the score (expectations and assumptions)—instantaneously identifies that the soloist has skipped a beat, an incident which also caused unavoidable consequent errors, and great distress to the soloist. The accompanist, having already been alert and picking up the soloist's signals—not only through intuition, but also by listening, monitoring, anticipating, and being attuned to the soloist's actions (communication)—responds to this incident by making fast decisions, reacting and immediately acting upon resolving the mishap (interaction). The accompanist restores the musical flow and ensures togetherness with the soloist by keeping calm, improvising their part, pre-empting the soloist's next actions, and scanning the score until they catch up with the soloist (interaction and support). At the same time, the accompanist supports the soloist emotionally as well as musically, by conveying with their demeanor that things are under control, and encouraging the soloist to keep going (support and communication). The accompanist aims to cover the error as seamlessly as possible, without giving an indication that something was amiss (expectations and assumptions).

Conclusion

The four thematic categories identified above formed the central part of a conceptual framework about professional piano accompaniment practice, providing a foundation for understanding the working practices of professional piano accompanists, in terms of the specific and general skills and roles exemplified in their practice: the skills and roles provide the basic structure of each accompanist's toolkit, and are tailored depending on the specific parameters of each engagement, *expectations and assumptions*, being taken for granted as attributes already possessed by the piano accompanist, whereas *interaction*, *communication*, and *support* unfold during practice. Each encounter is unique, influencing the decisions the accompanist makes as to which "tools" are needed to be utilized, causing a fluctuating cyclical process. Overall, this research contributes to the ensemble performance medium, providing fresh pedagogical insights into professional piano accompaniment practice. As the first attempt to rationalize the act of piano accompanying, it aims to encourage accompanist-practitioners to become more conscious and aware of their actions and to consider how they can improve their practice, and instrumental and vocal soloists to understand their piano accompanist's role in the solo–accompaniment partnership.

References

Adler, K. (1965). *The art of accompanying and coaching*. University of Minnesota Press.

Katz, M. (2009). *The complete collaborator. The pianist as a partner*. Oxford University Press.

King, E., & Roussou, E. (2017). The empathic nature of the piano accompanist. In E. King, & C. Waddington (Eds.), *Music and empathy* (pp. 267–81). Ashgate.

Roussou, E. (2017). *Exploring the piano accompanist in Western duo music ensembles: Towards a conceptual framework of professional piano accompaniment practice* [Doctoral thesis]. University of Hull.

Smith, J. A., Flowers, P., & Larkin, M. (2009). *Interpretative phenomenological analysis: Theory, method and research*. Sage.

12

Developing familiarity

Rehearsal talk in a newly formed duo

Jane Ginsborg and Dawn Bennett

Introduction

Researchers have long been interested in performers' cognitions about the music they learn, practice, and memorize for performance, and how these cognitions change as they become familiar with the music. The study of cognitive processes underlying ensemble performance is more recent. Cognitive processes occur within each individual performer and between ensemble members, thus both influence and are influenced by social processes. These, too, change as ensemble members become familiar with each other (see Chapters 1 and 5). Research questions concern the different aspects of the music to which they attend at different stages of practice and rehearsal, and the nature of performers' interactions with each other (see, for example, Chapters 21 and 23).

The present case study was inspired by two studies involving the preparation of unfamiliar repertoire. The first investigated changes in practice focus in the individual practice sessions and joint rehearsals of a singer and pianist-conductor (Ginsborg et al., 2006). This informed a framework of musical dimensions in line with Chaffin et al. (2005) (see the categories displayed in Fig. 12.1) and suggested that over time, musicians' focus shifts from structural and basic dimensions of the music (e.g. where section boundaries occur) to interpretative dimensions such as dynamics and rubato (e.g. determining how softly or loudly to play, how much to accelerate or decelerate), and finally to expressive dimensions (e.g. deciding what is to be conveyed to the audience, such as "yearning" or "joy," and how it is to be conveyed).

The other study investigated the roles of performers' familiarity with each other, and their expertise, as well as change over time (Ginsborg & King, 2012). Student and professional singer–pianist duos worked first with their regular duo partner and then with a same-expertise partner on the same songs. Finally, one student and one professional duo swapped partners and prepared a third new song. Analysis combined the musical dimensions framework informed by the work of Chaffin et al. (2005) with Bales' (1999) Interaction Process Analysis (IPA) for exploring positive and negative socio-emotional interactions and task answers and questions (see the categories displayed in Fig. 12.2). The professional duos' approach to rehearsal was more efficient: they sang and played more, and talked less than the students. Socio-emotional interaction was overwhelmingly positive, but the professionals were more likely to request and volunteer their own opinions to their rehearsal colleagues. The numbers of references made to structural, basic, interpretative, and expressive dimensions changed over time in similar ways for the students and professionals.

Jane Ginsborg and Dawn Bennett, *Developing familiarity* In: *Together in music.* Edited by: Renee Timmers, Freya Bailes, and Helena Daffern, Oxford University Press. © Oxford University Press 2022. DOI: 10.1093/oso/9780198860761.003.0012

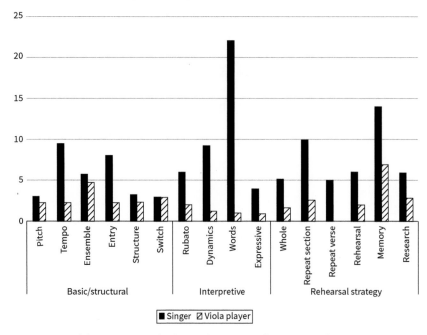

Figure 12.1 Musical dimensions and rehearsal strategies (by musician).

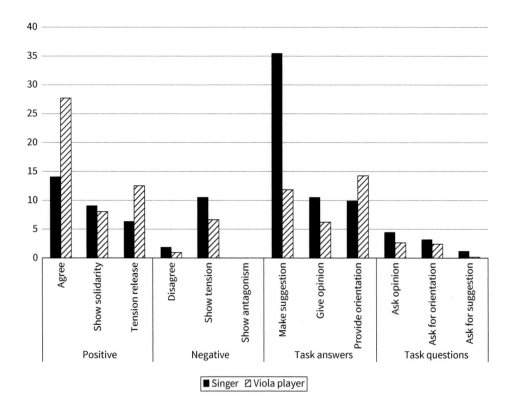

Figure 12.2 Interaction processes by musician.

Aim and research questions

The present case study asked how a newly formed duo—both expert performers—negotiates a shared understanding of an unfamiliar work. Two songs were learned over a seven-day period; each performer memorized one song. Practice sessions and rehearsals were audio-recorded and transcribed verbatim. A multistrategy approach was used to analyze and triangulate three sets of data:

1. Talk during rehearsal;
2. Singing and playing; and
3. Annotations made by the musicians on the scores after the final rehearsal and three public performances (Ginsborg & Bennett, 2021).

In this chapter, we consider the content analysis of rehearsal talk, addressing four research questions:

1. What topics (i.e. musical dimensions and rehearsal strategies) did the musicians discuss?
2. What were the musicians' interaction processes?
3. How did these topics and processes change over the course of rehearsals?
4. What differences were observable, if any, between the singer and viola player, memorizer and non-memorizer, and/or the two songs?

Method

Participants

The authors, a singer and a viola player, are experienced performers who had not previously worked together.

Materials

The work was *From Kipling* (1994): Boris Tchaikovsky's settings of Rudyard Kipling's poems "Far-off Amazon" ("Amazon") and "Homer," loosely translated into Russian.

Procedure

Over the course of seven days, the musicians practiced the songs independently and rehearsed together every day (see Table 12.1). Following their final rehearsal, they gave two performances. The viola player performed "Amazon" from memory, while the singer read from the score; the singer performed "Homer" from memory, while the viola player read from the score.

Table 12.1 Individual practice and joint rehearsal time (hours [h] and minutes [']), percentage consisting of talk, and proportions of talk relating to each of the two songs

Date (March 2014)	Individual practice	Rehearsal	Percentage of rehearsal spent talking	Proportion "Amazon:" "Homer"
24th	1h 17'	20'	33.8%	88:12
25th	17'	34'	53.6%	59:41
26th	33'	26'	73.5%	("Amazon" only)
27th	57'	28'	45.3%	31:69
28th	1h 04'	27'	43.4%	45:55
29th	–	33'	50.1%	80:20
30th	–	27'	44.1%	24:76
TOTAL	4h 08'	3h 24'	49.9%	61:39

Analyses

Quantitative analyses included calculations of time spent talking, numbers of exchanges (verbal dialogue between episodes of music-making), proportion of exchanges initiated by each musician, and total number of verbal utterances.

Qualitative analyses involved coding each utterance in terms of musical dimensions and/or as interaction process, as appropriate to the utterance. From a total of 302 utterances, 206 musical dimensions codes and 207 IPA codes were generated. To check reliability, each author coded one rehearsal of one song. Analysis using Cohen's *kappa* showed reliability to be excellent (0.98 and 0.93 for the two frameworks, respectively). The remaining coding was undertaken by J. G. and double-checked by D. B. Disagreements were resolved following discussion. In total, taking both speakers and both songs together, 582 musical dimensions codes were assigned, and 948 IPA codes.

Results

Quantitative characteristics

Almost exactly half the musicians' rehearsal time was spent on talking (49.9%). They rehearsed "Amazon" in all seven sessions, and "Homer" in six (see Table 12.1). Although "Amazon" was slightly shorter, they spent 8% more time rehearsing it, with a larger proportion of talk, than "Homer."

On average, there were more, and longer, exchanges in rehearsals of "Amazon" (10, mean of 14 utterances per exchange) than "Homer" (8, mean of 10.5 utterances per exchange). The singer initiated, on average, 62.7% of all exchanges: 65% in "Amazon" and 58.3% in "Homer."

Musical dimensions and rehearsal strategies

To identify the topics discussed by the musicians, the number of utterances made in each sub-category by each musician was calculated as a percentage of utterances in all rehearsals to which musical dimension codes had been assigned. For example, the two musicians' 336 utterances during seven rehearsals of "Amazon" included 22 references to *tempo* (6.55%) made by the singer and four by the viola player (1.19%). Their 246 utterances during six rehearsals of "Homer" included seven references to *tempo* made by the singer (2.85%) and three by the viola player (1.19%). Thus, 11.8% of all utterances referred to *tempo* (see Fig. 12.1).

Other basic dimensions mentioned comparatively often were *ensemble* (10.6%) and *entries* (10%). The most frequently mentioned interpretative dimensions were *dynamics* (10%) and *words* (23%), while the most frequently mentioned rehearsal strategies were *repeat section* (13%) and [work on] *memory* (21%). Comparisons between the mean numbers of utterances in each rehearsal referring to these seven dimensions were made using Mann–Whitney U tests. A Bonferroni correction having been applied, only in the category *words* did the singer make significantly more utterances ($M = 4.85$, $SD = 5.19$) than the viola player ($M = 0.23$, $SD = 0.44$, $U = 17.5$, $Z = -3.63$, $p < .001$).

Interaction processes

The musicians were most likely to *make suggestions* (47.4%), *agree* (41.8%), and *provide orientation* (24.2%); *disagreements* were rare (2.8%) and there was no *antagonism* between them (see Fig. 12.2). The only significant difference between the musicians was that the singer made more suggestions ($M = 13.46$, $SD = 10.27$) than the viola player ($M = 3.92$, $SD = 2.25$, $U = 24.5$, $Z = -3.01$, $p = .002$).

One change in the IPA codes was revealed by Kruskal–Wallis tests to be significant across rehearsals as the musicians became more familiar with each other, and with the music: *Showing solidarity* ($\chi [6] = 14.73$, $p = .022$) rose and fell with each rehearsal, as shown in Fig. 12.3.

Other observations

No differences between the musicians' references to musical dimensions were observed that might be attributable to the song having been memorized or not, but more requests for orientation were made by the viola player when rehearsing "Amazon" ($M = 2.21$, $SD = 2.46$) than "Homer" ($M = 0.17$, $SD = 0.39$, $U = 22$, $Z = -2.89$, $p = .004$), possibly because "Amazon" has several difficult passages for the viola that are somewhat similar but not exactly the same.

Conclusion

As the musicians developed familiarity with each other, and with the music, their talk consisted of references to musical dimensions and rehearsal strategies, and revealed the nature of

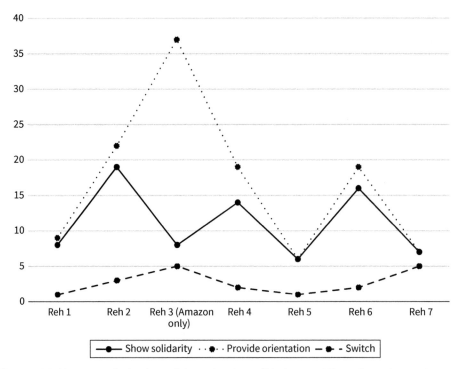

Figure 12.3 Utterances by both musicians *showing solidarity*, *providing orientation*, and referring to *switch* in each rehearsal.

their interaction processes. In terms of the latter, the musicians made suggestions and agreed with each other, provided orientation, showed tension, and relieved it using humour, but they also showed solidarity. The musical dimensions to which they referred most often were the meaning and subject matter of the songs, and memory, followed by tempo, ensemble, entries, and dynamics. Meaning and subject matter were particularly salient because of the discrepancies between Kipling's original poems and their reworking into Russian; memory was salient because of the musicians' different perspectives on the task: the singer was an experienced memorizer, but this was the first time the viola player had deliberately memorized her part. In terms of rehearsal strategies, they preferred to repeat sections shorter than a verse.

Analyses comparing the musicians revealed relatively few differences between them. The singer made more suggestions, related to the dimensions to which she referred most often: words, tempo, and sections to repeat. This may be because, as singer, she was responsible for conveying the meaning of the words, but in addition, she already had experience of conducting such studies. While there were no differences between them attributable specifically to their role as memorizer or non-memorizer, the two songs were different in style: there were fewer switches, for example, in "Homer." Finally, although there were differences between the nature and content of talk in the seven rehearsals, no clear progression—such as a focus on basic to interpretative and expressive content, for example—could be identified, as the musicians became more familiar with the music. Nor were there meaningful changes in the nature of their interactions as they became more familiar with each other, perhaps because they were both already experienced duo musicians with other partners.

The positive socio-emotional interactions found in the case study, and the musicians' requests for provision of orientation, echo those revealed by Ginsborg and King's (2012) study of student and professional singers and pianists. Unlike those participants, the singer and viola player in the present study rarely asked for or gave opinions, and were more likely to repeat sections than the whole song.

One limitation of case studies is that results cannot be generalized. There is nevertheless value in taking a "fly-on-the-wall" observational approach to the study of collaborative rehearsal and performance, not least for the musicians themselves who both feel they have learned something new about how they go about preparing for performance with co-performers (for example, the singer's tendency to make suggestions; being more aware of how rehearsal time is spent), and how this might be applied in other situations. We hope that this will also be of value to researchers curious as to the methods that can be applied to the study of collaborative performance, and of interest to other musicians who enjoy making music together.

References

Bales, R. F. (1999). *Social interaction systems: Theory and measurement*. Transaction.

Chaffin, R., Imreh, G., & Crawford, M. (2005). *Practicing perfection: Memory and piano performance* (2nd ed.). Psychology Press.

Ginsborg, J., & Bennett, D. (2021). Developing familiarity in a new duo: Rehearsal talk and performance cues. *Frontiers in Psychology: Performance Science, 12*, 222. doi:10.3389/fpsyg.2021.590987.

Ginsborg, J., Chaffin, R., & Nicholson, G. (2006). Shared performance cues in singing and conducting: A content analysis of talk during practice. *Psychology of Music, 34*, 167–94.

Ginsborg, J., & King, E. (2012). Rehearsal talk: Familiarity and expertise in singer-pianist duos. *Musicae Scientiae, 16*(2), 148–67.

PART 2

EXPRESSION, COMMUNICATION, AND INTERACTION

13

Embodiment, process, and product in ensemble expression

Renee Timmers

Introduction

In performing together, musicians create a shared, coordinated performance. Such ensemble performances are established dynamically and interactively, as well as through constructing a distributed notion of the outcomes of performance. An element of emergence and uncertainty will always be present in ensemble performance. Nevertheless, musicians develop ideas about musical aesthetics, style, and expression, and an in-depth familiarity with the sounding structures and cohering parts of music, particularly in score-based genres. This chapter will consider this dichotomy between ensemble performance as process and as product, giving priority to the former while reconciling the latter. By looking at process and product, it considers tensions between an embodied and enactive perspective on performance emphasizing real-time, distributed interaction between organism and environment, and a more (traditional) cognitive perspective that emphasizes the concepts, ideas, and representations that performers bring, and that inform performance. Perspectives on ensemble performance as embodied and as examples of a complex, dynamic system are finding increased support and traction in research (e.g. Glowinski et al., 2016; see also van der Schyff et al., 2018). This chapter enhances existing research by explicitly addressing how ensemble performance processes that have been primarily investigated from a cognitive perspective can be (better) understood as embodied and enactive. In doing so, it aims to deepen our understanding of expressive communication in ensemble performance, identifying gaps and future directions for research: how do musicians develop a shared performance on which they agree, how do they coordinate musically, and how may performance processes depend on musical context and ensemble aesthetics?

Processes of interaction and emergence

This first section discusses the first two questions of how musicians develop a shared performance on which they agree and what processes inform such musical coordination. Three issues are addressed, namely: (1) is there a need for shared cognitive representations of the music; (2) what processes are involved in addition to temporal coordination and how are they enactive and embodied; and (3) in what ways are these processes of coordination communicative and expressive?

Renee Timmers, *Embodiment, process, and product in ensemble expression* In: *Together in music*. Edited by: Renee Timmers, Freya Bailes, and Helena Daffern, Oxford University Press. © Oxford University Press 2022. DOI: 10.1093/oso/9780198860761.003.0013

Cognitive representation versus emergence and embodiment

What does it mean to have shared performance goals in an ensemble context? Does it mean that musicians agree, conceptually, on how the music is organized and structured and should sound? In a cognitive interpretation of ensemble performance, one may indeed expect that musicians develop a shared understanding of music and this gives rise to a successful performance. This may function analogously to the generation of expression from a cognitive interpretation of musical structure (Palmer, 1997). However, an embodied and enactive perspective would rather argue that "agreement" is obtained through real-time processes of coordination and synchronization without the need for musicians to agree in cognitive terms (i.e. mentally) on their expressive intentions, conceptualizations, and representations of the music, as long as the agreement is realized externally in terms of coordinated sounds and movements. Alignment of expressive intentions may strengthen as a consequence of the performance process, but they are not necessarily the origin, nor a prerequisite for a successful performance.

Empirical research has shown that familiarity with the parts and style of co-performers benefits successful synchronization (Hadley et al., 2015; Keller et al., 2007), strengthening the ability to predict the timing of the co-performer. Intriguingly, such ability to predict is associated with a high empathic personality trait (Novembre et al., 2019). While this suggests an important role for shared mental representations, a more embodied interpretation is possible too: familiarity with the actions or motor-repertoire of the co-performer will enhance synchronization, allowing for motor resonance with those actions, which causally contributes to accurate synchronization (Hadley et al., 2015). Indeed, empathy may have a strong embodied component and rely on motor mimicry (Novembre et al., 2019).

Other evidence for the importance of emergent, embodied action comes from studies that have shown that performers do not necessarily agree on the details of an otherwise coordinated performance and may show diverging interpretations of the music (Schober & Spiro, 2014). Furthermore, when looking at rehearsal behavior of ensembles, including what is talked about and how musical interpretations are developed, processes of agreement and coordination tend to be implicit and established through real-time music-making rather than conceptually agreed in verbal explanation and discussion. For example, Pennill (2019) found in a longitudinal study that musicians spend relatively little time discussing expressive aspects of performance, even though it was seen as an important objective for rehearsal.

Processes of alignment between ensemble performers

Concerning real-time processes of musical coordination, significant research has been dedicated to understanding the way in which performers achieve interpersonal synchronization (see also Chapter 17). Classical models of sensorimotor synchronization allocate a central role to a mental "timekeeper" that generates motor outputs and responds to external events (Repp & Su, 2013). Research on synchronized tapping models processes of synchronization as a combination of prediction (anticipation) of subsequent taps, and adaptation to discrepancies between taps (Keller, 2014). Furthermore, allocation of attention to others and oneself may influence the degree to which one adapts to each other. For example, in a string quartet, performers might adapt more strongly to the first violin than to other performers. In reality, patterns of interdependence turn out to be considerably more complex (Timmers et al., 2014; Wing et al., 2014).

Indeed, the complex interrelationships between performers is a major argument for investigating ensemble performance as a complex dynamic system. Within such a system, entrainment in time is modeled through the use of coupled oscillators, rather than linearly responding timekeepers (Loehr et al., 2011). Despite large differences in conceptualization and theorization, essential aspects of timekeeper models find their counterpart in entrainment models. In non-linear models, oscillators entrain to external stimuli through period resonance and phase coupling (Large & Jones, 1999), which can be seen as analogous to period prediction (anticipation) and phase correction (adaptation) in timekeeping models. Furthermore, the attunement of phase expectancy (precision of prediction) may sharpen or broaden, depending on contextual factors such as the degree of periodic regularity of the stimuli, and listeners' referent period (spontaneous tempo that is most stably produced) and focal attention ability (Drake et al., 2000). Such sharply or broadly defined attunement of phase expectancy influences coupling strength (Large & Jones, 1999), which can be seen as a parallel to attention allocation. Intriguing evidence has been found in support of models of oscillatory entrainment in demonstrations of correlations in brain wave periodicities between performers playing together (Sänger et al., 2012), and neurological responses to presented stimuli, including neurological oscillations correlated with periodicities that are implied but not physically present (Tal et al., 2017).

An important characteristic of the coupled-oscillators model is the assumption that different units form part of a larger system that behaves in a complex non-linear manner. To explore how this may work with respect to, for example, tuning, Fig. 13.1 shows a potential scenario of the tuning of five singers at a given moment in time, illustrated by five circles that represent the five singers singing at a certain relative pitch height (intonation), represented by their vertical position. If we assume that the relationships in tuning can be conceptualized as a form of pulling and pushing in converging directions (see arrows) as in a connected system, a singer who is more out of tune would encounter greater pull than a singer who is less out of tune, compared to the mean tuning. It follows that we may expect adjustments in the direction of the mean rather than strong patterns of coupling between pairs of performers.

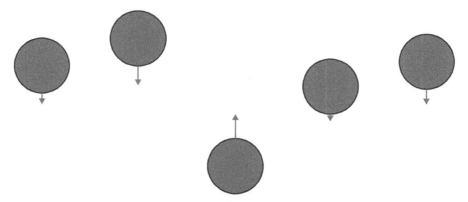

Figure 13.1 Illustration of a pull towards the mean in the tuning of notes by five singers, shown as five circles positioned at different vertical heights representing their relative tuning.

Table 13.1 Overview of pairwise correlations* between tuning deviations of singers at lag 0 and lag 1 (Analysis 1) and correlations for each singer between adjustments to the next note (difference in relative tuning) and deviation from general tuning (Analysis 2)

	Analysis 1				Analysis 2
	Lag 0		Lag 1		
	Max	Average	Max	Average	
S1	.054	.027	.265	.073	−.430
S2	.140	.040	.202	.045	−.511
S3	.071	.029	−.017	−.049	−.710
S4	.165	.103	.106	.025	−.588
S5	.165	.033	.111	.053	−.619

* Correlations are averages across six performances, with 42 notes per performance. Analysis 1 includes several correlations with different singers, and the maximum correlation and mean across those are presented.

To illustrate that this indeed provides a useful perspective on ensemble tuning, two analyses were conducted of previously collected data of tuning in a vocal quintet singing a brief homophonic piece six times (D'Amario et al., 2020). The tuning of each note of each singer (Singers 1–5, henceforth S1–5) was measured as deviation from equal temperament in cents ("relative tuning"). For the current analysis, only the data of the last rehearsal are examined.[1]

The first analysis assumes that performers adjust to each other in a pairwise fashion. This is similar to pairwise cross-correlation analyses conducted to examine processes of ensemble synchronization (Timmers et al., 2014). The hypothesis is that pairs of singers adjust to each other in tuning during each note of the music, leading to positive pairwise cross-correlations at "lag 0." Alternatively, singers may realize such adjustments with a lag, leading to positive cross-correlations at, for example, a lag of one note ("lag"). Table 13.1 shows the average of pairwise cross-correlations between singers at lag 0 and 1 (Analysis 1).

The second analysis assumes that the singers work as part of a system, as illustrated in Fig. 13.1. As mentioned, the hypothesis is that singers will adjust their tuning relative to the degree of deviation from general tuning. Such "general tuning" is estimated as the mean relative tuning across singers. This should lead to negative correlations between adjustments to the next note and deviation from general tuning for each singer. The right columns in Table 13.1 show the average correlations per singer arising from this analysis. It is evident from the table that while Analysis 1 leads to small cross-correlation values, Analysis 2 shows greater adjustments from individuals to the collective to increase in-tune singing.

Although Analysis 2 is a considerable simplification of the complex systems perspective, the findings provide an indication of the relative power of the perspective of considering the ensemble as a system, rather than looking at interactions between individual agents who respond individually to each other. It will be of interest to apply this perspective in future research to timing and dynamics as well as tuning.

---

[1] A complete analysis and explanation will be made available in work that is in preparation.

Sonic and bodily alignment as expressive communication

Having discussed processes contributing to the emergence of shared performances, we may wonder in what ways such a shared performance can be said to be expressive or communicative. Performance expression has traditionally been defined as referring to "the large and small variations in timing, intensity or dynamics, timbre, and pitch that form the microstructure of a performance and differentiate it from another performance of the same music" (Palmer, 1997, p. 118). Additionally, it has generally been understood that expressive variations serve the purpose of communicating a performer's interpretation of the structure, emotion, and character of the music (Palmer, 1997; Timmers, 2007). Offering a useful alternative, Ashley (2017, p. 479) argued for the definition of communication as "action intended to bring about alignment or coordination of states between individuals." If states are sounds and behaviors of ensemble performance, we can interpret much of what musicians do as communicative: synchronization, blending, harmonizing, and interlocking in time, but also coordination of bowing, breathing, gesturing, and looking. Nevertheless, we can additionally argue that the produced sounds and gestures may be expressive and carry referential meaning. It is noteworthy that in ensemble performance research, the emphasis has been on "coming together" rather than on deviating from the expected, as is central to the interpretation of "expression" in solo performance. The suggestion here seems to be that variations in tempo, dynamics, timbre, and tuning may emerge through performance, but a primary ensemble task is to do this jointly and to stay together. Nevertheless, realizing change at various moments in the music is a central aspect of ensemble performance and rehearsal. Processes to realize change may be different from what we have focused on so far. Change may require more of an intentional effort, such as a deliberate acting on cues in the score (such as sf or fff), cues from co-performers (looks or gestures), or verbal agreements.

With respect to possible referential meaning of ensemble sounds, we can argue that "embodied meanings" may specifically concern associations with energy levels, bodily tension and effort, sensations, feelings, and emotions, but also associations with movement patterns, gestures, actions, and interactions. However, embodied meaning also relates to contextual embedding, i.e. sounds become meaningful through sense-making interaction (Schiavio et al., 2017). As such, they may, for example, be experienced as religious, celebratory, motivational, or relaxing. Furthermore, we may act on sounds through drawing associations with other musical and non-musical sounds, from both within the music that is performed and beyond (Clarke et al., 2016).

Product concepts of ensemble performance

This last section considers conventions and aesthetic preferences related to ensemble performance that may shape and inform *the product* of performance practice. A growing body of research has documented the changes over time in practices and aesthetic concepts related to performance style. Developing from pioneering research by Philip (1992), among others, historical recordings provide evidence of changing performance practices (see also Chapter 22). Changes in performance style within western classical performance traditions include the type and amount of tempo rubato, the employment of vibrato in singers, strings and wind players, tempo choices, the use of dynamics, and the employment of portamento.

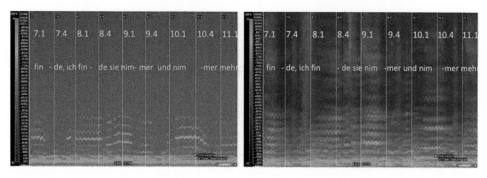

Figure 13.2 Spectrogram with timepoints indicating measure and half-measure onsets in the accompaniment. Left: Emma Eames, 1911; right: Gundula Janowitz, 1977.

Developments with respect to tuning preferences have been suggested too, although they are hard to reliably quantify (Devaney & Ellis, 2008). Various factors may lie behind changes in performance style, whether this concerns a possible push towards "objective perfection" driven by recording conditions or revivals of historical performance practices (see, for example, Day, 2000; Fabian, 2015). What is of relevance here is that many developments in performance style concern the ensemble as much as the individual performer.

For an illustration, consider Fig. 13.2 which shows spectrograms of an excerpt of Schubert's "Gretchen am Spinnrade" performed by Emma Eames and Henri Gilles in 1911[2] (left panel) and by Gundula Janowitz and Irwin Gage in 1977[3] (right panel). The visible panel relates to measures 7–11. The two performances are highly contrasting in tempo (73[4] versus 57 BPM), in the use of vibrato and portamento by the singers, and in tempo rubato (see Timmers, 2007). Moreover, a marked contrast can be observed between the temporal alignment of the voice and accompaniment. In the performance from 1977, the voice and accompaniment are strongly vertically aligned: the voice makes rapid note transitions, assuring that new pitch onsets coincide with the accompaniment (half measure onsets in the accompaniment are marked by vertical lines). Fluidity is present in dynamics (becoming softer at note endings) and vibrato (e.g. starting late with vibrato). In comparison, the relationship between voice and accompaniment is more flexible in the 1911 recording (left panel), where the voice regularly anticipates note transitions by leaving a note early and gradually descending (measures 7.1, 9.1, 10.4) or ascending into the next note (end of 8.4), and modifying alignment by early (9.4) or delayed timing (8.4). Such fluid relationships between accompaniment and melody have been observed in various genres, including jazz (Ashley, 2002) and popular music (Dibben, 2014). Hudson (1994) referred to this as tempo rubato in which time is "stolen" and subsequently "paid back" to restore alignment. This contrasts with the second type of tempo rubato in which vertical alignment is continuously maintained between voices that together vary gradually in tempo.

---

[2] Available at https://www.youtube.com/watch?v=y3q70UZsGbE, excerpt: 11–19 seconds. From *The Record of Singing I*. EMI RLS 724.

[3] Available at https://www.youtube.com/watch?v=XRm14vOr0Eg excerpt: 14–24 seconds. From *Schubert Lieder*. Deutsche Grammophon 453 082-2.

[4] The absolute tempo of historical recordings is hard to know for sure, as playback speed may have been adjusted by editors in the digitization of the recording.

Fluid vertical relationships between voices seem to pose a challenge to models of ensemble synchronization, in particular when interpreted from the perspective of noise-like deviation from a stable timekeeper. Interpreting synchronization as coupling within a complex system may offer a more flexible perspective. As Clayton (2012) explains, entrainment in phase and frequency may occur between systems with a great variety of characteristics, and the degree of coupling may vary. Coupling may occur between phases that are not strictly aligned such as anti-phase coupling or if one voice is performing ahead of another and entrainment may be induced with attractor ratios other than 1:1, 2:1, or 3:1. Interestingly, while entrainment may occur between non-periodic systems, periodicity is a strong feature of human movement. As Will et al. (2015) demonstrated, even in the absence of a clear musical pulse, for example in the *alap*, a rhythmically free improvised section of a raga, listeners refer to an inner pulse to tap along with the music, and align their taps with recurring temporal patterns in the music. Indeed, a pulse is often physically present in movement to support performances of an *alap* (Will et al., 2015).

What these examples demonstrate is the diversity of forms of entrainment in musical ensembles (see also Chapters 17 and 22), whether this concerns entrainment with uneven temporal proportions such as in performances of Balkan *aksak* rhythms (Clayton, 2015) or entrainment with rhythmically free musical improvisation. The role of movement coordination in such entrainment is of particular interest. For example, relatively independent voices may be entrained to by different motor effectors that are nevertheless experienced as coordinated, as when one taps a foot and gestures along to represent the (fluid) entrainment of the vocal line.

For ensemble performance, these differences in how parts align imply different styles of coordination, representing differences in ensemble aesthetics. Similarly, ensemble aesthetics may relate to ways in which ensembles blend harmonically and in terms of tuning. Experimental investigation has shown differences in synchronization for homophonic or polyphonic music (D'Amario et al., 2020). It will be of interest to extend these investigations to other performance dimensions and to consider the processes of coordination and their aesthetic implications. Perceptual studies that use different versions of musical coordination may be helpful in characterizing such aesthetic principles. For example, Marandola (2014) studied criteria regulating the "acceptability" of the interrelationships between voices in a Pygmy community. On the other hand, learning to physically entrain to an unknown genre may help one to learn some of that genre's aesthetic principles.

Conclusion

Ensemble performance is a prime example of complex behavior in which performers are coupled through sound and movement, making up a larger whole. Individual components may adjust locally to maintain equilibrium of the system, while simultaneously the system develops over time. The power of this perspective is that it allows for continuous, flexible adjustments and explains why there is no need for a fully fledged agreed representation of the ensemble, which is unlikely to happen. Performance develops in the moment and is relative to what immediately preceded it. Nevertheless, forms of interaction and outcomes of performance are subject to changes related to performance style and ensemble aesthetics. Familiarity with other performers' parts and style of performance facilitates entrainment and may strengthen the coupling. Within this complex dynamic, performers have agency to influence and shape the ensemble, both in terms of process and product. Through explicit and implicit communication, performers may introduce and develop innovative ensemble aesthetics. From an embodied perspective, ensemble aesthetics can be understood as related to the type of interrelationships between performers, and the movements, shapes, and textures associated with ensemble sounds. Performers' movements and playing techniques may be important drivers in the establishment of novel ensemble aesthetics. Indeed, innovation in music performance inevitably requires, through its embodied nature, action innovation.

Continuing the research, it will be of interest to investigate coupling processes in time, intensity, and intonation across different genres and styles: what types of discrepancy or "asynchronization" are minimized, or, more positively, what opportunities for unity and interdependence are explored/exploited? Similarly, it will be of interest to explore stylistic components of ensemble aesthetics: what makes up the repertoire of actions, sounds, and interrelations of an ensemble and which are identifiers for the ensemble as a whole? Other researchers have also interpreted ensemble performance as a complex system, investigated expressiveness from an embodied perspective, and pointed out the distributed and emergent characteristics of creative music-making (e.g. Clarke & Doffman, 2017; see also Fabian, 2015). The contribution of this chapter is to explicitly connect notions of expressive ensemble performance with processes of ensemble coordination and communication; to explore where embodied perspectives connect with, and deviate from, more traditional, cognitive perspectives; to move beyond a focus on timing and consider adaptive processes in intonation; and to balance perspectives on performance as process and as product.

Acknowledgments

I am very grateful to Sara D'Amario for sharing the tuning data. This research is an outcome of the White Rose College of the Arts and Humanities-funded PhD network on "Expressive nonverbal communication in ensemble performance."

References

Ashley, R. (2002). Do[n't] change a hair for me: The art of Jazz rubato. *Music Perception: An Interdisciplinary Journal, 19*(3), 311–32.

Ashley, R. (2017). Music and communication. In R. Ashley, & R. Timmers (Eds.), *The Routledge companion to music cognition* (pp. 479–88). Routledge.

Clarke, E. F., & Doffman, M. (Eds.). (2017). *Distributed creativity: Collaboration and improvisation in contemporary music*. Oxford University Press.

Clarke, E., Doffman, M., & Timmers, R. (2016). Creativity, collaboration and development in Jeremy Thurlow's Ouija for Peter Sheppard Skærved. *Journal of the Royal Musical Association, 141*(1), 113–65.

Clayton, M. (2012). What is entrainment? Definition and applications in musical research. *Empirical Musicology Review, 7*, 49–56.

Clayton, M. (2015). Aksak patterns and entrained interaction in Transylvanian Village Music. *Empirical Musicology Review, 10*, 292–301.

D'Amario, S., Daffern, H., & Bailes, F. (2020). A longitudinal study investigating synchronization in a singing quintet. *Journal of Voice, 34*(159), e1–12. http://doi.org/10.1016/j.jvoice.2018.06.011

Day, T. (2000). *A century of recorded music: Listening to musical history.* Yale University Press.

Devaney, J., & Ellis, D. P. (2008). An empirical approach to studying intonation tendencies in polyphonic vocal performances. *Journal of Interdisciplinary Music Studies, 2*, 141–56.

Dibben, N. (2014). Understanding performance expression in popular music recordings. In D. Fabian, R. Timmers, & E. Schubert (Eds.), *Expressiveness in music performance: Empirical approaches across styles and cultures* (pp. 117–32). Oxford University Press.

Drake, C., Jones, M. R., & Baruch, C. (2000). The development of rhythmic attending in auditory sequences: Attunement, referent period, focal attending. *Cognition, 77*(3), 251–88.

Fabian, D. (2015). *A musicology of performance: Theory and method based on Bach's solos for violin.* Open Book Publishers.

Glowinski, D., Bracco, F., Chiorri, C., & Grandjean, D. (2016). Music ensemble as a resilient system. Managing the unexpected through group interaction. *Frontiers in Psychology, 7*, 1–7. doi.org/10.3389/fpsyg.2016.01548

Hadley, L. V., Novembre, G., Keller, P. E., & Pickering, M. J. (2015). Causal role of motor simulation in turn-taking behavior. *Journal of Neuroscience, 35*(50), 16516–20.

Hudson, R. (1994). *Stolen time: The history of tempo rubato.* Clarendon Press.

Keller, P. E. (2014). Ensemble performance: Interpersonal alignment of musical expression. In D. Fabian, R. Timmers, & E. Schubert (Eds.), *Expressiveness in music performance: Empirical approaches across styles and cultures* (pp. 260–82). Oxford University Press.

Keller, P. E., Knoblich, G., & Repp, B. H. (2007). Pianists duet better when they play with themselves: On the possible role of action simulation in synchronization. *Consciousness and Cognition, 16*(1), 102–11.

Large, E. W., & Jones, M. R. (1999). The dynamics of attending: How people track time-varying events. *Psychological Review, 106*(1), 119–59.

Loehr, J. D., Large, E. W., & Palmer, C. (2011). Temporal coordination and adaptation to rate change in music performance. *Journal of Experimental Psychology: Human Perception and Performance, 37*(4), 1292–309.

Novembre, G., Mitsopoulos, Z., & Keller, P. E. (2019). Empathic perspective taking promotes interpersonal coordination through music. *Scientific Reports, 9*(1), 1–12. http://doi.org/10.1038/s41598-019-48556-9

Marandola, F. (2014). Expressiveness in the performance of Bedzan Pygmies' vocal polyphonies: When the same is never the same. In D. Fabian, R. Timmers, & E. Schubert (Eds.), *Expressiveness in music performance: Empirical approaches across styles and cultures* (pp. 200–16). Oxford University Press.

Pennill, N. (2019). *Ensembles working towards performance: Emerging coordination and interactions in self-organised groups* [Doctoral dissertation] University of Sheffield, White Rose eTheses Online.

Palmer, C. (1997). Music performance. *Annual Review of Psychology, 48*, 115–38.

Philip, R. (1992). *Early recordings and musical style: Changing tastes in instrumental performance, 1900–1950.* Cambridge University Press.

Repp, B. H., & Su, Y. H. (2013). Sensorimotor synchronization: A review of recent research (2006–2012). *Psychonomic Bulletin & Review, 20*(3), 403–52.

Sänger, J., Müller, V., & Lindenberger, U. (2012). Intra-and interbrain synchronization and network properties when playing guitar in duets. *Frontiers in Human Neuroscience, 6*, 312. http://doi.org/0.3389/fnhum.2012.00312

Schiavio, A., van der Schyff, D., Cespedes-Guevara, J., & Reybrouck, M. (2017). Enacting musical emotions. Sense-making, dynamic systems, and the embodied mind. *Phenomenology and the Cognitive Sciences*, 16(5), 785–809.

Schober, M. F., & Spiro, N. (2014). Jazz improvisers' shared understanding: A case study. *Frontiers in Psychology*, 5, 808. https://doi.org/10.3389/fpsyg.2014.00808

Tal, I., Large, E. W., Rabinovitch, E., Wei, Y., Schroeder, C. E., Poeppel, D., & Golumbic, E. Z. (2017). Neural entrainment to the beat: The "missing-pulse" phenomenon. *Journal of Neuroscience*, 37(26), 6331–41.

Timmers, R. (2007). Vocal expression in recorded performances of Schubert songs. *Musicae Scientiae*, 11(2), 237–68.

Timmers, R., Endo, S., Bradbury, A., & Wing, A. M. (2014). Synchronization and leadership in string quartet performance: A case study of auditory and visual cues. *Frontiers in Psychology*, 5, 645. http://doi.org/10.3389/fpsyg.2014.00645

Van der Schyff, D., Schiavio, A., Walton, A., Velardo, V., & Chemero, A. (2018). Musical creativity and the embodied mind: Exploring the possibilities of 4E cognition and dynamical systems theory. *Music & Science*, 1, 1–18.

Will, U., Clayton, M., Wertheim, I., Leante, L., & Berg, E. (2015). Pulse and entrainment to non-isochronous auditory stimuli: The case of North Indian alap. *PLoS One*, 10(4), e0123247. http://doi.org/10.1371/journal.pone.0123247

Wing, A. M., Endo, S., Bradbury, A., & Vorberg, D. (2014). Optimal feedback correction in string quartet synchronization. *Journal of The Royal Society Interface*, 11(93), 20131125. https://doi.org/10.1098/rsif.2013.1125

14

Gestures in ensemble performance

Alexander Refsum Jensenius and Çağrı Erdem

Introduction

The topic of *gesture* has received growing attention among music researchers over recent decades. Some of this research has been summarized in anthologies on "musical gestures," such as those by Gritten and King (2006), Godøy and Leman (2010), and Gritten and King (2011). There have also been a couple of articles reviewing how the term gesture has been used in various music-related disciplines (and beyond), including those by Cadoz and Wanderley (2000) and Jensenius et al. (2010). Much empirical work has been performed since these reviews were written, aided by better motion capture technologies, new machine learning techniques, and a heightened awareness of the topic. Still there are a number of open questions as to the role of gestures in music performance in general, and in ensemble performance in particular. This chapter aims to clarify some of the basic terminology of music-related body motion, and draw up some perspectives of how one can think about gestures in ensemble performance. This is, obviously, only one way of looking at the very multifaceted concept of gesture, but it may lead to further interest in this exciting and complex research domain.

From motion to gesture

Within this chapter, gesture is referred to as the *meaning* related to a perceived and/or performed action. In this context, "meaning" should not be understood as "meaningful," but rather in the sense of communicating "something." In a musical context, this could be information about the tempo, such as seen in the beat patterns of conductors. It could also be the expressive swaying of the upper body of a violinist in a string quartet, indicating the phrasing to her fellow musicians. How others experience such gestures are, of course, highly dependent on prior experience and cultural background. Thus, gesture is by definition a subjective term. This differentiates it from the related—but different—terms *motion*, *force*, and *action*. Motion refers to the physical displacement of an object in time and space, while force refers to the push or pull experienced in interaction with other objects. Both motion and force refer to physical phenomena, and can be studied objectively with various types of sensing devices (see, for example, Jensenius, 2018) for an overview of different methods for sensing music-related body motion). Motion and force are also interrelated: applying force to an object can set it in motion, and the motion of an object can lead to the experience of force.

While motion and force are terms that are drawn from the world of physics, and more precisely (bio)mechanics, we reserve action to describe the psychological experience of motion and force. An action can be understood as the *chunking* of continuous motion or force into what Godøy and Leman (2010) refer to as "cognitive units." Such a unit is a piece of

Alexander Refsum Jensenius and Çağrı Erdem, *Gestures in ensemble performance* In: *Together in music*. Edited by: Renee Timmers, Freya Bailes, and Helena Daffern, Oxford University Press. © Oxford University Press 2022. DOI: 10.1093/oso/9780198860761.003.0014

information that is held consciously in our focus of attention. Actions are often goal-oriented, that is, we think about them with respect to a particular goal: lifting a glass, opening a door, playing a key on a piano. It is usually easy to identify the goal, but it is more difficult to describe precisely when an action begins or ends. This has some implications for how we conceptualize and analyze actions. For example, think about an individual drum stroke, in which a drumstick is lifted and then dropped to hit the membrane of the drum. It is straightforward to identify when the excitation happens, but it can be very hard to say when the action began. This becomes more complex when multiple actions are combined into action series, which leads to *coarticulation*, the merging of individual actions into larger shapes of actions (Godøy et al., 2010). A challenge from an empirical research perspective is that a motion capture recording will only inform about the continuous displacement of markers attached to a musician's body. It is non-trivial to segment such a continuous motion stream into actions, since this will rely on the perspective from which one is looking, the temporal and spatial resolution, and so on. Defining the meaning-bearing components of such actions—the gestures—relies on yet another level of abstraction. The reason we emphasize these differences between motion/force, action, and gesture, is that they are sometimes used synonymously in the literature. This causes confusion and reduces the power of the term gesture.

Gesture

The power of the term gesture is that it goes beyond motion. In a linguistic context, it usually denotes bodily actions associated with speech, or what Kendon (2004, p. 7) referred to as "visible action as utterance." McNeill (1992) showed how hand motion and facial expressions do not just randomly accompany speech, but are an integral part of the communication itself. He classified gesture into five functional categories:

- *Iconics* represent a particular feature of an object and can be described in terms of the shape and spatial extent of the gesture. Iconic gestures are often used to illustrate an action, for example imitating a knocking movement with a hand while saying "knocking on the door;"
- *Metaphorics* are similar to iconics but represent an abstract feature of an object. An example of a metaphoric gesture could be to say "something happened" while holding up the hands to refer to "something;"
- *Beats* occur together with spoken words to highlight discontinuities and stress specific words. Beats are typically carried out as in/out or up/down movements, such as a nod, and may be seen as emphasizing the most important words in a narrative;
- *Deictics* indicate a point in space, for example pointing in a specific direction while saying "over there;"
- *Emblems* are stereotypical patterns with agreed meaning, such as the goodbye or OK sign.

To explain the relationships between gesture and speech, McNeill (1992, p. 37) outlined what he calls the *Kendon continuum*. This continuum goes from *gesticulation* on one end, in which gestures always co-occur with speech, to *sign language* on the other end, in which the gestures are linguistically self-contained. In between are the two cases of what he calls *emblems* and *pantomime*. Similar relationships between action and sound can be found in the case of *musical* gestures. Gestures linked to the sound-producing actions of musicians, for example, are strictly related to musical sound. A conductor's gestures, on the other hand, can take on many different functions along such an imagined continuum.

Musical gesture

How can we think about gestures from a musical perspective? The term musical gesture has, over the years, been used in quite different ways. One approach is that of Hatten (2004, p. 95) who argues that a musical gesture is "significant energetic shaping through time." He uses gesture in a metaphorical sense to describe motion-like qualities in the sound of music. This is quite different from the way the term is used to describe music-related body motion in some empirical music research. One definition that manages to combine these perspectives well—that is, between thinking about musical gesture as primarily related to sonic properties *or* to body motion—is the one presented by Gritten and King (2006, p. xx):

> [A] gesture is a movement or change in state that becomes marked as significant by an agent. This is to say that for movement or sound to be(come) gesture, it must be taken intentionally by an interpreter, who may or may not be involved in the actual sound production of a performance, in such a manner as to donate it with the trappings of human significance.

This definition implies that there is a flow of communication between the performer and the perceiver, and that the performer's motion "becomes" a gesture only if it is understood as such by the perceiver.

An interesting question then arises concerning consciousness: does an action have to be carried out consciously to be experienced as a gesture? Following the argument of Gritten and King (2006), gestures could be performed unconsciously but still be valid if they are observed as significant by the perceiver. From these definitions and theories, it is clear that gesture is a highly subjective phenomenon.

In summary, the term musical gesture is related to both motion and sound (the physical), as well as actions and sound objects (the perceptual), as sketched in Fig. 14.1. In some cases, the experience of a musical gesture may be driven primarily by sound, other times primarily by motion. In many cases, however, the combination of motion and sound leads to the experienced gesture.

Functional categories

When it comes to understanding more about motion/force, action, and gesture in ensemble performance, it is helpful to examine different types. Jensenius et al. (2010) suggested dividing music-related motion into four categories: sound-producing, sound-facilitating, sound-accompanying, and communicative. It is only the fourth of these—the communicative—that could be categorized as gestural by definition. The three others can also be considered as gestures, but only if there is a meaning-bearing component expressed by the performer and/or experienced by the perceiver. For example, when a pianist hits a key with the finger, it

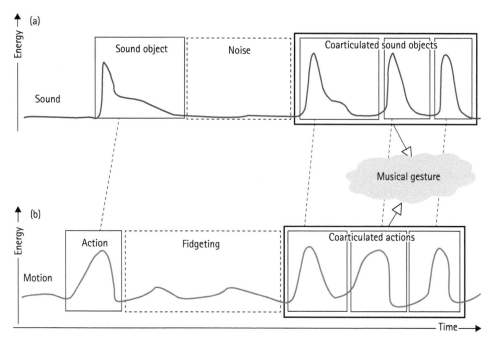

Figure 14.1 A visual summary of how a musical gesture can be thought of as the combination of experienced sound objects (a) and actions (b). These actions and sound objects are perceived from the continuous stream of sound (a) and motion (b).

involves motion and force and it can be experienced as a goal-directed action. However, it is not necessarily a gesture. It can be a gesture if the action is performed with a particular type of expressivity, or there is some other communicative element to the action. One such example could be a pianist playing the final chord of a piece with a dramatic action, hence signaling that this is the end of the piece. Such a musical gesture has a clear communicative element and is based on both sound-producing and sound-facilitating actions.

Gestures in ensembles

Ensemble performance is an excellent case for exploring musical gestures. After all, it is necessary to communicate to play together, and this often involves a combination of audition and vision. The type of communication, however, varies considerably, depending on several factors. In the following, we will investigate this from four perspectives: the *size and setup* of the ensemble, the *degrees of freedom* the musicians have over the music being played, how the *musical leadership* is distributed among musicians, and whether or not *machines* are involved in the musicianship.

Ensemble size and setup

Keller (2014) argues that interpersonal synchrony and leader–follower relations in ensembles are established using primarily head nodding, body swaying, and gaze patterns. As such, they provide "visual cues" that support the coordination within the ensemble. He further argues that if co-performers are denied visual contact, the performers increase their level of body sway to regulate the performance timing. Such gesturing, however, depends to a large extent on the size and setup of the ensemble in question, as this directly impacts the level of attention and details in the gestural communication.

The setup of an ensemble is related to what Jensenius et al. (2010) refer to as the performance *scene* (the volume over which the musicians are spread), their performance *position* within that scene, and their gesture *space* related to that position. The performance scene may be visually defined in the form of a concert hall stage, but it could also be a socially constructed area in the middle of a busy city street. The musicians' positions are defined within the boundaries of that performance scene. It may be tight and fixed, such as in the case of a string quartet sitting close together, even when they perform on a large stage. The musicians' positions may also be large and flexible, as seen in the way members of a rock band move around on a large stage. Thus, the gesture space of the musicians, that is, the physical volume they have at their disposal from their performance position, varies a lot.

The gesture space for members of a string quartet is constrained to a small "box" around their chair position, while it could cover the entire stage (and beyond) for rock musicians. These two extremes influence the different types of gestures one would typically see during such performances. A string quartet sitting relatively close to each other in a semi-circle makes it possible to pick up subtleties of each other's performance actions. This allows the musicians to use small gestures in their within-ensemble communication, in the form of a raised eyebrow, or a minute twist of the bowing arm.

Musical degrees of freedom

Another parameter that regulates the type and level of gestures found in ensemble performance is what may be called the "musical degrees of freedom" of the performance, that is, how much of the performance each individual musician is controlling. In this context, freedom does not mean "freedom in speech," but rather the number of independently variable factors affecting the performance. In a free improvisation group, for example, each musician has much freedom when it comes to controlling any aspect of the performance. This is quite different from a jazz trio playing a tightly synchronized Bebop tune or an orchestra playing a nineteenth-century concert. These differences in the musician's degrees of freedom necessarily influence the way they gesture.

The degrees of freedom of a musical performance may correlate with whether a score is used in the performance, and the level of detail in the notation of the score. Musical scores come in many different flavours, and some are more open for flexibility on the performer's side than others. However, even in performances based on very detailed score instructions, the musicians still have to create a meaningful performance as a group through the shaping of timbre/texture, the dynamics, and the timing of notes. Sawyer and DeZutter (2009) describe how the performances of a symphony orchestra can vary "from night to night," despite the presence of explicit leadership and a musical score. This depends to a large degree on the continuous communication between performers, in which gestures may also play an important part. These gestures can be based on expressive elements of sound-producing actions, such as to indicate the beginning of a passage, or upper body swaying to shape a phrase. Other times they may be purely communicative such as head nodding or facial expressions.

Freely improvising ensembles relies even more on gestural communication during a performance. If there are no/few predefined musical elements, this requires a high level of awareness within the ensemble to follow each other (Becker, 2000). Then all sorts of cues—including different types of gestures—are used to convey the intentions of the performers. Sometimes the performers may also use gestures to intentionally "sabotage" each other during the performance. One example of this can be found in "call and response" improvisation, during which the musicians may surprise each other, using both auditory and visual cues, to create more interesting and unexpected musical results (Schuiling, 2018, p. 46).

Musical leadership

While most musicians' primary focus is that of producing (musical) sound, the *musical leader* is also/instead focused on gestural communication with the rest of the ensemble and the audience. Such gesturing may be in the form of "indirect" sound production, through controlling individual onsets. It could also be more abstract, with the aim of creating a particular emotional feeling in the ensemble and audience.

Ensembles rely on different types of musical leadership such as the first violinist of a string quartet, the founder of a jazz band, the lead singer in a pop/rock band, or the conductor of a full-size orchestra. Davidson and Correia (2002, p. 243) describe how Annie Lennox takes on the role of leading the other members of her band in addition to her singing: "She is a narrator-interpreter in her use of illustrative and emblematic gestures with the co-performers and audience. She is a co-worker in her use of regulatory movements to coordinate musical entrances and exits." Leante (2014) argues that *khyal* singers in North Indian classical music communicate the lyrics through iconics or metaphorics, and perform abstract gestures along with the flow of the improvised sections. However, musical leadership is not always connected to a particular person. In a discussion of "shared intentionality," McCaleb (2014, p. 91) describes how the leadership varies within a string quartet, what he refers to as the "fluidity of ensemble roles." For this to happen, it is necessary that the musicians have knowledge of the musical material beyond their own part, and they also need to use non-verbal communication with their co-performers.

While such musical leadership is possible in small ensembles, larger ensembles often rely on a conductor as the *de facto* driving force in what Volpe et al. (2016) called "sensorimotor conversations" with the musicians. From a gestural perspective, the conductor is unique, being the only individual in the ensemble who does not have any direct influence on the sound production. They can instead be seen as an important communicator of emotional content, but they are also expected to provide temporal and structural information to the musicians. Using motion capture, Luck and Nte (2008) showed how conductors' motion trajectories induce the perception of temporal events. The role of the conductor is much more than only being a timekeeper, however, as orchestra musicians interact with each other in complex ways during performance (Ponchione-Bailey & Clarke, 2020). Wöllner and Auhagen (2008) have also shown that the perceived qualities of a conductor's gestures vary, depending on where the musicians sit in an orchestra. Their findings indicate that the frontal (woodwinds) and left-hand (first violinists) perspectives are better when it comes to receiving the "level of arousal" and "rhythmical clarity" of the conductor's gestures. This also shows the intrinsic relationship between the musical leadership and the size and setup of an ensemble.

The role of the conductor is institutionalized in Western (art) music traditions, and is largely focused around note-based scores. There are also cases in which the musical structure itself is conducted. One such example is John Zorn's *Cobra*, which features the composer as "prompting" the ensemble with a system of symbols printed on cue cards and lead sheets. This piece also relies on non-verbal interaction between the ensemble members: "*Cobra* exaggerates the degree to which all music performance depends on the communication of musical and other inter-personal signs—which may involve physical movement, including bodily and facial gestures, as much as sound" (van der Schyff, 2013, p. 6). An example of improvised leadership without the presence of a conductor can be found in traditional Turkish art. *Meşk* is a face-to-face teaching method in which the students emulate their master's way of performing. This leads to a participatory performance style, in which the musicians improvise according to the actions of the co-performers, but also with respect to the tradition. The performance can be seen as a "faithful repetition as a teaching method" (Özdemir, 2019, p. 148), which emerges as a performance concept for innovative improvisation, yet directed by the master and the tradition.

Machine musicianship

Until now, we have focused on gesturing found in ensembles with human performers. However, what happens when *machines*—from mechanical devices to computers—enter the stage? What Robert Rowe (2001) coined as *machine musicianship* is today prevalent in many musical settings. This can be in the form of machine-based instruments played by humans, robots playing acoustic instruments, or machines conducting human musicians. In the most extreme cases, one may even find completely autonomous machine-based musicianship.

A common complaint among audiences that experience machine musicianship has been the lack of causal relations between what is seen and heard: "As far as I could tell, they were all just checking their e-mail" (Trueman, 2007, p. 176). When performing with acoustic instruments, there is a direct energy transfer from musician to instrument, which can be seen/heard by other musicians and the audience. Machine-based instruments, and in particular digital musical instruments (DMIs), are based on the creation of *mappings* from action to sound. The creation of various types of "gestural controllers"—and meaningful mappings from these controllers to sound engines—have been a much-researched topic in the field of new interfaces for musical expression over recent decades (Jensenius & Lyons, 2017). This has been driven by the need for creating relationships between actions and sound that make sense, as well as an understanding of the power of gestures in music performance.

One form of machine musicianship that we find particularly interesting when it comes to the topic of ensemble gesture is that of *live coding*. This is a performance style in which the musician writes code on the computer, generating musical sound in real time. Since the musician typically sits in front of a computer during the entire performance, it has become common to project the written code on a screen behind the performer. Sometimes also a live video is shown of the musician's finger typing. This helps in "humanizing" an otherwise quite disembodied performance style. With better Internet technologies available, live coding is now also spreading to collaborative performances, in which many people type code in shared "virtual rooms." Here the performers' telematic typing actions can be seen as having a meaning-bearing component, hence becoming gestures in their own right (see Chapter 20 for more on live coding music ensembles).

Over the last decades, there has been a growing interest in forming laptop orchestras that explore the potentials of machine-based performance in a larger ensemble setting. Interestingly, this has also led to the need for more well-defined musical leadership within the ensemble. Some laptop orchestras have solved this by having a human conductor, while in other cases, a computer is assigned a conductor role. Then the messaging can come in the form of text messages or symbols on the screen. There are also ensembles exploring combinations of human and machine conductors. For example, in Dan Trueman's *PLahara*— inspired by the traditional North Indian *lahara* and composed for the 15-piece Princeton Laptop Orchestra (PLOrk)—the role of conductor is distributed among three conductors. The first uses a local network to add new layers and direct the tonal information of the piece. The second uses sign language to call particular sections, while the third uses a "knob box" to control various parameters of different instruments of PLOrk, over the network (Smallwood et al., 2008).

It is interesting to see that several laptop orchestras, and also other groups involving machine musicianship, incorporate various types of "gestural" controllers or actuators. In our machine-based performance practice, we have found it necessary to use gestural communication to play together. This includes using wearable sensors that capture motion or physiological data, live visuals, or physical objects that can "embody" the digitally produced sound. Without such visual references, it is often impossible to understand what is going on during a performance.

Conclusion

As the above discussion has shown, gestures are an essential (and integral) part of ensemble performance. The types of gestures, and who performs them, differ widely depending on musical genre and culture. Factors such as the size and setup of the ensemble and their musical degrees of freedom influence the way musicians gesture. How the musical leadership is organized is another important factor. If there is no conductor, the musicians need to communicate more directly with each other. This leads to different types of performance gestures than when a conductor is taking on the main communication role. Finally, machine musicianship challenges traditional ideas of what an ensemble is and paves the way for many new performance styles. Despite these differences, however, one thing that all types of music performance share is the production of musical sound as well as the need for meaningful communication between musicians and audiences.

References

Becker, H. S. (2000). The etiquette of improvisation. *Mind, Culture, and Activity, 7*(3), 171–6.

Cadoz, C., & Wanderley, M. M. (2000). Gesture-music. In M. M. Wanderley, & M. Battier (Eds.), *Trends in gestural control of music* (pp. 71–94). IRCAM.

Davidson, J. W., & Correia, J. S. (2002). Body movement. In R. Parncutt, & G. E. McPherson (Eds.), *The science and psychology of music performance. Creative strategies for teaching and learning* (pp. 237–50). Oxford University Press.

Godøy, R. I., Jensenius, A. R., & Nymoen, K. (2010). Chunking in music by coarticulation. *Acta Acoustica United with Acoustica*, *96*(4), 690–700.

Godøy, R. I., & Leman, M. (Eds.) (2010). *Musical gestures: Sound, movement, and meaning*. Routledge.

Gritten, A., & King, E. (Eds.) (2006). *Music and gesture*. Ashgate.

Gritten, A., & King, E. (Eds.) (2011). *New perspectives on music and gesture*. Ashgate.

Hatten, R. S. (2004). *Interpreting musical gestures, topics, and tropes: Mozart, Beethoven, Schubert*. Indiana University Press.

Jensenius, A. R. (2018). Methods for studying music-related body motion. In R. Bader (Ed.), *Handbook of systematic musicology* (pp. 567–80). Springer-Verlag.

Jensenius, A. R., & Lyons, M. J. (Eds.) (2017). *A NIME reader: Fifteen years of new interfaces*. Springer.

Jensenius, A. R., Wanderley, M. M., Godøy, R. I., & Leman, M. (2010). Musical gestures: Concepts and methods in research. In R. I. Godøy, & M. Leman (Eds.), *Musical gestures: Sound, movement, and meaning* (pp. 12–35). Routledge.

Keller, P. (2014). Ensemble performance: Interpersonal alignment of musical expression. In D. Fabian, R. Timmers, & E. Schubert (Eds.), *Expressiveness in music performance: Empirical approaches across styles and cultures* (pp. 260–82). Oxford University Press.

Kendon, A. (2004). *Gesture: Visible action as utterance*. Cambridge University Press.

Leante, L. (2014). Gesture and imagery in music performance: Perspectives from North Indian classical music. In T. Shephard, & A. Leonard (Eds.), *The Routledge companion to music and visual culture* (pp. 145–52). Routledge.

Luck, G., & Nte, S. (2008). An investigation of conductors' temporal gestures and conductor—musician synchronization, and a first experiment. *Psychology of Music*, *36*(1), 81–99.

McCaleb, J. M. (2014). *Embodied knowledge in ensemble performance*. Routledge.

McNeill, D. (1992). *Hand and mind: What gestures reveal about thought*. University of Chicago Press.

Özdemir, Ş. S. (2019). Discovering one's self through embodiment of tradition in meşk: An analysis of the mode of transmission in Turkish performative traditions. *Musicologist*, *3*(2), 151–70.

Ponchione-Bailey, C., & Clarke, E. F. (2020). Digital methods for the study of the nineteenth-century orchestra. *Nineteenth-Century Music Review*, 1–32.

Rowe, R. (2001). *Machine musicianship*. MIT Press.

Sawyer, R. K., & DeZutter, S. (2009). Distributed creativity: How collective creations emerge from collaboration. *Psychology of Aesthetics, Creativity, and the Arts*, *3*(2), 81–92.

Schuiling, F. (2018). *The instant composers pool and improvisation beyond jazz*. Routledge.

Smallwood, S., Trueman, D., Cook, P., & Wang, G. (2008). Composing for laptop orchestra. *Computer Music Journal*, *32*(1), 9–25.

Trueman, D. (2007). Why a laptop orchestra? *Organised Sound*, *12*(2), 171–9.

van der Schyff, D. (2013). The free improvisation game: Performing John Zorn's Cobra. *Journal of Research in Music Performance*, (Spring issue), 1–11.

Volpe, G., D'Ausilio, A., Badino, L., Camurri, A., & Fadiga, L. (2016). Measuring social interaction in music ensembles. *Philosophical Transactions of the Royal Society B: Biological Sciences*, *371*(1693), 20150377. http://doi.org/10.1098/rstb.2015.0377

Wöllner, C., & Auhagen, W. (2008). Perceiving conductors' expressive gestures from different visual perspectives. An exploratory continuous response study. *Music Perception*, *26*(2), 129–43.

15

Technologies for investigating large ensemble performance

Cayenna Ponchione-Bailey and Eric F. Clarke

Introduction

Large musical ensembles are complex social and musical assemblages, the study of which can be both exciting and challenging. While it can be difficult to define the boundaries of what constitutes a large ensemble, for the purposes of this chapter, the focus will be on Western classical ensembles of roughly 20 or more individuals that are often led by a non-instrument-playing, arm-waving conductor—in other words orchestras, wind bands, and choirs. To date, a substantial proportion of the research on large ensembles has focused on the relationship between musicians and the conductor: how conductors use gestures to communicate with musicians, what they communicate, and how they establish their authority or leadership style. Indeed, the focus has somewhat overlooked musician-to-musician communication, although some progress has been made in this area more recently.

Some of the questions that have been addressed by this literature are:

- How do conducting gestures (and conductors' non-verbal communication) work to convey information to musicians?
- What information do musicians use to stay together and to make decisions about how and when to play their parts?
- How do conductors establish leadership with a group and how do we know if they have achieved it?
- How do listeners respond to performances played under different types of leadership conditions?
- Do people evaluate performances differently depending on the perceived expressiveness, race, gender, or expertise of the conductor; and conversely, do they evaluate the expertise or expressiveness of a conductor based on the perceived quality of the ensemble?
- How do "objective" measures of performance (such as synchronization and togetherness) relate to listeners' and players' evaluations of performance?
- How are musicians' bodies affected by conductors' gestural communication and body posture?

Qualitative research methods from sociology and anthropology, such as observation, questionnaires, and interviews, have been used widely to collect data about aspects of large ensemble research—particularly its social aspects. However, there is a limit to the types of

Cayenna Ponchione-Bailey and Eric F. Clarke, *Technologies for investigating large ensemble performance* In: *Together in music*. Edited by: Renee Timmers, Freya Bailes, and Helena Daffern, Oxford University Press. © Oxford University Press 2022.
DOI: 10.1093/oso/9780198860761.003.0015

question that these methods can address and an increasing desire to coordinate qualitative evidence with quantitative measures of performance phenomena.

In an effort to broach these more quantitative questions, large ensemble research has benefitted greatly from technological developments. Whether one is interested in understanding musicians' or audiences' perceptions and actions, or analyzing the sounding outcomes of large ensemble performance, new technologies have started to open up large ensemble performance to empirical investigation. In addition to the challenges already faced by research on small ensemble performance (such as finding ways to capture and analyze non-verbal communication between individuals, make explicit otherwise tacit or procedural knowledge, or obtain quantitative measures of performance outputs), large ensemble research faces further impediments. The number of individuals involved and the unique role of the conductor, as well as financial and professional considerations, can make it difficult to gain access to large ensembles (e.g. for reasons of funding and the protection of precious rehearsal time).

Some large ensemble research questions can be explored with a small subset of players in a laboratory setting. But in an effort to obtain data from all of the members of an ensemble with the ecological validity of real-world rehearsal and performance settings, researchers have developed various technological tools to collect and analyze performance-related data. Experimentation with technology to investigate large ensemble performance began with the work of Harrer (1975), who was the first to attach sensors to a conductor to obtain biophysical data about their state of arousal while engaged in different musical tasks. And in a rather different implementation of technology, Clayton (1985) used video recording of the trajectory of an LED attached to the end of a conductor's baton, while simultaneously recording the playing and foot tapping of the conducted musicians. Since then, a number of more technologically developed methods have been implemented. The methods we cover here include: digital approaches to interviews and questionnaires, including media-stimulated recall (MSR) for obtaining performer perspectives, innovative uses of video and audio recordings to obtain insights into listener and viewer experiences, and audio and motion capture (MoCap) data to analyze interpersonal coordination and communication.[1] It is worth noting that there are, in principle, two distinct problems to address: technological solutions to the collection of appropriate data in the first place; and efficient and effective means to analyze the large amounts of data that such methods may generate—including the fundamental problem of defining both the nature and timing of an "event" in either audio or video data.[2] This chapter outlines a variety of technological tools for pursuing these goals, focusing on the methods used by the selected studies rather than reporting their findings.

Interviews and questionnaires

Qualitative data about performers' experiences, as obtained through one-to-one interviews, can provide valuable insights that external observation and other data collection methods are unable to access (e.g. Dobson & Gaunt, 2015). For example, though a core aspect of ensemble

---

[1] Some studies have also used biophysical and neurological data (e.g. surface electromyography, electrocardiograms, and functional magnetic resonance imaging) to provide insight into conductors' and performers' physiological and cognitive processes (e.g. Manternach, 2016; Marrin & Picard, 1998; Ono et al., 2015).

[2] Many instruments and voices produce notes that may be characterized by complex and fuzzily defined attributes of pitch, dynamic envelope, and timbre (deliberately variable pitch, slow rise times, constantly varying timbre).

performance involves listening and responding to other musicians, it is not yet possible to determine to whom or what a musician is auditorily attending, and to whom or what they are responding, without asking them directly (although there are studies discussed later in this chapter that demonstrate some new ways of approaching these questions).[3] Even eye tracking technologies, which have been used to investigate attention during tasks such as score reading, are not able to capture nuanced data about musicians' full attention, since players may be attending to sources of information throughout the ensemble while their eyes are directed elsewhere. However, obtaining and analyzing interview data can be time-intensive and impractical for ensembles of several dozen or more musicians. A possible substitute for the one-to-one interview is the online questionnaire. Online questionnaires have the advantage that they can be completed in participants' own time outside of the rehearsal and concert process, but can suffer from lower response rates and do not benefit from dialogue with the researcher to clarify answers or go into greater depth. Perhaps most critically for performance studies, they are less useful for obtaining detailed information from participants about very specific playing episodes, such as what they might have been thinking or doing during a particular passage of music in a performance or rehearsal.

In order to obtain qualitative data from musicians about their experiences while playing a targeted musical passage, a variation of the online questionnaire has been developed utilizing video-stimulated recall (VSR). VSR uses video recordings of participants' own activities to prompt recollections of their thought process and experiences during a specific task. The method has been used since the early 1980s to study cognitive processes in naturalistic environments. It is particularly useful for reflecting on activities that involve high levels of concentration, absorption, or "flow" which limit a participant's ability to provide commentary during the activity (such as speak aloud protocols) or to recall details of the event without an external prompt. In some circumstances, audio-stimulated recall (ASR) can also be effective, especially when combined with a musical score or other contextualizing information (Clarke et al., forthcoming).

It is not uncommon for VSR to be used in a one-to-one interview where a researcher will guide the participant through the process of remembering their experiences while watching video footage of their own activity. In order to upscale this method to capture the experiences of many ensemble musicians at once and to see how their experiences relate to one another at specific moments in a rehearsal or performance, Ponchione-Bailey (2016) developed an online platform to facilitate large-group MSR. Using the platform, participants leave time-stamped comments on the video or audio recording about what they were experiencing or thinking at specific moments. The advantages of this approach are that the research process does not disrupt the rehearsal or performance process, participants can complete the study in their own time, and their comments are attached (time-stamped) to very specific locations on the video or sound recording, allowing those observations to be related to others' experiences of precisely the same moment. The disadvantage is that the turnaround time between the musical event and the responses of the participants can be a day or more, and participation can be low. An alternative approach uses smartphone technology and an online polling application to conduct MSR in situ. The advantages of this approach are a very much shorter turnaround time between a playing experience and the stimulated recall (a minute or two)

---

[3] Interview methods cannot, of course, capture aspects of players' experiences of which they themselves are not consciously aware.

and a high response rate. The disadvantages are that participants cannot pause or review passages for further reflection, the procedure is disruptive to the natural rehearsal and performance process, and comments cannot be time-stamped to the recording, making them less specific (see Ponchione-Bailey, 2016; Ponchione-Bailey & Clarke, 2020).

Using video and audio recordings

Researchers have made use of video and audio recordings to tackle a variety of questions relating to the relationship between the aural and visual aspects of communication between musicians, between musicians and the conductor, and between the ensemble and the audience. This has included occlusion of specific parts of video recordings,[4] muting of audio, cross-pairing of video with other audio, extracting information from video using automated processes, and using video recordings in combination with MoCap systems to compare viewers' responses to point-light displays with their responses to full-view video.

Occluding part or all of a video and muting audio have been used by researchers to home in on the specific visual or aural information necessary for successful ensemble timing or the perception of expression. Wöllner (2008), for example, investigated which parts of a conductor's body convey most information to viewers about the conductor's expressive musical intentions, using partial occlusion of video footage of conductors (head only versus arms only), a softening of the sharpness of video footage (in an effort to simulate players' peripheral visual views of the conductor), and various AV combinations (with and without sound). The videos were made using standard video editing software and presented in a laboratory setting to participants who rated the expressiveness of the conductors in the various video and audio combinations.

More than ten years earlier, Fredrickson (1994) used VHS technology to explore the relative importance for ensemble coordination of listening to colleagues versus watching the conductor. Individual musicians in a laboratory setting were presented with a video of a conductor and the auditory feed of the ensemble playing, and were asked to play along. After the first 16 measures, the sound of the ensemble, the video of the conductor, or both ceased, and the player was asked to continue playing to the end of the piece (a total of 64 measures). Using a continuous response digital interface (CRDI), evaluators rated the degree to which the player successfully stayed with the audio recording under each condition.

Various CRDIs have been employed in music research, including sliders, dials, computer mice, and tablet interfaces, in an effort to track multiple dimensions of listeners' experiences such as arousal, valence, and shape (e.g. Küssner & Leech-Wilkinson, 2014). Such CRDIs have been used in combination with biophysical data from a conductor to investigate the concordance between the arousal levels of the conductor and the audience during the performance of a work, and the difference in this concordance between those who attended the live event versus a video screening of the concert (Nakra & BuSha, 2014).

The influence of the perceived quality of an ensemble's performance on evaluations of the expressiveness of the conductor, and conversely the influence of the perceived expressiveness, or perceived race of the conductor on evaluations of ensemble performance, have been investigated by cross-pairing audio recordings of ensembles with separate videos of conductors

---

[4] See Wöllner (2008, pp. 251–2) for an overview of occlusion in psychological research.

(e.g. Morrison et al., 2014; VanWeelden & McGee, 2007). In these studies, the challenge is to create credible combinations of video recordings of conductors and audio recordings of ensembles captured at different times. Researchers have tried to address this through careful selection of musical excerpts, the use of a metronome or click track to ensure consistent tempi between recordings, and video recording conductors against a green screen to allow replacement of the background with various concert hall views so as to create the impression of distinct and genuine performance situations. Participants then watch the videos and respond to questionnaires about their perceptions and evaluations of conductors and/or ensembles.

Audio capture and analysis

Studies that utilize audio recordings alone without the corresponding visual information provided by conductors' gestures are rare, as most large ensemble research is focused on the relationship between the conductor's gestures and the ensemble's performance as a whole. In small ensemble research, the analysis of audio to investigate interpersonal timing has been in use for more than three decades but has only recently been applied to a large ensemble context (see Chapter 16 for an overview of audio analysis in the study of vocal ensembles). Recordings of small and heterogeneous groups, with instruments or voices clearly identified by distinctive timbral or registral properties or very separate musical lines, can be manually or even automatically analyzed, but it is currently impossible to disaggregate individual players' lines from a standard mono or stereo audio recording of a large ensemble of homogeneous instruments such as the string sections of an orchestra.

In order to tackle the complex interpersonal timing within a string orchestra, the authors of this chapter have used a large array of contact microphones to simultaneously capture every individual player's sound while rehearsing and performing. These audio files can then be analyzed for various acoustical features, including note onsets and offsets, note transitions, pitch glides and vibrato, and relative dynamic level using analytical software such as Sonic Visualiser. In combination with various plug-ins, Sonic Visualiser provides a graphical interface for viewing and analyzing sound files to detect musical features, including note onsets and changes in pitch, amplitude, and timbre. While the software makes it possible to explore the sound files and extract features, the analysis of large amounts of data depends upon additional processing and is extremely labor-intensive. The hope is that ongoing research in music information retrieval (MIR) may result in effective methods for fast and more automated extraction of such musical features from large ensemble recordings.

Motion capture

The development of inexpensive and non-invasive MoCap technologies has been an exciting new turn in ensemble research, making it possible to capture and analyze the embodied communication central to group musical performance (see Chapter 14 for a discussion of "gesture" in ensemble performance). Within large ensemble research, this has primarily focused on those aspects of conductors' gestures that enable musicians to synchronize with the conductor, and the relationship between gestures and the temporal elements of an ensemble's performance. Researchers have also used MoCap to explore expression in conducting gesture, to track the direction of musicians' attention while playing, and to investigate communication and leadership in orchestras.

MoCap systems use magnetic, inertial, or optical technologies to capture information about musicians' movements (see Nymoen, 2013). While all of these technologies have been employed to study conducting and large ensemble performance, inertial and optical tracking methods predominate.[5] There are many off-the-shelf inertial MoCap devices now available, including mobile phones and watches that have in-built accelerometers, allowing data to be collected by Bluetooth. While there can be problems with measurement accuracy, these tools are inexpensive and easily accessible, and have featured in studies investigating automated gesture recognition for use in virtual ensemble environments. However, most researchers interested in understanding the nuanced connection between conducting gesture and sound, and player-to-player synchronization have used optical MoCap systems (for an overview of ensemble timing and synchronization research, see Chapter 17 and Chapter 23 for a case study of visual versus auditory cues for ensemble synchronization). These systems all use a combination of video cameras and computer vision algorithms to track musicians' movements. The cameras are of three varieties: "regular" digital video cameras, infrared (IR) video cameras, and depth video cameras (although this last variety has not yet been utilized for large ensemble research).

As an example of "regular" digital video, Salgian et al. (2007) used footage of a professional conductor in a live concert setting from a standard low-resolution digital camera, and employed computer vision techniques to isolate the pixels associated with the right hand of the conductor to track the hand's vertical position in relation to the pulse of the ensemble. The advantage of this approach is that data can be obtained from existing "normal" video footage of conductors or musicians, but because the image is only two-dimensional, the richness of the data is limited.

IR cameras have been more widely used by MoCap researchers due to the three-dimensional data that multiple IR camera systems can generate and the ability to synthesize and manipulate the resulting point-light displays. These cameras work by detecting IR light, either from IR-emitting diodes or from reflective markers attached to points on a person's body or instrument.[6] IR video cameras typically have sampling rates in the range of 120–1000 Hz, allowing for millisecond timing accuracy and extremely accurate spatial data.

MoCap technologies have enabled the quantification of musicians' movements and the separation of the kinematics of motion from embodiment more generally (e.g. through the creation of point-light displays), while retaining fine-grained synchronization between motion and sound. This makes possible automatic feature extraction and the controlled manipulation of point-light displays, enabling the transformation of specific gesture parameters or the morphing of multiple conductors' gestures into a composite stick figure. Researchers have exploited this aspect of motion capture to investigate the beat-inducing properties of conducting gestures (for a review, see Luck, 2011), the effect of conductors' gender and expertise on the perception and evaluation of conductors' gestures (e.g. Wöllner & Deconick, 2013; Wöllner et al., 2012), and the possible causal relationships between the gestures of conductors and musicians (e.g. d'Ausilio et al., 2012). MoCap can also be used to study facial

---

[5] The "conductor's jacket" (Marrin & Picard, 1998) uses magnetic MoCap technology.
[6] In the latter case, IR light emitted from a source near the camera is reflected from the markers back to the camera.

movements and has been used to investigate the influence of conductors' gestures and body postures on singers' physiological responses (Manternach, 2012).

By combining MoCap with computational approaches and statistical analysis, two research projects based in Italy[7] have studied social communication within ensembles utilizing the Granger causality test to attempt to identify causal relationships between the actions of conductors and musicians, and between the ensemble musicians themselves (d'Ausilio et al., 2012). The Granger causality test determines the probability that one time series (e.g. data from one individual's motion over time) is able to predict another time series (data from another individual's motion). The method has been used to detect the efficacy of a conductor's leadership (the degree to which a conductor's gestures appear to influence the motions of the musicians) and musician-to-musician relations, offering a quantitative approach to tracking the complex issue of leader–follower relations in an orchestral environment. The research team has also blended relatively "naturalistic" orchestral rehearsal settings with experimental arrangements of players' positions that vary their sightlines to the conductor, in order to tease out how the flow of communication changes when traditional seating arrangements, and thus lines of communication, are modified (Pauline et al., 2019).

Although the work described in this section is engaged in understanding interaction in large ensemble settings and has captured data from a number of musicians, it is still limited in scale. As with many of the research methods for exploring communication in ensembles, some work has yet to be done to upscale these tools to capture data from everyone in a large ensemble if a more rounded view of what is happening for all involved is to be obtained.

Conclusion

Large ensembles offer a fascinating, but challenging, context in which to study musical behaviors and processes. As we have shown, the overwhelming majority of this work has focused on the classical orchestra (implicitly or explicitly) and has been preoccupied with questions of leadership associated with the role of the conductor. One consequence is a serious neglect of many other equally fascinating contexts and questions. Large ensembles come in a huge variety of forms and cultural traditions (including jazz big bands, gamelans, ukulele orchestras, gospel choirs, and steel bands) and with manifestly different conditions of leadership. Recent work (Clarke et al., forthcoming; Dobson & Gaunt, 2015; Ponchione-Bailey, 2016; Ponchione-Bailey & Clarke, 2020) has started to address the complex and diverse mesh of musical and social dynamics that operate within, and extend out from the activities of, large ensembles. The presence and activities of conductors and/or leaders of large ensembles certainly affect these interpersonal dynamics, but the situation is much more complex than the centripetal and hierarchical model that is often assumed.

With this in mind, our own work has aimed to triangulate the data of players' experiences, listeners' evaluations and responses, and objective characteristics of the ensemble's playing itself. By manipulating the presence/absence of a conductor, and the instructions to players about how they should attend to one another and with what musical aim, controlled equivalents of spontaneously arising differences between ensembles can be introduced, and their effects upon players' experiences, listeners' evaluations, and the data of performance

---

[7] See http://siempre.infomus.org/ and https://entimement.dibris.unige.it/, accessed December 2, 2019.

(including timing, coordination, dynamic shaping, and pitch inflection) can be captured using the methods described earlier in this chapter. The technologies to do this work are increasingly available, but there is a need for more sophisticated and powerful ways both to capture interplayer interaction (visual and auditory) and to analyze the large amounts of data that even short periods of rehearsal or performance can generate. Equally, while the widespread public adoption of smartphone and other mobile technologies has facilitated relatively non-disruptive ways to gather the insights of participants, we are still a long way from capturing the full richness and flux of players' in situ experiences.

It may be that virtual reality (VR) or augmented reality (AR) technologies can also contribute to large ensemble research in the near future, as they have done for solo performers with audience simulators (e.g. Williamon et al., 2014). Placing individual players in VR environments that simulate their engagement with ensembles of various kinds under different kinds of leadership or direction may offer interesting ways to study interaction and togetherness under controlled conditions, with the possibility of monitoring the direction of gaze with the VR headset. Ensemble performance raises fascinating questions about the multimodal allocation of attention (auditory, visual, kinesthetic), and one of the tantalizing challenges is to develop methods that might allow access to this "private" world. Verbal report—with or without MSR—offers rich qualitative data but is compromised by the interventions of consciousness/self-consciousness, the passage of time, and the difficulty of capturing rapid changes in fixation and modality, and "parallel processing" (e.g. watching a leader while listening to a desk partner). The study of large ensembles is still in its infancy, but with technological innovation and researcher imagination, a rich and rewarding field beckons.

Acknowledgments

This research was supported by the Arts and Humanities Research Council grant no. AH/N004663/1 ("Transforming C19th Historically Informed Practice").

References

Clarke, E. F., Ponchione-Bailey, C., & Holden, C. (forthcoming). String sound in the round. Methods, outcomes and implications of experimental approaches to nineteenth-century string playing. In C. Holden, E. F. Clarke, & C. Ponchione-Bailey (Eds.), *Practice in context. Historically informed practices in nineteenth-century instrumental music.* Oxford University Press.

Clayton, A. M. H. (1985). *Coordination between players in musical performance* [Doctoral dissertation]. University of Edinburgh.

D'Ausilio, A., Badino, L., Li, Y., Tokay, S., Craighero, L., Canto, R., Aloimonos, Y., & Fadiga, L. (2012). Leadership in orchestra emerges from the causal relationships of movement kinematics. *PLoS One, 7*(5), e35757. http://doi.org/10.1371/journal.pone.0035757

Dobson, M. C., & Gaunt, H. F. (2015). Musical and social communication in expert orchestral performance. *Psychology of Music, 43*(1), 24–42.

Fredrickson, W. E. (1994). Band musicians' performance and eye contact as influenced by loss of a visual and/or aural stimulus. *Journal of Research in Music Education, 42*(4), 306–17.

Harrer, G. (1975). Das "Musikerlebnis" in Griff des naturwissenschaftlishen Experiments. In G. Harrer (Ed.), *Grundlagen der Musiktherapie und Musikpsychologie* (pp. 3–47). G. Fischer.

Küssner, M., & Leech-Wilkinson, D. (2014). Investigating the influence of musical training on cross-modal correspondences and sensorimotor skills in a real-time drawing paradigm. *Psychology of Music, 42*(3), 44–69.

Luck, G. (2011). Quantifying the beat-inducing properties of conductors' temporal gestures, and conductor–musician synchronization. In I. Deliège, & J. Davidson (Eds.), *Music and the mind: Essays in honour of John Sloboda* (pp. 325–38). Oxford University Press.

Manternach, J. N. (2012). The effect of nonverbal conductor lip rounding and eyebrow lifting on singers' lip and eyebrow postures: A motion capture study. *International Journal of Research in Choral Singing, 4*(1), 36–46.

Manternach, J. N. (2016). Effects of varied conductor prep on singer muscle engagement and voicing behaviors. *Psychology of Music, 44*(3), 574–86.

Marrin, T., & Picard, R. (1998). *The conductor's jacket: A device for recording expressive musical gestures.* International Computer Music Conference.

Morrison, S. J., Price, H. E., Smedley, E. M., & Meals, C. D. (2014). Conductor gestures influence evaluations of ensemble performance. *Frontiers in Psychology, 5,* 806. http://doi.org/10.3389/fpsyg.2014.00806

Nakra, T. M., & BuSha, B. F. (2014). Synchronous sympathy at the symphony: Conductor and audience accord. *Music Perception: An Interdisciplinary Journal, 32*(2), 109–24.

Nymoen, K. (2013). *Methods and technologies for analysing links between musical sound and body motion* [Doctoral dissertation]. University of Oslo.

Ono, K., Nakamura, A., & Maess, B. (2015). Keeping an eye on the conductor: Neural correlates of visuo-motor synchronization and musical experience. *Frontiers in Human Neuroscience, 9,* 154. http://doi.org/10.3389/fnhum.2015.00154

Pauline M. H., Leonardo, B., Alessandro, D., Gualtiero, V., Serâ, T., Luciano, F., & Antonio, C. (2019). Multi-layer adaptation of group coordination in musical ensembles. *Scientific Reports, 9,* 5854. http://doi.org/10.1038/s41598-019-42395-4

Ponchione-Bailey, C. (2016). *Tracking authorship and creativity in orchestral performance* [DPhil Thesis]. University of Oxford.

Ponchione-Bailey, C., & Clarke, E. F. (2020). Digital methods for the study of the nineteenth-century orchestra. *Nineteenth-Century Music Review.* https://doi.org/10.1017/S1479409819000661

Salgian, A., Pfirrmann, M., & Nakra, T. M. (2007). Follow the beat? Understanding conducting gestures from video. In G. Bebis, R. Boyle, B. Parvin, D. Koracin, N. Paragios, et al. (Eds.), *Advances in visual computing* (pp. 414–23). Springer.

Williamon, A., Aufegger, L., & Eiholzer, H. (2014). Simulating and stimulating performance: Introducing distributed simulation to enhance musical learning and performance. *Frontiers in Psychology, 5,* 25. http://doi.org/10.3389/fpsyg.2014.00025

VanWeelden, K., McGee, I. R. (2007). The influence of music style and conductor race on perception of ensemble and conductor performance. *International Journal of Music Education, 25*(1), 7–9.

Wöllner, C. (2008). Which part of the conductor's body conveys most expressive information? A spatial occlusion approach. *Musicae Scientiae, 12*(2), 249–72.

Wöllner, C., & Deconinck, F. J. A. (2013). Gender recognition depends on type of movement and motor skill. Analyzing and perceiving biological motion in musical and nonmusical tasks. *Acta Psychologica*, *143*(1), 79–87.

Wöllner, C., Deconinck, F. J. A., Parkinson, J., Hove, M. J., & Keller, P. E. (2012). The perception of prototypical motion: Synchronization is enhanced with quantitatively morphed gestures of musical conductors. *Journal of Experimental Psychology Human Perception and Performance*, *38*(6), 1390–403.

16
Understanding expressive ensemble singing through acoustics

Helena Daffern and Sara D'Amario

Introduction

The academic field of singing voice acoustics[1] is now well established and proving valuable across numerous disciplines, including pedagogy and performance. It also contributes to clinical communities where collaborations are informing voice therapies and treatments. The empirical study of acoustics in ensemble singing is much more sparse than for the solo voice. However, its investigation is highly valuable, as illustrated by Ternström's review of work in the field (2003), with meaningful applications within ensemble training, direction, and performance practices, and with implications for vocal health. This chapter illustrates the practical potential of studying ensemble singing through acoustics. The methodological approaches of initial experimental work are considered alongside how the insights gained in this area may be extended to develop our understanding of the processes of ensemble singing.

The unique characteristics of singing ensembles are born from the acoustic complexities and scope and range of the human voice as a musical instrument. When investigating multi-voice ensembles, a significant challenge is accounting for the variations of numerous acoustic variables for each individual, all of which may lead to adaptations of the same or additional acoustic features by the other singers within the group: there are many coincident relationships that are changing in real time and based on current technology, "the reality of choral performance is too complex to be studied all at once" (Ternström & Karna, 2002, p. 271).

Systematically identifying and investigating specific acoustic parameters provides a starting point from which a more holistic and practically useful picture can be built. Ternström and Karna (2002) demonstrate this value of systematic enquiry as they set out practical advice for choirs through the description and concatenation of the research findings and theories relating to specific acoustic factors relevant to choir performance. This chapter presents four acoustic attributes that are most analyzed within the literature addressing ensemble singing: intonation, vibrato, intensity, and timbre (the additional topic of synchronization is discussed in depth in Chapter 17).

---

[1] Here we refer to voice acoustics as the properties of the sound emitted when singing, which is one strand of voice science, the wider field of which also considers the physiological mechanisms involved in producing the sound and/or the perception of that sound.

Helena Daffern and Sara D'Amario, *Understanding expressive ensemble singing through acoustics* In: *Together in music.* Edited by: Renee Timmers, Freya Bailes, and Helena Daffern, Oxford University Press. © Oxford University Press 2022. DOI: 10.1093/oso/9780198860761.003.0016

Intonation

Tuning, or intonation, is a dominant topic in the practice of choral singing, in terms of both accuracy in note-matching when singing in unison and the tuning of intervals between parts. However, while many scholars have given impassioned perspectives on appropriate tuning systems, there is no ground truth of "good tuning" in *a capella* singing. Practitioners often promote just intonation, but issues of pitch drift in pieces with modulation then need addressing (Havrøy, 2013). Psychoacousticians distinguish between the perceived pitch, a subjective quantity, and the fundamental frequency (f_o) of a tone (the lowest partial in the acoustic spectrum of the voice, and the repetition rate with which the vocal folds vibrate), which is objectively measurable. They are closely correlated, but not identical. For assessing harmony, the f_o is the more relevant of the two, since consonance is closely tied to mathematical ratios of frequencies. The accurate measurement of each singer's f_o is essential to investigate tuning. However, it requires that individual voices be sufficiently separated at the point of recording. This section considers the different methods that have been employed to assess empirically the tuning behaviours of vocal groups, including the types of intonation that are employed and the adjustments individuals make in response to one another.

Tuning styles and accuracy

Devaney and colleagues developed AMPACT, a toolkit combining digital signal processing with MIDI files to extract the f_o of individual voices within a solo voice group from a mono or stereo recording (Devaney & Ellis, 2008). They incorporated machine learning to inform an analytical approach that accounts for the importance of both vertical and horizontal tuning tendencies.[2] Using AMPACT, Devaney et al. (2012) analyzed four three-part vocal groups performing a chord progression by Benedetti. They found an overall horizontal tendency for the groups to avoid pitch drift by tuning to equal temperament. They also found variation in the tuning of the major and minor third chords in the piece, with the groups utilizing just intonation, as well as equal tempered and Pythagorean tuning for these intervals. One ensemble narrowed their major thirds and widened their minor thirds even beyond the prediction for just intonation, leading the authors to suggest that tuning may contribute to group identity and be context-dependent within a piece.

In a different approach to extracting information from individual voices, studies have combined acoustic analysis with the use of electrolaryngographs. These devices allow direct assessment of vocal fold activity via two circular electrodes placed on the neck at the position of the thyroid cartilage (for a full description of the use of electrolaryngographs in choir research, see D'Amario & Daffern, 2017). In a study spanning five sessions over four months, an overall tendency towards equal temperament rather than just intonation was observed for the individuals of a singing quintet (D'Amario et al., 2018). f_o was analyzed through electrolaryngograph signals alongside the acoustic signal from small microphones placed close to the mouth of each singer. Harmonic major thirds were found to be tuned slightly closer to just intonation, while minor thirds remained closer to equal temperament.

---

[2] Horizontal tuning: the tuning of melodic intervals as a voice changes note; vertical tuning: the tuning of chords as voices tune to each other in creating harmonies.

The findings of these studies of solo-voice ensembles suggest that equal temperament dominates current practice, although the very small sample sizes and the varied quality of the ensembles make generalizations towards a "best practice" model inappropriate. However, the special treatment of thirds that has been identified, alongside a tendency towards equal temperament overall provokes a hypothesis for further testing: employing just intonation in the tuning of chords with more ambiguous targets such as thirds (for which equal temperament and just intonation predictions are most dissimilar) might enable affective "pure tuning" as a gold standard at such moments, while avoiding unwanted pitch drift through equal temperament at other times.

Investigating a larger ensemble and other processes of intonation, Jers and Ternström (2005) created multi-channel recordings of a 16-part choir singing in unison/octaves. They placed small microphones on the noses of the singers who were spaced just under one meter apart. The overall intonation of sections within the choir was measured (in terms of pitch matching rather than the tuning of intervals) by calculating the mean f_o value of each note and considering the deviation of intonation between singers and over time. Tuning was found to be more precise in slower performances, descending intervals were tuned more accurately than ascending intervals, and larger melodic intervals (fifths and octaves) were exaggerated.

Use of synthesis to assess tuning

The studies discussed previously illustrate ways to investigate tuning in multi-part recordings, which assess data from quite "natural" performance environments (in that the singers perform together in a real space in real time). Another approach which allows more systematic, but less natural experimental procedures is to use synthesis: controlling certain acoustic parameters in stimuli presented to the singer or singers allows robust assessment of the adjustments of an individual to those specific acoustic parameters.

Utilizing synthesis to investigate the tuning tendencies of ensemble singers, Howard et al. (2013) presented a synthesized quartet over headphones to the participant with their own part omitted. The participants sang their part, focusing on tuning the chords of the piece, which was specifically composed to exploit pitch drift in just intonation. The synthesized parts were presented in both just intonation and equal temperament. The female participants, who sang both the alto and soprano line, were most "out of tune" when singing with the just intonation model synthesized for the study. This supports the findings of the more ecological studies presented previously that singers tend towards equal temperament.

Ternström and Sundberg (1988) had previously used synthesis to assess the impact of acoustic factors beyond f_o on tuning in choirs—in particular, the effect of balance of loudness on the ease of intonation, and whether intonation accuracy is affected by spectral changes (associated with vowel and timbre) within the choir. In a first experiment, male subjects were asked to sing in unison with synthesized stimuli of different vowels (/a:/ and /u:/), intensity, and f_o. The results showed high accuracy in terms of pitch matching, although a perceptual pitch-amplitude effect was observed whereby the mean f_o of the singer would drop as the intensity of the stimulus increased, especially for the /u:/ vowel. Subsequently, a second set of stimuli were created that controlled the frequency of vibrato oscillations, the common partials (overlapping harmonics), and partials above f_o. The singers were asked to tune a third or fifth above the stimulus tone, with "pure" or just intonation used as the model for "in tune."

Vibrato was found to make intonation more difficult, while major thirds seemed easier to tune when higher partials were absent. It was also found that adding the first or all common partials for the interval of a fifth aided intonation. In a second experiment, presented in the same paper, stimuli were created from a pre-recorded choir of male voices. Analysis of the recordings confirmed the reinforcement/suppression of the common partials for the fifth, depending on the vowel, and the results support the finding of their synthesis experiment that the presence of the lowest common partial strongly influences intonation.

Tuning adaptations

More recently, the intonation behaviours of singers adjusting to each other when performing together have been explored in an investigation that measured the tuning of five live vocal quartets in three conditions: solo (performing their part, unable to hear the other singers); partial (where they could hear some but not all the other parts); and open (where all the singers could hear each other) (Dai & Dixon, 2017). The "isolated" singer sang in a different room to the rest of the quartet, with microphones and loudspeakers providing the audio capture and feedback, depending on the condition. As expected, the authors found evidence of adjustment in the interactive conditions, with note stability, pitch error (calculated as the difference between the scored and observed pitch for each singer and note), and melodic interval error increasing in these conditions, while harmonic interval tuning improved.[3] This study highlights the complex interactions that occur in group singing and begins to explore some of these relationships. It shows that when conducting tuning studies, the model against which intonation is judged needs careful consideration, since the "ground truth" may be shifting for both vertical and horizontal tuning as singers adapt to each other and potentially engage with different tuning styles throughout a piece. Timmers considers how these tuning adaptations might be approached as complex systems in Chapter 13.

Vibrato

Identified acoustically as periodic variations in pitch, intensity, and timbre, vibrato is a highly controversial characteristic of singing, especially in the context of vocal ensembles, and is often interwoven into arguments about tuning and the concept of choral blend (Galante, 2011). While vibrato might be consciously avoided or advised against during ensemble singing, it is still often employed to some degree, either intentionally or not—it may, for example, be used as a musical ornament even when not commonly adopted. This section focuses on the empirical work which seeks to investigate adaptations of vibrato in relation to other singers as they sing together, potentially contributing to the "blending" process between singers.

In their study investigating intonation through multi-channel choir recordings, which is discussed in the previous section, Jers and Ternström (2005) also measured the vibrato of individual singers as the standard deviation of the f_o of tones, and considered patterns of vibrato within long tones. They found that some singers did not employ vibrato, even over

---

[3] A model of equal temperament seems to have been used as "ground truth" for tuning in this study.

long tones, but in those who did, there was evidence of synchronization of the vibrato oscilla-tions. This finding was also reported in a case study of a newly formed vocal quartet recorded performing the same exercise three times over a nine-week intensive rehearsal schedule (Daffern, 2017). Daffern found that over the course of the sessions, singers reduced their vibrato production overall in terms of both the number of notes containing vibrato and the frequency extent of the oscillations. In the case of the final long chord of the piece, synchro-nization in the vibrato oscillations was observed. The findings of these two studies appear to concur, but there are limited data and therefore generalizations cannot be extrapolated. More experimental work is needed in this area. Vibrato is an acoustic parameter at the forefront of performers' conscious intentions, and future work could improve our understanding of vi-brato perception, how vibrato relates to intonation, the chorus effect, and choral "blend," as well as coordination and interactions in performance.

Intensity

Intensity is a key expressive parameter in ensemble performance, both in terms of inten-sity ranges communicating expressive dynamics and with respect to performer relationships within the ensemble. Performers need to adjust their dynamics relative to others in order to: balance intensity between parts; ensure ensemble cohesion; communicate an expressive interpretation of the music; and achieve optimal blend or isolation of voices as appropriate. This section considers how acoustic analysis has been employed to investigate intensity in singing ensembles and the implications of those findings for future research.

Exploring the impact of room acoustics on the output level and timbre of different types of choirs, Ternström (1993) investigated the dynamic range of a boys', mixed youth, and mixed adult choir in three different rooms (large church, basement room, and rehearsal hall). The analysis relied on the computation of long-term average spectra (LTAS), a technique com-puting the decibel (dB) measurement of the acoustic signal at each frequency averaged over time) using two microphones placed at an equal distance in front of the choir. Dynamic ranges (calculated as the maximum level difference) from pianissimo to fortissimo of 12 dB, 16 dB, and 20 dB for the boys', youth, and adult choir were reported, respectively. A lower power was observed for the youth and adult choirs in the rehearsal hall, which had relatively low room absorption, compared to the church, alongside a change in spectral slope in the absorbent room in the boys' choir. These results offer insights into how choirs might adapt to the acoustics of a space.

Building on research that measured the dynamic ranges of individual choral singers, Titze and Maxfield (2017) produced a model of a voice range profile[4] of a choir. From this, they ex-plored contributions of individual voices on the sound level range of a choir over a two octave range. The model predicts six different dynamic levels (*pp, p, mp, mf, f, ff*) between 3 and 6 dB. The model revealed that choir size does not significantly influence dynamic range (with only a 3 dB increase with each doubling of the choir size), and that dynamic range might be lim-ited if blend is prioritized over loudness in a non-homogeneous choir, whereby the loudness and loudness variations of the singers are varied.

---

[4]   Voice range profile (VRP) represents the sound pressure level range that a singer can produce over their f_o range.

Choral singing relies on the fact that each singer can hear their own voice (called Self) and the voices of the co-performers (called Other), avoiding the masking effect (i.e. the voice of one singer is so loud it masks that of another). Measuring the so-called Self-to-Other ratio (SOR)—the sound difference in decibels between Self and Other—enables investigation of the optimum sound levels between performers and any contributing practical factors. For instance, if the distance between singers increases, the SOR ratio will increase, as the Other will decrease relative to Self.

The SOR has been the topic of a number of empirical investigations conducted by Ternström and colleagues and has been shown to affect intonation. For example, an intensity difference larger than 25 dB sound pressure level (SPL) between singers was found to cause intonation issues in choral singing (Ternström & Sundberg, 1988).

In later experiments, they measured SOR values using binaural microphones in the context of chamber choir and opera chorus performances. Average SOR values of +4 dB were reported in a 20-singer chamber choir standing in a single row in a normal rehearsal hall (Ternström, 1994). Similar SOR values (average +3 dB) were also measured in another chamber choir of 30 singers in a large broadcasting studio (Ternström, 1995). However, much higher SOR values between +10 and +15 dB were measured for a soprano, mezzo-soprano, tenor, and baritone of the chorus of Opera Australia during a dress rehearsal on the Opera Theater stage of the Sydney Opera House (Ternström et al., 2005).

Singers' preferred SORs were also investigated in a perceptual experiment using synthesized choir sounds; results demonstrate high inter-subject variability (ranging from −1 and +15 dB) and small intra-subject variability (± 2 dB) of singers' preferences. This highlighted that the singers' preferred SOR varied largely across participants, but the singers' own choices were consistent across different production tasks (Ternström, 1999).

The differences observed around intensity between types of ensemble and preferences of individuals may be related to their different environmental situations and associated acoustic objectives. The requirements of an operatic stage, and associated vocal technique, may give rise to different priorities in terms of the blend of the ensemble, for which the SOR is likely to be a key parameter. While the perception of optimal SORs seems to differ consistently across participants, its production depends on multiple factors, including choir formation and room acoustics, voice type, and training. Future work on intensity needs to carefully consider and categorize these situations in order for results to be contextually relevant, especially in light of understanding potential effects on various other acoustic parameters, including intonation and spectral features, and their wider implications for concepts of blend.

Timbre

While timbre is a perceptual descriptor associated with many acoustic features, it encompasses certain measurable physical parameters such as the distribution of energy over frequency, which contributes to the blend of a vocal ensemble. Timbre is more challenging to measure than other features, such as intonation, especially for the human voice, because it is very broad in its range of timbral variation. The timbre produced by a voice is greatly affected by formants, which are peaks in a voice spectrum caused by the resonant frequencies of the vocal tract. The first three formants are usually responsible for the vowel that is perceived; however, singers adjust the frequency of their formants in a technique known as formant tuning for various acoustic affects, including adapting across vocal registers and maximizing vocal efficiency for vocal power, or blending to and isolating from other voices.

In a study of a single barbershop quartet recorded with small microphones on the noses of the singers, Kalin (2005) used inverse filtering to extract the positions of the formant frequencies for each singer in specific chords. He suggests that the formant tuning he observed, whereby the singers separated their formants apart from each other, might facilitate the idiomatic exact/pure tuning of the genre by allowing the singers to hear themselves more clearly. The tuning of formants to partials was also observed (although to a lesser extent) and is attributed to enhancing the characteristic "lock-and-ring" effect of barbershop's blended timbre.

Varying the intensity of formants, rather than or in addition to tuning them, is another technique that can affect the blend of an ensemble, depending on whether a singer wants their voice to fuse with that of the co-performers in the ensemble or be soloistic. Empirical investigations have analyzed the acoustic differences in vocal timbres between solo and choral singing, by comparing the LTAS for matched productions (i.e. passages with identical text and melody performed in solo and choral mode by the same singer) using acoustic recordings. Rossing et al. (1986, 1987) and Łętowski et al. (1988) found that male and female singers typically produce more energy in the singer's formant region (2 - 4 kHz) when performing liturgical passages in solo singing, compared with the choral singing technique. Łętowski et al. (1988) also found that untrained singers tended to use brighter singing quality, whereas trained singers tended to dampen their voice during choral singing. Goodwin (1980) found an increase in the level of the fundamental with fewer and weaker upper partials and weaker second and third formants, compared to the first, when the same singers blended to a recorded voice, compared to singing alone.

Reid et al. (2007) expanded this research among professional opera singers, analyzing the timbral differences between solo and choral timbres. This provides contrasting results to the earlier studies focused on the liturgical repertoire. In Reid et al. (2007), timbral characteristics were investigated by calculating the singing power ratio (SPR) and the energy ratio (ER) from the LTAS; these are comparison measures of the energy between high (2–4 kHz) and low (0–2 kHz) frequency bands, respectively, and represent the relative energy of the singer's formant region. The different analysis methods used here, involving measurement of energy in frequency bands rather than in specific partials, make comparison with the previous studies less direct. However, the results still point to inconsistencies between the findings. The differences observed may reflect (similar to the differences observed with the SOR) the idiomatic vocal technique of professional opera singers as well as the different performance objectives for opera choruses, compared to a choir or vocal ensemble.

In vocal ensembles, as for solo voice, formants play a major role in timbre; the studies above indicate that singers alter their formants when singing as part of a vocal ensemble to change the overall sound. However, this initial work suggests that the alteration of formant production varies dependent on context, including repertoire, genre, environment, and singers' musical expertise and vocal technique. Robust methodologies have emerged from this work, but it remains an area for fruitful future exploration—including considering timbre in these contexts, but also to consider the interactions of vowels, formants, and timbre and their role in the blend of an ensemble.

Future work

Studies to date provide valuable insights into singing ensemble performance parameters and reveal how technology can deepen this field of research and embed its usefulness for practicing musicians. Acoustic understanding has the potential to influence decision-making in singing, pedagogic and conducting/directing practices, informing performance objectives and environmental and situational choices. Vocal ensembles should be driven by performers' objectives (whether aesthetic or otherwise) informed by realistic acoustic possibilities and limitations. In turn, application of acoustics knowledge within practice can promote healthy voice use—for instance, avoiding ineffective vocal effort attempting to increase the dynamic range of a choir (Titze & Maxfield, 2017).

The focus of existing studies on specific isolated acoustic features—necessary due to the complexities of voice acoustics—might reduce the immediacy of their relevance to performance/performers. Data are often analyzed from isolated notes, or short exercises and on specific sustained vowels, rather than representing an ecologically "musical" framework of data capture or analysis. An acoustic feature that is notable by its absence in this regard, and is highlighted by Keller (2014) as an expressive performance parameter, is that of articulation. The incalculable possibilities available to the human voice pertaining to articulation (once text is involved) make its study particularly challenging. Onset detection alone (which is only one aspect of articulation) is particularly difficult for the singing voice, with acoustic characteristics varying greatly, depending on the consonant or vowel and phonation type (soft or hard) (see Chapter 17).

As digital tools advance, it will be increasingly feasible to explore more varied data sets that represent more fully the range of sounds produced by the singing voice. In addition to enabling the collection of more sophisticated and reliable data, new technologies are presenting possibilities to improve and expedite analytical processes. For instance, the automated analysis systems emerging in music information retrieval (see Chapter 15) are providing faster and more accessible ways to extract acoustic parameters from audio. Improving the usability of these tools and understanding their outputs are imperative to encourage a wider reach of user, especially for performers and educators.

As well as improving analysis techniques, study design can adapt with advancing technology. For instance, finely controlling specific acoustic parameters of set stimuli through synthesis has been shown to be valuable in exploring how individuals contribute to the process of singing together. However, it also presents limitations in the ecology of experimental design (and therefore the ability to extrapolate these findings across musical contexts). Emerging technologies such as virtual reality can provide plausible and immersive visual and auditory information that can be controlled independently, introducing new scope for future studies (Daffern et al., 2019).

Conclusion

The valuable work that has already been undertaken in the area of ensemble voice acoustics illustrates how anecdotal evidence can be translated into measurable acoustic characteristics. There is a corresponding need for this and future work to be effectively disseminated and accessible for it to be practically impactful, and to encourage more ensemble singers to undertake research in this area (as has emerged with solo voice acoustics). The knowledge base this research provides can guide the decision-making of practicing musicians, providing a meaningful contribution to the expressive performance processes of vocal ensembles.

References

Daffern, H. (2017). Blend in singing ensemble performance: Vibrato production in a vocal quartet. Journal of Voice, 31(3), P385.E23–385.E29. https://doi.org/10.1016/j.jvoice.2016.09.007

Daffern, H., Camlin, D. A., Egermann, H., Gully, A. J., Kearney, G., Neale, C., & Rees-Jones, J. (2019). Exploring the potential of virtual reality technology to investigate the health and well being benefits of group singing. International Journal of Performance Arts and Digital Media, 15(1), 1–22.

Dai, J., & Dixon, S. (2017). Analysis of interactive intonation in unaccompanied SATB ensembles. 18th International Society for Music Information Retrieval Conference, 599–605.

D'Amario, S., & Daffern, H. (2017). Using electrolaryngography and electroglottography to assess the singing voice: A systematic review. Psychomusicology: Music, Mind, and Brain, 26(4), 229–43.

D'Amario, S., Howard, D. M., Daffern, H., & Pennill, N. (2018). A longitudinal study of intonation in an a cappella singing quintet. Journal of Voice, 34(1), P159.E13–159.E27. https://doi.org/10.1016/j.jvoice.2018.07.015

Devaney, J., & Ellis, D. P. (2008). An empirical approach to studying intonation tendencies in polyphonic vocal performances. Journal of Interdisciplinary Music Studies, 2(1&2), 141–56.

Devaney, J., Mandel, M., & Fujinaga, I. (2012). A study of intonation in three-part singing using the Automatic Music Performance Analysis and Comparison Toolkit (AMPACT). 13th International Society for Music Information Retrieval Conference (ISMR 2012), 511–16.

Galante, B. (2011). On the voice – vibrato and choral acoustics: Common voice science issues for the choral conductor. Choral Journal, 51(7), 67–78.

Goodwin, A. (1980). An acoustical study of individual voices in Choral Blend. Journal of Research in Music Education, 28(2), 119–28.

Havrøy, F. (2013). "You cannot just say: 'I am singing the right note' ". Discussing intonation issues with Neue Vocalsolisten Stuttgart. Music + Practice, 1(1). http://doi.org/10.32063/0104

Howard, D. M., Daffern, H., & Brereton, J. (2013). Four-part choral synthesis system for investigating intonation in a cappella choral singing. Logopedics Phoniatrics Vocology, 38(3), 135–42.

Jers, H., & Ternström, S. (2005). Intonation analysis of a multi-channel choir recording. TMH-QPSR Speech, Music and Hearing: Quarterly Progress and Status Report, 47(1), 1–6.

Kalin, G. (2005). *Formant frequency adjustment in barbershop quartet singing* [Master's thesis]. KTH Royal Institute of Technology. http://www.speech.kth.se/prod/publications/files/1684.pdf

Keller, P. E. (2014). Ensemble performance: Interpersonal alignment of musical expression. In D. Fabian, R. Timmers, & E. Schubert (Eds.), Expressiveness in music performance: Empirical approaches across styles and cultures (pp. 260–82). Oxford University Press.

Łętowski, T., Zimak, L., & Ciołkosz-Łupinowa, H. (1988). Timbre differences of an individual voice in solo and choral singing. Archives of Acoustics, 13, 55–65.

Reid, K. L., Davis, P., Oates, J., Cabrera, D., Ternström, S., Black, M., & Chapman, J. (2007). The acoustic characteristics of professional opera singers performing in chorus versus solo mode. Journal of Voice, 21(1), 35–45.

Rossing, T. D., Sundberg, J., & Ternström, S. (1986). Acoustic comparison of voice use in solo and choir singing. The Journal of the Acoustical Society of America, 76, 1975–81.

Rossing, T. D., Sundberg, J., & Ternström, S. (1987). Acoustic comparison of soprano solo and choir singing. The Journal of the Acoustical Society of America, 82, 830–6.

Ternström, S. (1993). Long-time average spectrum characteristics of different choirs in different rooms. Voice, 2, 55–77.

Ternström, S. (1994). Hearing myself with the others—sound levels in choral performance measured with separation of the own voice from the rest of the choir. Journal of Voice, 84, 293–302.

Ternström, S. (1995). Self-to-other ratios measured in choral performance. Proceedings of the 15th International Congress on Acoustics, 2, 681–4.

Ternström, S. (1999). Preferred self-to-other ratios in choir singing. The Journal of the Acoustical Society of America, 105(6), 3563–74.

Ternström, S. (2003). Choir acoustics: An overview of scientific research published to date. International Journal of Research in Choral Singing, 1(1), 3–12.

Ternström, S., Cabrera, D., & Davis, P. (2005). Self-to-other ratios measured in an opera chorus in performance. The Journal of the Acoustical Society of America, 118(6), 3903–11.

Ternström, S., & Karna, D. R. (2002). Choir. In R. Parncutt and G. McPherson (Eds.), The science and psychology of music performance: Creative strategies for teaching and learning (pp. 269–84). Oxford University Press.

Ternström, S., & Sundberg, J. (1988). Intonation precision of choir singers. The Journal of the Acoustical Society of America, 84(1), 59–69.

Titze, I. R., & Maxfield, L. (2017). Acoustic factors affecting the dynamic range of a choir. The Journal of the Acoustical Society of America, 142(4), 2464. https://doi.org/10.1121/1.5004569

17

Ensemble timing and synchronization

Sara D'Amario and Freya Bailes

Introduction

Timing and synchronization are fundamental considerations in ensemble playing. Musicians in ensembles vary the degree of temporal alignment between the sounds that they produce, known as synchronization. This chapter is concerned with the synchronization that occurs as a result of music production, be that synchronization between the sounds produced or between the physical actions required to produce the sounds.

Research in this field has traditionally emphasized the tight synchronization that can be achieved between musicians in ensembles that include string quartets (Wing et al., 2014), piano duos (Goebl & Palmer, 2009), and classical singing formations (D'Amario et al., 2018a). The variability in note onset asynchronies between performers in Western classical professional ensembles is typically in the order of tens of milliseconds and decreases with increasing tempo. The average value of absolute asynchronies and the standard deviation of signed asynchronies are both typically between 30 and 50 ms during expressive performances of Western classical music; mean signed asynchrony is typically close to 0, falling often between −5 and +5 ms (Keller, 2014). Nevertheless, asynchronies between co-performers during ensemble playing are not only inevitable, but also often intentional (see also Chapters 13 and 22).

Existing review chapters have excellently summarized the main developments of our understanding of processes underlying interpersonal synchronization (e.g. Keller, 2014). In this chapter, we will focus on relatively recent developments in studies of ensemble synchronization that investigate variations of synchronization behavior across genres and styles, the influence of contextual factors on ensemble timing, and the broader aspects of interpersonal synchronization which not only concern the timing of tones, but also relate to entrainment between movements, bodies, physiology, and brains. We argue that there is a need for a greater recognition by the research community of variations in the degree to which synchronicity is the desired musical outcome. Different musical traditions can be expected to vary with respect to the degree and expression of temporal coordination appropriate to their aesthetic goals. Similarly, the phase relationships between musical parts can be more or less significant features of the music itself, depending on the musical tradition. Ensemble coordination comprises a wide range of synchronous behaviors. Beyond the synchronization of note onsets, musicians synchronously co-vary parameters, such as intensity, articulation, and tuning, for expressive purposes (see Chapter 13). Moreover, synchronization between musicians is not homogenous across the course of a piece of music: we hope to encourage a greater research emphasis on dynamic interpersonal patterns in ensemble performance.

Sara D'Amario and Freya Bailes, *Ensemble timing and synchronization* In: *Together in music.* Edited by: Renee Timmers, Freya Bailes, and Helena Daffern, Oxford University Press. © Oxford University Press 2022. DOI: 10.1093/oso/9780198860761.003.0017

Defining what constitutes synchronization between musicians in an ensemble is not a trivial matter. When measuring the degree of synchronization between the physical sounds produced by two or more musicians, this seemingly objective process still requires a subjective decision about the width of the temporal window within which the note onsets must occur in order for them to be considered as synchronous. An alternative approach embraces subjectivity by studying what it is that listeners *perceive* to be synchronous.[1] In this chapter, we extend our consideration of ensemble coordination beyond the measurable aspects of performance timing, to reflect on the importance of the perceived in addition to the realized timing. We structure our review around four central issues: (1) the factors that affect ensemble synchronization; (2) differences in approach to ensemble timing by musical tradition and genre; (3) the physiological patterns of the individual performers relating to interpersonal synchronization; and (4) the potential for incorporating listener/performer perceptions in studies of ensemble synchronization. Our goal in this chapter is to broaden the conceptual horizons of what has traditionally been considered of interest in studies of ensemble timing and synchronization. We also make suggestions for future research in timing and synchronization in music ensembles consistent with this aim.

Factors that affect ensemble synchronization

A number of contextual factors have been shown to affect interpersonal synchronization, for instance leader–follower relationships and the visual contact between musicians (D'Amario et al., 2018b; Palmer et al., 2019), as well as the note density of the music being performed and the auditory feedback from co-performer(s) (Goebl & Palmer, 2009). The distance between performers, the type of instrument being performed (with gradual or rapid onsets), and the acoustic conditions of the venue might also influence synchronization, although further studies are needed to shed more light in this respect. Fischinger et al. (2015), for example, studied the impact of altered virtual room acoustic characteristics (including different reverberation times and a dry condition) on intonation, tempo, and timing precision in choir singing. Results demonstrate that while intonation was not markedly affected by simulated room acoustics, tempo was slower and timing precision decreased when participants sang in virtual rooms of relatively large sizes with long reverberation times.

Cognitive factors such as the expertise and knowledge of the ensemble are bound to shape the extent to which they synchronize. For example, the ability of individuals within an ensemble to generate anticipatory auditory imagery is known to affect the coordination of their combined musical outcome (Keller & Appel, 2010). One obvious example is the role of an ensemble musician's familiarity with not only their part, but also the parts of the others in the group, as well as a mental image of the combined effect. Some research suggests that having played a co-performer's part before meeting and then playing with the co-performer for the first time can have a paradoxically *negative* impact on the ability to coordinate the timing of the piece (Ragert et al., 2013). This is thought to arise because of a perceptual mismatch between one's own mental image of the local timing variations associated with the part, and that being realized by the new co-performer. Research also highlights the tendency in humans

---

[1] Note that perceiving synchrony is distinct from judging performance quality as a measure of the degree of synchrony achieved.

to increase their pace unconsciously during joint action activities, e.g. clapping games and music ensemble performances; this seems to be an ubiquitous phenomenon, which can be attributed to the combination of two different mechanisms, named *phase advanced mechanism* (shortening single intervals) and a human-specific *period correction mechanism* (shortening the period of individual intervals by adjusting internal timekeepers) that can result in joint rushing (Wolf et al., 2019).

An increasing amount of research has investigated the body movements of musicians as they serve a facilitative role as visual sensorimotor signals between ensemble members. Certain spatiotemporal characteristics of cueing gestures enable synchronization; for example, in piano–piano duos, violin–violin duos, and violin–piano duos, peak acceleration in a leader's head-nodding gestures coincides with beat position, while gesture duration and periodicity of head and bowing hand gestures relate to tempo (Bishop & Goebl, 2018a). The finding regarding points of peak acceleration in head-nods to cue beat position has been corroborated by Bishop and Goebl (2018b), showing also that interpersonal synchronization at onsets improved as smoothness and magnitude of the gestures increased and the prototypicality decreased (i.e. the similarity between the gestures produced by co-performers, evaluated by assessing how similar each gesture was to all other gestures within the data set). It has been further found that during passages with irregular rhythms in same-instrument performances (i.e. piano–piano and clarinet–clarinet duos), musicians' movements became smoother. Importantly, these specific passages were characterized by stronger interpersonal coordination and increased visual interactions, compared with regularly timed passages (Bishop et al., 2019a, b; see also Chapter 23). Different performance conditions encourage different compensatory behaviors to enable temporal coordination. For example, Goebl and Palmer (2009) showed that pianists' head movements in piano duos became more synchronized when auditory feedback was reduced, and that the fingers of pianists who were acting as leaders were raised higher than those of the followers. It has also been shown that musicians' movements are more predictable when they play in an ensemble than alone (Glowinski et al., 2013), and that their movements differ with varying degrees of shared musical intentions between musicians (Glowinski et al., 2015). In summary, ensemble synchronization is shaped by characteristics of the music, acoustic conditions, sensorimotor cues, and the musicians' familiarity with their own and others' parts.

Influences of tradition on ensemble synchronization

Our current understanding of what might be meant by ensemble synchronization, how it works, and how important it is to musicians and listeners has been biased by a tendency to focus on a narrow range of musical genres and traditions. Most studies of ensemble timing and synchronization concern Western classical music and, to a lesser extent, jazz; yet studies of different musical genres and traditions, including non-Western examples, have shown variation in the extent to which strict synchronicity between ensemble musicians is the desired musical outcome. Moreover, aesthetic standards for ensemble synchrony change over time, and the chapter by Terepin in this book (see Chapter 22) reminds us of historical shifts in the production and reception of ensemble "togetherness" in Western classical music (see also Ponchione-Bailey & Clarke, 2020).

Body movements have been investigated in relation to jazz duos comprising a range of instruments, e.g. saxophone, double bass, electric bass, and drums (Eerola et al., 2018). Results suggest that ancillary body motion may vary according to the temporal regularity of the music, and may be more important for co-performer communication in non-pulsed, free improvisations than in standard jazz with a regular pulse. One feature common to many musical styles (e.g. funk, jazz) is groove, by which a repeated rhythmic pattern creates a strong drive to move to the beat. Groove can be described as arising from the rhythmic interactions between individuals engaging with the music (Keil & Feld, 1994). A positive relationship has been established between the experience of musical groove and the quality of sensorimotor coupling achieved when moving to the music (Janata et al., 2012). Thus, for a group of musicians performing groove-based music, the groove is a self-perpetuating form of synchronous interaction.

Ethnomusicological investigations on interpersonal coordination in ensembles involving Indian and Afro-Brazilian cultures observed a number of cases of music "entrainment." This phenomenon refers to two independent rhythmical systems that synchronize, interacting with each other to such an extent that they eventually assume the same or related period; in other words, two independent rhythms that stabilize and reassert this stabilization if that synchrony is momentarily stopped (Clayton, 2012). Cases of music entrainment have been observed between independent groups of musicians during Afro-Brazilian Congado performances, a form of ritual processional music (Lucas et al., 2011). Researchers analyzed audiovisual recordings of four different occasions during which two different groups played different music in close proximity. Findings revealed the occurrence of entrainment in phase, entrainment out of phase, and also no entrainment, depending on the proximity, visual contact, tempo similarity, and intention between the groups. Entrainment is important as a form of dynamic interpersonal adaptation. For adaptive timing between musicians to occur (Keller, 2014), an accurate perception of the musical pulse is required, which is rarely metronomic in its regularity, and so sensitivity to tempo change is also needed (Schulze et al., 2005).

A study investigating Indian classical music revealed complex relationships between tanpura players in an ensemble (Clayton, 2007). While the musicians' intentions were to keep independent tanpura rhythms, observational analysis of the performers' hand gestures revealed cases of tight coordination. When the accompanist fixed their visual attention on the soloist's back or shoulder, the tanpura rhythms stabilized in 3:2 relationships (the period of one plucking pattern was roughly 3 seconds, while the other was 2 seconds), suggesting the importance of visual contact between musicians in Indian classical ensembles.

In a rare study of listener perceptions, Neuhoff et al. (2017) manipulated the note onsets of drum-strokes in excerpts of Malian duet and quartet music, and presented these to expert listeners (professional percussionists and dancers from Mali). The research was not concerned with questions of ensemble per se, instead focusing on the discrimination of drumming patterns and perceptions of authenticity. There is certainly scope for research into the impact of varying temporal coordination between ensemble musicians on an audience's perceptions and subjective experiences of the music.

Another variety of ensemble coordination worthy of consideration is that required by polymetric music. Such music simultaneously presents multiple meters, with examples coming from West African drumming ensembles and jazz, as well as twentieth-century Western art music (Poudrier & Repp, 2013). Poudrier and Repp (2013) conducted initial research to investigate whether listeners are able to track multiple beat structures at once or whether these are integrated within one single metric framework. Listeners in their study were classically trained musicians, whose accuracy when judging the timing of a probe suggested an ability to attend to both of the concurrently presented meters when these were relatively simple. However, their probe task performance was no better than chance when presented with more complex rhythmic combinations. It seems probable that listeners who are highly experienced as performers of polymetric music would be better able to attend to more complex patterns. An interesting question arising from this research relates to the potential for ensemble size to impact on perceptions of polymetric music, given that large ensembles may combine more distinct lines. More research is needed to understand how ensemble musicians coordinate their parts when performing polymetric music, particularly in the absence of external time-keepers such as cues from a conductor.

Interpersonal synchronization between musicians has been also investigated in the context of Transylvanian (the central region of current Romania) village music. Research measured aksak patterns (rhythmic sequences of short and long beats executed based on un-interrupted reiterations) and entrained interactions between two professional Gypsy players (a violinist and a viola player) performing a repertoire known as "Gypsy song of sorrow," mostly performed during local celebration events (Bonini-Baraldi et al., 2015; Clayton, 2015). These studies measured asynchronies ranging from a few milliseconds to almost a second; asynchronies lasting less than 10% of the beat duration were defined as small-scale asynchronies, and those lasting from 20% to 50% of the beat duration were considered large-scale asynchronies. The authors argue that this variability was not the results of performers' errors, since the musicians were professional performers playing together for more than 40 years; these asynchronies, as the researchers suggest, should be understood as related to the corresponding rhythmic unit. Large-scale asynchronies were found to be relatively stable across different interpretations of the same piece; they may be highly dependent on the mu-sical structure of the melody in relation to the accompaniment, and therefore considered as rhythmic variations, rather than asynchronies at all. Small asynchronies instead were found to vary across repetitions, and thus may be related to a specific interpretation. In summary, with variations in musical structures across musical genres, we can similarly expect consid-erable variations in ensemble synchronization. Studies in this field contribute to the theory of rhythm and meter, as well as knowledge of interaction in ensemble playing.

Synchronization between brains, breathing, and cardiac activity during ensemble playing

Studies suggest that a tightly synchronized and interacting range of physiological parameters supports and facilitates synchronization in ensembles. Specifically, a network of motor brain areas allows the emergence and execution of an efficient social coordination during ensemble playing (for a review of the neurophysiological mechanisms allowing real-time interpersonal coordination, see Keller et al., 2014). It has been shown that interpersonally synchronized ac-tivities such as duo guitar performances are preceded and accompanied by intra- and inter-brain oscillatory activity (Sänger et al., 2012), with coupled brain activity in the alpha and beta frequency ranges between the guitarists (Sänger et al., 2013). The directionality of such between-brain couplings was found to discriminate the musical roles of leader versus fol-lower (Sänger et al., 2013). A later investigation further investigated the extent and functional significance of synchronization of cortical activity across multiple brains, through the simultaneous recording of the electroencephalogram (EEG) activity of four guitarists playing in ensemble (Müller et al., 2018). Results indicate complex hyperbrain network interactions during quartet performances, characterized by higher frequencies for intrabrain communication and lower frequencies for interbrain connections. Modulations in the cortical activity were also investigated during quartet performances of professional saxophonists and compared with a resting state; results suggest a relationship between temporal coordination of actions during ensemble performances and cortical activity (Babiloni et al., 2011).

Recent work has further focused on the neurocognitive mechanisms that enable synchronization with a co-performer in music, by investigating the roles of motor expertise and visual information, in addition to auditory information (Timmers et al., 2020). This study applied double-pulse transcranial magnetic stimulation (dTMS) to musicians with varying levels of piano expertise while synchronizing rhythm, articulation, and dynamics with those of pre-recorded performances of a pianist, presented as audio-only, audio-video, or audio-animation. The application of dTMS enabled an analysis of the relevance of the dorsal premotor cortex associated with motor resonance with co-performer actions, and the relevance of the intraparietal sulcus associated with multisensory binding. Results demonstrate that in order to beneficially use a co-performer's visual and motor information for sensorimotor synchronization, high levels of relevant motor expertise are needed.

At a larger temporal level, interpersonal synchronization can involve the temporal coordination of other physiological elements, such as breathing and cardiac activity, in addition to the coordination of body movements described above. Investigations focused on the musical domain have shown a tight synchronization of such elements during ensemble performances. For example, patterns of cardiac and respiratory synchronization have been found in choir singing, with phase synchronization between respiration and heart rate variability increasing during singing, compared with a rest condition, and also increasing when singing in unison rather than singing with multiple voice parts (Müller & Lindenberger, 2011). Tight coordination of cardiac activity between singers has also been reported in a study investigating heart rate variability of singers in relation to the musical structure of the piece being sung. Results show a connection between song structure, heart rate, and respiration, and synchronization in frequencies and phases of respiration and cardiac cycles between singers (Vickhoff et al., 2013). Such intra-interpersonal synchrony is necessarily complex in its relationship to the production and perception of the ensemble's sound.

Incorporating listener/performer perceptions in studies of ensemble synchronization

Empirical studies concerned with ensemble musicians' perceptions of their own temporal co-ordination are fewer than those which consider physically measured patterns of synchrony. Although important, measures of the degree of sound-producing synchronization achieved in ensemble performance are limited as a source of information about the ensemble's aesthetic intentions, as well as the resulting musical effects. One project, which triangulated each of these perspectives, tracked the rehearsals of a vocal quintet, obtaining objective measures of the synchrony between voices using audio and laryngograph recordings, an analysis of the verbal interactions between the singers during rehearsals, as well as a separate survey of listeners' perceptions of the degree of ensemble achieved. Results demonstrate that synchronization improved across rehearsals, although the extent to which it did so depended on the complexities of the piece performed (D'Amario et al., 2018a) and did not seem to be the result of any rehearsal strategies to target synchronization, as articulated during rehearsal (D'Amario et al., 2018a). Listeners, including singers who performed the pieces, were not able to perceive differences in narrow or wide synchronization as measured in the homophonic piece, irrespective of their musical expertise (D'Amario et al., 2019). This triangulation of measured synchronization, verbal interactions, and listener perceptions demonstrates that there is not always a clear agreement between such different measures, and so researchers should not assume an isomorphic relationship between what is realized, what is perceived, and what is intended. Ensemble timing is complex, suggesting the need to undertake the simultaneous investigation of different aspects of music-making at once.

A number of research questions relating to the perception of synchronization are as yet neglected. Firstly, what is the impact of varying temporal coordination between musicians on audience's perceptions? Secondly, how do differences in aesthetic norms affect the subjective interpretation of a coordinated ensemble performance? Systematic studies of audience expectations of stylistic norms and perceptions of the music as they relate to both intended and realized musical performances would represent useful contributions to knowledge with respect to both questions. More research is needed relating to ensemble musicians' aesthetic goals, and we might ask how their intended degree of interpersonal synchrony varies as the music progresses from start to finish.

Conclusion

Timing and interpersonal synchronization in ensembles are key performance elements, and the aim of our chapter has been to broaden the conceptual horizons of what has traditionally been considered of interest in studies of timing and synchronization in music ensembles to date. Timing and synchronization can be impacted by a number of contextual factors, vary by genre, and are associated with a complex and highly interconnected range of physiological mechanisms. The simultaneous investigation of such different aspects alongside the cognitive dimensions of the musicians' approach with a wide range of music aesthetic goals has the potential to provide a deep understanding of interpersonal coordination, while revealing the processes supporting interpersonal synchronization in music ensembles.

References

Babiloni, C., Vecchio, F., Infarinato, F., Buffo, P., Marzano, N., Spada, D., Rossi, S., Bruni, I., Rossini, P. M., & Perani, D. (2011). Simultaneous recording of electroencephalographic data in musicians playing in ensemble. *Cortex*, *47*(9), 1082–90.

Bishop, L., Cancino-Chacón, C., & Goebl, W. (2019a). Eye gaze as a means of giving and seeking information during musical interaction. *Consciousness and Cognition*, *68*, 73–96.

Bishop, L., Cancino-Chacón, C., & Goebl, W. (2019b). Moving to communicate, moving to interact: Patterns of body motion in musical duo performances. *Music Perception*, *37*(1), 1–25.

Bishop, L., & Goebl, W. (2018a). Beating time: How ensemble musicians' cueing gestures communicate beat position and tempo. *Psychology of Music, 46*(1), 84–106.

Bishop, L., & Goebl, W. (2018b). Communication for coordination: Gesture kinematics and conventionality affect synchronization success in piano duos. *Psychological Research, 82*, 1177–94.

Bonini-Baraldi, F., Bigand, E., & Pozzo, T. (2015). Measuring aksak rhythm and synchronization in Transylvanian village music by using motion capture. *Empirical Musicology Review, 10*(4), 265–91.

Clayton, M. (2007). Observing entrainment in music performance: Video-based observational analysis of Indian musicians' tanpura playing and beat marking. *Musicae Scientiae, 11*(1), 27–59.

Clayton, M. (2012). What is entrainment? Definition and applications in musical research. *Empirical Musicology Review, 7*(1–2), 49–56.

Clayton, M. (2015). Aksak patterns and entrained interaction in Transylvanian village music. *Empirical Musicology Review, 10*(4), 292–301.

D'Amario, S., Daffern, H., & Bailes, F. (2018a). A longitudinal study investigating synchronization in a singing quintet. *Journal of Voice, 34*(1), 159.e1–159.e12. https://doi.org/10.1016/j.jvoice.2018.06.011

D'Amario, S., Daffern, H., & Bailes, F. (2018b). Synchronization in singing duo performances: The roles of visual contact and leadership instruction. *Frontiers in Psychology, 9*, 1208. http://doi.org/10.3389/fpsyg.2018.01208

D'Amario, S., Daffern, H., & Bailes, F. (2019). Perception of synchronization in singing ensembles. *PLoS One, 14*(6), e0218162. https://doi.org/10.1371/journal.pone.0218162

Eerola, T., Jakubowski, K., Moran, N., Keller, P. E., & Clayton, M. (2018). Shared periodic performer movements coordinate interactions in duo improvisations. *Royal Society Open Science, 5*, 171520. https://doi.org/10.1098/rsos.171520

Fischinger, T., Frieler, K., & Louhivuori, J. (2015). Influence of virtual room acoustics on choir singing. *Psychomusicology: Music, Mind, and Brain, 25*(3), 208–18.

Glowinski, D., Dardard, F., Gnecco, G., Piana, S., & Camurri, A. (2015). Expressive non-verbal interaction in a string quartet: An analysis through head movements. *Journal on Multimodal User Interfaces, 9*, 55–68.

Glowinski, D., Mancini, M., Cowie, R., Camurri, A., Chiorri, C., & Doherty, C. (2013). The movements made by performers in a skilled quartet: A distinctive pattern, and the function that it serves. *Frontiers in Psychology, 4*, 841. https://doi.org/10.3389/fpsyg.2013.00841

Goebl, W., & Palmer, C. (2009). Synchronization of timing and motion among performing musicians. *Music Perception, 26*(5), 427–38.

Janata, P., Tomic, S. T., & Haberman, J. M. (2012). Sensorimotor coupling in music and the psychology of the groove. *Journal of Experimental Psychology: General, 141*(1), 54–75.

Keil, C., & Feld, S. (1994). *Music grooves*. University of Chicago Press.

Keller, P. E. (2014). Ensemble performance: Interpersonal alignment of musical expression. In D. Fabian, R. Timmers, & E. Schubert (Eds.), *Expressiveness in music performance: Empirical approaches across styles and cultures* (pp. 260–82). Oxford University Press.

Keller, P. E., & Appel, M. (2010). Individual differences, auditory imagery, and the coordination of body movements and sounds in musical ensembles. *Music Perception, 28*(1), 27–46.

Keller, P. E., Novembre, G., & Hove, M. J. (2014). Rhythm in joint action: Psychological and neurophysiological mechanisms for real-time interpersonal coordination. *Philosophical Transactions of the Royal Society of London. Series B, Biological Sciences, 369*, 20130394. https://doi.org/10.1098/rstb.2013.0394

Lucas, G., Clayton, M., & Leante, L. (2011). Inter-group entrainment in Afro-Brazilian Congado ritual. *Empirical Musicology Review*, *6*(2), 75–102.

Müller, V., & Lindenberger, U. (2011). Cardiac and respiratory patterns synchronize between persons during choir singing. *PLoS One*, *6*(9), e24893. https://doi.org/10.1371/journal.pone.0024893

Müller, V., Sänger, J., & Lindenberger, U. (2018). Hyperbrain network properties of guitarists playing in quartet. *Annals of the New York Academy of Sciences*, *1423*, 198–210.

Neuhoff, H., Polak, R., & Fischinger, T. (2017). Perception and evaluation of timing patterns in drum ensemble music from Mali. *Music Perception*, *34*(4), 438–51.

Palmer, C., Spidle, F., Koopmans, E., & Schubert, P. (2019). Ears, head and eyes: When singers synchronize. *Quarterly Journal of Experimental Psychology*, *72*(9), 2272–87. https://doi.org/10.1177/1747021819833968

Ponchione-Bailey, C., & Clarke, E. F. (2020). Digital methods for the study of the nineteenth-century orchestra. *Nineteenth-Century Music Review*, 1–32. https://doi.org/10–1017/S1479409819000661

Poudrier, È., & Repp, B. H. (2013). Can musicians track two different beats simultaneously? *Music Perception*, *30*(4), 369–90.

Ragert, M., Schroeder, T., & Keller, P. E. (2013). Knowing too little or too much: The effects of familiarity with a co-performer's part on interpersonal coordination in musical ensembles. *Frontiers in Psychology*, *4*, 368. https://doi.org/10.3389/fpsyg.2013.00368

Sänger, J., Müller, V., & Lindenberger, U. (2012). Intra- and interbrain synchronization and network properties when playing guitar in duets. *Frontiers in Human Neuroscience*, *6*, 312. https://doi.org/10.3389/fnhum.2012.00312

Sänger, J., Müller, V., & Lindenberger, U. (2013). Directionality in hyperbrain networks discriminates between leaders and followers in guitar duets. *Frontiers in Human Neuroscience*, *7*, 234. https://doi.org/10.3389/fnhum.2013.00234

Schulze, H. H., Cordes, A., & Vorberg, D. (2005). Keeping synchrony while tempo changes: Accelerando and ritardando. *Music Perception*, *22*(3), 461–77.

Timmers, R., MacRitchie, J., Schabrun, S. M., Thapa, T., Varlet, M., & Keller, P. E. (2020). Neural multimodal integration underlying synchronization with a co-performer in music: Influences of motor expertise and visual information. *Neuroscience Letters*, *721*, 134803. https://doi.org/10.1016/j.neulet.2020.134803

Vickhoff, B., Malmgren, H., Åström, R., Nyberg, G. F., Ekström, S.-R., Engwall, M., Snygg, J., Nilsson, M., & Jörnsten, R. (2013). Music structure determines heart rate variability of singers. *Frontiers in Psychology*, *4*, 334. https://doi.org/10.3389/fpsyg.2013.00334

Wing, A., Endo, S., Bradbury, A., & Vorberg, D. (2014). Optimal feedback correction in string quartet synchronization. *Journal of the Royal Society Interface*, *11*, 20131125. https://doi.org/10.1098/rsif.2013.1125

Wolf, T., Vesper, C., Sebanz, N., Keller, P. E., & Knoblich, G. (2019). Combining phase advancement and period correction explains rushing during joint rhythmic activities. *Scientific Reports*, *9*, 9350. https://doi.org/10.1038/s41598-019-45601-5

18

Ensemble interaction in indeterminate music

A case study of Christian Wolff's *Exercises*

Emily Payne and Philip Thomas

Introduction

The exploration of social organization through the use of indeterminate notation has been a recurring concern of the music of experimental composer Christian Wolff (b. 1934) since the late 1950s. In 1973, he embarked upon a series of pieces titled *Exercises* for (mostly) unspecified instrumentation and numbers of players. Since then, he has returned to the title to extend the number of works to, currently, 37;[1] they are among his most frequently performed pieces. The notation Wolff employs in these pieces is skeletal and there are no separate parts: every musician reads from the same set of instructions and musical score. Consequently, players negotiate a way of working with the score and with each other, making decisions prior to, and during, the moment of performance. Orchestration, tempo, dynamics, sequence, coordination, and much else are all "up for grabs," and can differ radically from performance to performance. Consequently, the *Exercises* offer considerable potential for navigating approaches to ensemble interaction and for exploration of performance possibilities. Exactly how these possibilities are exercised in practice is the focus of this case study.

Exercises performed by Apartment House

The case study addressed in this chapter is a recording session that took place in London on March 21–24, 2017, in which the ensemble Apartment House (with whom Philip Thomas plays the piano) combined a selection of different *Exercises* from the earliest to some of the most recent.[2] The session was conceived as a professional (rather than research) project, resulting in a CD recording. It was observed and video recorded by Emily Payne, who undertook subsequent interviews and stimulated recall sessions with the musicians.[3] An interview was undertaken with Wolff in the months after the

---

[1] A number of additional pieces include the word in their title, such as *Winter Exercise* (2013) and *Apartment House Exercise* (2002). For a more detailed account of Wolff's small ensemble music, see Fox (2010).

[2] Apartment House is an experimental music ensemble founded in 1995 under the leadership of Anton Lukoszevieze. See Lukoszevieze and Fox (2016) for an interview with Lukoszevieze about the group's history and performance ethos.

[3] Stimulated recall is a method whereby participants view or listen to recorded material during an interview and are invited to comment on any aspects that seem noteworthy to them (see, for example, Clarke et al., 2016). All interviews were transcribed and analyzed using thematic analysis (Braun & Clarke, 2012) to identify emergent themes.

Emily Payne and Philip Thomas, *Ensemble interaction in indeterminate music* In: *Together in music.* Edited by: Renee Timmers, Freya Bailes, and Helena Daffern, Oxford University Press. © Oxford University Press 2022. DOI: 10.1093/oso/9780198860761.003.0018

Table 18.1 Overview of empirical material collected during the project

Date	Event	Location	Data	Personnel
March 21, 2017–March 24, 2017	Recording session	Craxton Studios, London	Audiovisual	Apartment House, Simon Reynell (sound recordist), EP
June 29, 2017	Interview	School of Music, University of Leeds, Leeds	Audio	Christian Wolff, EP, PT
August 22, 2017	Interview and stimulated recall session	New Cross, London	Audio	Mira Benjamin, EP
August 28, 2017	Stimulated recall session	Sheffield	Text[a]	PT
September 22, 2003	Interview and stimulated recall session	Oxford	Audio	Christopher Redgate, EP

[a] For reasons of time, Thomas was not interviewed in person but watched the video footage and made notes during and immediately after each take. He did not listen to Benjamin's interview before doing this, nor did he read any of Payne's notes on her observations.

session (see Table 18.1 for an overview of the empirical material collected during the project).[4]

Our discussion focuses in particular on *Exercise 4*, of which four takes were recorded by Thomas (PT; piano), Christopher Redgate (CR; oboe), and Mira Benjamin (MB; violin) on March 22, 2017.

The notation for *Exercise 4* (see Fig. 18.1) is minimal, with a number of parameters unspecified, e.g. clefs, tempo, articulation, dynamics, and timbre. The rhythmic beaming is suggestive of phrasing, but Wolff provides no instructions regarding its interpretation. Indeed, aside from the directive "must" in the final sentence, the accompanying instructions read more like gentle suggestions than a prescribed approach:

> In general the point of reference, where more than one player plays the same material (the normal situation), is unison. But, as rhythm and speed, articulation, amplitude, colour, and modes of playing are all flexible, any player may try to establish what the point of reference for unison is at any point in the course of playing. If, however, a movement by a player, say, in the direction of faster is not generally picked up by the rest, he must return to the prevailing speed. (Wolff, 1974, p. 1)

Wolff's words are indicative of a concern with the social relations of performance, and a reluctance to subscribe to the hierarchies that conventionally condition chamber music performance. But what does it mean for performance to say that unison is a "point of reference," rather than the primary shared intention that is typically assumed to underpin group music-making? Where do the limits lie, and what makes for a "successful" performance?

---

[4] The project received ethical approval from the School of Music, Humanities and Media at the University of Huddersfield. Informed consent was provided by all participants before data collection commenced.

Figure 18.1 Christian Wolff: *Exercise 4*
Edition Peters No. 66589
© 1974 by C. F. Peters Corporation, New York
Reproduced by permission of Peters Edition Limited, London

The trio did not rehearse before recording, and throughout the recording session, no single performer took a lead; instead there were moments when the musicians operated as individuals, in pairs, or more collectively. The first take was characterized by confusion and hesitation, and was followed by a brief conversation between the players. However, very little was said after this, rather the "discussion" took place in the playing itself. As Thomas commented at the beginning of the session, "We could try and make some decisions as to who plays what, or we could just play actually, and see what happens." In the following sections, we identify three different forms of interaction in the musicians' playing as they engaged with Wolff's notation: working responsively, independently, and emergently. We conclude by reflecting on what these ways of working might bring to discussions of ensemble performance.

Working responsively

Take two of *Exercise 4* began in a fairly coordinated manner, with the trio breathing together before synchronous entries from Redgate and Benjamin, followed shortly by Thomas. A steady tempo was maintained throughout the performance, with few sudden shifts in speed, apart from some occasional accelerations from Thomas. Benjamin and Redgate sometimes matched each other's articulation with *pizzicato* or *staccato*, respectively, and occasionally slowed down together on particular phrases. Benjamin and Redgate finished synchronously with a brief smile at one another, with Thomas finishing soon after. Thomas felt that take two was more cohesive than their previous playing, commenting on watching the footage that it "shows more signs of listening to each other, and greater confidence. There's more playfulness with the interaction of lines, and at the same time less trying to muck around with the sound." A specific example of Benjamin responding to Redgate by matching her sound to his playing occurred about halfway through the second take where, having been playing in a legato manner, Redgate began line 5 with *staccato* articulation and at a soft dynamic, and Benjamin echoed him with gentle *pizzicato*. Similarly, Redgate reflected that at the beginning of this take, he was seeking a sound that would not be too strong in character and would blend with Benjamin's. Watching the footage, he commented:

> [A]n obvious modification I could have done was to flutter tongue here. The problem with flutter, especially down there, it tends to be very loud and dominating, so I rejected it. Because I wanted to get into her sound world, but I realised that I couldn't do it with the flutter. It would just be too overpowering [. . .].

Benjamin characterized this take as "chamber music," and Redgate's reflections certainly suggest a concern with cohesion and the ensemble's collective sound.

Working independently

In contrast to the cooperative strategies described above, there were instances of the musicians making decisions to modify the material in unexpected ways, apparently independently from, rather than in response to, one another. In take one, Redgate introduced some trills, afterwards asking the others for their feedback:

Talking about modifying things: what do you think about, because on the line you [Benjamin] have got lovely *pizzicato*, you've got the harmonics, and all the different bow things. Do you think trills and trems are allowed? Once or twice I was picking bits and tremming two notes.

Thomas and Benjamin agreed to Redgate's suggestion, and in take two, Redgate employed this technique more frequently, particularly around repeated dyads, e.g. at the beginning of line 3. He repeated this approach in all subsequent takes.

For Benjamin, too, opportunities for independent decision-making lay in timbre, but she took quite a different approach to Redgate, playing *pizzicato* throughout take four. Her decision to employ this technique was conceived of, and applied separately from, any consideration of the others. As she commented in interview: "I love being surprised by what's coming up. So 'OK, I'm just going to do *pizz.* for the entire thing.'" Thomas later reflected on the effect that Benjamin's decision had on how he experienced the piece, and on the performance as a whole:

Mira's decision to play entirely *pizz.* was canny – it made everything slow down a little (although the full performance was not slower) and highlighted the canonic potential in the piece. It also I think made both Chris and myself listen more carefully, aware that Mira's playing changed the character (pace, volume, articulation) of the piece.

Working emergently

The moments of interaction discussed so far have been focused on decisions made by the musicians, but there was an episode in take one of *Exercise 4* that unfolded somewhat less predictably. About halfway through the take, Redgate and Benjamin (reading the score in treble clef) played the repeated D4 figure halfway through line 4 quite freely; then Thomas entered assertively with the same phrase but read in the bass clef as F2; by that point, Redgate and Benjamin had reached the beginning of line 6 and played the first two phrases in unison, and because they played an F4, it sounded like an echo of Thomas. Watching back over the footage, Benjamin reflected on the serendipity of this interaction:

[Sometimes] you notice that something has happened and then you decide to try and keep that going a little bit. [...] You realise, "Hey that was really cute what just happened", or "That was a wonderful sound, I'm going to try and make it last". And then as soon as you try to make it last it starts to deflate and then it leaves, but it's these little experiences of liking what you hear. [...] So right there we landed on this F really loudly, together, totally by accident at the same time. That was quite fun, and I think what follows is that little moment.

"Collaborative emergence" describes a phenomenon in ensemble performance whereby unpredictable outcomes are determined by the group as a whole rather than any single individual; to use a well-worn phrase that tends to be most often used in relation to improvised ensemble interaction, "the whole is the greater than the sum of the parts" (Sawyer, 2003, p. 11;

see also Chapter 1). In these indeterminate circumstances, despite the presence of music notation, the unexpected outcome is one of momentary coordination, rather than innovation, where Redgate and Benjamin seemed to pair up and respond to Thomas spontaneously. This moment of interaction was not repeated in any of the subsequent takes.

Conclusion

The above brief episodes––some of which only lasted for a few seconds––only scratch the surface of the kinds of interactions going on in the session, but they demonstrate how the players responded to the situation and to Wolff's notation in radically different ways across takes. The distribution of creative authority was neither uniform nor static within the ensemble, with the performers moving between different kinds of interaction: sometimes working responsively or independently, sometimes in pairs or emergently as a collective. The notation acts like something of a puzzle to be solved in the moment, or rather, given there are infinite solutions, a provocation to act, to create (as also discussed in Chapter 2). Like the Apartment House musicians, some performers might opt not to talk about anything but just to dive straight in and play, and then play again; others might engage in prolonged conversation about possibilities and what might and might not "work." Wolff (1984/2017, p. 85) has written that the notation is one element in a conversation "before the fact:" it provides a text for musicians to work with, setting out limits, possibilities, rules, and choices. The score is upheld as facilitating work to be done, discussions to be had, and solutions to be proposed, discarded, subverted, and enacted. As Wolff reflected during interview, "exercise"––understood as both noun and verb––is particularly apposite as a title: "to try out […] not necessarily an end in themselves." Processes of interaction and exchange are granted an importance equal to, and quite possibly greater than, the end result. People get lost playing, or there might be points at which no one plays–– confusion and disruption can be a feature of this music. Wolff's *Exercises* thus prompt a rethinking of what it means to play together: cooperation is necessary, but the resultant ensemble interaction might be characterized by uncertainty, surprise, or even complete breakdown.

Acknowledgments

We are grateful to Christian Wolff and Apartment House for their participation in this research project.

References

Braun, V., & Clarke, V. (2012). Thematic analysis. In H. Cooper, P. M. Camic, D. L. Long, A. T. Panter, D. Rindskopf, & K. J. Sher (Eds.), *APA handbook of research methods in psychology* (Vol. 2, pp. 57–71). American Psychological Association.

Clarke, E., Doffman, M., & Timmers, R. (2016). Creativity, collaboration and development in Jeremy Thurlow's *Ouija* for Peter Sheppard Skærved. *Journal of the Royal Musical Association*, *141*(1), 113–65.

Fox, C. (2010). Exercising the ensemble: Some thoughts on the later music of Christian Wolff. In Thomas, P., & Chase, S. (Eds.), *Changing the system: The music of Christian Wolff* (pp. 125–39). Ashgate.

Lukoszevieze, A., & Fox, C. (2016). 20 years of Apartment House: Anton Lukoszevieze in interview with Christopher Fox. *Tempo*, *70*(275), 78–82.

Sawyer, K. (2003). *Group creativity: Music, theater, collaboration*. Lawrence Erlbaum Associates.

Wolff, C. (1974). *Exercises [1–14]: For any number of instruments*. Edition Peters.

Wolff, C. (1984/2017). On notation. In C. Wolff, *Occasional Pieces: Writings and Interviews, 1952–2013* (p. 85). Oxford University Press.

19

Using performance sociograms to investigate inter-performer relationships in music ensembles

Christoph Seibert

Introduction

A crucial aspect of joint music performance is the experiential relationship between co-performers. However, assessing the mutual experience of musicians during their performance on stage involves methodological challenges for balancing data quality against invasiveness. This chapter introduces the use of performance sociograms as a method to visualize and investigate relationships between musicians. A case study with a contemporary music ensemble exemplifies a methodological approach that provides insights on a phenomenological level by minimally affecting the performance itself.

Originally developed by Moreno (1934) as a method to describe and visualize the structure of interpersonal relations in a group situation, a sociogram is a network plot with nodes representing individuals and edges representing interpersonal relations. Relationships are characterized based on quantitative or qualitative data, for example in terms of valence and directionality, which are visualized using distinctive colors or other graphical elements. Within the context of joint music performance, a sociogram can be applied to display various aspects of the relationships between co-performers. This chapter illustrates the use of performance sociograms and discusses their potential for research on ensemble performance.

Method

Participants of the study were the eight members of a newly formed contemporary music ensemble (aged 26–36; three females, five males) who were enrolled in an academic program for contemporary music ensemble playing. A ninth musician withdrew from the program and was replaced by a substitute who took part in the research concerts without participating in the study.

The ensemble performed three identically programmed concerts throughout the year, featuring three contemporary pieces. Iannis Xenakis' *Plektó*, 1993 (for seven musicians—flute, clarinet, piano, percussion, violin, cello, and conductor) was the final piece and the focus of the current analysis. All concerts were preceded by a dress rehearsal and performed in the same small chamber music hall with an audience.

Christoph Seibert, *Using performance sociograms to investigate inter-performer relationships in music ensembles* In: *Together in music*. Edited by: Renee Timmers, Freya Bailes, and Helena Daffern, Oxford University Press. © Oxford University Press 2022.
DOI: 10.1093/oso/9780198860761.003.0019

Directly after the performance of each piece, during the dress rehearsals and the concerts, the musicians filled out a questionnaire with closed and open-ended questions. The topics addressed in the questionnaire that are part of the analysis presented in this chapter include:

- The quality of the ensemble's performance;
- The communication within the ensemble during performance;
- The atmosphere within the ensemble during performance;
- The quality of the individual's performance;
- The quality of the individual's preparation for the performance;
- Unique and critical moments during the performance;
- An as detailed as possible description of the individual's experience during the performance (inter alia with co-performers as one given aspect on which to focus).

During the two days following each concert, interviews were conducted with each musician, in which their concert experience was explored and their questionnaire answers discussed further. The interviews were audio recorded and lasted between 25 and 144 minutes (mean: 53 minutes). In the final interview, they were asked to draw a sociogram reflecting their relationships with co-performers during the performance of *Plektó* in the third concert. They were given colored pencils and a template showing the relative positions of members of the ensemble (see Fig. 19.1).

The data (six questionnaires and three interviews per musician) were analyzed using qualitative content analysis alongside the performance sociograms. Several steps of data analysis were conducted. An initial analysis of the questionnaire data generated a set of keywords (e.g. "contact," "connection," name of a co-performer's instrument, name of a co-performer), which were used to filter the data and extract relevant references. Subsequently, extracted passages were sorted in accordance with the specified communicative relation (*who* is saying something about *whom*, e.g. Musician 1 mentions Musician 5, Musician 3 mentions the ensemble as a whole).

Thematic categories were identified from these processed data to capture the different characterizations of co-performer relations. Categories were developed using a process of subsumption and refinement, i.e. adding new categories up to a satisfactory degree of saturation and selectivity (Schreier, 2012, p. 115ff). All data-driven categories were found to have an evaluative character. Scaled sub-categories were generated to specify these evaluations using an ordinal scale from 1 (very negative) to 5 (very positive). These scales were used to define the valence of the relations between co-performers, which was plotted in the performance sociograms as described below. The resulting categories and the coding framework are presented in Table 19.1. Two researchers independently coded all the material in line with the coding framework, with discussion of discrepancies to achieve consensus.

Performance sociograms were generated to interpret and visualize the data (see Fig. 19.1). Circles indicate the positions of the musicians, and a rectangle specifies the position of the conductor. Red, dashed red, gray, dashed green, and green arrows indicate the valence of the relation to a co-performer on a five-point scale from very negative to very positive. To define valence, all evaluative sub-categories of the coded passages associated with the corresponding dyad and concert were taken into account. Rather than taking a simple average, a weighted mean across evaluative codings was used alongside interpretation of the passage itself. Similarly, directionality of the communication was determined after interpreting relevant passages in the qualitative data. Bidirectional arrows indicate that the contact was somehow confirmed by the co-performer in question, and unidirectional arrows indicate that it was not confirmed. No arrows indicate that a co-performer was not experientially present for the participant, or that they simply were not mentioned. When these basic graphical elements were not sufficient to convey the performance situation according to the data, additional graphical elements were used (see Fig. 19.1, Musician 4, Concert 1). Example results for two musicians are presented in results as a proof of concept of the method. Each performance sociogram provides a view on the respective performance situation from an individual musician's perspective. Beyond that, the comparison of several sociograms provides insights into the difference between individuals in one concert and individual developments from concert to concert.

Results

As a result of the qualitative content analysis, four core themes emerged from the participants' statements about the individual experiences concerning the relation to co-performers: contact, performance, way of playing, and affect. Descriptions of these main categories and example references for the evaluative sub-categories are presented in Table 19.1.

These main categories were considered in the course of the generation of performance sociograms by means of the scaled sub-categories. The sociograms generated by the musicians in their final interview could be used to validate the data-driven sociograms for the third concert. To demonstrate the use of performance sociograms, those derived from the perspective of Musician 4 and Musician 8 are presented here (see Fig. 19.1).

In the performance sociogram generated for the first concert for Musician 4, she seems isolated from the rest of the ensemble, as indicated by a dashed red circle surrounding her. This can be grounded by relevant passages of the qualitative data: "I was paying attention to rhythm and cues … but I was concentrated on myself than rather paying attention to the ensemble"[1] (Musician 4, Concert 1). She chose an individual strategy for her performance and tried to maintain a high level of energy without breaking the line. In doing so, she rather blended out the other players and was just in rudimentary contact with the conductor (Musician 6).

The performance sociogram for Concert 2 indicates a wider focus, even if still selective. There are four positively valenced dyads associated with co-performers that were present for her and had a positive affective impact. "Some were very present for me, providing a feeling of safety and confidence" (Musician 4, Concert 2). The same relations are displayed in the data-driven sociogram of Concert 3. These are confirmed by the musician's self-created sociogram, which, although indicating connections with all performers, indicates more positively valenced connections with the same performers.

The performance sociograms for Musician 8 provide another perspective. The one generated for Concert 1 exhibits only very negative connections to the co-performers, which are observed in the qualitative data: "No one is listening, they are all just playing for themselves" (Musician 8, Concert 1). She was frustrated and annoyed, since no one seemed to play as it

---

[1] All quotations in the main text and in Table 19.1 were translated by the author, except those of Musician 6 as they were already in English.

Table 19.1 Categories and coding framework of qualitative data

Category	Description	Generalized example	Evaluative sub-categories (poles of scale)	Example
Contact	Evaluation of contact with co-performer	"The contact within the ensemble/to co-performer Y while playing was like X."	(1) Very negative	"… on Musician 5 I can … [4s] I can hardly say anything, actually, [2s] Um, [3s] because I am disregarding him, which I'm not proud of [laughing]." (Musician 1, Concert 3)
			(5) Very positive	"Great contact with Musician 4." (Musician 1, Concert 2)
Performance	Evaluation of performance quality	"I evaluate/describe the ensemble's/co-performer Y's performance as X."	(1) Very negative	"Musician 2 is not safe." (Musician 8, Concert 1)
			(5) Very positive	"[The ensemble's performance] was very intensive and concentrated and musical" (Musician 6, Concert 2)
Way of playing	Evaluation of style, expression, and interpretation	"There was a specific way of playing of the ensemble or individual co-performer Y that affected me in a certain manner."	(1) Very negative	"The vibrato is bothering me a lot." (Musician 1, Concert 2)
			(5) Very positive	"Musician 10 is very attentive." (Musician 5, Concert 2)
Affect	Affective responses to other(s)	"I had a certain feeling/ I was in a specific mood with regard to what was going on during the performance."	(1) Very negative	"[T]here was a lot of stress in the air, [2s] and not everyone can deal with it equally well." (Musician 8, Concert 3)
			(5) Very positive	"[The atmosphere within the ensemble during performance could be characterized as] well concentrated, right tension and a feeling of trust." (Musician 6, Concert 3)

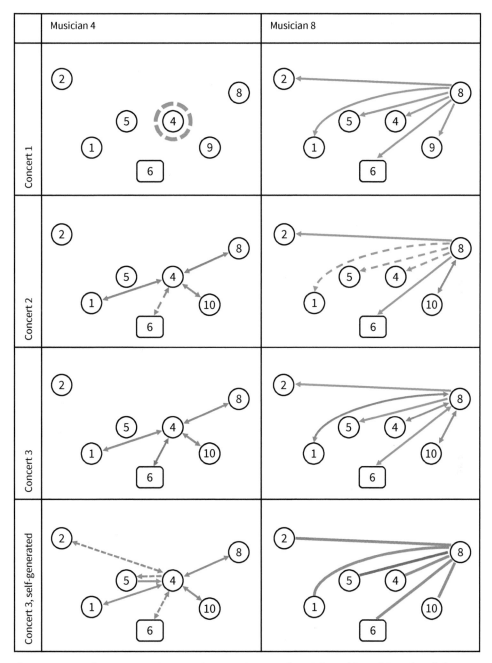

Figure 19.1 Performance sociograms for Musician 4 and Musician 8 (data-driven for all three concerts and self-generated after the third concert). Numbers correspond to the participants. Circle = musician position; rectangle = conductor position. Red, dashed red, gray, dashed green, and green arrows indicate the valence of the relation to a co-performer from very negative to very positive. Bidirectional or unidirectional arrows indicate confirmation of contact by the co-performer. No arrows = a co-performer was not experientially present or was not mentioned. Additional graphical elements were based on qualitative data (see Musician 4, Concert 1).

had been agreed upon during the rehearsals. She was well prepared and performed quite well (according to her self-reports) but had no chance to support her co-performers and could not connect with them.

The performance sociogram for Concert 2 indicates a very positively valenced connection with the substitute Musician 10. In contrast, the connections to all other co-performers remain negative, particularly to Musicians 2 and 6. "Musician 10 was wonderful. [2s] Well, we had an incredible amount of contact, that was nice. Very very nice. [...] And for example, Musician 2 is always such a precarious issue [...]" (Musician 8, Concert 2).

The data-driven sociogram of the third concert indicates that Musician 8 had very positively valenced contact with Musicians 1, 4, and 10, whereas there was explicitly no good connection to the other musicians. In comparison, the self-created sociogram gives a more positive impression. Here, except for the neutrally characterized contact with Musician 5, the relation to all co-performers was very positive.

As demonstrated by these two examples, performance sociograms provide an effective tool to illustrate individual and context-dependent characteristics of inter-performer relationships. In addition, for each performer, they are able to indicate changes in the individual experience of co-performer relations from concert to concert. The self-generated sociograms from these two examples appeared to be more positively valenced than the corresponding data-driven ones.

Discussion

In this chapter, performance sociograms have been presented as a tool to visualize and investigate relationships between musicians during ensemble performance as they are subjectively experienced. This section discusses their value in the light of the method and the example results presented here.

Performance sociograms reduce a large amount of data to a condensed, but informative visual representation. However, they are based on interpretations of the data and should be transparent with regard to their context. The plotted structure of interpersonal relations is dependent on the research question, the study design, and the methods used for data collection and analysis. These aspects are a constitutive part of performance sociograms and must be reported along with them. In the study presented here, the categories that constitute the performance sociograms (see Table 19.1) are informed by the interpretation of coded passages to extract the meaning of the visual representation. For instance, the representation of Musician 4 as an isolated individual in their sociogram for Concert 1 (see Fig. 19.1) is understood as a conscious use of a specific performance strategy once the qualitative data are considered.

Although a single performance sociogram might contain rich information, in general, the relations between multiple performance sociograms are particularly valuable. There are several possibilities for comparative analyses: between individuals, between points of measurement, or differentiated with regard to diverse categories or themes revealed by a qualitative content analysis. By considering sociograms of multiple performers over several performances, this study captures the differing perspectives of musicians' relations as experienced during the same performances: while Musician 4 started with a highly individual approach and subsequently expanded her focus, Musician 8 started with a wide focus and was trying to gain contact with her co-performers, gaining in success over performances.

In the study presented here, performance sociograms have been created by the musicians themselves for data generation, in addition to being used as a tool for data analysis and presentation. Beyond providing validation for sociograms based on data analysis, self-generated sociograms might be a useful pedagogical tool that invites musicians to reflect on communicative structures within the ensemble and help to make them explicit.

Conclusion

Performance sociograms might serve as a powerful tool for ensemble performance analysis and data assessment that can be adapted for use within several research contexts and musical practices. They offer the possibility to go beyond existing models of ensemble communication that have primarily focused on behavioral measures such as synchronization, gesturing, and eye contact, and include the systematic investigation of subjective phenomenological aspects of inter-performer relationships. Sociograms are able to integrate qualitative and quantitative data and can be combined with a variety of methods from ethnography to computational approaches.

Acknowledgments

I would like to thank the editors for their helpful comments, my colleagues and the staff members at the Max Planck Institute for Empirical Aesthetics who supported this study, Ari Kanemaki for assisting in the qualitative content analysis, and the ensemble for their cooperativeness and openness.

References

Moreno, J. L. (1934). *Who shall survive?: A new approach to the problem of human interrelations.* Nervous and Mental Disease Publishing Co.

Schreier, M. (2012). *Qualitative content analysis in practice.* Sage.

20

Together in cyberspace

Collaborative live coding of music

Ryan Kirkbride

Introduction

Technology has developed at an increasing rate since the turn of the twentieth century and its utility in music has become ever more present and impactful. The digital age has given rise to new methods for recording, creating, and even listening to music. It has also enabled new forms of musical interaction between performers that challenge the traditional conventions of ensemble performance. One practice that has emerged relatively recently, in terms of the history of music, is live coding, the improvised creation of electronic music through algorithms written live during performance. Typically, a live coder will project their screen for an audience and begin writing computer code to define some properties of the musical performance, such as rhythm, pitch, or a filter that affects timbre. While an algorithm is running, a live coder will adjust these properties to their liking based on what they hear. In contrast to more traditional forms of computer programming, in which code must be saved, compiled, and then run, this is all happening simultaneously as part of a performance. Live coding is still a new and developing practice and many more technologies for performing in this way are created every year. This case study introduces the collaborative live coding editor Troop[1] and examines its effect on musical interaction within ensemble live coding through live performance and user evaluation.

Motivation

The focus on improvisation in live coding draws many comparisons to improvised jazz music as each performance is typically unique (Magnusson, 2014). Research suggests that jazz audiences want "to be close to the musicians, see them interact with each other and see them play as clearly as they could hear them" (Brand et al., 2012, p. 9), which suggests that seeing the creative interactions accounts for as much of its appeal as the music itself. However, the performative actions of laptop musicians are far more often heard as opposed to seen: "At its most paradoxical the 'laptop performer' may move little and think a lot: the clues of will, choice, and intention will be inferred from the sounding flow or through apparent responses to the sounds of other performers" (Emmerson, 2007, p. 112).

---

[1] https://github.com/Qirky/Troop

Ryan Kirkbride, *Together in cyberspace* In: *Together in music*. Edited by: Renee Timmers, Freya Bailes, and Helena Daffern, Oxford University Press. © Oxford University Press 2022. DOI: 10.1093/oso/9780198860761.003.0020

Live coders attempt to combat these issues by projecting their screens for the audience, which gives them a visual "representation of what occurs in the sonic domain" (Magnusson, 2011) (see Chapter 14 for a discussion on musicianship in live coding and "humanizing" this process). Projecting code is made more difficult, however, when multiple performers wish to display their screen as part of collaborative performances and audiences are not often privy to the musical exchanges that take place as a result. There are many existing interfaces for collaborative live coding that allow users to share timing information, such as TidalCycles (McLean & Wiggins, 2010), as well as code, such as Extramuros (Ogborn et al., 2015) and The Republic (de Campo, 2014). However, many of these systems do not enable performers to collaborate directly within the same code, especially in a way that is visible to audiences. The primary motivation for developing the Troop interface was to provide performers with a method for writing code together enabling them to interact in a meaningful way and share with the audience the creative interactions that take place during improvised performance.

Troop: An interface for collaborative live coding

Troop is a shared live-coding text editor that allows multiple users to write code simultaneously within the same text buffer. It can be used with multiple live-coding languages, such as SuperCollider and TidalCycles, allowing users to create a variety of music, ranging from electroacoustic to dance music. It is one of several projects developed as part of the present author's practice-led-research PhD in collaborative live coding (Kirkbride, 2020), funded by the White Rose College of the Arts and Humanities (WRoCAH).

Troop uses an operational transformation algorithm similar to those used in popular collaborative word processing programs, such as Google Docs, which allows code to be entered with almost no lag and ensures that the text is identical for every connected user. Troop uses a client–server model to function; a single instance of the server application resides on a computer accessible over a network, such as the Internet or local Wi-Fi, and users connect to it using the client application. The server application keeps track of the "master" version of the text and passes important information, such as keystroke and mouse clicks, to each connected client.

Over the course of a performance, the text buffer naturally begins to fill up as more code is written by performers. With multiple collaborators, it would not always be possible to separate the individual contributions and it becomes unclear as to whom has written what, even to the performers themselves. This problem was identified by Xambó et al. (2016, p. 6), stating there is a challenge in "identifying how to know what is each other's code, as well as how to know who has modified it." To allow both audiences and performers to differentiate performers' code, each user is given a different colored font and named label mapped to the location of their text cursor (see Fig. 20.1). This allows performers to leave visible traces of their work throughout the communal text. This is an example of one of Donald Norman's user-centered design principles: using technology "to make visible what would otherwise be invisible, thus improving feedback and the ability to keep control" (Norman, 1998, p. 192). Editing another performer's code interweaves both their font colors and also their thought processes, creating a lasting visual testament to a collaborative process.

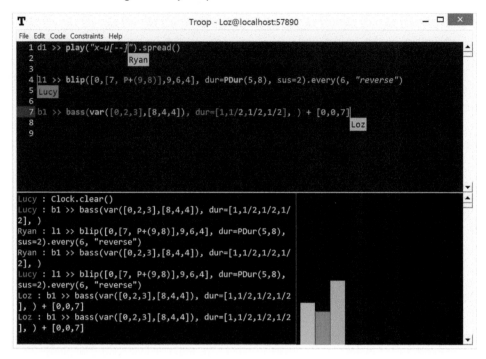

Figure 20.1 Screenshot of the Troop interface with three connected users.

User evaluation

Throughout Troop's development, it has been used in performance by The Yorkshire Programming Ensemble (TYPE),[2] a group of live coders, including the present author, based in the north of England, that perform improvised experimental dance music. This case study aims to evaluate the Troop interface using criteria defined by Gifford et al. (2017): the notion of "trust" in the interface, the ability to achieve "flow," and the sense of "immediacy." As part of the research carried out by Kirkbride (2020), members of TYPE were interviewed together and asked to evaluate Troop with these in mind. When asked about "trust," the group was more concerned about trust in their co-performers as opposed to the interface itself:

> I guess the trust level is more about how we play together. I feel like something that's really nice about Troop is that I can see what everyone else is working on really easily. [...] So it's really immediate in that sense. I can see exactly what everyone is up to and then I can, in terms of taking risks, try stuff out I know when it's an appropriate time. (P1)

Furthermore, this sense of trust and familiarity was developed through regular rehearsals, which mostly took place over the Internet: "[Troop] also allowed us to practice together loads in a really low-maintenance and low-effort way, which has enabled us to build that trust up" (P1).

---

[2] https://typeensemble.wordpress.com/

Trust between ensemble members is very important in improvisation and this holds true for live coding. Interestingly, Troop seems to strengthen the level of trust between performers by giving them a real-time overview of the process of coding and helps inform performers' creative decisions, such as when musical changes should be introduced. Practicing together over the Internet also enabled them to develop trust as they were able to do so more frequently than if they'd had to rehearse in person. When asked whether Troop helped or hindered them in achieving flow, members of TYPE felt they did not necessarily achieve an individual sense of flow, but the trust in their co-performers helped them stay in the moment:

> Compared to when I'm playing gigs on my own, if something goes wrong when I'm playing with TYPE, it takes me out of it less because it's easier to recover because there are more of us. [...] You guys can help fix it and recover and turn it round. It's partly to do with Troop because obviously we're all working together and we can all support each other [...] but I also think, from a confidence and capacity perspective, it's easier to stay in the flow and to keep things going with Troop compared to playing solo. I think that's a combination of the software and also just of the nature of playing with other musicians. (P1)

As opposed to achieving a sense of individual flow, it seems that TYPE were experiencing "group flow" (Sawyer, 2006) as a result of using Troop. This is when flow is achieved as a collective unit and "everything seems to come naturally; the performers are in interactional synchrony." This would also help explain why the members of TYPE did not worry when things went wrong during a performance in the same way they would when performing solo. Members of TYPE were also asked about the sense of immediacy Troop offered them in reacting to each other's musical changes:

> I find Troop pretty good for stuff like that because you can see what everybody's up to. So I can see if someone is creating a new player at the same time as me and I can kind of feed off that. (P1)

Being able to see code written in real time in the same text box meant that users were more cognizant of the musical changes being made by their co-performers and allowed them to be more proactive about their own musical decisions. Sawyer states that in group flow, "each of the group members can even feel as if they are able to anticipate what their fellow performers will do before they do it," which is exactly what is occurring here while using Troop.

Potential in pedagogy

While Troop has demonstrated its merit as a tool for performance, it also has some potential as a pedagogical tool. Music has been used as a useful teaching analogy for computer science in younger age groups, as demonstrated by software such as Scratch (Ruthmann et al., 2010) and Sonic-Pi (Aaron, 2016), and collaborative live coding can help move student thinking "from an individual to a social plane" (Xambó et al., 2016). Using Troop as a teaching tool would allow workshop leaders to write code to demonstrate specific functions and users could immediately change values and listen to how it affects the sound. In a typical workshop session, users must read the text from a screen or projector and write the code themselves, which becomes susceptible to syntax errors if even one character was copied incorrectly. A teacher would then have to visit each student with an error and go through the problem multiple times. Using Troop, however, would allow teachers and workshop leaders to address these issues quickly and directly using the program.

Conclusion

Using Troop as a medium for collaborative improvisation helped performers achieve group flow during live coding performance and created a sense of "interactional synchrony" between performers. Group flow "can inspire musicians to play things that they would not have been able to play alone, or that they would not have thought of without the inspiration of the group" (Sawyer, 2015, p. 95) and is an important part of successful group improvisation. Troop's ability to facilitate rehearsals over the Internet also helped performers rehearse more frequently and develop trust among the ensemble, which may have contributed to the increased sense of group flow. Troop is unique in that it necessitates working within the same textual material and consequently enables live coders to easily share and combine ideas to create novel musical sequences without separating coding and communication in the process.

References

Aaron, S. (2016). Sonic pi – performance in education, technology and art. *International Journal of Performance Arts and Digital Media*, *12*(2), 171–8. https://doi.org/10.1080/14794713.2016.1227593

Brand, G., Sloboda, J., Saul, B., & Hathaway, M. (2012). The reciprocal relationship between jazz musicians and audiences in live performances: A pilot qualitative study. *Psychology of Music*, *40*(5), 634–51.

de Campo, A. (2014). Republic: Collaborative live coding 2003–2013. *Dagstuhl Reports*, *3*(9), 152–3.

Emmerson, S. (2007). *Living electronic music*. Ashgate Publishing Ltd.

Gifford, T., Knotts, S., Kalonaris, S., & McCormack, J. (2017). Evaluating improvisational interfaces. In T. Gifford, S. Knotts, & E. McCormack (Eds.), *ICW2017: Proceedings of the Improvisational Creativity Workshop*.

Kirkbride, R. (2020). *Collaborative interfaces for ensemble live coding performance* [Doctoral dissertation]. University of Leeds.

Magnusson, T. (2011). Algorithms as scores: Coding live music. *Leonardo Music Journal*, *21*, 19–23.

Magnusson, T. (2014). Herding cats: Observing live coding in the wild. *Computer Music Journal*, *38*(1), 8–16.

McLean, A., & Wiggins, G. (2010). Tidal – pattern language for the live coding of music. *Proceedings of the 7th Sound and Music Computing Conference* (pp. 331–4).

Norman, D. A. (1998). *The design of everyday things*. MIT Press.

Ogborn, D., Tsabary, E., Jarvis, I., Cárdenas, A., & McLean, A. (2015). Extramuros: Making music in a browser-based, language-neutral collaborative live coding environment. *Proceedings of the First International Conference on Live Coding* (pp. 163–9).

Ruthmann, A., Heines, J. M., Greher, G. R., Laidler, P., & Saulters II, C. (2010). Teaching computational thinking through musical live coding in scratch. *Proceedings of the 41st ACM technical symposium on computer science education* (pp. 351–5).

Sawyer, R. K. (2006). Group creativity: Musical performance and collaboration. *Psychology of Music, 34*(2), 148–65.

Sawyer, R. K. (2015). Group creativity: Musical performance and collaboration. In R. Caines, & A. Heble (Eds.), *The improvisation studies reader: Spontaneous acts* (1st ed., pp. 87–100). Routledge.

Xambó, A., Freeman, J., Magerko, B., & Shah, P. (2016). Challenges and new directions for collaborative live coding in the classroom. *International Conference of Live Interfaces 2016* (pp. 65–73). REFRAME Books.

21

"Crystal clear" or "as clear as mud!"

Verbalized imagery as successful communication between singers and choir directors

Mary T. Black

Introduction

This case study examines the imagery which directors verbalize during rehearsals and how it affects what choir members sing. Based on data from PhD research which examined the roles of imagery in choral rehearsals, it presents a fresh exploration of the effectiveness of imagery as a communication tool and its ability to clarify director explanations.

Understanding imagery utilized in choral rehearsals

Verbal imagery is regularly employed in choral rehearsals, in which context it can be defined as "*an image, metaphor, analogy, simile or other figurative language, employed verbally by choral directors in rehearsals, to enhance explanations and whose function is to affect singers' responses*" (Black, 2015, p. xv). Directors include imagery with the intention of changing the response to a note, word, or phrase and learn its success through experience, as director Ken[1] noted: "I've found out what works and I use what works." Spitzer (2004, p. 99) explains how a change in response is enacted: "the imagery […] inspires thought; it sets into motion imaginative reflection." The imagery directors use sets in motion the singer's imagination of the sound to be produced, then the singer creates a sound related to that image.

Imagery enables explanation of two invisible aspects central to singing: firstly, the vocal mechanism. The complexity and variability of the voice combined with the part concealment and subconscious workings of the mechanism make description of the required vocal sound and its production seem impossible. However, directors need to attempt this so singers can create the type of sound the director seeks. (See also Chapter 4 for metaphorical expressions in string quartets.)

The second invisible aspect does not appear in the notation but is heard in the sung sound, often termed expression or interpretation. The second of Ortony's (1975, p. 48) theses of metaphor is extremely useful in this setting, making the invisible tangible: "metaphor enables the predication by transfer of characteristics which are unnameable." Ortony is not referring to a metronome mark for example, but to ideas and concepts and their inability to be described precisely. Director Sam provides an example: "I think a word like *dance* is good because it lifts it into a different kind of sphere and gets [them] to think about the physicality and dance-like

---

[1] Directors are anonymized; for further details, see Table 21.1.

Mary T. Black, *"Crystal clear" or "as clear as mud!"* In: *Together in music*. Edited by: Renee Timmers, Freya Bailes, and Helena Daffern, Oxford University Press. © Oxford University Press 2022. DOI: 10.1093/oso/9780198860761.003.0021

nature of the rhythms." Imagery creates a connection between the singer's vocal function and thought processes, emphasizing the important interaction between mind and physiology.

Summary of research

In order to explore the roles of imagery in choral rehearsals, a five-year investigation was undertaken. This employed a multi-method approach, using videoed observations, questionnaires, and interviews through which 21 directors and 332 choir members across 15 choirs contributed (see Table 21.1).

During the interviews, participants were shown short extracts of their previous rehearsal at a point where the choir sang a particular note, word, or phrase, and the director employed an image relating to that phrase, followed by another sung rendition of the phrase; participants were asked to compare pre- and post-imagery vocal responses. Interpretative phenomenological analysis was chosen as the most appropriate approach, as it is concerned with how participants make sense of their experiences, i.e. how they described any changes heard in their responses to the imagery.

A set of categories was devised[2] to define what vocal effect had been created by the singers; category titles are shown in Fig. 21.1.

A crucial aspect of the interviews was to discuss the vocal responses to the imagery in the rehearsal context, i.e. participants reflected on the sonic output. The image was examined alongside the phrase, note, etc., to which it related, rather than disconnecting it, analyzing the image alone. This is important for two reasons; firstly, the results of the imagery were the phenomena being evaluated, i.e. the effect on the vocal sound as determined using the categories. These are subjective judgments made by directors during rehearsals, based on their aural perceptions at that time, rather than analyzing audio files out of context.

The second reason is limitations in what can be explained in words, i.e. the singers' understanding of the imagery is expressed in sound. Criticism that imagery is ambiguous or imprecise, for example Miller (1998, pp. 41–2), frequently relates to verbal explanations of imagery without reference to the music or rehearsal context. However, it is not necessary for singers to recollect or explain specific words, to respond vocally, so this is irrelevant to normal rehearsals. Paivio and Begg (1981, p. 194) found that students had better "memory for meaning than memory for wording of linguistic material." This is extremely pertinent when referring to aspects of singing, for example *head voice* or *vocal line*, which may appear to amateur singers to be physically non-existent, though may become evident in vocal studios.

A lack of precision has been a particular obstacle for describing vocal technique, as demonstrated by decades of debate placing imagery in opposition to more scientific terms (Ware, 2013, p. 413). A persuasive compromise is provided by Ware (2013, p. 415), who proffers the term "anatomically informed imagery," meaning images based on scientific or technical principles, for example *column of air* to signify sub-glottal pressure.

Another objection to the use of imagery is that singers across the choir would provide different vocal responses. However, the choral setting is a communal context, so this almost guarantees differences in perception and vocal response. Each singer contributes their own

---

[2] Categories were developed during the research, but originally informed by Jacobsen (2004), among others, and trialled during initial stages.

Table 21.1 Participant information and types of data collected

Participants			Types of data collected			
Director code	Type of choir (see notes)	No. in choir[1]	Observations	Video recordings	Questionnaires	Interviews: group/ individual
Bill	V		✓			
Joe	ACS		✓			
Rob	C		✓	✓		
Sam	U	32	✓	✓	✓	Grp
Pete	AU	21	✓	✓	✓	Grp
Neil	C/U	8			✓	
Maria	C/U	6			✓	
Laura	U	8			✓	
Carla	U	10			✓	
Colin	U	16			✓	
Richie	AU	18			✓	
Lyn	AU	10			✓	
Val	C/U	10			✓	
Ant	AU	23			✓	
Gary	AU	19			✓	
Emma	AU	7	✓	✓	✓	5 grp, 12 individ
Ken	ACS	101	✓	✓	✓	
Tim	G	43	✓	✓	✓	
Walter	X/AU				✓	Individ
Paul	P				✓	Individ
Graham	AU				✓	Individ

Notes:

[1] Number contributing to research

Type of choir:

ACS, auditioned choral society; AU, auditioned university student; C, community; G, gospel; P, professional; U, university student; V, volunteer; X church.

Voice type:

All choirs were SATB, except Lyn SA; Emma S/S/A/A/T/Bar/B; Tim SAT.

(See Black (2015, pp. 227–31)).

interpretation of the imagery together with their distinct timbre. Even if a director's explanation is "crystal clear," singers will not produce identical responses to each other, whether or not imagery is used, though they may imitate each other. It is fundamental to the director's role to blend the vocal responses into the desired choral sound. (See Chapter 16 for details of choir acoustics.)

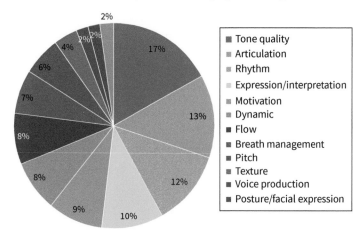

Figure 21.1 A pie chart showing categories of vocal effects in responses to 336 verbal imagery examples provided by directors in the research.

Responses to imagery and categories of vocal effect

It was expected that the research would show imagery was usually used to describe expression and interpretation. However, the data indicated that tone quality (including resonance, timbre, register, and tonal differences) was the most frequently encountered vocal effect, with 17% of 336 images, as opposed to 13% for expression (see Fig. 21.1). The second most frequently used category, articulation, included consonants, vowel shape or formation, glottal stops, diction, and pronunciation, for example Sam's comment, "did you hear the S of dress? It was like a pipe bursting!"

Further examples are provided in Table 21.2. It was especially true that imagery replaced technical terminology when directors were trying to counteract problems of the invisibility of the instrument.

In Example 1, Emma's focus was on matching the tone colors in her seven-voiced chamber choir. As a highly skilled and experienced singer, it was perfectly possible for her to have employed appropriate technical terms, for example head resonator, but she chose not to.

Director Tim had no vocal training and frequently used imagery, with fewer examples of technical vocabulary; Example 2 was his description of *head voice*. Director Ken had chosen to take vocal lessons in order to improve his understanding of technical vocabulary, though he frequently employed imagery, as in Example 3, which was clearly focused on a precise timbre.

Directors were asked specifically whether singers had achieved their intended effects and their answers were affirmative. Example 4 demonstrates this happened during the rehearsal and that singers had understood and remembered his image and associated effect. Directors are the sole arbiters of whether their intentions have been achieved by singers in rehearsals, so in this research, their judgments were relied upon.

Table 21.2 Examples of imagery

	Images describing tonal quality	Director (singer)
1	It's quite difficult to make your singing light, in order to blend.	Emma
2	That's a heavenly kind of voice.	Tim
3	Make that really strong, you know, very bell-like.	Ken
	Image understood and achieved by singers	
4	[Image: *Brow*] I want to feel that there's a real resistance at the beginning. Now sing that phrase again and think about that moment. [Choir sang whole phrase]. That's it!	Ken
	The transition between the B and R's a particularly difficult one, so I think he's trying to get across the difficulty of that; the B provides the resistance, making it trickier to get into the R.	Singer 4, Ken's choir (interview)
	Director's vocal knowledge	
5	I liken it to a car, the clutch, when you find the bite then the engine will really go with its full power.	Tim

Director communication in rehearsals

Director's vocal experience

As expected, the director's vocal knowledge and experience are vitally important in communicating the vocal effects to be achieved. In Tim's choir, there occurred several mismatches between Tim and his singers, or disagreement between singers, about what type of effect Tim was intending when using imagery. In Table 21.2, Example 5, Tim tried to explain swift phonation followed by instant air-flow at the beginning of a phrase, but his lack of vocal training led to confusion among some of his singers.

Singers should be able to rely on both their director's knowledge of the appropriate anatomy and physiology and more importantly on their vocal experience and ability to apply that knowledge. Only then will directors know exactly what they are trying to describe and how it can be produced. Jacobsen (2004, p. 30) stresses that "imagistic language can best support function [only] if one knows what the function is."

The appropriateness of the image is important; it must be remembered that directors are not producing the sound themselves but are helping singers create it. Directors need to know their singers in terms of their current and prior experience and abilities. A strong rapport can be developed when singers and director are well accustomed to each other; director Ken changed strategies and choice of language, depending on which choir he directed. Directors must also possess a sufficiently fluent and creative vocabulary to be able to communicate their requirements to the singers. This is essential, as Jacobsen (2004, p. 76) observes: "through study of voice science, vocal pedagogy and resultant imagery are based in technical and mechanistic vocal function to which creativity is applied."

Consistency of vocabulary

Clear communication will be aided if directors are consistent with images they use. This stems partly from directors trying to build conceptual understanding of difficult ideas with their singers. In one example, Tim used the word *sharp*, meaning alert and prepared for the next entry, rather than in relation to pitch. Later, he said, "It's slightly sharper, it cuts through the rhythm," referring to a focused tonal quality which allowed the word to be heard despite complex rhythms; this inconsistency is open to misinterpretation, especially with amateur singers.

Director's aural skills

During rehearsals, directors usually review singers' vocal responses and either amend or confirm as appropriate. This would be true whether the director's input was imagery or any other strategy.[3] This emphasizes the director's aural analysis skills, focused not only on error detection, but also on analyzing their singers' reaction to specific images and the vocal effect singers produced in that precise context. Directors need to be responsive in real time to the sounds they hear, enabling them to adapt promptly. Effective directors will understand that not everything they say and do will always be understood by everyone, nor the correct response produced by every singer, so they should employ a variety of images or strategies to counteract this. All directors in the research used imagery and stated it was *sometimes* or *very effective* (Black, 2015, p. 253). They employed it as a vital way of communicating with their singers, especially when attempting to create particular vocal effects.

Conclusion

There are two main points to emphasize here. Firstly, directors employed imagery to affect all categories of sound, for example rhythm or expression, but most frequently to influence tone quality. This does not correlate, however, with the reasons most directors gave for employing imagery, which were to inspire singers and to interpret the music (Black, 2015, p. 254). Secondly, directors found imagery to be a valid and useful strategy in helping them create the sounds they required and addressing hidden aspects of expressive singing. Directors continuously employed imagery as one of their strategies, using immediate aural assessments to check success. Several directors repeated images from one rehearsal to another, showing conviction of their efficacy. Other directors can therefore have confidence in employing imagery, knowing it can produce appropriate results. Many accepted terms, for example *legato* or *in the mask*, are also imagistic and open to a wide range of interpretations, so the complexities of interpreting directors' words are not restricted to imagery.[4]

---

[3] Strategies studied in the research included gesture, vocal demonstration, and technical explanations; for comparisons, see Black (2015, p. 116).

[4] See previous footnote.

Imagery can be influential in many ways, most importantly in developing singers' understanding of the concepts involved and in enabling singers to create and modify vocal sounds in response to their director's requests.

References

Black, M. T. (2015). *Let the music dance! The functions and effects of verbal imagery in choral rehearsals* [Doctoral dissertation]. University of Leeds.

Jacobsen, L. L. (2004). *Verbal imagery used in rehearsals by experienced high school choral directors: An investigation into types and intent of use* [Doctoral dissertation]. University of Oregon.

Miller, R. (1998). The reluctant student. *Journal of Singing, 54*(3), 41–3.

Ortony, A. (1975). Why metaphors are necessary and not just nice. *Educational Theory, 25,* 45–53.

Paivio, A., & Begg, I. (1981). *Psychology of language.* Prentice-Hall Inc.

Spitzer, M. (2004). *Metaphor and musical thought.* Chicago University Press.

Ware, R. (2013). The use of science and imagery in the voice studio. A study of voice teachers in the United States and Canada. *Journal of Singing, 69*(4), 413–17.

22

An historical perspective on ensemble performance

Asynchrony in early recordings of the Czech Quartet

Christopher Terepin

Introduction

In 1928, the Czech String Quartet, formerly known as the Bohemian Quartet, recorded the famous String Quartet Op.96 "American" by Antonin Dvorak. Founded in Prague in 1892, this ensemble had been at the forefront of Czech musical life for decades, as influential performers and teachers. They had also enjoyed a close connection with Dvorak until his death in 1904, and while there had been some changes in personnel by the time of recording, violinists and founder members Karel Hoffman and Josef Suk had both worked with the composer on his quartets. That this group was recorded affords us a tantalizing glimpse of an historically significant approach to ensemble performance.

There are, of course, limits on the knowledge one can reliably obtain from recordings, and especially those dating from the early twentieth century. One must be wary of the dangers of over-extrapolation on both technological and philosophical grounds; nonetheless, such sources raise many important questions. To what extent can evidence of historical performance styles help to nuance our understanding of normative ensemble practices? And more broadly, how does this kind of evidence relate to critical and theoretical discourses of performance? The following case study draws on the Czech Quartet's playing to explore the relationship between early twentieth-century style, music analysis, and differing values of "togetherness."

Early twentieth-century style

Hearing the Czech Quartet on record, one is immediately confronted with many of the paradigmatic stylistic features that scholars associate with early twentieth-century performance (https://www.youtube.com/watch?v=O8jhjYSRoh8). Such characteristics include unnotated tempo changes, detailed gradations of tone, abundant between-player asynchronies, frequent portamenti, and varied use of vibrato. Robert Philip (2004, p. 21) describes this group's approach to ensemble in particular as "what now seems a strange mixture of homogeneity and looseness, and with none of the modern ideas of control or precision." Their example thus fits neatly within a broadly accepted narrative of historical change, in which the "emotional-pictorial" (Leech-Wilkinson, 2009, p. 252) orientation of late nineteenth- and early twentieth-century styles was gradually superseded by the greater textual literalism

Christopher Terepin, *An historical perspective on ensemble performance* In: *Together in music.* Edited by: Renee Timmers, Freya Bailes, and Helena Daffern, Oxford University Press. © Oxford University Press 2022. DOI: 10.1093/oso/9780198860761.003.0022

and more rigorously hierarchical organizational schemes that characterized many later approaches to performance (though not all; see Fabian, 2015).

While Philip is careful to point out that there is nothing intrinsically superior about present styles, and that tastes have simply changed, the value attached to ensemble precision—and especially temporal synchronization—in the intervening years poses special challenges to understanding how this kind of performance might have made sense to contemporary performers and listeners. One of the most interestingly unfamiliar aspects of the Czech Quartet's playing is the apparent decoupling of large-scale shaping strategies such as tempo modification, which are quite easily understood as coordinated and intentional, from the seemingly irrational local fluctuations that Philip identifies. Against the backdrop of a modern discourse of ensemble performance that habitually elevates shared intentions, unified "interpretations," and quasi-telepathic connections between co-performers, the unusual synthesis in this group's playing—between sharply profiled collective gestures and an apparent disinclination towards the monitoring of group synchronization—demands special attention.

Some of the clearest examples of such a collective approach to large-scale shape can be found in the Czech musicians' performance of the Lento movement of Dvorak's Op.96. For instance, in two analytically parallel places (Fig. 22.1a (mm.49–57) and Fig. 22.1b (mm.68–76)), these players approach the climactic first inversion harmonies with a striking (and entirely un-notated) tempo variation of 30% in just three measures. Cellist Ladislav Zelenka begins to generate momentum in the pizzicato bassline (mm.52; mm.71); his colleagues respond enthusiastically, and within a few moments, they jointly conjure the strong impression of rolling down an incline. Arrival at the phrase's climax just two measures later (mm.54–55; mm.73–74) instigates an equally precipitous slowing, and with it a sense of broadening in multiple dimensions simultaneously. While this shape is conspicuously audible in both sections, its expressive effect is no mere duplicate, but is subtly distinguished between iterations. The second time, the peak tempo is perceptibly lower (quaver = 112 in mm.73, against the original quaver = 118 in mm.54), and the expressive quality of the melodic resolution is unmistakably transformed.

How are we to reconcile such cooperative and interventionist shaping with what appears, at best, to be profoundly inconsistent attention to the maintenance of ensemble? This may be a false dichotomy, informed more by modern assumptions about "good ensemble" than by any historical understanding of the potential expressivity of asynchronous timing. For while it is impossible to know the precise extent to which their playing remained stable over the decades, the performance witnessed by the following reviewer surely resembled the group's own recording(s) more closely than it did "modern" playing: "… they excel in a style of delicious refinement as well as a perfect mécanique and a discriminating sense of their various composers' texts … all went well and the ensemble was perfect" (A. M., 1899, p. 185).

It is a distinct possibility that consistent synchrony was not always a prerequisite for positive responses to ensemble performance, and that asynchronous nuance may once have been a marker of high sophistication. Given evidence of this kind, the once-standard framing of discussions of ensemble in terms of a value-laden binary (of maintenance against deviation) now appears as historically incurious as it is analytically limiting. (See Chapter 17 in this volume for further discussion.) It can be illuminating, then, to treat group synchronization not as a normative state but a spectrum: a complex and contingent variable that plays a role in shaping the "energetic and tensional morphologies" of performance (Cook, 2013, p. 93).

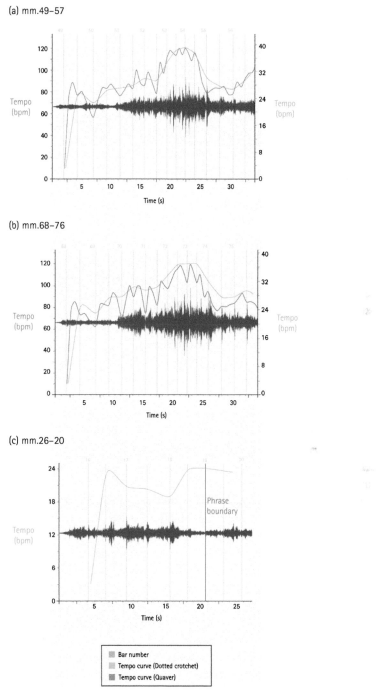

Figure 22.1 Dvorak: String Quartet in F Op.96, as performed by Czech String Quartet (1928): (a) mm.49–57; (b) mm.68–76; (c) mm.16–20.

Theory

In attempting to understand these practices, it will be useful briefly to situate ensemble within two broader models of change in performance style: Nicholas Cook's (2013, p. 70) recent distinction between "rhetorical" and "structuralist" concepts of performance, and an older discourse that postulated an opposition between the "vitalist" and the "geometrical" in art. "Vitalism" as an aesthetic category was drawn from a selection of nineteenth-century philosophical and scientific ideas which hypothesized the role of a "life force" in distinguishing life from non-life; in musical performance, it came to be associated with the projection of feeling states through (often significant and usually un-notated) fluctuations in tempo and intensity.[1] Cook's (2014, p. 19) observations about changes in piano playing offer a memorable touchstone for these stylistic contrasts:

> Pianists whose style was formed before the First World War aimed to draw the greatest possible emotion out of particular points in the music, resulting in a very detailed, even intricate style of performance that, from the mid-century perspective, must have seemed hopelessly cluttered in the same way as the antimacassars and knick-knacks of the Edwardian interior.

That there are striking parallels here with changes in ensemble performance suggests that we can get a little closer to understanding the Czech Quartet's playing if we regard the impulse towards constant synchronization as a specific, historically situated phenomenon—that is, as an archetypal feature of "geometrical style." Such a move would shift the character of ensemble discourse closer to that of keyboard playing, in which asynchronous "clutter" has reliably been afforded historical significance, despite considerable swings in the *critical* reception of those same practices. This curious sense of concurrency in pianistic reception has arguably been intensified still further by the turn towards "historically informed performance." By incentivizing players to experiment with styles previously considered obsolete (see Peres da Costa, 2012), this ideology has served further to complicate the already contentious relationship between historical curiosity and aesthetic value. Comparable work on asynchrony in ensembles, though similarly inspired by historical precedent, has until recently been considerably rarer, and this imbalance hints at some subtle (and historically traceable) variation in the values and beliefs that underpin these related musical subcultures.

Change in performance style also generates tensions with more abstract music-theoretical models. Cook notes of the pianist Eugen d'Albert (1864–1932), for instance, that the unevenness and irregularity of his "rhetorical" style is especially challenging because of the high esteem in which his musicianship was held by contemporary musical authorities, the theorist Heinrich Schenker among them. If the latter's theorizing, underpinned as it was by the search for deep order in the great works of tonal music, might seem in its structuralist rigor to exhibit a certain kinship with the new world of "geometrical" art, it is surely significant that his own concept of his analytical ideas' *application in performance* remained deeply entwined with the "vitalist" aesthetic and the now unfamiliar styles of performers like d'Albert (Cook, 2013, pp. 57–70). Similarly, more recent attempts to model the dynamics of musical performance

---

[1]   Richard Taruskin (1995, pp. 110–14) has drawn heavily on this historical dialectic in his well-known and extensive critique of "authenticist" performance ideology.

map less than cleanly onto pre-war styles, such as Todd's (1992) model of "phrase arching," which, in some ways, form a performative analog for the hierarchical organizational schemes of Schenkerian and post-Schenkerian analysis. That is not to say that there is no validity in such models, only that they should be thought of as appropriate to certain paradigms of how music sounds in performance. Taken together, these contexts suggest that there might indeed be ways of accounting for the Czech Quartet's style without imposing an opposition between a loose, cluttered surface and more "structural" shaping strategies (that appear to be more explicitly coordinated).

Asynchrony

What kind of function(s) might between-player asynchrony have served in the Czech Quartet's style, if we are to understand such asynchronies as part of an integrated performance aesthetic, at least in principle? In the absence of period ears, I focus on a potentially rewarding point of intersection between the irregular ebbs and flows of the "vitalist" conception and the more predictable "ball-throwing trajectories" of Todd's phrase arching model. This comparison may afford the modern observer a revealing, if historically anachronistic, window onto some potential expressive and structural functions of ensemble asynchrony.

The strophic structure of Dvorak's score is more than incidentally useful here, for it allows us to see how clear, notated boundaries are handled in this paradigmatically "rhetorical" style. At the close of the first main section (b.1–18), for instance, the norms of "structuralist" performance would likely yield a certain relaxation in tempo and dynamics, a conventional coupling of parameters which serves to clarify the division between "A" and "B" material. This kind of integrated lightening gesture constitutes a familiar strategy for structural articulation in modern(ist) performance. What is so interesting about the Czech Quartet's approach to this moment is that they too, like good structuralists, mark the phrase boundary by significantly releasing b.18. The difference is in the parameters: instead of linking tempo and dynamics, these musicians use a combination of *asynchrony and dynamic* to give the impression of lightness.

The effect actually starts in the previous measure (mm.17), when a large agogic accent in the cello melody results in a dislocation with the first violin of at least a quaver beat. By measure 18, all three upper voices have come apart, as the second violin rushes to catch up with the first, who continues to play unevenly, over-syncopating the rhythmic figure. The violins become synchronized only in the final moments of the phrase, by which time they have reached a considerably quieter dynamic—*but not a slower tempo*. This can be seen in Fig. 22.1c; the moment of transition does not yield the lowest point of the tempo curve, as might be considered normative in structuralist performance; in fact, their tempo here is both quicker and more consistent than at any other point in the phrase. By contrast, the arrival at the new material (mm.19) is marked by precise synchronization between all parts, the subtlest of portamenti from first violinist Karel Hoffman notwithstanding. Thus, the textural distinction between an asynchronous, diffuse "tail" of the old phrase (mm.18) and the precise, synchronous start of the new one (mm.19) also serves subtly to "mark" the boundary between sections.

Away from phrase boundaries, one can also hear some close correspondences between this ensemble style and the abundant, well-theorized asynchronies of early twentieth-century piano playing. Between mm.31–42, for instance, the Czech Quartet engages in some strikingly pianistic "contrapuntal" dislocation of lines, which it achieves by overlaying several clearly defined, contrasting rhythmic profiles: portentous, speech-like timing in the viola gestures, rubato and notes inégales in the second violin, and a soft-edged, quasi-vocal flexibility in violin and cello (epitomized by the delayed portamenti in mm.41). And the "accompanying" chords of the coda, alternately bowed and plucked by the top three voices, are given such varied treatment that each seems to have a different pattern of arpeggiation to its neighbor. The final three measures of the piece, by contrast, are remarkably consistent in both tempo and arpeggiation. Given this variety, ensemble asynchrony need not be associated with specific expressive or structural functions; instead, it seems best understood as a contextual variable, held in constant tension with other aspects of performance. It is the constantly evolving quality of those relationships that underpins the irregular and multi-layered patterning one hears in "vitalist" performance styles.

Conclusion

These brief examples only scratch the surface of a profoundly unfamiliar concept of ensemble, but even these may stimulate significant further reflection both on the impermanence of stylistic conventions and on the potential meanings of "togetherness." While it would, of course, be naïve to extrapolate too many wider conclusions from the evidence of this group alone, when considered alongside other contemporary sources, such obsolete styles certainly guard against treating aesthetic premises of ensemble as lying "outside history." Attempts to rationalize, justify, and account for such elusive aspects of performance will never allow us to hear these musicians as contemporaries did; nor am I suggesting that modern musicians should feel pressured into recovering this way of playing on the basis of historicity alone. Perhaps the real value of early recordings lies instead in their capacity to reveal our own priorities, terminologies, and biases with clarity, and this is surely as true of ensemble as of any other aspect of musical performance.

References

A. M. (1899). The Bohemian string quartet. *Musical Standard*, *11*(273), 185.

Cook, N. (2013). *Beyond the score*. Oxford University Press.

Cook, N. (2014). Between art and science: Music as performance. *Journal of the British Academy*, *2*, 1–25.

Fabian, D. (2015). *A musicology of performance theory and method based on Bach's solos for violin*. Open Book Publishers.

Leech-Wilkinson, D. (2009). Recordings and histories of performance style. In N. Cook, E. Clarke, D. Leech-Wilkinson, & J. Rink (Eds.), *The Cambridge companion to recorded music* (pp. 246–62). Cambridge University Press.

Peres Da Costa, N. (2012). *Off the record: Performing practices in romantic piano playing*. Oxford University Press.

Philip, R. (2004). *Performing music in the age of recording*. Yale University Press.

Taruskin, R. (1995). *Text and act: Essays on music and performance*. Oxford University Press.

Todd, N. (1992). The dynamics of dynamics: A model of musical expression. *The Journal of the Acoustical Society of America*, *91*(6), 3540–50.

Discography

Dvorak, A. (1928). *String Quartet in F Op.96, ii. Lento* [Recorded by Czech String Quartet; 78rpm]. Polydor/95085.   Available   at   https://www.discogs.com/The-Bohemian-Quartet-Smetana-Dvo%C5%99%C3%A1k-And-Suk/release/13996914

23

Beyond synchronization

Body gestures and gaze direction in duo performance

Laura Bishop, Carlos Cancino-Chacón, and Werner Goebl

Introduction

Successful coordination during music ensemble performance is supported by dynamic, multimodal interactions among ensemble members. Most critical is the musicians' attention to each other's audio signals: this alone is sufficient for an ensemble to maintain synchronization much of the time (see Chapter 17). Visual interaction is largely peripheral to successful synchronization, though performers may choose to exchange visual signals when timing of the music is uncertain.

While successful synchronization provides a foundation for a high-quality performance, coordination of other parameters is important as well. In the Western classical music tradition, expressive parameters such as dynamics and phrasing must be carefully aligned. Coordinated manipulation of such parameters—which are imprecisely specified (or omitted) in the score—is important for ensembles who want to establish an interpretation of the piece that distinguishes their unique group playing style.

What role visual interaction plays in coordinating an expressive performance remains unclear. To date, few studies have considered the possibility that its contribution may be social, rather than related to the basic mechanics of synchronization. We propose that visual interactions among ensemble performers may help with achieving complex expressive goals and, more specifically, may serve as a social motivator that allows performers to confirm and guide each other's attention. Ultimately, this may promote creative risk-taking.

In this chapter, we focus on two main categories of visual interaction: body gestures and gaze direction. Our focus on body gestures is motivated by research showing that gesture patterns often change during joint action tasks to become more predictable (van der Wel et al., 2016; see also Chapter 14). Moreover, coordination sometimes emerges between musicians at the level of body sway (Chang et al., 2017). Our focus on gaze direction was motivated by the fact that gaze can serve simultaneously as a means of obtaining information about the world and as a means of communicating one's own attention and intent.

We carried out a study with musical duos to test two broad, competing hypotheses. On one hand, we considered the possibility that visual interaction supports basic coordination as a supplement to auditory interactions, resulting in musicians being more visually interactive during difficult-to-coordinate parts of a performance and during the early stages of rehearsal, when they are unsure of how each other might play. The competing hypothesis is that visual interaction supports engagement and creativity among co-performers, resulting in musicians being more visually interactive during the later stages of rehearsal, when performers

Laura Bishop, Carlos Cancino-Chacón, and Werner Goebl, *Beyond synchronization* In: *Together in music.* Edited by: Renee Timmers, Freya Bailes, and Helena Daffern, Oxford University Press. © Oxford University Press 2022. DOI: 10.1093/oso/9780198860761.003.0023

are more sure of the notes and more confident about experimenting with new interpretive ideas. Our methods and results are presented in detail elsewhere (Bishop et al., 2019a, b). The current chapter draws our results together into a discussion of how visual interaction may enhance performers' experience of playing together and audiences' perceptions of performance quality.

Methods and results

Ten clarinet duos and ten piano duos, all comprising highly trained professional or semi-professional musicians, participated in the study. Each duo spent one hour rehearsing a new piece, and recorded four complete performances of the piece during the course of the rehearsal period.

At the start of the session, musicians were instructed to practice together rather than independently, and to focus on preparing an expressive interpretation of the piece. We pointed out that some elements of the score were deliberately ambiguous (e.g. there were no tempo ranges given), and told the musicians to make their own decisions about how the piece should sound. They were told that the purpose of the study was to look at how musicians interact during rehearsal, and were not given any specific instructions regarding where to look or how to move.

The piece was specially composed for the purpose of the study, and contained a number of potential challenges for coordination, including a section with no notated meter. Motion capture recordings were collected using a ten-camera OptiTrack system, and SMI wireless eye tracking glasses were used to collect gaze data. Audio and (for pianists) MIDI data were also recorded.

Duos were arranged face-to-face, a short distance apart, and were allowed to use the score throughout the session (see Fig. 23.1a, b, c). Duos performed the piece once at the start of the session (i.e. while sight-reading), once halfway through a free joint rehearsal period, and twice at the end of the session. The fourth performance was given under no-visual-contact conditions (i.e. performers were blocked from seeing each other); all other performances were given under normal visual contact conditions.

Effects of musical structure

We investigated the effects of musical structure on eye gaze patterns and head kinematics. Of primary interest was the comparison between the unmetered section of the piece, where timing was fairly irregular, and the metrical, more regularly timed sections. The unmetered section allowed for greater freedom of interpretation, and was likely more difficult for duos to coordinate.

Coordination of head motion between performers was stronger during the unmetered section than elsewhere in the piece. In Fig. 23.1d, this is shown by the uptake in red and yellow coloring that occurs in the unmetered section around lag 0, and is particularly visible in the third performance (lower plot). Also notable in the third performance is the increase in coordination strength (i.e. red uptake) that occurs immediately prior to the unmetered

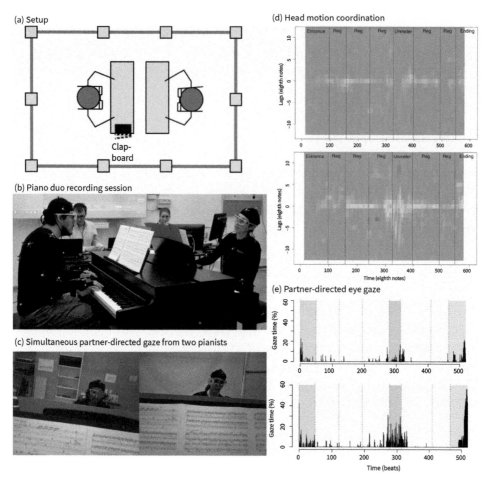

Figure 23.1 Illustration of research methods. (a) The experimental setup. (b) Pianists are shown performing with motion capture and eye tracking. (c) Video captured by the eye tracking glasses is shown for two pianists; blue circles indicate gaze position. (d) The strength of primo-secondo head coordination, measured using a rolling-window cross-correlation method and averaged across pianists, for the first (upper plot) and third (lower plot) performances; blue areas indicate negative correlations and red areas indicate positive correlations. (e) The percentage of performance time that pianists spent watching their partner in the first (upper plot) and third (lower plot) performances; gray dotted lines indicate metrical boundaries the beginning and ending piece sections are in blue and yellow, and the unmetered section is in pink. Note that beats were counted differently for plots in (d) and (e), resulting in different total beat numbers.

Reproduced with permission from Bishop, L., Cancino-Chacón, C. E., & Goebl, W. (2019a). Eye gaze as a means of giving and seeking information during musical interaction. Consciousness and Cognition, 68, 73–96; and Bishop, L., Cancino- Chacón, C. E., & Goebl, W. (2019b). Moving to communicate, moving to interact: Patterns of body motion in musical duo performance. Music Perception, 37, 1–25.

section, which likely indicates a coordinated transition between sections or preparation for the less predictable unmetered section.

Performers were also found to exchange cueing gestures (exaggerated head nods) during the unmetered section. Drawing on some previous studies of ours, which showed that beats are primarily communicated through gesture acceleration (Bishop & Goebl, 2018), we conducted a search for cueing gestures by comparing head acceleration curves at each beat of the piece to head acceleration curves given just prior to piece onset (at the moment where cueing-in gestures were exchanged). Acceleration curves more closely replicated those associated with cueing-in gestures at fermatas, suggesting that performers exchanged visual signals to help align the chords that followed these pauses.

Musicians spent a larger percentage of performance time watching their partner during the unmetered section than during the regularly timed sections, though most musicians did occasionally look at their partner during regularly timed sections as well (see Fig. 23.1e). There was also an uptake in partner-directed gaze at the very start of the piece (which started with a synchronized chord) and in the final beats of the piece (where most duos introduced a *ritardando*). Also, importantly, we found no evidence that the "leader" (i.e. the partner playing the melody) looked less at the "follower" (i.e. the partner playing the accompaniment) than the follower spent looking at the leader. This suggests that visual information traveled both ways, rather than exclusively from leader to follower.

Effects of rehearsal

The effects of rehearsal on eye gaze and head kinematics were also assessed. Our analyses of head gestures revealed that quantity of movement and the strength of coordination between performers were higher at the end of the session than at the start (see Fig. 23.1d). The percentage of time that musicians spent watching their partner also increased from the start to the end of the session (see Fig. 23.1e).

Effects of visual contact

A comparison between the final two performances was made for gesture kinematics, to test whether head movements were more communicative when musicians could see each other than when visual contact between performers was occluded. We found that the quantity of movement and the strength of coordination between performers' head movements were both greater when musicians could see each other than when they could not.

The quality of synchronization that musicians achieved during their final two performances was also assessed, by looking at the magnitude of primo-secondo note onset asynchronies. Synchronization did not differ between performances, indicating that visual contact—and the strengthened gestural coordination that occurred during the third performance—had no noticeable effects on synchrony.

Discussion

Our findings show how duo musicians' use of visual interaction techniques changes across different performance conditions. When predictability of timing is low (as during our unmetered section), performers seem motivated to supplement their auditory interactions with visual signals. Cueing gestures were exchanged as performers tried to resynchronize following fermatas. Performers also spent more time watching each other during the unmetered section. These findings suggest that visual signals may sometimes be used to facilitate coordination. On the other hand, we observed no difference in synchronization success between the final two performances (with versus without visual contact). Thus, we might predict that performers' use of visual signals during the unmetered section does more to raise their confidence than it does to affect coordination.

Performers moved more, and their movements were more coordinated after rehearsing than before; likewise, the time they spent watching each other increased. Performers were therefore more visually interactive when they were more familiar with the music (and their partner). Musicians' expectations for how the piece should sound may be more concrete after some rehearsal, and their visual interaction may reflect a more driven attempt to ensure successful coordination. A second (not mutually exclusive) explanation is that once musicians are more comfortable with the notes, their focus shifts more towards their partner, with whom they become more engaged, making both partners more willing to experiment with alternate interpretations. In this respect, visual interaction may come to serve a social–motivational function.

Our hypothesis that visual interaction among ensemble members may serve a primarily social function is motivated by recent research on group flow, a state characterized by a shared sense of absorption, intrinsic reward, and effortlessness (Hart & Di Blasi, 2015). Musicians associate a lack of self-consciousness and individuality with the experience of group flow, but also require a clear understanding of their role in the collaboration. The possibility for dynamic, fine-grained interaction between musicians is thought to be critical for establishing a sense of "shared social presence." We propose that visual interaction may encourage an external (partner/task-directed), rather than internal (self-reflective), focus and strengthen the resonance that emerges between co-performers.

We also propose that visual interaction may benefit performance quality from the audience's perspective. Some research has shown that viewers are sensitive to the social dynamics portrayed by interacting musicians (e.g. dominance or insolence); however, further study is needed to determine which types of (audio and visual) cues are meaningful to audiences.

During public performance, the audience's overt response can feed back to the performer, shaping their performance as it unfolds. Performer–audience interaction is present during Western classical concerts, though perhaps less obvious than in some other musical scenes. We would argue that musicians trained in the Western classical tradition (where public performance is typically the goal) are, even in rehearsal, influenced by the response of a hypothetical audience. Thus, musicians may "play for" this hypothetical audience during rehearsal, as they anticipate potential audience responses. We would therefore hypothesize that our participants' recorded performances included a similar, if not underestimated (due to lowered arousal), degree of visual interaction than would occur among duo musicians during public performance.

The current study was designed to maximize ecological validity within a laboratory setting, but the question remains: how generalizable are our results to real-world performances? Musicians encounter variability in performance conditions on a regular basis (e.g. in acoustic conditions, lighting conditions, positioning and spacing on a stage, the presence/absence of an audience, etc.). Skilled musicians are expected to adapt to these variable conditions, and indeed tend to do so successfully. This means, of course, that researchers run the risk of capturing musicians' abilities to adapt to a new, but artificial set of constraints, rather than their "real-world" behavior. We would encourage other researchers to test the replicability of our findings with musicians of different traditions, playing different instruments, and positioned relative to each other in different ways.

Conclusion

This study tested two potentially complementary functions of visual interaction in a duo performance setting. Our results suggest that skilled musicians draw on visual signaling when trying to coordinate irregularly timed music. More generally, visual interaction seems to serve a social–motivational function, as musicians seem eager to engage visually with each other, despite this offering no benefit to synchronization. Future research should consider how visual interaction affects performance quality beyond the level of synchronization and, in particular, how it shapes the subjective experiences of performers and audience members.

Acknowledgments

This research was funded by the Austrian Science Fund (FWF), grant P-29427, and the European Research Council (ERC), under the EU's Horizon 2020 Framework Programme, grant 670035 (project "Con Espressione").

References

Bishop, L., Cancino-Chacón, C. E., & Goebl, W. (2019a). Eye gaze as a means of giving and seeking information during musical interaction. *Consciousness and Cognition, 68*, 73–96. doi: 10.1016/j.concog.2019.01.002

Bishop, L., Cancino-Chacón, C. E., & Goebl, W. (2019b). Moving to communicate, moving to interact: Patterns of body motion in musical duo performance. *Music Perception, 37*, 1–25. doi: 10.1525/mp.2019.37.1.1

Bishop, L., & Goebl, W. (2018). Communication for coordination: Gesture kinematics and conventionality affect synchronization success in piano duos. *Psychological Research, 82*, 1177–94. doi: 10.1007/s00426-017-0893-3

Chang, A., Livingstone, S. R., Bosnyak, D. J., & Trainor, L. J. (2017). Body sway reflects leadership in joint music performance. *Proceedings of the National Academy of Sciences, 114*(21). doi: 10.1073/pnas.1617657114

Hart, E., & Di Blasi, Z. (2015). Combined flow in musical jam sessions: A pilot qualitative study. *Psychology of Music, 43*(2), 275–90. doi: 10.1177/0305735613502374

van der Wel, R. P. R. D., Sebanz, N., & Knoblich, G. (2016). A joint action perspective on embodiment. In Y. Coello, & M. Fischer (Eds.), *Foundations of embodied cognition* (pp. 165–181). Oxford: Psychology Press.

PART 3

PARTICIPATION, DEVELOPMENT, AND WELLBEING

24

Ensembles for wellbeing

Gunter Kreutz and Michael Bonshor

Introduction

Human beings have performed music together since ancient times across all known cultures and societies (Mithen, 2005). Importantly, access to music ensembles in those prehistoric times appears to have been inclusive rather than being granted on the basis of enhanced levels of individual aptitude or training. In contrast, in urban and industrialized societies, the concept of the musician as an expert with special skills has become widespread (Levitin, 2006). Nowadays, learning to play musical instruments in readiness for formal participation in Western musical culture usually requires long-term commitment, training, and deliberate practice. This often begins in childhood, even if professional levels are not reached by the majority of ensemble players (Lehmann & Ericsson, 1997). Long-term commitment and motivation to play music together can be seen as intrinsic sources of individual growth and wellbeing (Deci & Ryan, 2015). Therefore, ensemble playing offers one context in which self-determination (i.e. the satisfaction of human needs such as competence and autonomy) (Deci & Ryan, 2000) can be achieved across the lifespan (Hallam et al., 2017), with significant implications for healthy aging in both professional and amateur musicians (Gembris, 2012).

Instrumental music ensemble playing has many aspects in common with other forms of collective musical participation, such as singing and dancing, but there are also some aspects that are unique to playing musical instruments in ensemble. Therefore, their potential psychological, physiological, and social benefits and challenges are worth considering separately and in comparison to other musical activities (MacDonald et al., 2012). Instrumental ensemble playing usually demands high levels of performance and training, partly due to the physical characteristics of musical instruments and the psychophysiological implications of collective rehearsal and performance. However, preliminary evidence shows that instrumental ensemble playing can enhance individual wellbeing and health in a similar way to participation in other leisure musical activities (Juniu et al., 1996; Williamson & Bonshor, 2019). The main focus of this chapter will therefore be upon the wellbeing effects of playing in instrumental ensembles.

Models of wellbeing

The World Health Organization (1946, p.1) definition of health is "a state of complete physical, mental and social well-being and not merely the absence of disease or infirmity." In 1986, this definition was expanded to include health promotion, prevention of ill-health, resilience, empowerment, and self-actualization. Currently, there is a consensus that improvement of wellbeing, in general, can positively influence people's lives in a variety of ways. Indeed,

Gunter Kreutz and Michael Bonshor, *Ensembles for wellbeing* In: *Together in music*. Edited by: Renee Timmers, Freya Bailes, and Helena Daffern, Oxford University Press. © Oxford University Press 2022. DOI: 10.1093/oso/9780198860761.003.0024

wellbeing is often understood as a multi-dimensional construct that is difficult to dissociate from other concepts such as standard of living, living conditions, and health (Halleröd & Seldén, 2013). For example, Seligman's PERMA model (Seligman, 2011, 2018), is a construct that comprises five dimensions: Positive emotions, Engagement, Relationships, Meaning, and Accomplishment. This suggests that individual wellbeing originates from the interdependence and covariation of several elements or dimensions, which interact with physical and mental health.

Previous work shows that the PERMA model can be successfully applied theoretically (Croom, 2015) and empirically (Lee et al., 2017) to music learning and practice. According to Croom (2015), Seligman's PERMA model has been highly influential in the development of Positive Psychology (Seligman & Csikszentmihalyi, 2014) and has fostered novel approaches to education, including music learning and practice. Croom presents a review of the literature that is related to each of the PERMA components. To begin with, his review reveals a research focus on music listening as a mood-enhancing self-regulatory strategy. Even though performers are also listeners, participation in musical ensembles has rarely been researched with respect to eliciting positive emotions (P) or relationships (R) among the performers. The second PERMA component, engagement (E), which may give rise to "flow" experiences (Csikszentmihalyi, 1990; see also Chapter 25), has been studied from the perspectives of deliberate practice and expert piano playing (de Manzano et al., 2010) in individual performers, but it is also highly relevant to ensembles. Croom (2015) also identified "Meaning" as mediating wellbeing in terms of the PERMA model (the model's M), and this has been explored in studies on the impact of live music events on its attendees and their identity formation (e.g. Lamont, 2011). Findings support the notion that there exists no "passive listening." In fact, the participation of festival audiences, including singing and dancing, can be seen as informal but active music group activities, which contribute to wellbeing (Packer & Ballantyne, 2011).

Interestingly, Croom (2015) turns to studies on music therapy interventions in spinal injury patients to build a case for music participation as relevant to accomplishment (the final A in the PERMA model). The authors of the cited study invited their participants to a collaborative electronic music project, which seemed to foster "motivation, self-esteem and a feeling of creativity" (Lee & Nantais, 1996, pp. 367–8). In sum, Croom (2015) appears to have constructed a solid case to promote music participation as contributing in a variety of ways (and for a wide range of target groups) to the facilitation of individual flourishing and wellbeing in terms of the PERMA model. However, with few exceptions, Croom's review is highly focused on receptive music activities, which are mainly represented by music listening in everyday, educational, and therapeutic contexts.

Aaron Antonovsky's (1997) salutogenetic approach to wellbeing and health has been highly influential in medical research during recent decades. In brief, "salutogenetic" stands in opposition to "pathogenetic," a commonly acknowledged medical term representing the search for causes of illness, while "salutogenetic" represents the search for causes of health. Considering the role of music, Kreutz (2015) developed a contextual model of musical activities as enhancing wellbeing on the basis of Antonovsky's construct of Sense of Coherence. According to this, behaviors can be beneficial if they are perceived as intelligible, manageable, and meaningful. This construct is in many respects similar to "flow," which means that a person who is fully engaged in a challenging, but achievable activity experiences a particularly high level of enjoyment and fulfillment, which other activities may not offer in that moment (Csikszentmihalyi, 1990). In other words, the specific nature of an activity in itself is of less relevance to enhancing wellbeing, as long as an individual is able to find value and motivation in it that exceed the activity per se. However, activities such as active music-making by singing, dancing, or playing musical instruments offer themselves as particularly beneficial as they fulfill the salutogenetic criteria par excellence (Kreutz, 2015). Kreutz et al. (2012) argued that studying psychophysiological markers, including hormones and neurotransmitters, as indicators of stress and immune functions, could provide insights into the psychobiological mechanisms underlying affective states, and the perceived benefits of musical activities. This is mainly because many of these markers represent facets of stress regulation, immune system competence, and social bonding that may significantly contribute to holistic wellbeing (see also Fancourt et al., 2014).

To conclude, the PERMA model and the salutogenetic model are both suitable as frameworks to guide research concerning the effects of music ensemble activities on wellbeing and health. However, these models are neither mutually exclusive nor sufficiently comprehensive. They are therefore subject to continued discussion, and researchers have only recently begun to address the potential benefits of music ensemble practice by using rigorous methodologies.

Empirical evidence

Choral singing

Choral singing has perhaps been the most researched ensemble music activity over the past two decades when it comes to its effects on wellbeing (see Clift, 2012 for a critical review). There is initial evidence to suggest that singing together in groups has beneficial effects on wellbeing, positive emotions (Busch & Gick, 2012; Clift et al., 2010; Fancourt et al., 2016b; Stone et al., 2018), and quality of life (Johnson et al., 2013). Group singing can be successful in strengthening social bonding (Bullack et al., 2018; Good & Russo, 2016; Kreutz, 2014) to provide benefits for individuals living with mental or physical health issues (Coulton et al., 2015; Skingley et al., 2014). However, the beneficial effects of singing may be influenced or even compromised by psychophysiological and social demands that are associated with this activity. For example, it is not clear to what extent the demands of solo singing may induce different stress responses when compared with group singing (Beck et al., 2000; Fancourt et al., 2015). Moreover, group singing may entail negative social experiences that can reduce its positive psychological value (Kreutz & Brünger, 2012).

Although there are still several issues to be explored and a range of methodological challenges to be met with respect to group singing research (Dingle et al., 2019), the available evidence points towards group singing as a relatively low-risk and rewarding musical ensemble activity, which can enhance many aspects of wellbeing (Daykin et al., 2018).

Instrumental ensembles

The impact of playing music in ensembles on individual wellbeing has been studied from a variety of perspectives, including educational (e.g. Hallam, 2010; Iadeluca & Sangiorgio, 2009) and therapeutic (e.g. Ansdell & DeNora, 2016; Fancourt et al., 2016a), and as a leisure activity (e.g. Hallam et al., 2017). Researchers have also examined specific ensembles with different levels of proficiencies (Ascenso et al., 2018; Williamson & Bonshor, 2019). It is of note that, in general, although amateur performers may be dedicated and proficient, they do not depend on playing music as a source of income, as professionals do. It therefore appears only natural that non-musical aspects, such as social interaction, might play a greater role as sources of potential reward when playing music in amateur ensembles (Appelgren et al., 2019). Several studies have concluded that playing music together can bring important extra-musical benefits. Burnard and Dragovic (2015), for example, conducted an observational study on collaborative music learning as an extracurricular activity at school. Pupils and teachers were interviewed as part of this project, and the authors observed that collaborative musical engagement fulfilled basic psychological features of wellbeing, including self-discovery and embodiment of the played music, along with significant group experiences and feelings of togetherness (Burnard & Dragovic, 2015).

A study of 17 school-based music activity programs in Australia (Lee et al., 2017) identified 128 statements that could be directly related to the PERMA wellbeing model outlined in this chapter. The music participation programs thus not only increased musical skills and abilities, but also improved students' psychosocial wellbeing. The success of such programs appeared to be highly dependent on the heads of schools, teachers, staff, and local people in the community, such as parents, music entrepreneurs, and musicians. Building positive relationships among students and within the wider community was therefore interpreted as the dominant component in providing the benefits described by the PERMA model (Lee et al., 2017).

Empathy is a social enabler, and researchers have begun to ask whether musical interaction serves to enhance empathic experiences and behaviors. For example, Rabinowitch et al. (2013) conducted an experiment in which they assigned cohorts of 8- to 11-year-old children either to a group engaging in interactive musical games such as collective rhythmic improvisation and imitating each other's musical phrases, or to a control group. The findings suggested that children who played the musical games benefitted in terms of empathy and emotion processing. However, this result was due to lower baseline scores in the target groups, i.e. the groups differed with respect to empathy levels at the beginning of the intervention and were more similar at the end. In the absence of alternative interventions, the results could also be interpreted as classic experimenter effects. This means that the observed changes may be due to demand characteristics of the research, or enhanced attention towards the experimental group, rather than the intervention per se. Single blinding by separating intervention and assessment procedures may be necessary to minimize such systematic influences in future studies.

Participating in amateur music-making is a popular leisure activity across the lifespan. Hallam et al. (2017) addressed making music as a lifelong leisure activity from a psychological perspective. Their review of studies on amateur ensemble practices concluded that beneficial effects seemed to arise from both individual and social experiences within such settings. Specifically, among interviewees of different age groups from the Music For Life Project (Creech et al., 2014), similar improvements were reported in terms of emotional aspects such as self-regulation, mood enhancement, social reward, and feelings of pride. Importantly, music-making in later life can also be a significant cognitive stimulation that benefits a wide range of processes such as attention, memory, and motivation (see Chapter 30). Therefore, the authors propose that a lifelong-learning perspective appears appropriate for investigating the long-term costs and benefits of active music participation in terms of mental, physical, and social wellbeing and health (Creech et al., 2014).

Brass bands are often intergenerational, offering a lifelong community with whom to make music. Williamson and Bonshor (2019) investigated the potential health benefits of ensemble practice and performance in a cohort of brass players. Three hundred and forty-six survey responses were analyzed under a line by line coding, segmentation, and thematic analysis regime (Braun & Clarke, 2006), resulting in a total of 1658 individual quotations. Several themes emerged mainly relating to physical (82%), social (97%), and psychological benefits (95%). Although emotional (14%) and spiritual benefits (3%) were less prominent, the authors concluded that an overwhelming majority of statements expressed positive responses to regular participation in brass ensemble playing. In contrast, negative effects such as stage fright, weight gain attributed to sedentary rehearsals, or hearing problems were relatively rarely mentioned. Physical aspects of wellbeing were highlighted, with participants characterizing the psychophysical demands of brass playing as having some therapeutic effects. Self-reported improvements included posture, muscle tone, core strength, general fitness, stamina, manual dexterity, flexibility, cardiovascular function, and, to a particularly high degree, respiration. Interviewees further indicated that their brass band playing contributed to social bonding and community building among players, often with opportunities to include their families in the social life of the band. There were only occasional reports of associated social problems, mainly in relation to dealing with committee work. Participants also interpreted the cognitive demands of brass band playing as positive stimulation; the challenges of rehearsing and performing can maintain and enhance mental capacities through learning and memorizing new musical material. In other words, brass ensembles share many characteristics of self-descriptions that can be found for sports teams (Nowak, 2014) as well as in singing groups (Clift & Hancox, 2001), including a somewhat strong sense of self-actualization and achievement, which generally supports many aspects of holistic wellbeing, in line with the "A" (achievement) of the PERMA model outlined in this chapter.

Limitations

We have reviewed the initial evidence to suggest that playing music in amateur ensembles may have positive effects on different aspects of wellbeing. However, these findings need to be treated with some caution. First of all, access to music learning in childhood and in later life is subject to socioeconomic influences, individual differences, and a range of other factors that could systematically influence the observed and reported associations. Many studies rely on correlational designs which preclude the assessment of temporal changes and the identification of the direction of causality. Qualitative approaches play an important role in revealing potential domains and moderators of wellbeing effects, but they do not allow for generalization. Therefore, to consolidate the preliminary evidence, there is a need for methodologically rigorous empirical studies, which can be subsequently incorporated in high-quality systematic reviews and meta-analyses. The development of novel research instruments, which particularly target musical activities and wellbeing, will also facilitate the implementation of increasingly rigorous and appropriate methodologies with respect to the target groups and behaviors (Krause et al., 2018).

Conclusion

Performing music in amateur ensembles may have beneficial effects on many different aspects of wellbeing, while adverse effects or health risks appear less prominent. This provides a striking comparison with some of the reported negative effects related to the lifestyle, career stressors, and performance challenges reported by professional musicians (Gross & Musgrave, 2016). Although high levels of job satisfaction and wellbeing may still be present for many professional musicians (Ascenso et al., 2018), amateur ensemble players bear comparatively fewer psychological and physical health risks and may therefore be more likely to experience the significant positive wellbeing effects associated with leisure-time musical activities (Bonde et al., 2018).

References

Ansdell, G., & DeNora, T. (2016). *Musical pathways in recovery.* Routledge.

Antonovsky, A. (1997). *Salutogenese. Zur entmystifizierung der gesundheit.* dgvt-Verlag.

Appelgren, A., Osika, W., Theorell, T., Madison, G., & Bojner Horwitz, E. (2019). Tuning in on motivation: Differences between non-musicians, amateurs, and professional musicians. *Psychology of Music, 47*(6), 864–73.

Ascenso, S., Perkins, R., & Williamon, A. (2018). Resounding meaning: A PERMA wellbeing profile of classical musicians. *Frontiers in Psychology, 9.* https://doi.org/10.3389/fpsyg.2018.01895

Beck, R. J., Cesario, T. C., Yousefi, A., & Enamoto, H. (2000). Choral singing, performance perception, and immune system changes in salivary immunoglobulin A and cortisol. *Music Perception, 18*(1), 87–106.

Bonde, L. O., Juel, K., & Ekholm, O. (2018). Associations between music and health-related outcomes in adult non-musicians, amateur musicians and professional musicians—Results from a nationwide Danish study. *Nordic Journal of Music Therapy, 27*(4), 262–82.

Braun, V., & Clarke, V. (2006). Using thematic analysis in psychology. *Qualitative Research in Psychology, 3*(2), 77–101.

Bullack, A., Gass, C., Nater, U. M., & Kreutz, G. (2018). Psychobiological effects of choral singing on affective state, social connectedness, and stress: Influences of singing activity and time course. *Frontiers in Behavioral Neuroscience, 12.* https://doi.org/10.3389/fnbeh.2018.00223

Burnard, P., & Dragovic, T. (2015). Collaborative creativity in instrumental group music learning as a site for enhancing pupil wellbeing. *Cambridge Journal of Education, 45*(3), 371–92.

Busch, S. L., & Gick, M. (2012). A quantitative study of choral singing and psychological wellbeing/Étude quantitative sur le chant choral et le bien-être. *Canadian Journal of Music Therapy, 18*(1), 45–61.

Clift, S. (2012). Singing, wellbeing and health. In R. MacDonald, G. Kreutz, & L. A. Mitchell (Eds.), *Music, health, and wellbeing.* (pp. 113–24). Oxford University Press.

Clift, S., & Hancox, G. (2001). The perceived benefits of singing: Findings from preliminary surveys of a university college choral society. *The Journal of the Royal Society for the Promotion of Health, 121*(4), 248–56.

Clift, S., Hancox, G., Morrison, I., Hess, B., Kreutz, G., & Stewart, D. (2010). Choral singing and psychological wellbeing: Quantitative and qualitative findings from English choirs in a cross-national survey. *Journal of Applied Arts and Health*, *1*(1), 19–34. https://doi.org/10.1386/jaah.1.1.19/1

Coulton, S., Clift, S., Skingley, A., & Rodriguez, J. (2015). Effectiveness and cost-effectiveness of community singing on mental health-related quality of life of older people: Randomised controlled trial. *British Journal of Psychiatry*, *207*(3), 250–5.

Creech, A., Hallam, S., Varvarigou, M., & McQueen, H. (2014). *Active ageing with music: Supporting wellbeing in the third and fourth ages*. Institute of Education Press.

Croom, A. M. (2015). Music practice and participation for psychological well-being: A review of how music influences positive emotion, engagement, relationships, meaning, and accomplishment. *Musicae Scientiae*, *19*(1), 44–64.

Csikszentmihalyi, M. (1990). *Flow: The psychology of optimal experience*. Harper Collins.

Daykin, N., Mansfield, L., Meads, C., Julier, G., Tomlinson, A., Payne, A., Grigsby Duffy, L., Lane, J., D'Innocenzo, G., Burnett, A., Kay, T., Dolan, P., Testoni, S., & Victor, C. (2018). What works for wellbeing? A systematic review of wellbeing outcomes for music and singing in adults. *Perspectives in Public Health*, *138*(1), 39–46.

de Manzano, Ö., Theorell, T., Harmat, L., & Ullén, F. (2010). The psychophysiology of flow during piano playing. *Emotion*, *10*(3), 301–11.

Deci, E. L., & Ryan, R. M. (2000). The "what" and "why" of goal pursuits: Human needs and the self-determination of behavior. *Psychological Inquiry*, *11*, 227–68.

Deci, E. L., & Ryan, R. M. (2015). Self-determination theory. In *International Encyclopedia of the Social & Behavioral Sciences* (pp. 486–91). Elsevier.

Dingle, G. A., Clift, S., Finn, S., Gilbert, R., Groarke, J. M., Irons, J. Y., Bartoli, A. J., Lamont, A., Launay, J., Martin, E. S., Moss, H., Sanfilippo, K. R., Shipton, M., Stewart, L., Talbot., S., Tarrant, M., Tip, L., & Williams, E. J. (2019). An agenda for best practice research on group singing, health, and well-being. *Music & Science*, *2*. https://doi.org/10.1177/2059204319861719

Fancourt, D., Aufegger, L., & Williamon, A. (2015). Low-stress and high-stress singing have contrasting effects on glucocorticoid response. *Frontiers in Psychology*, *6*, 1242. https://doi.org/10.3389/fpsyg.2015.01242

Fancourt, D., Ockelford, A., & Belai, A. (2014). The psychoneuroimmunological effects of music: A systematic review and a new model. *Brain, Behavior, and Immunity*, *36*, 15–26.

Fancourt, D., Perkins, R., Ascenso, S., Carvalho, L. A., Steptoe, A., & Williamon, A. (2016a). Effects of group drumming interventions on anxiety, depression, social resilience and inflammatory immune response among mental health service users. *PLoS One*, *11*(3), e0151136. https://doi.org/10.1371/journal.pone.0151136

Fancourt, D., Williamon, A., Carvalho, L. A., Steptoe, A., Dow, R., & Lewis, I. (2016b). Singing modulates mood, stress, cortisol, cytokine and neuropeptide activity in cancer patients and carers. *Ecancer*, *10*, 631. https://doi.org/10.3332/ecancer.2016.631

Gembris, H. (2012). Music-making as a lifelong development and resource for health. In R. A. R. MacDonald, G. Kreutz, & L. Mitchell (Eds.), *Music, health, and wellbeing* (pp. 368–82). Oxford University Press.

Good, A., & Russo, F. A. (2016). Singing promotes cooperation in a diverse group of children. *Social Psychology*, *47*(6), 340–4.

Gross, S. A., & Musgrave, G. (2016). *Can music make you sick? Music and depression. A study into the incidence of musicians' mental health part 1: pilot survey report*. https://www.helpmusicians.org.uk/assets/publications/files/can_music_make_you_sick_part_1-_pilot_survey_report_2019.pdf

Hallam, S. (2010). The power of music: Its impact on the intellectual, social and personal development of children and young people. *International Journal of Music Education, 28*(3), 269–89.

Hallam, S., Creech, A., & Varvarigou, M. (2017). Well-being and music leisure activities through the lifespan. In R. Mantie, & G. D. Smith (Eds.), *The Oxford handbook of music making and leisure* (pp. 31–60). Oxford University Press.

Halleröd, B., & Seldén, D. (2013). The multi-dimensional characteristics of wellbeing: How different aspects of wellbeing interact and do not interact with each other. *Social Indicators Research, 113*(3), 807–25.

Iadeluca, V., & Sangiorgio, A. (2009). Bambini al Centro: Music as a means to promote wellbeing. *International Journal of Community Music, 1*(3), 311–18.

Johnson, J. K., Louhivuori, J., Stewart, A. L., Tolvanen, A., Ross, L., & Era, P. (2013). Quality of life (QOL) of older adult community choral singers in Finland. *International Psychogeriatrics/IPA, 25*(7), 1055–64. https://doi.org/10.1017/S1041610213000422

Juniu, S., Tedrick, T., & Boyd, R. (1996). Leisure or work?: Amateur and professional musicians' perception of rehearsal and performance. *Journal of Leisure Research, 28*(1), 44–56.

Krause, A. E., Davidson, J. W., & North, A. C. (2018). Musical activity and well-being. *Music Perception: An Interdisciplinary Journal, 35*(4), 454–74.

Kreutz, G. (2014). Does singing facilitate social bonding? *Music and Medicine, 6*(2), 51–60.

Kreutz, G. (2015). The value of music for public health. In S. Clift, & P. Camic (Eds.), *Oxford textbook of creative arts, health, and well-being. International perspectives on practice, policy, and research* (pp. 211–17). Oxford University Press.

Kreutz, G., & Brünger, P. (2012). A shade of grey: Negative associations with amateur choral singing. *Arts & Health: An International Journal of Research, Policy and Practice, 4*(3), 230–8.

Kreutz, G., Quiroga, C., & Bongard, S. (2012). Psychoneuroendocrine research on music and health: An overview. In R. A. R. MacDonald, G. Kreutz, & L. Mitchell (Eds.), *Music, health, and wellbeing* (pp. 457–76). Oxford University Press.

Lamont, A. (2011). University students' strong experiences of music. *Musicae Scientiae, 15*(2), 229–49.

Lee, B., & Nantais, T. (1996). Use of electronic music as an occupational therapy modality in spinal cord injury rehabilitation: An occupational performance model. *American Journal of Occupational Therapy, 50,* 362–9.

Lee, J., Krause, A. E., & Davidson, J. W. (2017). The PERMA well-being model and music facilitation practice: Preliminary documentation for well-being through music provision in Australian schools. *Research Studies in Music Education, 39*(1), 73–89.

Lehmann, A. C., & Ericsson, K. A. (1997). Research on expert performance and deliberate practice: Implications for the education of amateur musicians and music students. *Psychomusicology: A Journal of Research in Music Cognition, 16*(1–2), 40–58.

Levitin, D. (2006). *This is your brain on music: Understanding a human obsession.* Penguin.

MacDonald, R., Kreutz, G., & Mitchell, L. (2012). What is music, health, and wellbeing and why is it important? In R. MacDonald, G. Kreutz, & L. Mitchell (Eds.), *Music, health, and wellbeing* (pp. 3–11). Oxford University Press.

Mithen, S. (2005). *The singing neanderthals: The origins of music, language, mind and body.* Phoenix.

Nowak, P. F. (2014). Amateur sports of the elderly: A chance for health and a higher quality of life. *Advances in Aging Research, 3*(3). https://doi.org/10.4236/aar.2014.33031

Packer, J., & Ballantyne, J. (2011). The impact of music festival attendance on young people's psychological and social well-being. *Psychology of Music*, *39*(2), 164–81.

Rabinowitch, T.-C., Cross, I., & Burnard, P. (2013). Long-term musical group interaction has a positive influence on empathy in children. *Psychology of Music*, *41*(4), 484–98.

Seligman, M. E. P. (2011). *Flourish*. Free Press.

Seligman, M. E. P. (2018). PERMA and the building blocks of well-being. *The Journal of Positive Psychology*, *13*(4), 333–5.

Seligman, M. E. P., & Csikszentmihalyi, M. (2014). Positive psychology: An introduction. In M. Csikszentmihaly (Ed.), *Flow and the foundations of positive psychology* (pp. 279–98). Springer Netherlands.

Skingley, A., Page, S., Clift, S., Morrison, I., Coulton, S., Treadwell, P., Vella-Burows, T., & Shipton, M. (2014). "Singing for breathing": Participants' perceptions of a group singing programme for people with COPD. *Arts & Health: An International Journal of Research, Policy and Practice*, *6*(1), 59–74.

Stone, N. L., Millar, S. A., Herrod, P. J. J., Barrett, D. A., Ortori, C. A., Mellon, V. A., & O'Sullivan, S. E. (2018). An analysis of endocannabinoid concentrations and mood following singing and exercise in healthy volunteers. *Frontiers in Behavioral Neuroscience*, *12*. https://doi.org/10.3389/fnbeh.2018.00269

Williamson, V. J., & Bonshor, M. (2019). Wellbeing in brass bands: The benefits and challenges of group music making. *Frontiers in Psychology*, *10*. https://doi.org/10.3389/fpsyg.2019.01176

World Health Organization. (1946). Constitution of the world health organization. *Basic Documents*, 1–19. https://apps.who.int/iris/handle/10665/268688

25

Ensemble musicians' health and wellness

Naomi Norton

Introduction

In the preamble to its constitution[1] the World Health Organization (WHO) defines health as "a state of complete physical, mental and social well-being and not merely the absence of disease or infirmity". Wellness is defined as "the optimal state of health of individuals and groups," with two foci relating to people achieving their fullest potential and fulfilling role expectations in various settings (WHO, 2006, p. 5). Music can facilitate health and wellness by fostering creativity, fulfilling fundamental human needs of competence, connection, and autonomy, motivating people, encouraging them to exercise, diminishing or alleviating tension, anxiety, or other disorders, and promoting work–life balance (Philippe et al., 2019). These positive relationships between music, health, and wellness are explored in the other chapters of this third part of the book; in contrast, this chapter focuses on the potential for music-making to disrupt ensemble musicians' health and wellness by causing or exacerbating physical and psychosocial disorders that affect professional and leisure activities (Philippe et al., 2019).

Participative music-making is a musical and social act and one that influences personal skill development, identity, confidence, and motivation (see Hewitt & Allan, 2013): the primary purpose of a given ensemble may relate more strongly to one or more of these dimensions and individual members' motivations for participation in any given ensemble can also vary (Parker et al., 2019). Ensemble contexts create complicated physical and social environments, opportunities, beliefs, and values that must be negotiated by members and those who work with them to enable the ensemble and its members to thrive.

Given the uniqueness of each ensemble, it is vital to consider the original context of the research on which evidence-based recommendations that are designed to improve performing ensemble musicians' health and wellness are made. To date, most research has focused on professional classical orchestral musicians and, as a result, this chapter draws on eight publications situated in this context (Andersen et al., 2013; Cohen & Bodner, 2019; Dobson & Gaunt, 2015; Guptill, 2012; Jacukowicz, 2016; Rickert et al., 2013; 2014; Wright-Reid & Holland, 2008). Instrumental and vocal music students have also been the focus of a fair amount of research and three publications from this context are referred to (Jacukowicz, 2016; Matthews & Kitsantas, 2012; Parker et al., 2019). Freelance professional musicians are less commonly investigated, but this chapter includes four publications involving musicians from a variety of genres (Dobson, 2011; Hernandez et al., 2009; MacDonald & Wilson, 2005; Parker et al., 2019) and one with a professional classical vocal ensemble (Lim, 2014). Research with pre-professional and amateur ensembles is harder to find, but a study focusing

---

[1] Available at https://www.who.int/about/who-we-are/constitution

Naomi Norton, *Ensemble musicians' health and wellness* In: *Together in music*. Edited by: Renee Timmers, Freya Bailes, and Helena Daffern, Oxford University Press. © Oxford University Press 2022. DOI: 10.1093/oso/9780198860761.003.0025

on members of a competitively auditioned Scottish youth symphony orchestra and concert band (Hewitt & Allan, 2013) and another in-depth study with members of an amateur choral ensemble (Bonshor, 2017) are included to represent insights from outside the professional context.

Research with other populations indicates that maximizing health and increasing productivity are dependent on creating healthy cultures and environments; however, the majority of musicians' health and wellness research has focused on interventions designed to change *individual* musicians' beliefs and behaviors (Rickert et al., 2013). In contrast, the recommendations identified in this chapter focus on factors beyond individuals' capability, drawing on insights from a behavior change framework called "The Behaviour Change Wheel" developed by psychologists from the University College London Centre for Behaviour Change (Michie et al., 2014). An overview of this framework and its applications to musicians' health and wellness research can be found in Norton (2020). Four topics identified as causes of musicians' physical and psychosocial stress—which can play a role in the development of physical and psychosocial disorders (Jacukowicz, 2016; Parker et al., 2019; Rickert et al., 2013)—are addressed in the current chapter: (1) venue characteristics and configurations; (2) rehearsal organization, goals, and flow; (3) ensemble culture and social norms; and (4) social support and competition. The following sections are intended as a means of stimulating thought and discussion regarding the variety of environmental factors that can affect ensemble musicians and could be addressed to enhance health, wellness, and performance for all.

Venue characteristics and configurations

Rehearsal and performance spaces come in a wide variety of forms, from custom-designed venues through to the famous garages used by rock bands, and, in some cases, are not covered spaces at all (e.g. open air concerts, busking, or marching bands). Even in spaces that are designed for music, it is important to remember that the design is generally intended to facilitate "perfection of sound" rather than performers' health and wellness (Andersen et al., 2013, p. 127). There are characteristics that affect musicians within any venue: for example, temperature can affect blood flow, lighting can affect the ability to see the music and other performers, acoustics can increase or decrease noise exposure, and inter-performer space can affect posture and confidence. Research indicates that musicians who play in environments that are noisy, dark, and cramped are less satisfied than those who have space, can see, and are not subject to poor acoustics (Kenny et al., 2016). Even if the natural acoustics of a room are not optimal for music-making, it is possible to enhance the acoustics using strategies such as acoustic insulation (Wright-Reid & Holland, 2008). Beyond basic physical characteristics, it is important to consider the purpose of a space and associated norms: for example, many jazz and popular ensembles play in venues that are primarily intended for social events, and so usually include a bar serving alcoholic drinks and people taking advantage of that service. As a result, it becomes more socially acceptable, and possibly even expected, for musicians to drink alcohol during or surrounding their set (Dobson, 2011; MacDonald & Wilson, 2005). Understanding the influence of venue on musicians' behavior is an important step in identifying ways to reflect upon and modify behaviors.

There are considerations to be made within venues in terms of ensemble and audience layout and the positioning of individual members within the ensemble. Most ensembles probably do consider this but their focus is likely to be primarily on improving sound quality rather than promoting members' health and wellness; however, there are strategies that can enhance health and wellness as well as performance, or at least balance musicians' needs against achieving the optimal musical product. Research conducted by the Association of British Orchestras (ABO) resulted in a list of recommendations for reducing noise exposure without compromising on sound quality, and in some cases even enhancing it (Wright-Reid & Holland, 2008). They recommend thinking about "soundlines" from a musician to the audience: i.e. does the sound have to travel through people or objects upon leaving the instrument? If it does then that may dampen the sound, which can force the player to increase volume and expose human barriers to raised noise exposure. Soundlines can be enhanced by moving sections within an ensemble around, using staging or encouraging musicians to stand, using baffles to direct sound, or spacing players out to decrease sound exposure and allow sound to pass forward. It is worth noting that acoustic screens are often recommended as a means of reducing noise exposure, but Wright-Reid and Holland (2008) emphasize that this approach must be used cautiously as it can actually increase the overall noise exposure by reflecting sound at musicians on both sides of the screen and may also increase the physical demands on the player behind a screen who must play louder to be heard. Rotating individuals' positions within ensembles can help to reduce noise exposure as well as enabling people to experience different visual and oral perspectives and become more aware of other musical sections as well as the challenges of "tuning in" their musical radar from different positions (Dobson & Gaunt, 2015). As a cautionary note when recommending such changes, it is vital that layouts and strategies that will be used for a performance are practised in rehearsals to enable musicians to learn their surroundings and adapt their sound production and expectations accordingly (Bonshor, 2017; Wright-Reid & Holland, 2008).

The strategies above originate from research with professional classical orchestral musicians but could be used by other ensembles. However, they should be used cautiously, ensuring musicians' understanding and support and with consideration of members' comfort, confidence, and expertise. In contrast with recommendations regarding rotating positions, research with amateur choral singers highlights the importance of a consistent position within a familiar ensemble layout to support members' confidence and performance (Bonshor, 2017). Similarly, in contrast to preceding research with highly trained vocal ensembles, amateur vocal singer participants in their research by Bonshor (2017) disliked large gaps between singers and "mixed voice" layouts as they felt such configurations reduced their ability to hear and derive confidence from each other. Dobson and Gaunt (2015) also observed different findings from studies regarding coordination and communication in large-scale ensembles, depending on their focus on musical rather than social outcomes. These contrasting findings highlight the need for ensemble musicians to consider both the original context and aims of research used to develop recommendations for promoting health, wellness, and performance, and the importance of conducting context-specific research to investigate the transferability of such recommendations to new environments.

Rehearsal organization, goals, and flow

Ensemble rehearsals and concerts are often scheduled and organized at least to some extent. This trait is perhaps most evident for classical orchestras where rehearsals are directed by a chosen conductor, last for a specified length of time, and are intended to prepare pre-selected repertoire for concerts that are expected to be of a set duration. The duration, intensity, and frequency of rehearsals and practice sessions contribute to musicians' workloads and can play a role in the development of musculoskeletal pain and injury (Guptill, 2012; Jacukowicz, 2016; Kenny et al., 2016; Lim, 2014; Rickert et al., 2013). In addition, ensemble musicians are likely to have less personal choice than solo musicians in terms of planning how breaks and playing periods are structured within rehearsals (Andersen et al., 2013). Quotations from Danish professional classical orchestral musicians demonstrate their commitment to the music and perceived inability to take a break to relieve pain or tension while their section has music to play (Andersen et al., 2013): this is particularly the case for string players who have long passages and rare opportunities to rest their arms. Scheduled breaks within long rehearsals give musicians an opportunity to rest their hearing, voice, musculoskeletal system, and attention: recommendations from healthcare professionals suggest that breaks should take place approximately every 20–30 minutes, something unheard of in most rehearsals. However, astute ensembles and their directors (if applicable) can facilitate breaks within rehearsals by choosing varied repertoire to avoid overusing certain instruments and techniques, planning rehearsals to vary the intensity for individual players and sections, and rehearsing shorter sections to allow musicians to return to rest more regularly.

Conductors have a vital role to play in facilitating or disrupting the health, wellness, and performance of musicians in their ensembles. A key strategy for reducing noise exposure is to ensure that the conductor supports that aim as they can encourage the ensemble to play more quietly during rehearsals as well as selecting and rehearsing repertoire with varying dynamics to enable hearing to recover (Wright-Reid & Holland, 2008). Conductors' musical and organizational decisions influence young musicians' decisions to initiate and maintain their involvement in an orchestra (Hewitt & Allan, 2013) or, with professional musicians, their commitment to the ensemble's shared goals (Andersen et al., 2013). Research indicates that a conductor's goal orientation can affect ensemble members' collective beliefs, communication, concentration, capacity to achieve their potential, and strategies for dealing with challenge. A mastery or task-focused goal orientation involves developing skills and prioritizing processes leading to excellence, whereas pursuing performance or ego-oriented goals involves demonstrating competence relative to others (Matthews & Kitsantas, 2012). Matthews and Kitsantas (2012) reported that by using mastery rather than performance goals the conductor in their study created an environment in which higher education students in orchestral and band ensembles concentrated better, experienced a greater sense of belief in their own performance and that of the group, felt that failures related to inefficient strategies rather than a lack of ability, were able to create more effective strategies, and performed to a high standard. Goal orientation should be considered by all ensembles—not just those with a conductor—because performance goals have been identified as risk factors for performance anxiety among musicians (Lacaille et al., 2005). That said, it is once again vital to consider the context of this research and acknowledge that the outcomes of research with pre-professional instrumentalists studying on a higher education course may not transfer readily to professional or vocal ensembles, those with musicians of different ages, or those that are created to fulfil a purpose different to that of an auditioned university ensemble.

The concept of "flow", which involves individuals being "completely immersed and fully concentrated in an activity [experienced as] enjoyable and intrinsically rewarding" (Cohen & Bodner, 2019, p. 422), was first proposed by Csikszentmihalyi (1975). Flow has since been characterized by occupational science literature as a desirable state that is positively related to health and wellness (Guptill, 2012). Research indicates that many orchestral musicians experience a high state of flow during their musical activities (Cohen & Bodner, 2019; Guptill, 2012) and it has been suggested that interventions could be designed to help musicians achieve this state because it has been found to have a significant negative relationship with music performance anxiety (Cohen & Bodner, 2019) and a positive relationship with peak performance for ensembles through group flow (see Dobson & Gaunt, 2015). Paradoxically, because receding awareness of the body and a distorted sense of time are characteristics of a flow state, musicians experiencing flow may expose themselves to an increased risk of musculoskeletal injury by not taking regular breaks or being aware of their physical state (Andersen et al., 2013; Guptill, 2012). Professional musicians in Guptill's (2012) research described strategies that they use in their private practice to consciously *disrupt* flow to enable them to monitor their body to avoid injury: for example, using timers to break up practice, taking breaks, not playing pieces from start to finish, and playing a balance of challenging and relaxing repertoire. Many of these strategies are not immediately suited to most ensemble rehearsals and cultural change would likely be needed to make them possible or acceptable in ensemble environments. Research with athletes indicates that focusing on mastery rather than performance goals may be a key factor in achieving a state of flow (Stavrou et al., 2015), meaning that the suggestion of encouraging conductors to prioritize mastery goals could have implications for enhancing flow and thus reducing anxiety that would need to be balanced against the potential for increasing the risk of musculoskeletal injury. Unpicking the complicated interactions between flow, goal orientation, physical health, and psychological wellness will be vital to ensure that interventions designed to address one aspect of ensemble musicians' health and wellness do not inadvertently cause damage in other ways.

Ensemble culture and social norms

Within every ensemble there are "rules" or beliefs—some of which may be explicit and others that are unwritten—governing members' behaviors: it is these collectively created beliefs that are referred to as social norms (Rickert et al., 2014). The culture within an ensemble relates to these beliefs but also encompasses the attitudes and values that influence how group members behave, think, and react within the ensemble environment (Rickert et al., 2014). A particularly potent example of this relates to musicians' priorities, as explained by Andersen et al. (2013, p. 127): "musicians are raised in a culture that places the highest priority on creating the best possible sound rather than on considering the strain or potential damage to the body". This relates to the belief outlined in the preceding section suggesting that musicians feel they cannot stop to rest and relieve tension when the ensemble is playing: there is nothing physically preventing them from stopping, but the culture is such that it may be perceived as socially unacceptable. It is only a short step from not stopping to rest to performing while in pain or injured, which has been found to be a problem since some musicians still feel embarrassed, shameful, or guilty as they believe that injury is a sign of weakness and is associated with failure or poor technique (Rickert et al., 2014). A related influence on this type of behavior is the belief that pain is a natural consequence of being a musician (Andersen et al., 2013). Such beliefs should be challenged to ensure that musicians' health and wellness are valued as much as their performance and recognized as a means of achieving peak performance.

The insecure and freelance nature of many professional ensembles can, by itself, have a negative influence on musicians' physical and psychological health and wellness (Jacukowicz, 2016; MacDonald & Wilson, 2005; Parker et al., 2019), but it also makes it particularly important for aspiring ensemble members to be aware of, and able to adapt to, ensembles' social norms. Dobson (2011) refers to "professional sociability" as the need to be sociable and liked by peers as a means of finding and retaining work: this often involves a perceived need to socialize with members of an ensemble, frequently in the presence of alcohol. Dobson's (2011) exploration of drinking in socio-professional contexts highlights how socializing can be a bonding process that helps create and maintain group identity among freelance players but can be problematic in terms of potentially disadvantaging those who do not want to partake in such activities or for whom it could negatively influence their health and wellness. Above an expected baseline of musical excellence, social and interpersonal skills have been identified as crucial for professional orchestral musicians in relation to their ability to "tune in" to the ensemble and contribute to optimal performance (Dobson & Gaunt, 2015). It is possible that musicians perceive sociability outside the performance space either as a means of measuring peers' ability to cooperate within the performance space or as a means of enhancing that ability by building social bonds. More explicit awareness of this concept, and its personal and professional implications, could help existing and aspiring ensemble musicians to judge how to react to this social norm in terms of protecting and promoting their own and others' health and wellness. Research by Parker et al. (2019) also suggests that individual musicians should be aware of their motivations for pursuing an ensemble position and taking part in related socio-professional activities because motivation focused towards *having* to do something (as opposed to *wanting* to) was found to predict higher rates of problem drinking for those with uncertain job security.

Sometimes social norms and culture do not need to be changed, they simply need to be learned; unfortunately, guidance relating to ensemble etiquette is not often included in musicians' training. Research conducted with professional ensembles highlights the importance of pursuing shared ensemble goals and subsuming personal goals (Dobson & Gaunt, 2015; Lim, 2014; MacDonald & Wilson, 2005). This means that ensemble members may express distaste or disdain for those who conduct "brash or ostentatious warm-up routines" (Dobson & Gaunt, 2015, p. 12) or who follow their own impulses in performance at the expense of the ensemble (MacDonald & Wilson, 2005). Unless this is known, aspiring musicians may fall into the trap of wanting to show off their excellent musical skills in the hopes of impressing potential colleagues, an action that can have quite the opposite effect. Aspiring musicians recognize the value of participating in an ensemble to develop the skills needed for social integration into future professional and amateur musical environments (Hewitt & Allan, 2013) but that may not fully prepare them for what to expect in professional ensembles, especially as each is unique. Lim (2014) refers to the concept of joining a "community of practice" and suggests that one way of learning the social norms and culture of an ensemble is to attend, observe, and participate in peripheral tasks prior to becoming a core member. More explicit discussion of social norms, culture, and etiquette could help all ensemble musicians to become consciously aware of collectively created beliefs and decide whether they should be retained and taught to incoming members through modeling and education or training, modified somewhat, or abandoned entirely as a means of enhancing members' health, wellness, and performance.

Social support and competition

Musicians have relationships with others who they derive support from and support in turn: these networks facilitate musical engagement, can help to reduce stress and protect musicians' health and wellness (Hewitt & Allan, 2013; Jacukowicz, 2016; Parker et al., 2019; Philippe et al., 2019; Rickert et al., 2013), and contribute to the cooperation that is essential for group performance (Andersen et al., 2013). Positive social experiences within ensembles contribute strongly to young musicians' ongoing involvement in music (Hewitt & Allan, 2013) and strong social support has been associated with reaching a high level of achievement in music (Philippe et al., 2019). Bonshor (2017) highlights the potential benefits of group music-making for amateur musicians, with support from research by Lim (2014, p. 310) who states that it can "strengthen social attachment and weaken psychological boundaries between the self and the group" (see also Chapter 27). This becomes more challenging when membership of an ensemble forms part of a musician's occupation as there can be artistic, financial, and career consequences (Lim, 2014); however, among professional musicians there is recognition of the need to support peers through cooperative relationships, comradeship, and communication that does not need to form deep friendships but does establish interdependent working relationships (Dobson, 2011). Strong intra-ensemble bonds can create problems as musicians may play while in pain to avoid what they perceive as letting their colleagues down (Andersen et al., 2013). The level of dedication to music that leads many musicians to be subsumed within a musical world that defines their professional, leisure, and social activities can also prove problematic if they are forced to withdraw from an ensemble for any reason (Guptill, 2012). Improving social support within ensembles could be pursued as a means of improving musicians' health and wellness, but it would seem wise to balance it with encouragement for musicians to develop external social support networks that can provide variety and perspective as well as alternative means of support when internal ensemble networks are strained or removed.

The strain on social support networks increases when musicians are under pressure or in intense environments, for example while touring. Hernandez et al. (2009) conducted a detailed psychological profile of the members of a touring rock band: underlying psychological difficulties relating to ensemble goals and individual members' family situations, health, and identities indicated that there was a high likelihood of interpersonal difficulties developing. The authors suggest that psychologists could play a role in helping ensembles develop communication skills, self-reflection, and group expectations, particularly under stressful situations. This type of support and skill-building could be useful to all ensembles, something that has been recognized in professional sport teams with the inclusion of sport psychologists. Lim's (2014) presentation of the interpersonal relationships within The Swingle Singers (a full-time touring ensemble) suggests that the ensemble developed a culture whereby they recognize the value of conflict and develop strategies to resolve it satisfactorily, reflect on past crises to identify how to move forward, share decision-making, and maintain relationships while retaining the ability to adapt to new members. The means of achieving social and organizational harmony described by members of that ensemble could be used as reflection stimuli, particularly for touring ensembles.

There is an ongoing tension for musicians in terms of the potential for other musicians to act as both social support and also competition, as Dobson (2011, p. 248) summarizes: there is an "underlying tension … between regarding peers as competitors for future work, yet simultaneously acknowledging that the same people hold the potential to lead to new work opportunities." Rivalry and peer comparison can contribute to musicians doubting themselves and worrying about their reputation and career aspirations, which can negatively affect their health, wellness, and performance (Dobson, 2011; Jacukowicz, 2016; Kenny et al., 2016). Within an ensemble, work is inherently collaborative and recognition of this shared purpose may mediate the effects of competition at least to some extent. Unfortunately, bullying has been identified as an issue for musicians both in research (e.g. Kenny et al., 2016) and from industry sources,[2] but guidance and support for musicians are increasing.[3] Some of the topics already covered in this chapter hint at ways of enhancing social support while reducing competition: for example, changing an ensemble's goals to focus on mastery rather than performance can enhance collective efficacy (Matthews & Kitsantas, 2012), reflecting on social and organizational structure can help to promote harmony (Lim, 2014), encouraging musicians to learn about their own motivations and how to take advantage of social support can buffer them against health problems (Parker et al., 2019), and helping musicians to understand how reputations are formed and maintained could reduce self-doubt and comparison with peers (Dobson, 2011).

Conclusion

Using research drawn from a variety of musical contexts, this chapter outlines key physical and psychosocial environmental factors that can affect the health, wellness, and performance of ensemble musicians. To date, research has primarily focused on changes that can be made by individual musicians to enhance personal skills, strength, and stamina: this is vitally important, but there is a further need to make changes at a societal and environmental level to support individual change. One of the key considerations when developing or implementing interventions is to ensure that the original context or purpose of the research on which recommendations are based is compatible with the context in which the intervention is to be applied. Furthermore, behavior change theories indicate that it is vital to consider both the planned consequences and the potential side-effects of interventions aimed at improving health and wellness to ensure that enhancing one aspect does not prove detrimental to others (see Michie et al., 2014). The cultural and environmental factors that have been identified in this chapter are often perceived as unchallengeable. However, ensemble cultures, and the behaviors that they engender, can be changed although it may require a broadening of the health promotion toolkit to consider strategies that go beyond education and training: for example, by using intervention strategies such as modeling, environmental restructuring, training, and enablement as identified in behavior change literature (see Michie et al., 2014). The key to enhancing health and wellness may, at times, be the process by which ensemble musicians learn and navigate social norms. Enhancing ensemble musicians' health and wellness through a focus on environment, culture, and opportunity will need to involve a range

[2] See, for example, a report published by the Incorporated Society of Musicians (ISM) in conjunction with Equity and The Musicians' Union: https://www.ism.org/news/dignity-in-study-arts-students-at-risk-of-discrimination-bullying-and-sexual-harassment-finds-equity-ism-and-the-musicians-union
[3] Another webinar in the British Association for Performing Arts and Medicine (BAPAM) and ISM health and wellbeing series deals specifically with resilience and bullying in the workplace: https://www.ism.org/professional-development/webinars/health-in-the-gig-economy-2

of individuals and organizations including ensemble members and leaders, conductors, ensemble management, venue providers, support organizations, and educators. This chapter provides stimulus for discussion among these stakeholders in relation to environmental factors that can affect the biological, psychological, and social health of musicians performing in ensembles.

References

Andersen, L. N., Roessler, K. K., & Eichberg, H. (2013). Pain among professional orchestral musicians: A case study in body culture and health psychology. *Medical Problems of Performing Artists*, *28*(3), 124–30.

Bonshor, M. J. (2017). Confidence and choral configuration: The affective impact of situational and acoustic factors in amateur choirs. *Psychology of Music*, *45*(5), 628–44.

Cohen, C., & Bodner, E. (2019). The relationship between flow and music performance anxiety amongst professional classical orchestral musicians. *Psychology of Music*, *47*(3), 420–35.

Csikszentmihalyi, M. (1975). *Beyond boredom and anxiety*. Jossey-Bass.

Dobson, M. C. (2011). Insecurity, professional sociability, and alcohol: Young freelance musicians' perspectives on work and life in the music profession. *Psychology of Music*, *39*(2), 240–60.

Dobson, M. C., & Gaunt, H. F. (2015). Musical and social communication in expert orchestral performance. *Psychology of Music*, *43*(1), 24–42.

Guptill, C. (2012). Injured professional musicians and the complex relationship between occupation and health. *Journal of Occupational Science*, *19*(3), 258–70.

Hernandez, D., Russo, S. A., & Schneider, B. A. (2009). The psychological profile of a rock band: Using intellectual and personality measures with musicians. *Medical Problems of Performing Artists*, *24*(2), 71–80.

Hewitt, A., & Allan, A. (2013). Advanced youth music ensembles: Experiences of, and reasons for, participation. *International Journal of Music Education*, *31*(3), 257–75.

Jacukowicz, A. (2016). Psychosocial work aspects, stress and musculoskeletal pain among musicians. A systematic review in search of correlates and predictors of playing-related pain. *Work: A Journal of Prevention, Assessment & Rehabilitation*, *54*, 657–68.

Kenny, D. T., Driscoll, T., & Ackermann, B. J. (2016). Is playing in the pit really the pits? Pain, strength, Music Performance Anxiety, and workplace satisfaction in professional musicians in stage, pit, and combined stage/pit orchestras. *Medical Problems of Performing Artists*, *31*(1), 1–7.

Lacaille, N., Whipple, N., & Koestner, R. (2005). Re-evaluating the benefits of performance goals: The relation of goal type to optimal performance for musicians and athletes. *Medical Problems of Performing Artists*, *20*(1), 11–16.

Lim, M. C. (2014). In pursuit of harmony: The social and organisational factors in a professional vocal ensemble. *Psychology of Music*, *42*(3), 307–24.

MacDonald, R., & Wilson, G. (2005). Musical identities of professional jazz musicians: A focus group investigation. *Psychology of Music*, *33*(4), 395–417.

Matthews, W. K., & Kitsantas, A. (2012). The role of the conductor's goal orientation and use of shared performance cues on collegiate instrumentalists' motivational beliefs and performance in large musical ensembles. *Psychology of Music*, *41*(5), 630–46.

Michie, S., Atkins, L., & West, R. (2014). *The Behaviour Change Wheel: A guide to designing interventions*. Silverback Publishing.

Norton, N. (2020). Considering musicians' health and wellness literature through the lens of the Behaviour Change Wheel. *Journal of Music, Health, and Wellbeing, Autumn,* 1–25. Available to download from https://musichealthandwellbeing.co.uk/publications/naomi-norton-considering-musicians-health-and-wellness-behaviour-change-wheel

Parker, S. L., Jimmieson, N. L., & Amiot, C. E. (2019). Persisting with a music career despite the insecurity: When social and motivational resources really matter. *Psychology of Music, 49*(1), 138–56. https://doi.org/10.1177/0305735619844589

Philippe, R. A., Kosirnik, C., Vuichoud, N., Williamon, A., & von Roten, F. C. (2019). Understanding wellbeing among college music students and amateur musicians in Western Switzerland. *Frontiers in Psychology, 10*(820). https://doi.org/10.3389/fpsyg.2019.00820

Rickert, D. L., Barrett, M. S., & Ackermann, B. J. (2013). Injury and the orchestral environment: Part 1. The role of work organisation and psychosocial factors in injury risk. *Medical Problems of Performing Artists, 28*(4), 219–29.

Rickert, D. L., Barrett, M. S., & Ackermann, B. J. (2014). Injury and the orchestral environment: Part 2. Organisational culture, behavioural norms, and attitudes to injury. *Medical Problems of Performing Artists, 29*(2), 94–101.

Stavrou, N. A. M., Psychountaki, M., Georgiadis, E., Karteroliotis, K., & Zervas, Y. (2015). Flow theory – goal orientation theory: Positive experience is related to athlete's goal orientation. *Frontiers in Psychology, 6,* 1499. https://doi.org/10.3389/fpsyg.2015.01499

World Health Organization. (2006). *Health promotion glossary update.* https://www.who.int/healthpromotion/about/HPR%20Glossary_New%20Terms.pdf

Wright-Reid, A. W., & Holland, M. W. (2008). *A Sound Ear II: The Control of Noise at Work Regulations 2005 and their impact on orchestras.* http://www.iayo.ie/admin/wp-content/uploads/A-Sound-Ear-II.pdf

26
Musical interaction, social communication, and wellbeing

Tal-Chen Rabinowitch and Satinder Gill

Introduction

It has long been appreciated that music may contribute to social-emotional wellbeing (Aristotle, 335 BC/1941; Plato, ca. 375 BC/2006; Schopenhauer, 1819/1950). In recent years, this conventional wisdom has gained growing empirical support, and details have begun to emerge about how and under what conditions wellbeing may be most affected by music. Such studies engage participants in various musical activities, typically involving group interpersonal interaction, and compare the effects on diverse quantitative measures of wellbeing, with control groups performing equivalent, but non-music-related activities (Ings et al., 2012). Joint music activity has been shown to offer positive social and emotional affordances, for example in the context of aging (Creech et al., 2013), and perinatal stress (Chang et al., 2015; Perkins et al., 2018; Sanfilippo et al., 2019). Studies have further substantiated a role for music, including music listening, in alleviating conditions such as depression (Erkkilä et al., 2011; Maratos et al., 2008; Odell-Miller et al., 2018) and anxiety, such as in preoperative patients (Bradt et al., 2013).

How can engagement with music and, in particular, musical interaction affect wellbeing in such a positive way? To address this question, it is instructive to consider additional effects of group music-making that are not necessarily directly related to wellbeing, and to study the possible links between them. For example, it has been suggested that musical interaction may, in general, provide a sense of purpose, control, and self-affirmation, which could indirectly underlie increased wellbeing. This direction is discussed in greater detail in two chapters of this volume by Burland (see Chapter 27) and by English (see Chapter 28). Evidence exists also for physiological responses to musical interaction that could have an effect on wellbeing, such as reduced cortisol levels, increases in the immune response, and decreased inflammatory activity (Perkins et al., 2016). These remain outside of the scope of the current chapter. Instead, we will focus on joint music-making and its positive effects on behaviors such as sharing, empathy, and cooperation (Cho, 2019; Cross et al., 2012; Good & Russo, 2016; Keller et al., 2016; Kirschner & Tomasello, 2010; Rabinowitch et al., 2013), which have broad social and emotional impact that could readily apply to wellbeing. In particular, we will consider a fundamental feature of music-making, synchrony—the temporal alignment of the movements of interacting individuals[1]—and how experiencing such an attunement of body and perception may project on different aspects of wellbeing, at both short and long timescales.

---

[1] See Chapter 17 for a review of research relating to ensemble timing and synchronization, which extends the definition of musical synchronization to encompass the sounds produced as well as the physical actions required to produce the sounds.

Tal-Chen Rabinowitch and Satinder Gill, *Musical interaction, social communication, and wellbeing* In: *Together in music*. Edited by: Renee Timmers, Freya Bailes, and Helena Daffern, Oxford University Press. © Oxford University Press 2022. DOI: 10.1093/oso/9780198860761.003.0026

Entrainment in music and its social-emotional outcomes

In our everyday interactions with others, we are able to perceive and move in time and mutu-ally co-adapt to each other with the movements of our bodies and voices, sometimes without even intending to do so. Thus, we tend to automatically adjust our gait (Nessler & Gilliland, 2009; Zivotofsky et al., 2012) and speech (Richardson et al., 2008) to each other when we walk and talk together, and we are capable of performing a range of joint tasks that rely on periodic timing, such as team rowing or acrobatics. This fundamental social capacity to synchronize our different actions, to fuse individual motions into a joint coherent, rhythmic sequence is termed *entrainment*, and appears to underlie also how we typically make music together (Clayton et al., 2005). Since, for the most part, music is a highly temporal and rhythmic me-dium, it requires players to entrain their movements (tapping, strumming, pulling, blowing) to those of other players, but also to the intended beat of the music itself, producing in this way music of various speeds and characters. Indeed, even just listening to music entails an entrainment to its tempo, evident in the movements of the body and the mood that it evokes, as entrainment may constitute a potent emotion induction mechanism (Juslin et al., 2010; Vuilleumier & Trost, 2015). Rhythm and beat may influence our respiration and cardiovas-cular systems in similar ways as emotion-induced physiological changes occur (Scherer, 2004). This strong relation between music and entrainment has prompted some to propose that both may have co-evolved in the course of human evolution (Cross, 2003; Knight & Lewis, 2017; Merker, 1999). Perhaps, our basic ability to entrain emerged from some primor-dial musical behavior, and vice versa, mutually reinforcing each other as music and entrain-ment became more and more beneficial, culturally, socially, and emotionally, to human social existence (Cross, 2003).

Does interpersonal coordination such as entrainment and synchronization indeed have a direct positive influence on social-emotional behavior? A considerable body of research performed over the past two decades has provided broad evidence for the positive effects of interpersonal synchrony on a large range of social behaviors and attitudes (reviewed in Mogan et al., 2017; Rennung & Göritz, 2016; Vicaria & Dickens, 2016). These have been documented in adults (e.g. Hove & Risen, 2009; Lakens & Stel, 2011; Macrae et al., 2008; Miles et al., 2009; Valdesolo & DeSteno, 2011) as well as in children (e.g. Cirelli et al., 2014; Rabinowitch & Cross, 2019; Rabinowitch & Knafo-Noam, 2015; Rabinowitch & Meltzoff, 2017a, b; Tunçgenç & Cohen, 2016a, b). It does not seem to matter if participants are dir-ected to actively synchronize with other participants, such as tapping with them (e.g. Hove & Risen, 2009) or walking with them (e.g. Wiltermuth & Heath, 2009), or if they are being passively moved in synchrony with other individuals, such as being rocked (Cirelli et al., 2014) or swung (Rabinowitch & Meltzoff, 2017a, b). The results consistently show increases in measures of cooperation (Rabinowitch & Meltzoff, 2017a; Wiltermuth & Heath, 2009), helping behavior (Cirelli et al., 2014), perceived closeness and similitude (Rabinowitch & Knafo-Noam, 2015), affiliation (Hove & Risen, 2009), self-esteem (Lumsden et al., 2014), and empathy (Koehne et al., 2016) among participants who had engaged in synchrony experi-ence, compared to asynchrony or no experience at all.

Although the social-emotional impact of synchrony has been broadly characterized in ex-isting research, there remain several key open questions about how synchrony experience induces behavioral or motivational changes. So far, the impact of synchrony has been mostly examined immediately following the synchrony experience. It remains unclear how long

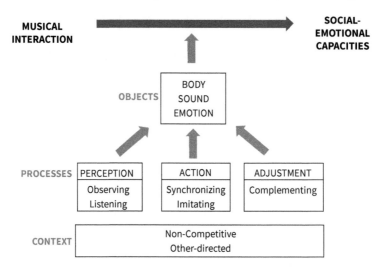

Figure 26.1 Model connecting musical interaction and social-emotional capacities.

these effects may last, whether repeated synchrony experience may extend the influence to the longer term (as in Pearce et al. (2015) who looked at the long-term effects of singing together), whether synchrony experience with one individual may alter one's rapport also with others who had not shared this experience, or whether other experiences, such as asynchrony, may counteract the effects of synchrony experience. Another understudied area is the impact of synchrony experience on individual measures of subjective wellbeing,[2] including physiological and mental balance, happiness, and satisfaction. Finally, the specific mechanisms that underlie behavioral and psychological outcomes of synchrony experience require thorough investigation. To this end, we describe in the next section a theoretical working model that could help explain or at least generate hypotheses about how synchrony, specifically as it occurs in joint music-making, may lead to enhanced social-emotional functioning.

A working model

Here we present a working model that is able to produce testable predictions that can help investigate and tune the way music can be harnessed to support wellbeing. We have previously developed such models that highlight several factors such as joint intentionality and intersubjectivity in musical group interaction and how they may be postulated to mediate music-induced boosting of beneficial interpersonal rapport and empathy (Cross et al., 2012; Rabinowitch, 2017; Rabinowitch et al., 2013). We will focus on basic processes that underlie group music-making and, in particular, synchronization within musical interaction—*perception*, *action*, and *adjustment* (see Fig. 26.1)—and consider how accumulated proficiency and experience may serve to enhance social aptitude and wellbeing also outside of the musical setting.

---

[2] https://www.hsph.harvard.edu/health-happiness/research-new/positive-health/measurement-of-well-being/

First, however, it is important to consider how context shapes the music interaction that is taking place. As we have previously emphasized, what matters is not so much *what* form of music is being played, but *how* it is being played (Cross et al., 2012; Rabinowitch, 2017; Rabinowitch et al., 2013). In many instances, musical interaction may readily turn into an activity that concentrates on competitiveness, stress, and self-focus (see Chapter 25). Such emphasis on promoting self, and on outperforming others, is a natural human tendency that can motivate hard work and lead to notable achievements. However, it is a rather poor background for fostering sensitivity towards others, or for promoting a sense of community and mutual care. Instead, a more balanced, less competitive, other-directed context for musical interaction is desired. This can be achieved in group music activities designed for promoting wellbeing and other social-emotional outcomes by a facilitator that structures and guides the interaction so that it is more collaborative, and focuses on the joint experience of the group's synergies rather than on differential skill, or on the quality of the musical piece ultimately produced (Rabinowitch et al., 2013). We posit that such an atmosphere of outward-looking joint music-making can set the foundations for enabling the transfer of social and emotional capacities, gained during joint music engagement, to other domains of social interaction outside music, in everyday life, for example with friends and family, and in organizational work practices.

Similar to other forms of joint action, group music engagement entails basic processes of perception, action, and adjustment, which are strongly tied to each other (see Chapters 13 and 17). These processes are directed towards multiple objects: *body, sound,* and *emotion* (see Fig. 26.1). Participants perceive the physical movements of their collaborators, listen to the sounds that are being produced, and may experience the same musical emotion (whether through expression and/or perception). As suggested by several studies mentioned above, it seems that entrainment may occur at a physical and emotional level (Juslin et al., 2010; Rabinowitch, 2017; Vuilleumier & Trost, 2015). The temporal rhythmic structure of the music lends itself to synchronization in movement and state of mind, as do the periodicity and expression in the movements of performers (e.g. Peckel et al., 2014; Zentner & Eerola, 2010). These perceptual aspects of joint music-making go hand in hand with action. Participants coordinate their movements to create a collective beat. Synchronization plays a key role here, as well as imitation of each other's movements and sounds. The ongoing cycle of synchronized action and perception (Keller et al., 2014) implies that the movements of others are perceived in relation to one's own movements, and each participant's movements feed back into the collective action. Thus, musical interaction requires from participants the ability and skill to continuously adjust their actions according to the perceived intentions of other group members, and to complement and co-adapt to them, attending to others' states and dynamics and joining in these dynamics without the need for explicit instructions. To some extent, this ability is innate. It can be observed, for example, in infant–parent interactions (Feldman, 2007; Trevarthen & Malloch, 2000). However, we reason that repeated experiencing of joint musical engagement and the proficiency gained during these interactions in reading others' intentions, in moving in synchrony with others, in being part of a collective, and in contributing in subtle ways to the joint process may generalize to other non-musical contexts, potentially refining the capacity to observe others, to notice nuances in their demeanor, and to recognize their emotions. Such capacity can be self-empowering because it enables a person to participate in a community and reaffirms them as being an organic part of it.

Conclusion

Growing evidence is available to show that musical interaction as well as synchrony (in either a musical or a non-musical context) can positively modulate a range of social-emotional behaviors. Given these findings, it is suggested that group music-making could provide an especially collaborative and allocentric context for experiencing synchrony. Indeed, we propose that synchrony experience may induce behavioral modification. We have outlined basic processes that take place during synchrony experience in joint music-making and inferred that this experience could benefit social-emotional behavior and capacities such as cooperation, closeness, and social bonding. Essentially, it is also possible that synchrony experience enhances wellbeing by increasing a sense of belonging and being part of a group, which may, in turn, help to decrease loneliness, depression, stress, and their physiological and mental manifestations.

What is currently missing is direct evidence for the effects of synchrony on wellbeing, and an empirical evaluation of the relation between action and perception in this process. The links between music, synchrony, and wellbeing encompass a broad range of disciplines, including musicology, music therapy, psychology, education, social work, and medicine. Therefore, it will be important to examine the direct links between synchrony experience and wellbeing from different perspectives and to align these results in order to obtain a more coherent and complete picture of the outcomes of musical interaction. Further experimental research will be needed to determine whether additional features of musical interaction, beyond synchrony, contribute to enhancing social and emotional competencies. Conversely, it will be instructive to compare the effects of synchrony in musical versus non-musical contexts. Another key assumption of our working model that requires empirical validation is that the manner in which joint music is performed matters. It will be important to compare in a controlled way the effects of self-directed (i.e. focus on how I perform, how I compare to others, how central I am) versus other-directed (i.e. attention to what others are doing, sharing the experience, collaborating) musical interaction.

The model's key assumption is grounded in a proposal that there are intrinsic relations between the processes of perception and action in group music interaction, shaped in how these processes are directed towards body, sound, and emotion. In doing so, it offers a relational conceptual mapping between the directing of these processes, for example co-adaptation, and their effects, which in the case of "co-adaptation" may include reading each other's states/ minds (intentions). Hence, this relational mapping (between intrinsic relations and their effects) may involve recognizing others' emotions and enable a person to be part of a community in emotion, body, and sound. The model extends the discussions on synchronous processes in musical interaction by proposing that synchronization is directed to people and other's emotions and expressions and that this directing, if done well, has effects. The model needs empirical validation, and its application may offer us further insights, as well as raise critical questions, into how contextual factors in group musical interaction, including synchrony, may affect wellbeing.

References

Aristotle. (1941). Poetics. In R. McKeon (Ed. & Trans.), *The basic works of Aristotle*. Modern Library.

Bradt, J., Dileo, C., & Shim, M. (2013). Music interventions for preoperative anxiety. *Cochrane Database of Systematic Reviews*, 6. https://doi.org//10.1002/14651858.CD006908.pub2

Chang, H. C., Yu, C. H., Chen, S. Y., & Chen, C. H. (2015). The effects of music listening on psychosocial stress and maternal–fetal attachment during pregnancy. *Complementary Therapies in Medicine*, *23*(4), 509–15.

Cho, E. (2019). The relationship between small music ensemble experience and empathy skill: A survey study. *Psychology of Music*. https://doi.org/10.1177/0305735619887226

Cirelli, L. K., Einarson, K. M., & Trainor, L. J. (2014). Interpersonal synchrony increases prosocial behavior in infants. *Developmental Science*, *17*(6), 1003–11.

Clayton, M., Sager, R., & Will, U. (2005). In time with the music: The concept of entrainment and its significance for ethnomusicology. *European Meetings in Ethnomusicology*, *11*, 1–82.

Creech, A., Hallam, S., Varvarigou, M., McQueen, H., & Gaunt, H. (2013). Active music making: A route to enhanced subjective well-being among older people. *Perspectives in Public Health*, *133*(1), 36–43.

Cross, I. (2003). Music and evolution: Causes and consequences. *Contemporary Music Review*, *22*(3), 79–89.

Cross, I., Laurence, F., & Rabinowitch, T.-C. (2012). Empathic creativity in musical group practices. In G. McPherson, & G. Welch (Eds.), *The Oxford handbook of music education* (pp. 337–53). Oxford University Press.

Erkkilä, J., Punkanen, M., Fachner, J., Ala-Ruona, E., Pöntiö, I., Tervaniemi, M., Vanhala, M., & Gold, C. (2011). Individual music therapy for depression: Randomised controlled trial. *The British Journal of Psychiatry*, *199*(2), 132–9.

Feldman, R. (2007). Parent–infant synchrony and the construction of shared timing: Physiological precursors, developmental outcomes, and risk conditions. *Journal of Child Psychology and Psychiatry*, *48*(3–4), 329–54.

Good, A., & Russo, F. A. (2016). Singing promotes cooperation in a diverse group of children. *Social Psychology*, *47*(6), 340–4.

Hove, M. J., & Risen, J. L. (2009). It's all in the timing: Interpersonal synchrony increases affiliation. *Social Cognition*, *27*(6), 949–60.

Ings, R., Crane, N., & Cameron, M. (2012). Be creative be well: Arts, wellbeing and local communities – an evaluation. Arts Council England. https://www.artscouncil.org.uk/sites/default/files/download-file/Be_Creative_Be_Well.pdf

Juslin, P. N., Liljeström, S., Västfjäll, D., & Lundqvist, L. O. (2010). How does music evoke emotions? Exploring the underlying mechanisms. In P. N. Juslin, & J. Sloboda (Eds.), *Handbook of music and emotion: Theory, research, applications* (pp. 605–42). Oxford University Press.

Keller, P. E., Novembre, G., & Hove, M. J. (2014). Rhythm in joint action: Psychological and neurophysiological mechanisms for real-time interpersonal coordination. *Philosophical Transactions of the Royal Society B: Biological Sciences*, *369*(1658), 20130394.

Keller, P., Novembre, G., & Loehr, J. (2016). Musical ensemble performance: Representing self, other and joint action outcomes. In S. S. Obhi, & E. S. Cross (Eds.), *Shared representations: Sensorimotor foundations of social life* (pp. 280–310). Cambridge University Press.

Kirschner, S., & Tomasello, M. (2010). Joint music making promotes prosocial behavior in 4-year-old children. *Evolution and Human Behavior*, *31*(5), 354–64.

Knight, C., & Lewis, J. D. (2017). Wild voices: Mimicry, reversal, metaphor, and the emergence of language. *Current Anthropology*, *58*(4), 435–53.

Koehne, S., Hatri, A., Cacioppo, J. T., & Dziobek, I. (2016). Perceived interpersonal synchrony increases empathy: Insights from autism spectrum disorder. *Cognition*, *146*, 8–15.

Lakens, D., & Stel, M. (2011). If they move in sync, they must feel in sync: Movement synchrony leads to attributions of rapport and entitativity. *Social Cognition*, *29*, 1–14.

Lumsden, J., Miles, L. K., & Macrae, C. N. (2014). Sync or sink? Interpersonal synchrony impacts self-esteem. *Frontiers in Psychology*, *5*, 1064. https://doi.org/10.3389/fpsyg.2014.01064

Macrae, C. N., Duffy, O. K., Miles, L. K., & Lawrence, J. (2008). A case of hand waving: Action synchrony and person perception. *Cognition*, *109*, 152–6.

Maratos, A., Gold, C., Wang, X., & Crawford, M. (2008). Music therapy for depression. *Cochrane Database of Systematic Reviews*, *1*. https://doi.org/10.1002/14651858.CD004517.pub2

Merker, B. (1999). Synchronous chorusing and the origins of music. *Musicae Scientiae*, *3*(1_suppl), 59–73.

Miles, L. K., Nind, L. K., & Macrae, C. N. (2009). The rhythm of rapport: Interpersonal synchrony and social perception. *Journal of Experimental Social Psychology*, *45*, 585–9.

Mogan, R., Fischer, R., & Bulbulia, J. A. (2017). To be in synchrony or not? A meta-analysis of synchrony's effects on behavior, perception, cognition and affect. *Journal of Experimental Social Psychology*, *72*, 13–20.

Nessler, J. A., & Gilliland, S. J. (2009). Interpersonal synchronization during side by side treadmill walking is influenced by leg length differential and altered sensory feedback. *Human Movement Science*, *28*(6), 772–85.

Odell-Miller, H., Fachner, J., & Erkkila, J. (2018) Music therapy clinical practice and research for people with depression: Music, brain processing and music therapy. In V. Karkou, & A. Zubala (Eds.), *Arts therapies and the treatment of depression* (pp. 154–71). Jessica Kingsley.

Pearce, E., Launay, J., & Dunbar, R. I. (2015). The ice-breaker effect: Singing mediates fast social bonding. *Royal Society Open Science*, *2*(10), 150221.

Peckel, M., Pozzo, T., & Bigand, E. (2014). The impact of the perception of rhythmic music on self-paced oscillatory movements. *Frontiers in Psychology*, *5*, 1037. https://doi.org/10.3389/fpsyg.2014.01037

Perkins, R., Ascenso, S., Atkins, L., Fancourt, D., & Williamon, A. (2016). Making music for mental health: How group drumming mediates recovery. *Psychology of Well-Being*, *6*(1), 11. https://doi.org/10.1186/s13612-016-0048-0

Perkins, R., Yorke, S., & Fancourt, D. (2018). How group singing facilitates recovery from the symptoms of postnatal depression: a comparative qualitative study. *BMC Psychology*, *6*(1), 1–12.

Plato. (2006). *The republic*. R. E. Allen (Ed. & Trans.). Yale University Press.

Rabinowitch, T.-C. (2017). Synchronisation – a musical substrate for positive social interaction and empathy. In E. King, & C. Waddington (Eds.), *Music and empathy* (pp. 89–96). Routledge.

Rabinowitch, T.-C., & Cross, I. (2019). Joint rhythmic tapping elicits distinct emotions depending on tap timing and prior musical training. *Emotion*, *19*(5), 808–17.

Rabinowitch, T.-C., Cross, I., & Burnard, P. (2013). Long-term musical group interaction has a positive influence on empathy in children. *Psychology of Music*, *41*(4), 484–98.

Rabinowitch, T.-C., & Knafo-Noam, A. (2015). Synchronous rhythmic interaction enhances children's perceived similarity and closeness towards each other. *PLoS One*, *10*, e0120878.

Rabinowitch, T.-C., & Meltzoff, A. N. (2017a). Enhancing preschoolers' cooperation through experience with synchronized movement. *Journal of Experimental Child Psychology, 160*, 21–32.

Rabinowitch, T.-C., & Meltzoff, A. N. (2017b). Joint rhythmic movement increases 4-year-old children's prosocial sharing and fairness towards peers. *Frontiers in Psychology, 8.* https://doi.org/10.3389/fpsyg.2017.01050

Rennung, M., & Göritz, A. S. (2016). Prosocial consequences of interpersonal synchrony. *Zeitschrift für Psychologie, 224*(3), 168–89.

Richardson, D., Dale, R., & Shockley, K. (2008). Synchrony and swing in conversation: Coordination, temporal dynamics, and communication. In I. Wachsmuth, M. Lenzen, & G. Knoblich (Eds.), *Embodied communication in humans and machines* (pp. 75–94). Oxford University Press.

Sanfilippo, K. R. M., McConnell, B., Cornelius, V., Darboe, B., Huma, H. B., Gaye, M., Ramchandani, P., Ceesay, H., Glover, V., Cross, I., & Stewart, L. (2019). A study protocol for testing the feasibility of a randomised stepped wedge cluster design to investigate a Community Health Intervention through Musical Engagement (CHIME) for perinatal mental health in The Gambia. *Pilot and Feasibility Studies, 5*(1), 1–8.

Scherer, K. R. (2004). Which emotions can be induced by music? What are the underlying mechanisms? And how can we measure them? *Journal of New Music Research, 33*(3), 239–51.

Schopenhauer, A. (1819/1950). *The world as will and representation.* E. F. J. Payne (Trans.). Dover Publications.

Trevarthen, C., & Malloch, S. N. (2000). The dance of wellbeing: Defining the musical therapeutic effect. *Nordisk tidsskrift for musikkterapi, 9*(2), 3–17.

Tunçgenç, B., & Cohen, E. (2016a). Interpersonal movement synchrony facilitates pro-social behavior in children's peer-play. *Developmental Science, 21*(1), e12505.

Tunçgenç, B., & Cohen, E. (2016b). Movement synchrony forges social bonds across group divides. *Frontiers in Psychology, 7*, 782. https://doi.org/10.3389/fpsyg.2016.00782

Valdesolo, P., & DeSteno, D. (2011). Synchrony and the social tuning of compassion. *Emotion, 11*, 262–6.

Vicaria, I. M., & Dickens, L. (2016). Meta-analyses of the intra- and interpersonal outcomes of interpersonal coordination. *Journal of Nonverbal Behaviour, 40*, 335–61.

Vuilleumier, P., & Trost, W. (2015). Music and emotions: From enchantment to entrainment. *Annals of the New York Academy of Sciences, 1337*(1), 212–22.

Wiltermuth, S. S., & Heath, C. (2009). Synchrony and cooperation. *Psychological Science, 20*(1), 1–5.

Zentner, M., & Eerola, T. (2010). Rhythmic engagement with music in infancy. *Proceedings of the National Academy of Sciences, 107*(13), 5768–73.

Zivotofsky, A. Z., Gruendlinger, L., & Hausdorff, J. M. (2012). Modality-specific communication enabling gait synchronization during over-ground side-by-side walking. *Human Movement Science, 31*(5), 1268–85.

27

Ensemble participation and personal development

Karen Burland

Introduction

The value of leisure in everyday life is far-reaching—offering a range of personal, social, and emotional benefits, including wellbeing, coping with negative life events and workplace stress, and managing physical/mental health. Rather than focus on named activities (like music or sport), the literature has tended to examine the level of engagement in "leisure pursuits" alongside individuals' motivations to participate (Haworth, 1997). Research focusing on musical activities demonstrates that the benefits of musical participation are similar to those associated with leisure activities more generally (Pitts, 2005), although until recently, only a relatively small number of studies have examined specifically the characteristics, functions, and value of collective music-making in ensembles. "Personal development" is often described as an outcome of musical participation and includes aspects relating to autonomy, confidence, self-awareness, social competence, and persistence. Much of the research exploring the impact of musical participation on personal development has directly involved children and young people, since there are many potential benefits for learning and general development. There is perhaps an implicit assumption that personal development occurs for adults within the workplace more than in extracurricular spaces; this chapter challenges that position, suggesting that ensemble participation for adults provides a valuable space for development which has benefits for both personal and working life.

One of the reasons that individuals are motivated to participate in any activity (be it for work or pleasure) relates to our identities and sense of self. We have as many identities as we have roles in our lives, and these influence our motivations, behaviors, and who we perceive ourselves to be—our sense of self. Music plays an important role in the formation, development, and maintenance of identity (DeNora, 2006) and a growing body of work suggests that musical identities influence an individual's sense of self, motivate behavior, and offer a sense of emotional and psychological wellbeing (Burland & Magee, 2014; MacDonald et al., 2017). Since learning and development (and our identity formation) take place within the myriad social contexts of daily life, there is good reason to suggest that the social dimensions of ensemble participation may also offer opportunities for individuals to develop, refine, or maintain personal identities. This chapter builds on a recent research study (Burland, 2017) to propose a theoretical framework for evaluating the ways in which ensemble participation influences personal development. The proposed framework is first introduced and subsequently discussed within the context of the existing literature in order to explore its implications for education, musical learning, and wellbeing. For the purposes of this chapter,

Karen Burland, *Ensemble participation and personal development* In: *Together in music.* Edited by: Renee Timmers, Freya Bailes, and Helena Daffern, Oxford University Press 2022. © Oxford University Press 2022. DOI: 10.1093/oso/9780198860761.003.0027

personal development is understood to encapsulate aspects of self-awareness, social competence, confidence, openness to learning, resilience, motivation, and satisfaction.

Identities at work and play

Understanding the value of ensemble participation for personal development relies, in part,
on how experiences within that context compare to other activities. Musical leisure activities
in adulthood are often undertaken to complement everyday or working life and examining
the contrasts in these contexts can usefully frame the ways in which ensemble participation
can influence personal development.

In order to gain deeper insight into the specific functions of musical leisure that influence the development and maintenance of identity, members of four amateur instrumental
ensembles based in South Yorkshire, UK, were invited to participate in a qualitative study.
Questionnaires (n = 47) gathered information about musical histories and levels of musical
engagement, working life, self-perceptions, and motivations to attend. A small number of respondents volunteered to participate in a follow-up interview (n = 9) and diary study (n = 5).
The semi-structured interviews gathered richer insights about the information provided
in the questionnaire, and the diaries captured the impact of daily experiences of work, life,
and music. Data were analyzed using Interpretative Phenomenological Analysis (Smith &
Osborn, 2003), a technique which prioritizes and uncovers the meaning attributed by individuals to their experiences. Full explanation of the method and results are in preparation.
Here the framing model will be explained and discussed.

Individuals spoke about the ways in which ensemble participation complemented their
professional (work-related) and personal identities (Burland, 2017). The data suggest that
ensemble participation can be characterized by five dimensions: group affiliation, opportunities for learning, pleasure and rejuvenation, wellbeing, and identity. These dimensions also
reflect other research in this area and provide a useful framework for understanding the ways
in which ensemble participation can influence personal development, particularly when it is
perceived as a positive or constructive experience. The dimensions highlight the interface of
musical participation with personal, professional, and musical identities.

Five dimensions of amateur musical ensemble participation

Group affiliation

The sense of belonging to a group of like-minded others lies at the heart of this dimension.
Enjoyment relates to the social aspects of group music-making, but also to the challenge associated with the collective effort; playing with others is more challenging than solo playing,
and more rewarding when there is noticeable improvement and success. The collective
sound, that can only be created by everyone together, is immersive but also makes individuals
feel valuable, valued, and as if they make a meaningful contribution. Group affiliation also
involves feelings of friendship and belonging. Meeting new people, seeing them regularly,
and feeling part of a community of shared interests provides a sense of responsibility to the

ensemble which goes beyond an individual desire to make music. Individuals are motivated to make music with other like-minded people in a context that stretches and broadens their range of experience.

Opportunities for learning

This dimension is characterized by a desire to learn and develop new skills, to feel challenged in a supportive learning environment. The right amount of challenge is crucially important, as participants are motivated by the right atmosphere, in which the camaraderie of the group supports learning, ignores mistakes, and allows individuals to feel encouraged and not overwhelmed. Learning derives from musical directors or other players or singers, as well as from the simple opportunity to make music regularly. It is important that ensemble rehearsals provide a space for something more than the act of preparing music for performance or improving overall standard: the process or act of getting together and "having a go" is an important feature of this kind of musical leisure. This overall ethos can sustain participation and has a positive impact on enjoyment and confidence.

Pleasure and rejuvenation

Ensemble participation often offers fun, enjoyment, pleasure, and joy. This dimension overlaps with *group affiliation* because it is, in large part, the process of making music with others that offers this level of pleasure. However, pleasure is not simply the result of its social context—as described by one of my participants, "Music is an environment that makes me feel free, it gives back much more than it takes and only takes as much as you want to give" (male, aged 56–65 years). Music-making in this context is not perceived to demand anything of its players—musical participation, in and of itself, is a rewarding and satisfying activity. Participants report that enjoyment and feelings of commitment to the group motivate attendance, and rehearsals offer rejuvenation which overcomes the tiredness and anxiety associated with a day at work, for example.

Wellbeing and health

Ensemble participation is perceived as immersive, such that individuals lose track of time (or experience a sense of "flow") due to the levels of concentration required and the physical or mental challenge of playing the music while listening to the other players. Making music with others provides opportunities for individuals to forget about work, or even themselves, and this offers a way to relax and relieve stress. For older participants, the "mental agility" afforded by group music-making is a desirable outcome. For others, with young families alongside busy jobs, ensemble participation offers a structured activity over which they feel protective—time for them to do something for themselves. The demands of ensemble participation (with the right amount of challenge) prevent any possibility of thinking about other aspects of life and this contributes to making it relaxing and fulfilling.

Music and identity

Ensemble participation is perceived as a crucial and vital activity. Participants often describe it as essential to life and as a core part of individuals' sense of being and their enjoyment of life. Shared musical activity provides personal and, for some, spiritual fulfillment. But more than that, playing music with others offers confidence that might be lacking in other contexts. One of my participants said: "I'm more confident, equal I guess … I feel special because it's like I belong to an elite group of people in the world. I think being a musician makes me a more interesting person and being part of this group adds to that" (female, aged 26–35 years). Ensemble participation helps the individual to "fill in the gaps" left by other experiences—tough times or a lack of confidence at work, externally driven demands on time, or the need to feel fulfillment from achievement and learning not offered by other activities—playing in ensembles offers the opportunity to complete and fulfill the self.

These five dimensions provide a theoretical framework for understanding how ensemble participation may foster personal development. For those participants with busy personal and working lives, ensemble participation provided a space for refocusing on—and, in some instances, rebuilding—the self. The relationship between the possible positive and negative characteristics of the workplace and the five dimensions of ensemble participation is shown in Table 27.1. The illustrative quotes provided in italics within the table are indicative of the ways in which the respondents identified that their ensemble participation helped to address some of the more negative aspects of the workplace while complementing more positive experiences. The enjoyable aspects of work on the left-hand side are the often sought and valued aspects of the workplace and everyday life, and many of these are also associated with ensemble participation. For example, respondents described how the pleasure and energy derived from playing with others compensated for some of the more solitary and repetitive aspects of work. The data suggest that the positive impact of group music-making on an individual's sense of wellbeing overrides, or at least offers temporary relief from, the negative emotional experiences associated with the workplace/everyday life, as well as what can be challenging working conditions—long hours and high workload, for example. This is underpinned by an individual's sense of who they are—at work and at play—and these different identities complement each other and contribute to the individual's overall sense of who they are. The complementarity of our identities offers a sense of health and wellbeing and a secure sense of self, and it is this which keeps us open to new experiences, challenges, and ultimately opportunities for personal development.

The theoretical framework described above proposes that individuals are motivated to seek out opportunities to engage in activities that extend and complement the enjoyable and satisfying (and sometimes negative) aspects of their working or everyday lives. Ensemble participation allows individuals to "fill in the gaps" by providing opportunities for development, enjoyment, satisfaction, achievement, and positive social relationships. Being part of a larger collective and contributing to creating a big sound that can only be achieved with others, the camaraderie of working on challenges with others, and the feeling of satisfaction which comes from playing and mastering challenging music provide an important source of enjoyment and satisfaction. Personal development depends upon the conditions created by the combination of the five dimensions; without a supportive, secure, and stimulating environment, the willingness to take risks and put oneself "out there" is hard to achieve. When

Table 27.1 Applying the five dimensions to the positive and negative characteristics of work

Positive@work →	Dimensions	← Negative@work
Social factors	**Group affiliation**	
(friendship, teaching, supporting others)	*A chance to be sociable, and an opportunity to play with others, being part of a community of shared interests*	
Achievement and satisfaction	**Pleasure and rejuvenation**	**Dissatisfaction**
(goals, impact, difference, change)	*Even if I'm tired I forget about everything else and find new energy*	(solitary, repetition, slow progress, burdensome workload or tasks)
Skills, learning, and opportunities	**Opportunities for learning**	
(autonomy, creating knowledge, creativity, problem-solving)	*I like the challenge and the fact that mistakes don't matter as the group plays on regardless. It's nice to be directed and challenged to push the boundaries of what I think I can play*	
	Wellbeing and health	**Negative emotion**
	I'm concentrating on what I'm playing and not thinking about anything else	(stress, politics, upsetting experiences, negative relationships, lack of respect)
	I find it relaxing to use my brain in a different way to how I do at work	**Working conditions**
		(pressure, working pattern, workload, poor management)

Music and professional (and other) identities

SELF

I feel music is a core part of my being. It stimulates and relaxes and I could not imagine enjoying life without it.

Note: The arrows suggest the ways in which individuals turn to music to complement, or counteract, aspects of working or daily life. Illustrative quotations from participants are provided in italics.

this all sits in balance, the benefits can, of course, lead to an overall improvement in the collective sound and progress of the ensemble too, with collective musical, as well as personal, outcomes.

Contextualizing ensemble participation and personal development

The next section explores the occurrence of the five dimensions in a range of contexts. Studies investigating ensemble participation are often focused case studies of particular contexts rather than large-scale investigations. Methods for capturing and measuring the impact of ensemble participation are varied, according to researchers' interests and expertise, or what is appropriate to each research context. It can be challenging to compare the findings of different studies in order to gain a comprehensive understanding of *why* ensemble participation is associated with particular outcomes or benefits; it is also difficult to consider the limits to which new knowledge can be applied in different contexts. For example, are the outcomes for vocal groups the same as those associated with instrumental ensembles? Are there differences in the experiences of ensemble members according to the genre of music involved? Is there a continuum of outcomes/experiences and what are the influential factors? Do outcomes/experiences vary across the lifespan? To what extent are the findings the result of the *musical* content, or the result of the *social* dimension of the activity? How does the experience of working with a group of musicians compare to playing a team sport, acting in a piece of theatre, or being a member of a book club? The extent to which ensemble participation provides a space for personal development that is beneficial outside of the rehearsal room also needs to be scrutinized and explored in more detail.

There is relatively little literature which draws direct connections between ensemble participation and personal development in adulthood; the research has tended to focus on the impact of musical participation in educational settings (school and university) or, alternatively, focuses on individual motivations for participation in community music contexts, as well as the implications for wellbeing or quality of life (cf. Hallam & MacDonald, 2016). One area of burgeoning interest that encapsulates the context of the Five Dimensions of Amateur Musical Ensemble Participation is that of workplace choirs. There has been a significant amount of research exploring the benefits of singing in choirs (cf. Clift et al., 2008) in a range of contexts, including with prisoners (Cohen, 2009), the homeless (Bailey & Davidson, 2002), those living with mental illness (Dingle et al., 2012), and for neurological rehabilitation (Särkämo, 2017). These studies highlight the social, emotional, psychological, cognitive, and physiological benefits of participating in choirs. Some of these studies are interventions, aimed to raise quality of life, enhance inclusion, and support those living with long-term illness; others provide snapshots of the ensemble participants' motivations and perceptions of the benefits of singing in a group. Workplace choirs are an interesting case to consider within the context of the discussion so far. Such activities are often introduced as part of wellbeing initiatives to improve the health and wellbeing of employees and to improve psychosocial working conditions (Nielsen et al., 2010). Studies suggest that workplace choirs can change the way that colleagues perceive each other, with the potential to transform the workplace (Balsnes & Jansson, 2015). Workplace choirs necessitate the suspension of established hierarchies and relationships and often involve people operating outside out of their everyday comfort zones in a way that facilitates learning experiences that can have a positive impact on workplace collaboration (Balsnes & Jansson, 2015). It is worth highlighting some reason for caution when considering this literature. Some research has demonstrated that men are less likely to participate in choirs, which suggests that workplace choirs may not appeal equally to all employees (Vaag et al., 2014). For a cultural intervention to facilitate the kind of environmental change evidenced in Balsnes and Jansson's study, for example, it should be widely implemented since "disparities could promote negative effects that may override any collective benefits that may have otherwise occurred" (Vaag et al., 2014, p. 59). Nielsen et al. (2010) echo this suggestion and emphasize that interventions are usually aimed at stress management, concluding that more work is needed to help understand how health interventions can promote personal growth and engagement. While this chapter is not focused on health interventions per se, this is relevant as it highlights the extent to which relatively little is known about the impact of ensemble participation on personal development (which includes, but is not limited to, health and wellbeing) in adulthood.

One interpretation of *how* choral singing can foster personal development is that it offers a challenge which, when met by the singers, offers reward and an opportunity to grow. In a study which aimed to explore the experience, meaning, and implications of choir singing, Tonneijck et al. (2008, p. 176) found that the singers felt connected to others, as well as distracted from the routines of daily life, which provided them with a sense of "wholeness:"

> … choir singing led to an experience of wholeness, feeling at one with one's own behavior and emotions, and not being separated from others. Participants perceived that engaging in choir singing provided a feeling of unity, brought about relaxation and energy, and generated intense feelings, which were highly valued. The choir seemed to function as a platform which supported the process of engaging with others and enacted and created wholeness, which was satisfying and gave pleasure.

While theirs was a small-scale case study with six respondents drawn from a single amateur choir, the implications of "wholeness" for understanding how ensemble participation can foster personal development are worth brief reflection. The interplay between our different identities contributes to our overall sense of who we are, and it could be argued, therefore, that ensemble participation provides one space through which to "complete the self." One implication of Tonneijck et al.'s (2008) research (and the proposed framework) is that people participate in ensembles as a *reaction to* the workplace or routine life. However, the relationship should be considered as mutually beneficial; the personal development afforded by ensemble participation has the potential to permeate other contexts and activities such that the sense of "ensemble musician" identity brings confidence and resilience to other identities and, ultimately, one's overall sense of self.

While research on choir participation dominates the literature, there are examples of other instrumental contexts, for example laptop ensembles (Cheng, 2019), orchestras (Arrowsmith, 2016), community and company bands (Sheldon, 1998), flute choirs (Taylor et al., 2011), and community bands for older adults (Dabback, 2008), and such work highlights the social, musical, and health benefits of participation, as well as indicating that there are additional benefits for community engagement and inclusion, and social democracy (cf. Chapter 28). There is little discussion in these studies of personal development as it has been defined in this chapter, although Cheng's (2019) study comparing participants in an acoustic orchestra or laptop ensemble highlights that leadership, motivation, decision-making, interpersonal communication, oral communication, and problem-solving were all developed through participation. In addition, it is suggested that the technologically oriented problem-solving nature of performing in a laptop ensemble provides generic skills that are fundamental for working in the rapidly changing landscape of a digital era. For an older population, ensemble participation has been found to offer opportunities for personal transformation, particularly through "the construction, reclamation and revision of musical identity" (Dabback, 2008, p. 282) in the context of identity loss after retirement (cf. Chapter 30). In addition, belonging to an ensemble provides structure and purpose and the sense of being a valuable contributor to the larger group. An additional point worth noting here is that good leadership is crucial if ensembles are to foster a safe and supportive context for personal development. Musical ensembles which have directors who are nurturing and supportive, and work to create a positive community spirit are valued over those who are driven by musical achievement (Taylor et al., 2011; see also Chapter 10).

The discussion so far has highlighted the benefits of ensemble participation for personal development, but it is worth highlighting that this is a potential bias in the research caused by the tendency to seek out information focusing on positive outcomes. Some research suggests that not all experiences of group music-making are positive, for reasons such as the negative impact of competition culture (Williamson & Bonshor, 2019) and negative social interactions with music directors and other ensemble members (Kreutz & Brünger, 2012), as well as frustration relating to self-perceived levels of competence (Taylor et al., 2011). Understanding the richness of both positive and negative experiences of ensemble participation, and recognizing that there is not a one-size-fits-all explanation for the impact of making music with others, is undoubtedly of value in order for ensemble directors and participants to understand how such experiences can be optimized (see Chapter 25).

Conclusion

This chapter has presented a framework for evaluating ensemble participation for personal development. Making music with others helps us to formulate and refine our identities in ways that enable us to "complete the self"—to counteract the impact of negative experiences at work or in everyday life, for example. Ensemble participation is characterized by group affiliation, opportunities for learning, pleasure and rejuvenation, wellbeing, and identity work, and these elements combine to create a space for individuals to learn about and challenge themselves, to develop new skills, and to connect with others; such outcomes permeate our other roles and activities and therefore offer opportunities for personal development in non-musical contexts too.

There is still much to learn about the wide variety of instrumental ensemble contexts that now exist within increasingly different communities, and understanding their impact for different groups of participants, across the lifespan, should now be a priority. While this chapter has focused primarily on adults and working life, there is scope to understand more about those who are full-time carers or unemployed, work part-time, or who are experiencing transitions (into caring roles, ill-health, retirement, and new jobs). This chapter speculates about the value of ensemble participation, specifically for personal development, as there has been little research until now; more focused research to understand and verify the myriad ways in which ensemble participation interacts with everyday and working life will undoubtedly enhance our understanding about the value of making music with others more broadly.

References

Arrowsmith, J. D. (2016). *Paradigms, perspectives and participation: Reconceptualising amateur orchestras as unique socio-musical communities of practice* [Unpublished doctoral dissertation]. College of Business, Arts and Social Sciences, Brunel University.

Bailey, B. A., & Davidson, J. W. (2002). Adaptive characteristics of group singing: Perceptions from members of a choir for homeless men. *Musicae Scientiae, 6*(2), 221–56.

Balsnes, A. H., & Jansson, D. (2015). Unfreezing identities: Exploring choral singing in the workplace. *International Journal of Community Music, 8*(2), 163–78.

Burland, K. (April 3–5, 2017). *Understanding the psychological dimensions of music ensemble culture* [Conference presentation]. Society for Education, Music and Psychology Research Conference on Musical Cultures. University of Hull.

Burland, K., & Magee, W. M. (2014). Music technology in therapy and its relevance to identity. In W. M. Magee (Ed.), *Music technology in therapeutic and health settings* (pp. 327–48). Jessica Kingsley Publishers.

Cheng, L. (2019). Musical competency development in a laptop ensemble. *Research Studies in Music Education, 41*(1), 117–31.

Clift, S., Hancox, G., & Morrison, I. (2008). *Choral singing, well-being and health: Summary of findings from a cross-national study.* Canterbury Christ Church University. https://www.artshealthresources.org.uk/wp-content/uploads/2017/02/2008-Clift-Cross-national-survey-of-singing-and-health.pdf

Cohen, M. (2009). Choral singing and prison inmates: Influences of performing in a prison choir. *Journal of Correctional Education, 60,* 52–65.

Dabback, W. M. (2008). Identity formation through participation in the Rochester New Horizons Band programme. *International Journal of Community Music, 1*(2), 267–86.

DeNora, T. (2006). Music and self-identity. In A. Bennett, D. Shank, & J. Toynbee (Eds.), *The popular music studies reader* (pp. 141–7). Routledge.

Dingle, G. A., Brander, C., Ballantyne, J., & Baker, F. A. (2012). "To be heard": The social and mental health benefits of choir singer for disadvantaged adults. *Psychology of Music, 41*(4), 405–21.

Hallam, S., & MacDonald, R. (2016). The effects of music in community and educational settings. In S. Hallam, I. Cross, & M. Thaut (Eds.), *Oxford handbook of music psychology* (2nd ed.) (pp. 775–88). Oxford University Press.

Haworth, J. T. (1997). *Work, leisure and wellbeing.* Routledge.

Kreutz, G., & Brünger, P. (2012). A shade of grey: Negative associations with amateur choral singing. *International Journal for Research, Policy and Practice, 4*(3), 230–8.

MacDonald, R., Hargreaves, D. J., & Miell, D. (Eds.) (2017). *Handbook of musical identities.* Oxford University Press.

Nielsen, K., Randall, R., Holten, A.-L., & González, E. R. (2010). Conducting organizational-level occupational health interventions: What works? *Work & Stress, 24*(3), 234–59.

Pitts, S. E. (2005). *Valuing musical participation.* Ashgate.

Särkämo, T. (2017). Music for the ageing brain: Cognitive, emotional, social and neural benefits of musical leisure activities in stroke and dementia. *Dementia, 17*(6), 670–85.

Sheldon, D. A. (1998). Participation in community and company bands in Japan. *Update: Applications of Research in Music Education, 17*(1), 21–4.

Smith, J. A., & Osborn, M. (2003). Interpretative phenomenological analysis. In J. A. Smith (Ed.), *Qualitative psychology: A practical guide to methods* (pp. 53–80). Sage.

Taylor, D. M., Kruse, N. B., Nickel, B. J., Lee, B. B., & Bowen, T. N. (2011). Adult musicians' experiences in a homogenous ensemble setting. *Contributions to Music Education, 38*(1), 11–26.

Tonneijck, H. I. M., Kinébanian, A., & Josephsson, S. (2008). An exploration of choir singing: Achieving wholeness through challenge. *Journal of Occupational Science, 15*(3), 173–80.

Vaag, J., Saksvik, P. E., Milche, V., Theorell, T., & Bjerkeset, O. (2014). "Sound of Well-being" revisited – Choir singing and well-being among Norwegian municipal employees. *Journal of Applied Arts and Health, 5*(1), 51–63.

Williamson, V. J., & Bonshor, M. (2019). Wellbeing in brass bands: The benefits and challenges of group music making. *Frontiers in Psychology, 10,* 1176. https://doi.org/10.3389/fpsyg.2019.01176

28

Empowering ensembles

Music and world-building past and present

Helen J. English

Introduction

There is a growing body of research into the benefits of membership of a music ensemble. These range across dimensions of psychosocial wellbeing and encompass broad areas of social connections, identity formation, personal growth, and emotional health (see also Chapters 25, 26, and 27). Within these dimensions, some specific areas, notably agency, accomplishment, and meaning-making, contribute to what is termed empowerment. The use of the term empowerment suggests a referral to individuals and groups who lack power in some way. The term therefore often surfaces in relation to societal groups who experience inequities such as women, youth, older people, the less able-bodied, refugees, ethnic minorities, Indigenous people, and prisoners. In this chapter, I review some current research into ensemble music-making in relation to empowerment and then share my own recent comparative research into historic and current music ensembles in a continent characterized by waves of immigration beginning 60,000 years ago. As a further point of comparison with historic settlers' music-making, the chapter closes by reviewing some social justice ensembles created by and for migrants and refugees.

Empowerment and contributing factors

The majority of literature investigating the benefits of ensemble membership focuses on choirs. This is, in part, a flow-on effect from choral research in the early 2000s demonstrating positive effects, some remarkable, such as the regaining of language through singing for stroke survivors (Marley et al., 2018) and significant self-affirmation for people at the bottom of society (Bailey & Davidson, 2005; Davidson, 2011; Silber, 2005). It is also because, as accessible ensembles that are easy to establish, choirs are numerous; they do not require instrumental skills, and often no music reading skills or even a strong voice. Community choirs tend to be open to anyone. They may encompass a wide socioeconomic and age range and are inclusive of less able-bodied individuals.

A choral singing effect has been noted where choir participants' bodies entrain as their heart rates align and they breathe together (Vickhoff et al., 2013). This synchronization enhances members' perceptions of interconnectedness (Pearce et al., 2015); it may also give a sense of being part of something larger than oneself (see Chapter 27). Singing in choirs can also have very positive outcomes for dementia sufferers and their carers with noted

Helen J. English, *Empowering ensembles* In: *Together in music.* Edited by: Renee Timmers, Freya Bailes, and Helena Daffern, Oxford University Press. © Oxford University Press 2022. DOI: 10.1093/oso/9780198860761.003.0028

improvements through arousal, leading to raising of mood, enhanced communication, and increased wellbeing (Anderson & Sheets, 2017).

Published research into instrumental or electronic ensembles is less in evidence. Current research includes a focus on drumming circles (Ascenso et al., 2018), ukulele groups, swing bands (English et al., 2018), and brass bands (Williamson & Bonshor, 2019). Research into specially formed groups includes a MIDI keyboard ensemble (Pike, 2011) and an all-women rock band (Laes, 2015). Overall, research into instrumental groups reveals that many of the same benefits come with participation as have been found in choirs, for example social connectedness, emotional wellbeing, and sense of accomplishment. Interestingly, participants tend to like their ensemble sound-world better than that of others, whether it be a male harmony chorus or a brass band (English et al., 2018). This is most likely due to an attunement to that specific timbral world, as well as other factors, including affinity, familiarity, and group bias through attachment to the group (Shelemay, 2011). Such is the loyalty developed in these ensembles, members often offer long-term commitment to their group.

Ensemble participation is often described as empowering (Ascenso et al., 2018; Creech et al., 2013; Laes, 2015). Empowerment has been identified as a multi-layered concept that includes developing agency, sense of control (or autonomy), purpose, meaning-making, and accomplishment (see Chapter 4 for a detailed study of musical agency). In ensembles, these aspects develop during rehearsals, usually weekly, and therefore some, such as accomplishment, take time. Not all ensembles choose to perform, but for many of those that do, performance adds another dimension, through firstly the achievement of performing, and secondly the communication between performers and audience (Bailey & Davidson, 2005; Silber, 2005). Experiences of self-worth and communication with others flow through to empowerment, which often continues after the performance event (Bailey & Davidson, 2005). Participating and performing in an ensemble can potentially be empowering for anyone, but its effects are especially notable when the participants are disadvantaged in some way (Bailey & Davidson, 2005; Silber, 2005). Therefore, ensembles for demographic groups such as the homeless, prisoners, and older people isolated by infirmity can potentially reveal significant impacts and benefits within the context of their everyday sense of powerlessness (see also Chapter 10).

Work by Ascenso et al. (2018) exemplifies the empowering benefits of a drumming group for people with mental health issues. They found increased agency expressed by all participants as an enhanced ability to make choices and take initiatives. This flowed into greater engagement both within the drumming sessions and outside. Empowerment also grew from a sense of control in participants' lives through the structure of regular sessions that, in turn, led to increased confidence. In relation to a rock band intervention for older women (70+), Tuulikki Laes (2015, p. 55) argues that empowerment comes through an "expansion of agency." In her study, this related to the women's exploration of a music world that they had not experienced before as active participants. Here empowerment was related to the disruption of stereotypical ideas about what was suitable for older women—one participant referring to "depressing old people's music" (p. 59) as the usual musical experience on offer. Actively engaging in a music genre outside of stereotypes fostered a sense of accomplishment, specifically through the meaning-making associated with this new experience.

For some members of ensembles, experiences of performing for others bring a sense of empowerment through being given a voice usually denied by circumstance. In the case of a choir for homeless men in Canada, participants described their performances as empowering because of the real-time exchange that took place between performers and audience. The men felt recognized as people of worth, seen in a new light because of their role as musical communicators (Bailey & Davidson, 2005). Bailey and Davidson (2005) compared the men's sense of empowerment with that of a middle-class choir and found that the level of empowerment and its experience was significantly higher for the homeless men. A choir for women prisoners in Israel revealed similar benefits. Members of the choir, which was in a maximum-security prison, felt that they were seen and listened to differently through choral performances, that "we're really not animals or the way they describe us on the outside" (Silber, 2005, p. 267). However, for this sense of empowerment and connection with the audience to occur, much groundwork was first achieved in areas of trust, listening, and cooperating with the conductor. Resultant changes in behavior were associated with a sense of self-control, a shift to allowing connections with others and working as a team. The final performance at a songfest outside the prison gave members a sense of purpose and musical achievement (Silber, 2005).

Musical accomplishment is an important factor in empowerment. A recurring theme from music ensemble participants is surprise at what they are able to learn musically and the confidence they gain in holding their own in a musical group and even performing despite previous doubts. In the rock group project for older women, empowerment followed from ways in which the women met the challenges of learning a new style of music and its instruments: electric guitar and bass, keyboard, and drumkit. Learning to play the instruments, the rock music style, and reaching the performance level required a high level of commitment and motivation. The effort required and the unlikeliness of a third-age rock band seemed to increase the sense of achievement and empowerment experienced (Laes, 2015). Highlighting historical parallels, the next section describes the empowerment that music ensembles brought to settler communities in rural New South Wales (NSW), Australia, as signs of culture and accomplishment.

Settler music ensembles

Settler ensembles in historic Australian communities conferred some of the same benefits on members in terms of accomplishment and purpose, with self-worth (described as respect) an important aspect for the individual and community. Details of ensembles in mining townships near Newcastle, NSW, and their activities have been gleaned from extensive and careful examination of both local and metropolitan colonial newspapers, including the *Newcastle Chronicle* (1866–76) and *Miners' Advocate* (1873–76). Miners came out to the Newcastle region from Britain looking for work in what came to be known as the Coalopolis. Some had lost their jobs as reprisal for involvement in strikes, such as the 1844 Strike in Northumberland and Durham, England. Although their first homes were often bark huts in settlements with very little infrastructure, men and women from British coalfields were quick to form the same ensembles that were important to them in Britain: chiefly choirs and bands, of which brass bands became a strong part of Newcastle region's identity. The sound-worlds of these recreated ensembles and their repertoire connected settlers back to past lives, places, and relationships (English, 2020). Both choirs and brass bands were sources of empowerment for their communities who were eager to establish them as named for their townships, such as Wallsend Brass Band and Lambton Choral Union (English, 2017). These two ensemble types were empowering in distinct ways which related to their use and membership.

Brass bands came from British communities where they were closely associated with miners and their unions. In the Newcastle region, each band's importance to its community is demonstrated by their accompanying every social and civic activity, performing in processions, at picnics, on trains and steamers, and for dances and theatre. Bands played at union meetings and held their own outdoor concerts. Their central role comes through strongly in accounts of miners' demonstrations, such as one in 1874 when four bands marched alongside miners from the local collieries. Their sound carried through the air and across the cliffs, signaling the power and solidarity of the miners to onlookers through their brass sound and repertoire that had meaning for the communities (English, 2020).

While brass bands were strongly working class, choirs were collaborations between working and emerging middle classes and their performances were always attended by leading citizens, such as mine managers and aldermen of the town. Choirs were empowering in part because of their repertoire, which was viewed as high status. Empowerment for settler miners came from gaining self-respect and then gaining the respect of others in a period when miners were often vilified and characterized in racial terms with their coal-stained hands and faces (English, 2020). Singing in choirs or practicing in brass bands brought a sense of musical accomplishment and cultivation in the pursuit of something for itself and not for financial gain.

The non-denominational choirs were open to anyone and there were plenty of pathways into them from Sunday school singing classes to adult education such as *Singing for the Million!*, a movement that drew on simplified notation developed in the nineteenth century. The township choirs performed a range of repertoire, among which sacred works, including oratorios, were important. These works held particular prestige in the nineteenth century, a time when music was often regarded as the most spiritual and sublime of the arts. It was also in the nineteenth century that the consumption of art music (as opposed to music that was to gain the appellation "popular") became associated with status. This association afforded miners the opportunity to change firstly their own self-respect and then perceptions from power-brokers in Sydney of their respectability and worth (English, 2020). Newspaper reporting on events conveys the ongoing prejudices with which miners had to grapple and the real impact that their public choral performances had towards dissipating these. One event in particular makes this clear when a concert was held to mark a visit in 1879 by the Honorable Saul Samuel, Postmaster General for the NSW colony. Reflecting on this concert, "well calculated to disarm an unjust prejudice," Samuel was "most agreeably surprised at the very superior style of singing … and the pleasing class of people he had met with." The importance of this announcement for the local mining community is highlighted in local reporting that referred to the concert as "long remembered in the annals of Wallsend" (English, 2017, pp. 117–18).

Ensembles today in the Newcastle region

Today in the same region of Australia, comprising Newcastle, Lake Macquarie, and the Hunter Valley, there are a wide range of amateur ensembles, including brass bands, wind and jazz bands, ukulele groups, orchestras, and choirs. Six of these ensembles were the focus of a research project in 2017 (English et al., 2018). Themes of connections, accomplishment, purpose, control, and meaning-making emerged, which fed into a sense of empowerment. Music's capacity to bring back memories was another significant source of self-discovery and power.

Music has been shown to be one of the most powerful triggers for memory. In a process called anamnesis, music may bring back details from past hearings, including a sense of the self in the past and connections to others and to place (DeNora, 2000). The sense of connecting to the past, particularly past selves, can be renewing and empowering and seems to become more powerful as we grow older. For older adults, a recurring theme is that of reconnecting to something lost, of being given the opportunity to develop a passion that was denied in childhood or adolescence. This suggests that an aspect of empowerment for older music ensemble members may stem from the connection music affords to their youthful selves. In research into older participants' ensemble experiences, Creech et al. (2013, p. 97) found that music-making could be a means for "redefining one's identity or rediscovering a lost 'possible self'." The connection to the past experienced as nostalgia is especially powerful when it links back to our teenage years. Because experiences from this period of self-discovery are emotionally charged, memories are more likely to be embedded. We recall these as important through a process described as tagging (Levitin, 2006).

The theme of rediscovery of a "musical self" surfaced in comments from members of Newcastle region ensembles regarding reconnecting with something whose importance participants had forgotten or discovering abilities they had not thought they had. A frequently held perception was that as a child, they were not musical—this was often expressed in terms of siblings who were. The late discovery of their own capacity to acquire musical skills was a source of surprise and joy for many, especially older members. In focus group discussions with members of two ukulele groups based in Newcastle and Lake Macquarie, comments such as "I feel wow even at my age I can actually play a musical instrument and feel as if I can do it not too badly" and "I never, ever, would have thought that I could do, learn music" were common from these ensemble members. Other members spoke of discovering in themselves a great passion for music theory, or of overcoming doubts to perform solo with their group. In brass bands, because learning is often intergenerational, empowerment comes also from the sense of history and moving into the future, as well as musical accomplishment. Members of a Lake Macquarie brass band spoke of the band as a family tradition and took great pleasure from playing alongside children and parents.

In 2014, Community Music Victoria (Australia) initiated a street music project (*Street Sounds*) with the intention of starting a movement for community music in both metropolitan and rural Victoria. As a result, street music groups now proliferate across the state. In early 2018, a community street opera, the culmination of two years' preparation and rehearsals, was performed at Pentridge Prison in Coburg, Melbourne. The opera retold the story of Adela Pankhurst's imprisonment there and of women who sang under her window in support. Over 100 amateurs, mainly singers, took part and rehearsed over a five-month period. Focus groups with members of the collective brought up themes of connections to the past, wellbeing, and lifelong learning leading to empowerment (English & Davidson, 2020). Because of the historical and political focus, themes of restoration and activism also emerged. In keeping with other community ensembles, participants experienced personal growth through the project as they met the challenges of acquiring new skills. The sense of reconnection to the past and a "lost self" came through strongly. The re-enactment of the imprisonment of Adela Pankhurst and the positive actions of local women at the time led to many expressed feelings of recovering the past, of putting things right with respect not only to this suppressed history, but also to other war histories and to rebutting prevailing positive war stories. Participants commented on their contribution, noting, for example, the project was "kind of restoring from ourselves as to what was really important and what's worth doing, what's worth spending time on" and "I feel very privileged to be a part of that … incredible story and it was great that it was told" (English & Davidson, 2020).

Empowerment also came from singing alongside people with the same convictions, people who "proudly sing Solidarity Forever and The Red Flag." The connection to the past was mirrored by connections to participants' own past. For some, it was the political content that "reconnected that part of me and my life;" for others, it was the chance to engage with their past musical self: "I've done amateur singing in my very younger days um I haven't done it for a long, long time so it's almost reconnecting with that," and from a male participant who described how the opera provided something "that I'm missing and that was music and I thought, Oh, how could I have forgotten music is absolutely essential for my life!" (English & Davidson, 2020).

For the nineteenth-century migrant miners, music brought solace and a sense of connection back to relinquished places and traditions. The community groups who practice today draw on memories of youth and intergenerational learning for self-discovery in the present. Migrants and refugees experience the same challenges as the settlers, encountering unfamiliar surroundings, and at the same time coping with language challenges and barriers. Often for such groups, music ensembles offer a connection to the past and a means of navigating the present.

Ensembles that recreate music from the members' culture

In communities across the globe, cultural music groups meet for a variety of reasons, including to connect with others who are linked to specific places, culture, and memories, and to preserve their heritage. It is also important for many to share their musical culture with people from other backgrounds. Such groups are proliferating in Australia: examples include those dedicated to preserving culture, such as the Melbourne-based Bosnian group *Behar* and the Italian groups *Voce della Luna* and *Coro Furlan*. These vocal ensembles sing repertoire from their musical heritage in their languages: Bosnian, Italian, and Furlano. The music connects them to memories of places, ways of being and doing, and a sense of themselves at an earlier time. For example, members of the Bosnian choir *Behar* speak of connections to memories and an old lifestyle (Joseph & Southcott, 2018). *Coro Furlan*, an all-male choir, is open to anyone "with a passion for Italian music" and aims to preserve Friuilian musical culture for coming generations. *La Voce della Luna* (The Voice of the Moon) is an all-female choir of first, second, and later generations of Italian Australians. These ensembles help establish and maintain their cultures' distinctiveness.

While performances of music of a particular heritage have such positive benefits, they also have the potential to be exclusionary or divisive. This emerges when considering aspects such as the music's use historically, the cultural group the music represents (and the ones it does not), and the ways the music is re-presented. For example, in Sydney, a Turkish music ensemble which seeks to share its heritage with other non-Turkish Australians presented a concert "The City of the Sultans, The Sultan of the Cities: Istanbul." The organizers aimed to celebrate the city as an exemplar of multiculturalism through music and images. However, such re-creations are not straightforward, since memory is always selective and nostalgia is an emotional state that tends to idealize the past. In this instance, the performers sought to promote music associated with the cultural revolution of the Turkish Republic through the image of Istanbul, thereby replicating the revolution's strategic use of music "to construct national histories" (Senay, 2009, p. 77). Performances such as "Istanbul" therefore evoke an imagined and idealized place constructed from memories and may not represent everyone. This said, such performances are important for the performers and their communities as personal and collective confirmation of their identity through culture.

For migrant groups, music is often a connective vehicle to their identity and pasts (albeit reimagined) and a means of keeping their heritage alive. It is also a means of sharing and connecting to other cultures through the enjoyment of music. This was seen in a recent project *Songs from my Grandmother*, developed by the Multicultural Museums Victoria in association with the Australian Research Council's Centre of Excellence for the History of Emotions (CHE), focused on the music-making of grandmothers in Melbourne.[1] The project came to fruition with a performance at the Islamic Museum, Melbourne, in 2018. At the event, *La Voce della Luna* performed in company with Yiddish, Celtic, and Macedonian groups in a sharing of different musical cultures. This event promoted intercultural exchange and recognition through the encompassing theme of grandmothers. The diverse program called on accommodation of diverse tastes and styles by both performers and audience that afforded opportunities to listen beyond cultural boundaries of distinction. While cultural distinction is key to identity and separateness of one group from another, its performance can also be a means to connect across cultures.

Inclusive intercultural ensembles

Another way music can help refugee and migrant communities is through cross-cultural shared music experiences, such as those found in refugee choirs and other ensembles. Examples of such multi- and cross-cultural groups are the two refugee choirs *Citizens of the World* and *Sing for Freedom Choir*, both in London, and the *Lullaby Choir* in Melbourne. The *Lullaby Choir* was developed by VICSEG New Futures (Victorian Cooperative on Children's Services for Ethnic Groups) together with Samantha Dieckmann and Jane Davidson, as part of the project *Music, Emotion and Conciliation* funded by CHE. VICSEG New Futures is a not-for-profit community organization whose role is to provide support and training to newly arrived migrants, asylum seekers, and refugees. Lullabies were chosen as familiar and meaningful songs that are universal, yet distinctive within different cultures. The collaborative intent of the Choir which developed from a Lullaby Swap Meet (Dieckmann & Davidson, 2018) is to form meaningful connections through a shared theme of lullabies both between migrants from different nations and between migrants and established communities. Participants learn lullabies that other members grew up with and teach their own in turn, thus sharing an important piece of their cultural makeup. The choir comprises two groups: refugees and the VICSEG staff. Both groups have experienced empowerment—many

---

[1] https://www.sbs.com.au/language/english/audio/songs-from-my-grandmother-a-history-of-emotions

of the first group were reluctant to sing and perform publicly at first but moved through a process of gaining confidence and a sense of control and accomplishment to performing with enthusiasm. Performing for the second group provides an antidote to the challenges and stories they deal with every day, engendering a sense of positivity and emotional connections to each other.

Conclusion

In this chapter, different styles of ensembles have been presented, ranging from choirs to brass bands and drumming circles. The demographic of the ensembles is also varied, including older adults, settler miners, the homeless, migrants, and refugees. In these different ensembles and their contexts, the question is what sort of empowerment is evident and whether there is any variation due to ensemble type. It appears from existing research that whether vocal or instrumental, there is potential for empowerment through developing skills, agency and control, connections to past selves, accomplishment, and meaning-making. Ensembles that facilitate links to personal and/or historical pasts may reinforce empowerment through strengthening the self in the present. Performance adds to potential empowerment when ensemble members communicate through music and feel they are heard. For those who generally feel invisible or stigmatized, this is an especially powerful experience.

While reporting on positive effects from ensemble membership is widespread, it is important to challenge any assumption that "one size fits all." As Laes (2015) advises, listening to potential ensemble members and uncovering their aspirations or purpose are key to their self-realization. Performing in a rock group is empowering for a group of older women who want to defy stereotypes, whereas another ensemble's empowerment may come from its connection to history and tradition, as with brass bands. Leaders are also important, as is careful choice of repertoire for its meaning to the group. Leaders also have to tread a careful path between progress and accomplishment versus perfectionism and burnout. This second experience can eventuate for members of competitive ensembles such as brass bands and harmony choirs, both of which are often tied into national and international competition circuits.

Music has such strong potential to build connections, to communicate non-verbally, and to promote wellbeing and achievement that, when harnessed for good, ensembles serve as vehicles for positive experiences. As seen with choirs for historical migrants, refugees, and the homeless, drumming circles that promote mental wellbeing, and projects that celebrate musical diversity, ensembles can lead to feelings of self-worth and achievement that are potentially empowering for both the individual and the group.

References

Anderson, Z., & Sheets, D. (2017). Musical connections: A descriptive study of community-based choirs for persons with dementia and their caregivers. *Arbutus Review*, 8(1), 72–81.

Ascenso, S., Perkins, R., Atkins, L., Fancourt, D., & Williamon, A. (2018). Promoting well-being through group drumming with mental health service users and their carers. *International Journal of Qualitative Studies on Health and Well-Being*, 13, 1484219. https://doi.org/10.1080/17482631.2018.1484219

Bailey, B. A., & Davidson, J. W. (2005). Effects of group singing and performance on marginalized and middle-class singers. *Psychology of Music, 33*(3), 269–303.

Creech, A., Hallam, S., McQueen, H., & Varvarigou, M. (2013). The power of music in the lives of older adults. *Research Studies in Music Education, 35*(1), 87–102.

Davidson, J. W. (2011). Musical participation: Expectations, experiences and outcomes. In J. W. Davidson, & I. Deliege (Eds.), *Music and the mind* (pp. 65–87). Oxford University Press.

DeNora, T. (2000). *Music in everyday life.* Cambridge University Press.

Dieckmann, S., & Davidson, J. W. (2018). Resistance, harmony and dissonance in a multicultural lullaby choir. *The World of Music, 7,* 155–78.

English, H. J. (2017). Singing and identity formation in Newcastle, 1860–1880: Choirs, cultivation and connectedness. *Journal of Australian Colonial History, 19,* 95–118.

English, H. J. (2020). *Music and world-building in the colonial city: Newcastle, NSW, and its townships, 1860–1880.* Routledge.

English, H. J., & Davidson, J. W. (2020). Music for good: Reflections on a community music project through the lens of historical nostalgia. *International Journal of Community Music.* https://doi.org/10.1386/ijcm_00021_1

English, H., Monk, S., & Davidson, J. W. (2018). Music and world-building in Newcastle, New South Wales, Australia. *International Journal of Community Music, 11,* 245–63.

Joseph, D., & Southcott, J. (2018). Music participation for older people: Five choirs in Victoria, Australia. *Research Studies in Music Education, 40*(2), 176–90.

Laes, T. (2015). Empowering later adulthood music education: A case study of a rock band for third-age learners. *International Journal of Music Education, 33*(1), 51–65.

Levitin, D. J. (2006). *This is your brain on music: The science of a human obsession.* Dutton.

Marley, J., Matthias, B., Worrall, L., Guest, M., & Allan, C. (2018). From soundwaves to brainwaves: The effects of choral singing on recovery from stroke and aphasia. *British Journal of General Practice, 68*(suppl 1). https://doi.org/10.3399/bjgp18X696821

Pearce, E., Launay, J., & Dunbar, R. I. M. (2015). The ice-breaker effect: Singing mediates fast social bonding. *Royal Society Open Science, 2,* 150221. https://doi.org/10.1098/rsos.150221

Pike, P. D. (2011). Using technology to engage third-age (retired) leisure learners: A case study of a third-age MIDI piano ensemble. *International Journal of Music Education, 29*(2), 116–23.

Senay, B. (2009). Remembering the "Timeless City": Istanbul, music and memory among the Turkish migrants in Sydney. *Journal of Intercultural Studies, 30*(1), 73–87.

Shelemay, K. K. (2011). Music communities: Rethinking the collective in music. *Journal of the American Musicological Society, 64*(2), 349–90.

Silber, L. (2005). Bars behind bars: The impact of a women's prison choir on social harmony. *Music Education Research, 7*(2), 251–71.

Vickhoff, B., Malmgren, H., Åström, R., Nyberg, G., Engwall, M., Snygg, J., Nilsson, M., & Jornsten, R. (2013). Music structure determines heart rate variability of singers. *Frontiers of Psychology, 4,* 334. https://doi.org/10.3389/fpsyg.2013.00334

Williamson, V. J., & Bonshor, M. (2019). Wellbeing in brass bands: The benefits and challenges of group music making. *Frontiers in Psychology, 10,* 1176. https://doi.org/10.3389/fpsyg.2019.01176

29

Ensembles in music therapy

Stuart Wood and Irene Pujol Torras

Introduction

Histories of music and medicine provide evidence of music's use in most societies as a tool for mediating and moderating the inner, outer, and other world (Horden, 2000; Tyler, 2000). Nevertheless, only in the late 1960s did a discipline called music therapy really take shape in the UK. This period saw the establishment of professional associations, training courses, and career structures, shored up by the trappings of professional and academic status. In 1999, music therapy became a state-registered health profession in the UK. Now, it is regulated by the Health and Care Professions Council (HCPC). Since its beginnings, music therapy has been built on diverse and sometimes competing models, and while sometimes its formats of practice bear common signatures, often they contain a diversity of rationales, personnel, and vocabularies (Tyler, 2000).

In view of this diversity, we have adopted the notion of *assemblage* as a way of thinking about ensembles in music therapy. This notion, drawn primarily from the work of Deleuze and Guattari (1987), proposes that ensembles manifest in unique and context-specific circumstances, not only by virtue of people gathering in one space or under the rubric of a formalized process of group music therapy. Ensembles in music therapy may consist of acknowledged group members, often in closed formats, but may also at other times include observers, audiences, assistants, professional music therapists, music therapy assistants, or supporting musicians. Ensembles in music therapy will often be heavily influenced by the social spaces in which they take place, the physical objects such as musical instruments, architecture, or furniture that are present, the types of human voices within them, and less tangibly the underpinning values or processes of prevailing organizations, statutory policies, professional guidelines and codes, political movements, musical and cultural forces, or cultures of health and wellbeing. In other words, professionalized modes of grouping framed as music therapy are themselves contextual manifestations of long-standing musical practices of health promotion (Ansdell, 2014; Stige & Aaro, 2012).

It could be argued that any music therapy encounter is an experience of ensemble, because the practice is built on the belief that music brings people together in a state, place, and time where they are enabled to be with others. Claims for therapy-induced changes are made variously with respect to the processes of interpersonal musical experience, including heightened self-awareness induced by the participants' verbal interpretation of the meaning of the shared musical playing, the non-verbal dynamics of musical relating, or alternatively to music's physiological effects, as manifested in medical or other formal settings. These varied claims are often underpinned by assertions that music is a unique medium as compared with other modes of therapeutic interaction.

Stuart Wood and Irene Pujol Torras, *Ensembles in music therapy* In: *Together in music.* Edited by: Renee Timmers, Freya Bailes, and Helena Daffern, Oxford University Press. © Oxford University Press 2022. DOI: 10.1093/oso/9780198860761.003.0029

The practice of bringing people together in music therapy has, in recent times, developed into a wide diversity of approaches and practices that go beyond categorization as either "individual" or "group" work within the jargon of the profession. Nonetheless, the term "group music therapy" often performs the rhetorical function of embracing any music therapy that is not in an individual or 1:1 format. In practice, the ways in which people gather in music therapy have developed to include a closed trio (for example, of child, parent, and therapist) and small groups, but also large circumstantial gatherings and formats:

> such developments need to be unembarrassed to revisit essential questions ... What are the differences and similarities between dyadic, triadic, quartets, larger ensembles in music therapy (and do these matter?). How might music therapists best represent a collection of people with an astonishing variation of physical, mental, and social capacities and limitations who at times mutually enact sophisticated, flexible, shared social musical synchronicities? (Pavlicevic, 2016, p. 679)

Our response to this challenge from Pavlicevic is to engage actively with the rhetorics and registers that comprise the field of published music therapy literature. In the following sections, we explore how the term "group music therapy" operates as a rhetorical device to denote a modality of therapeutic intervention. In counterpoint to this, we employ a second rhetoric that opens up how music manifests more broadly within social narratives of health promotion with further opportunities for musical ensemble experience.

Rhetorics of music therapy ensembles

Structures, formats, and soundscapes

Although ensembles in music therapy take diverse shapes, they often share common signatures and underpinning modes of practice. Prime among these is the role of musical improvisation, which is one of the common principles of group music therapy, particularly in the UK. Sometimes this may take the form of a conventional free group improvisation through the use of voice and accessible instruments, whereas on other occasions, an "improvisatory approach" to music-making is embedded in the use of pre-composed musical material. This provides a wide spectrum of possibilities ranging from free improvisation to themed improvisations, songs that are modified or adapted, songwriting and composition (see Chapter 33), use of musical arrangements with space for personal improvisational moments, playing to pre-recorded tracks from social media sites such as Spotify or YouTube, listening to music together in an open-ended experiential way, adapting well-known songs to incorporate the contributions of ensemble members, or performing live. The combination of original and pre-composed material in music therapy ensembles can take on many different forms and structures.

Similarly, contexts and settings for music therapy ensembles are highly varied and often variable within themselves. From closed groups with a stable membership within health settings to community-based open or drop-in groups where the sense of identification with the group is more fluid, music therapy can stretch and contract within seconds to accommodate a range of participants. This invites people to adopt different roles of greater or lesser predominance in the ensemble, where they can experiment with how much they want to show of themselves and how they want to be seen or identified. Consequently, the music that emerges from music therapy groups can not only be varied, but also be documented, understood, and valued according to the musical, social, personal, and therapeutic explorations that take place.

Monitoring, description, and evidence

So far we have suggested that ensembles in music therapy can emerge in a proliferation of practice, tradition, theory, and format. Similar proliferations exist within the discipline's reflective methodologies. Three main strands are considered here: professional requirements of monitoring and evaluation, scholarly enquiries that describe practice, and research that seeks to build an evidence base.

In the UK, it is a professional requirement that music therapists should be able to monitor their practice such that they are able to exercise their own professional judgment, maintain records, review practice, and ensure its quality (Health and Care Professions Council, 2013). Models of monitoring and assessment from within music therapy have only recently begun to address specifically the question of how the broad diversity of ensembles can be understood, and how this might relate to individualized claims for therapeutic change where they arise (Stige & Aaro, 2012).

The Music Matrix (Wood & Crow, 2018) is a recent example of documentation that reframes individualized notions such as symptom-based intervention from a more communal perspective. The trend in published music therapy research is predominantly towards evaluation approaches or methods that are specific to diagnosis (Wood, 2016). Within this trend, it is common to find evaluation represented in the form of symptom-specific interventions (such as assessing reduction in anxiety among people with dementia), increasingly designed for use within para-medical situations. This approach tends to reduce the person to specific functions and to illustrate how functions improve by the strategic application of music. The Music Matrix is an example of monitoring and evaluation documentation that responds to this trend, including aspects of individual clinical function, but also profiling aesthetic attributes and social interaction that emerge from a communal notion of selfhood and wellbeing. This is achieved via close description of what happens across a set of experiential dimensions often determined by the participants or stakeholders in collaboration with the music therapist.

Scholarly works involving rich description of ensembles in music therapy have a clear lineage from phenomenological roots to the current trend for ethnographically informed music therapy research among authors such as Ansdell (2014) or Tsiris (2018), for example. In such accounts, often taking the form of case studies, the agendas of professional monitoring or evidencing give way to investigations via narratives, thick description (Geertz, 1973), and participant-observation for the purposes of understanding how people come together inside musical social formations. These accounts tend also to address both the professional frame of music therapy and the broader field of health promotion within a wide social context.

One area that warrants further development concerns which forms of evaluation and assessment practices are appropriate for broad-based social approaches in music therapy. The social approach typically prioritizes how the person (or indeed their social context) is manifest while music is happening, rather than seeking to provide evidence of the effect of the music therapy through the language of "pre-" and "post-" intervention measurement. The questions that inform this approach to music therapy evaluation may focus on changes in contextual elements such as music in the person's daily life, their family or carer relations, and their preferred formats of recreational music-making, as well as their achievement of functional goals or the apparent success of a treatment method. The music therapy profession has made important progress in the area of evaluation and assessment as applied to social approaches (Stige & Aaro, 2012), but there is room for more dialogue on this topic, as both the values and practices of evaluation and rich description are not always easy to align.

Research methods that test the effectiveness of interventions, such as randomized controlled trials, have not produced a definitive and comprehensive evidence base for music therapy in ensemble formats. To date, a small body of research offers evidence for the effectiveness of group music therapy for various client groups. For example, evidence can be claimed for the effectiveness of music therapy groups in the treatment of psychiatric disorders such as schizophrenia, particularly on negative symptoms, motivation for treatment, and depression (Carr, 2014). Group music therapy with children with Autistic Spectrum Disorder (ASD) may also claim positive research outcomes linked to peer interaction (Kern & Aldridge, 2006). Similarly, studies looking at the effects of group music therapy with people with learning disabilities have identified benefits in regulating behavior, improving communication skills, and enhancing quality of life (Savarimuthu & Bunnell, 2002). Research is growing in the field of group music therapy interventions for dementia and there is evidence for its effectiveness in treating overall symptoms (Koger et al., 1999). This is becoming an increasingly active area of research in music therapy, where groups comprising carers and family members often form the mode of therapeutic intervention.

Alongside systematic tests of the effectiveness of group music therapy, other forms of evidence emerge from case studies, smaller-scale experimental research, and practice- or arts-based research methods (see Chapter 34). These often highlight the important role of music therapy in engaging participants in a lively and active network of social interactions that might differ from the realm of interpersonal connectedness which they are able to access in other areas of their daily life, be that due to difficulties with communication, cognition, mental health, dementia, or other social, environmental, political, or physical factors (Ansdell, 2014).

Numerous unaddressed issues remain with regard to the effectiveness of group music therapy. Specifically, the concept of "dosage," which explores the effects of duration and frequency of music therapy groups, warrants further critical reflection. For example, Carr (2014) showed beneficial aspects of intensive, rather than protracted, group music therapy. Similarly, many active groups have received only little attention from research, such as ensembles for parents and babies, which are increasingly prevalent in the United States. Central aspects of practice require investigation, such as evaluations of specific (innovating or novel) music therapy techniques used in different ensembles.

The systematic investigation of specific music therapy techniques is not without controversy. One instance where this is strongly apparent is in the creation of practical manuals to guide research or practice interventions. While some of the overarching professional structures of music therapy research and governance tend towards such systematic approaches, it is also argued that manualization sits uncomfortably with the underlying multiplicity of music therapy experiences and practices. Perhaps in response to this tension between systematization and improvisation, hybrid research methodologies are starting to appear in the literature, for example in the creative use of mixed methods designs (e.g. Ettenberger et al., 2017) or in the promotion of arts-based interdisciplinary collaborations (Leavy, 2018).

Traditions, theories, and approaches

Music-making is an inherently social activity (Malloch & Trevarthen, 2009). Using music therapy in diverse group formats is therefore a natural affordance of the musical medium itself. The natural use of music's social properties in music therapy is underpinned by a rich array of traditions and theories, producing, as mentioned, many formats of practice. Within the psychoanalytic tradition, however, group experience was something of an innovation when it began to emerge as a field of psychotherapeutic treatment in the 1960s (Foulkes, 1964). Nonetheless, many ideas from group psychotherapy literature influence current thinking about group music therapy, along with musicology, child development, holistic medicine, and the substantial emerging branches of music therapy theory.

From an evolutionary perspective, music therapy has drawn from theories proposing that music arose from a need for humans to socially advance. This includes theories that link specific social functions to music-making, such as large group socialization, group cohesion, and conflict resolution (van der Schyff & Schiavio, 2017). Other accounts provide rich and complex views of the origins of human musicality, keeping at the core of the discipline music's unique non-verbal, interactional, and adaptable properties in enabling social groups to function and thrive (Stern, 2010). Some of these primal musical features of being in groups are at the center of thinking around music therapy groups, such as how people can come together and experience a sense of unity and belonging in group music-making, or as Pavlicevic (2003, p. 14) describes, "the compelling power of groups in music and the power of music to create electrifying collective experiences of social bonding."

As well as opportunities for meaningful socialization, music therapy groups can address many other domains which are more or less relevant in different contexts of health or social care. For example, other areas of emphasis may be: emotional expression, cognitive stimulation, agency, learning opportunities, stress reduction, hedonic experiences, mindfulness, behavioral modeling, and the reduction of sedentary behaviors (Fancourt, 2018). This variety of therapeutic functions of music therapy groups is what renders them a rich, flexible, and adaptable therapeutic tool which can meet a variety of needs. What motivates the possibilities for personal growth in various areas is nicely described by Davies and Richards (2002, p. 23) as:

> a particular sense of belonging when a musical improvisation is shared in a group where the instruments and many voices of sound seek a place to be alongside each other, affecting or resonating with each other rather than being indifferent. Here the uniqueness of the individual sound or instrument makes up the meaning of the whole. Members of a music therapy group, irrespective of verbal skills or the availability of words, can have an enriched experience, expressive as well as receptive, of themselves and others.

In recent years, the social properties of music therapy have been explained increasingly from a sociological orientation, offering a legitimizing platform for many music therapists to integrate diverse ensemble experience into their music therapy tradition (Pavlicevic, 2016). The sociological view frames ensembles in music therapy as a social manifestation of health promotion. This view adopts three broad themes. First, the ensemble can be seen in terms of how it is a vehicle for social movements in which health or social care are advocated, enacted, or promoted (see Chapter 28). Examples may take the form of musical theatre, carnival, protest, public health campaigns, or similar. Numerous accounts of this can be found in Stige and Aaro's (2012) rich volume on community music therapy, and include improvisational collectives such as the Otoasobi Project in Japan, a Children's Welfare Musical in Norway, and music education projects in a Palestinian refugee camp.

Second, the ensemble can operate as a focal point for the performance of fluid health and social identities, enabling pathways between, and beyond, sites of treatment. Ansdell's account of the *Smart Singers* group in London is a prime example of this approach, in which membership of a musical ensemble enables participants to manage their involvement in community mental health services over time (Ansdell, 2014). *Smart Singers* is a group hosted by the Chelsea Community Music Therapy Project in London. Although their base is a high-street mental health organization, they identify as an amateur singing group. Through rehearsals and performances which occupy both healthcare and community territories, participants can experience transformation in their habitual forms of belonging, their sense of social inclusion, and their role as producers of culture, not only as recipients of treatment.

Finally, the ensemble can be viewed in terms of how music impacts on people beyond the main client or patient, its impact occurring in what is often termed a "ripple effect" across an organization both among named clients or patients but also among beneficiaries such as family, onlookers, or careworkers (Pavlicevic & Ansdell, 2004; Wood, 2016). This model of understanding ensembles in music therapy draws from ecological theories, whose "premise is that changes in one will lead to changes in the other. To help an individual is not then a separate enterprise from working with contextual change" (Stige & Aaro, 2012, p. 45).

Conclusion

In this chapter, we adopted the concept of *assemblage* as a way of thinking about ensembles in music therapy, so as not to impose a singular basis for how, why, or in what format they manifest. Instead, we framed ensembles in music therapy as configurations of multiple elements that are rooted in a specific place and time. Ensembles in music therapy emerge from specific conditions, governed by the ethos, materials, and professional apparatus available. Ensembles in music therapy may not conform to standard or received classifications of tradition, theory, or approach, and pose methodological puzzles for monitoring, description, and evidence.

We have been mindful of rhetorical conventions that categorize music therapy experiences according to the status of "individual" or "group." This is not an accurate representation of contemporary nor, indeed, historical music therapy practices. Since its inception, music therapy has offered experiences and theory according to a fluid set of considerations, and thus many music therapists acknowledge the need for choirs, performance moments, ad hoc improvisations, itinerant or mobile social music-making, or specialized arrangements for groups of musicians (Pavlicevic & Ansdell, 2004) in their professional practice. Consequently, music therapists will continue to draw on a changing set of musical and interpersonal aptitudes related to ensemble work that may at times include accompaniment, conducting, workshop leading, special pedagogies, mentorship, community building, and event planning, as integral parts of their practice.

References

Ansdell, G. (2014). *How music helps in music therapy and everyday life*. Ashgate.

Carr, C. (2014). *Modelling of intensive group music therapy for acute adult psychiatric inpatients* [Doctoral thesis]. Queen Mary University of London. http://qmro.qmul.ac.uk/xmlui/handle/123456789/26966

Davies, A., & Richards, E. (Eds.) (2002). *Music therapy and group work, sound company*. Jessica Kingsley Publishers.

Deleuze, G., & Guattari, F. (1987). *A thousand plateaus: Capitalism and schizophrenia*. University of Minnesota Press.

Ettenberger, M., Rojas Cárdenas, C., Parker, M., & Odell-Miller, H. (2017). Family-centered music therapy with preterm infants and their parents in the Neonatal Intensive Care Unit (NICU) in Colombia – A mixed-methods study. *Nordic Journal of Music Therapy, 26*(3), 207–34.

Fancourt, D. (2018). *Arts in Public Health* [Paper presentation]. An Introduction to Arts and Health Conference, the Institute of Education.

Foulkes, S. H. (1964). *Therapeutic group analysis*. (Reprinted, 1984). Karnac Books.

Geertz, C. (1973). *The interpretation of cultures: Selected essays*. Basic Books.

Health and Care Professions Council. (2013). *The standards of proficiency for arts therapists*. https://www.hcpc-uk.org/standards/standards-of-proficiency/arts-therapists/

Horden, P. (Ed.) (2000). *Music as medicine: The history of music therapy since antiquity*. Routledge.

Kern, P., & Aldridge, D. (2006). Using embedded music therapy interventions to support outdoor play of young children with autism in an inclusive community-based child care program. *Journal of Music Therapy, 43*(4), 270–94.

Koger, S. M., Chapin, K., & Brotons, M. (1999). Is music therapy an effective intervention for dementia: A meta-analytic review of literature. *Journal of Music Therapy, 36*(1), 2–15.

Leavy, P. (2018). *Handbook of arts-based research*. Guildford Press.

Malloch, S., & Trevarthen, C. (Eds.) (2009). *Communicative musicality: Exploring the basis of human companionship*. Oxford University Press.

Pavlicevic, M. (2003). *Groups in music*. Jessica Kingsley Publishers.

Pavlicevic, M. (2016). Group music therapy reconsidered: Of musics, contexts, and discourses. In J. Edwards (Ed.), *Oxford handbook of music therapy* (pp. 669–83). Oxford University Press.

Pavlicevic, M., & Ansdell, G. (2004). *Community music therapy*. Jessica Kingsley Publishers.

Savarimuthu, D., & Bunnell, T. (2002). The effects of music on clients with learning disabilities: A literature review. *Complementary Therapies in Nursing and Midwifery, 8*(3), 160–5.

Stern, D. N. (2010). *Forms of vitality. Exploring dynamic experience in psychology, the arts, psychotherapy, and development*. Oxford University Press.

Stige, B., & Aaro, L. E. (2012). *Invitation to community music therapy*. Routledge.

Tsiris, G. (2018). *Performing spirituality in music therapy: Towards action, context and the everyday* [Doctoral thesis]. Goldsmiths, University of London. http://research.gold.ac.uk/id/eprint/23037

Tyler, H. (2000). The music therapy profession in modern Britain. In P. Horden (Ed.), *Music as medicine: The history of music therapy since antiquity* (pp. 375–93). Ashgate.

van der Schyff, D., & Schiavio, A. (2017). Evolutionary musicology meets embodied cognition: Biocultural coevolution and the enactive origins of human musicality. *Frontiers in Neuroscience, 11*, 519. https://doi.org/10.3389/fnins.2017.00519

Wood, S. (2016). *A matrix for community music therapy practice.* Barcelona Publishers.

Wood, S., & Crow, F. (2018). The music matrix: A qualitative participatory action research project to develop documentation for care home music therapy services. *British Journal of Music Therapy, 32*(2), 74–85.

30

Ensemble participation in late adulthood

Jennifer MacRitchie and Sandra Garrido

Introduction

What does it mean to be part of a musical ensemble as we grow older? Health and wellbeing throughout aging can be supported by an individual's continued ability to achieve things that are important to them (World Health Organization, 2015). Within this context of change, where an individual's self-perception, as well as society's perception of that individual, tends to alter (and can be subject to societal and internalized stigma associated with growing older), some aging adults commence new activities or continue to pursue meaningful activities such as playing a musical instrument. Conducting these activities in social contexts can serve to reinforce an individual's sense of identity such as being a musician or, more generally, a healthy and active aging adult (Dabback & Smith, 2012; see also Chapter 27).

In addition to the advantages that lifelong musical training offers for speech processing (Kraus & White-Schwoch, 2014) and the potential for cognitive growth provided by learning to play a musical instrument as a novice in later adulthood (Schneider et al., 2018), playing together in an ensemble presents an opportunity for socializing, and is a frequent motivator for aging adults to initiate and sustain engagement in music-making (Roulston et al., 2015). Having an avenue for self-expression, and opportunities to coordinate with others, fosters individuals' sense of belonging to a group (see Chapter 26): this may ameliorate feelings of isolation and loneliness that can arise with retirement (Creech et al., 2014) which may be particularly important for continued mental health. The motivations and experiences of individuals in late adulthood have been documented in research about newly formed music ensembles, but they are seldom examined in the context of continued long-term associations. In such a situation, these individuals may have to renegotiate their identity as a musician within the group as they experience the changes in lifestyle and health associated with aging.

This chapter will highlight the benefits and challenges of ensemble participation in late adulthood, focusing on a case study which considers the continued involvement of aging adult participants in a community orchestra. This was part of a broader study (MacRitchie & Garrido, 2019), but in this chapter, we focus on a subset of players in the orchestra who were aged 50 and over. Here, we investigate the perceived mental, emotional, and social benefits, as well as the challenges, of continued participation.

Case study: A community orchestra in Sydney, Australia

Data were collected from a survey of orchestral members, followed by individual interviews. Interviews were semi-structured, using prepared open-ended questions to frame the discussion. Survey participants were asked to select the most appropriate answer from a list

Jennifer MacRitchie and Sandra Garrido, *Ensemble participation in late adulthood* In: *Together in music*. Edited by: Renee Timmers, Freya Bailes, and Helena Daffern, Oxford University Press. © Oxford University Press 2022. DOI: 10.1093/oso/9780198860761.003.0030

of statements about their motivation to join the orchestra and their rehearsal and practice strategies, and to rate agreement with statements according to their feelings of confidence and self-efficacy (the belief in their own capacity to execute actions). Players' intellectual, social, and emotional engagement was gauged in the survey by Likert scale questions designed by Brown and Novak (2007) adapted to focus on the context of playing music rather than music consumption. Subsets of questions asked participants to rate their "captivation" (producing a Captivation Index) (e.g. "<the orchestra> gives me an opportunity to be absorbed in music in a way I don't find anywhere else"), "Intellectual Stimulation" (e.g. "I generally understand the music we play and 'get' what the composer is trying to communicate"), "Emotional Resonance" (e.g. "playing with the orchestra is therapeutic for me in an emotional sense"), and "Social Bonding" (e.g. "I feel a sense of belonging and connectedness with the rest of the orchestra"). Participants in the individual interviews were then asked to comment on their motivation and experience of rehearsing and performing with the orchestra. This included their connection and absorption in the music, effects on their physical and mental health, the level of challenge and intellectual stimulation, and connection to the other musicians.

Of the individuals who took part in the study, 15 participants were aged 50 and over ($M = 60.5$, $SD = 8.6$ years). Three of these participants took part in the subsequent interview. These participants were mostly individuals who had been playing their instrument since childhood (14 participants began at the age of 10 or under, one participant began in their forties), and who had been associated with the orchestra for a number of years (12 participants had been members for five years or more).

Physical and mental benefits and challenges

When asked about which experiences had the strongest impact on them in terms of being involved in music generally, the majority (12 participants) reported being inspired by "experiences of playing in ensembles." When asked about the most inspiring part of their involvement with this specific orchestra, survey answers selected from a list most often related to aspects of captivation and absorption, and intellectual stimulation (e.g. "The music itself"—six participants; "The gradual feeling of mastering new pieces as rehearsals progress"—four participants). The interview statements reflected a close tie between these mental benefits and the physical challenge required to achieve them.

> It's just a great, it's a big challenge and it's really, it keeps me occupied, it's very rewarding when you get through the concert and say "I did that hopefully not too badly." (P2, *M*, new member, working full-time)[1]

> The main challenges is having some music which initially you can't play you think "ok I got to get this working." That happens sometimes, it's just a matter of working at it, trying to find the time to do the required practice but that's the main challenge, the technical performance of it. (P2, *M*, new member, working full-time)

These views were confirmed by the survey results demonstrating that the orchestra's ensemble context was mentally engaging for players in late adulthood (Captivation Index $M = 8.2$,

---

[1] "P2, *M*" indicates participant number 2, male.

SD = 1.9, maximum possible score of 10; Intellectual Stimulation M = 7.8, SD = 1.7, maximum possible score of 10). However, the challenge of the material and how rehearsals were designed around this had a physical impact for players. Continually repeating demanding passages in rehearsals added to the physical challenges of coping with both rehearsals and concert performances, and were described as producing some stress for players.

> ... sometimes we feel like we're massive work horses ... I actually do feel that the conductor requires too much sometimes in rehearsals, in terms of like, volume, which really, obviously, if you're continually playing a difficult <passage> it's quite physical, it's quite demanding and we're all getting older. (P3, *F*, long-term member, working part-time)

Emotional benefits and challenges

The Emotional Resonance subscale overall had high scores among the aging adult survey participants (M = 13.0, SD = 2.1, maximum possible score of 15). From the interviews, high expectations appeared to create a level of pressure on all the participants interviewed. Rehearsals were noted by some as particularly stressful in comparison to the concerts themselves. The degree of stress associated with rehearsals was strongly related to whether performers felt they had played well and the amount of criticism they received during rehearsal.

> if it's a negative one then there's nothing you can do about it because that was the opportunity to say "right I've achieved this, this and this, next week I'll be able to work on ..." so the frustration lingers unfortunately because there's no other way of resolving ... (P1, *F*, long-term member, working full-time)

> so if that happens that could make you quite annoyed or angry. You've gone to all this effort and all they can do is criticise what you're doing, so that can be a downer sometimes. (P3, *F*, long-term member, working part-time)

> now in rehearsals there's a lot of frustration, its interrupted, we go over things, ... there's annoyances, there are difficulties ... so in rehearsals you get a lot more ... ups and downs a lot. (P3, *F*, long-term member, working part-time)

Performances, on the other hand, could be less stressful than rehearsals since players tended to be more "in the moment" and potentially more resigned to accept what happened.

> ... A performance somehow I've accepted is a one-off thing. It is what it is. You do your best, if it all goes to hell in a hand basket well that's just the way it is. (P1, *F*, long-term member, working full-time)

The same participant noted that performances could also be more stressful as everything needs to be correct on the first try. Rehearsals provided the opportunity to relax and try things out.

But to actually put the whole thing together and to play for 45 mins is a different thing even though you can play all the different ... putting it all together that is another thing again, and, you know you feel pretty exhausted by the end and you can't focus, you know what I mean? So a performance is more of a sort of a marathon sort of thing whereas sometimes in rehearsal you can do it a bit and its spot on and its great and you can, you know, have a laugh ... its [an] entirely different circumstance. (P1, *F*, long-term member, working full-time)

The emotional impact of being involved in the orchestra appeared to stem mainly from whether or not a high standard of playing was achieved in the final performance.

Social benefits and challenges

Previous ensemble experiences were a major influence for survey participants in terms of being involved in music generally, and "Social Bonding" was rated highly ($M = 4.3$, $SD = 0.7$, maximum possible score of 5). However, when asked in the survey about their inspiration to be involved in this specific orchestra, reasons that linked with social engagement were less often chosen: "feeling of synchronizing with so many other musical voices in a group setting" was selected by only three of the 15 participants in late adulthood.

Participants tended to have built up long-term social friendships over their extended period with the orchestra, but there was little time for new social connections to be made in the context of the rehearsal breaks. Despite this, there was an acknowledgement of participating in an activity with other people, and creating something as a group.

I feel very connected to this orchestra ... with quite a few of the people I've known them for 20 years or so, and you know, socialise with them on other occasions as well, so I feel it to be a very strong sort of social group as well for me. (P1, *F*, long-term member, working full-time)

The connection at the break, well one, it's relatively short, you know its 15 minutes or something. We have a cup of tea and all of that that so it's nice to be able to speak to some other people. (P3, *F*, long-term member, working part-time)

Where you're doing something you like doing, and so you love doing that with other people, and when it turns out really, really well you feel really good about everybody in the orchestra. You feel like you're a real group together, you've come together and you've created something. (P3, *F*, long-term member, working part-time)

Discussion

From this case study, it appears that individuals in late adulthood in a continued association with a community orchestra experience enduring mental, emotional, and social benefits, as well as challenges. Players were particularly captivated by the standard of repertoire, and were emotionally impacted by being able to achieve a high standard as an ensemble. Rehearsing and performing as a group provided a sense of social bonding across a group of people in their community despite the low level of individual interactions that occurred outside of the time spent physically playing music.

This study did not look at how these benefits and challenges change across time as individuals cope with aging. Future studies could investigate this longitudinally in order to understand how community orchestras can continue to benefit from and support players in late adulthood. Community ensembles provide not only cultural opportunities for members of their local communities, but can also provide other benefits as well, both to audience members and players (Garrido & Macritchie, 2018). There are opportunities for community ensembles in general to consider ways in which they can further support individuals in late adulthood. Navigating the physical and mental stresses that may arise, for example, could be considered in the structure of rehearsals (see Chapter 25), thus facilitating ongoing involvement in these important community structures. Increasing occasions for social interaction may also assist in traversing players' changing motivations and abilities throughout their association with the ensemble. Being able to acknowledge and accommodate varying players' abilities while balancing their continued endeavor and appreciation for high standards of ensemble playing would facilitate long-term involvement throughout later adulthood. Dementia-friendly ensembles, for example, may allow older adults in the community experiencing increasing cognitive impairments to commence or continue interacting with others through music playing.

Conclusion

In general, this case study of players in a community music ensemble illustrates that ensemble playing in later adulthood offers a mix of challenges and opportunities. Pursuing ensemble musical activities provides physical, mental, and emotional benefits, enhancing quality of life at this and later stages of life. Of equal importance is the need for community music organizations to address and adapt to the changing needs of their members so these benefits can be sustained throughout aging.

References

Brown, A. S., & Novak, J. L. (2007). *Assessing the intrinsic impacts of a live performance*. Wolfbrown. https://www.culturehive.co.uk/wp-content/uploads/2013/04/ImpactStudyFinalVersion.pdf

Creech, A., Hallam, S., McQueen, H., & Varvarigou, M. (2014). *Active ageing with music: Supporting well being in the Third and Fourth Ages*. IOE Press.

Dabback, W. M., & Smith, D. S. (2012). Elders and music: Empowering, learning, valuing life experience and considering the needs of aging adult learners. In G. E. McPherson, & G. F. Welch (Eds.), *The Oxford handbook of music education* (Vol. 2) (pp. 229–42). Oxford University Press.

Garrido, S., & Macritchie, J. (2018). Audience engagement with community music performances: Emotional contagion in audiences of a "pro-am" orchestra in suburban Sydney. *Musicae Scientiae, 24*(2), 155–67.

Kraus, N., & White-Schwoch, T. (2014). Music training: Lifelong investment to protect the brain from aging and hearing loss. *Acoustics Australia, 42*(2), 117–23.

MacRitchie, J., & Garrido, S. (2019). Ageing and the orchestra: Self-efficacy and engagement in community music-making. *Psychology of Music, 47*(6), 902–16.

Roulston, K., Jutras, P., & Kim, S. J. (2015). Adult perspectives of learning musical instruments. *International Journal of Music Education, 33*(3), 325–35.

Schneider, C. E., Hunter, E. G., & Bardach, S. H. (2018). Potential cognitive benefits from playing music among cognitively intact older adults: A scoping review. *Journal of Applied Gerontology, 38*(12), 1763–83.

World Health Organization. (2015). *World report on ageing and health.* https://www.who.int/ageing/events/world-report-2015-launch/en/

31

Emotional, cognitive, and motor development in youth orchestras

A two-year longitudinal study

Donald Glowinski, Cecile Levacher, Florian Buchheit, Chiara Malagoli, Benjamin Matuszewski, Simon Schaerlaeken, Chiara Noera, Katie Edwards, Carlo Chiorri, Frédéric Bevilacqua, and Didier Grandjean

Introduction

This chapter discusses the results of a longitudinal study on the impact of collective music practice carried out through three youth orchestras created by the Philharmonie de Paris's *Demos* program. The *Demos* program is a network of public and private stakeholders coordinated by the Philharmonie de Paris devoted to providing instrumental music education to children between 6 and 14 years old from all socioeconomic backgrounds. It aims to make music training and orchestral practice more widely available to students with little or no access to classical instrumental music education.

The longitudinal study was led by the Swiss Center for Affective Sciences at the University of Geneva in collaboration with the IRCAM-STMS lab and the University of Genoa, combining approaches from psychology, neuropsychology, and engineering. The goal of the study was to understand how orchestral practice can foster the development of children's executive functions (e.g. working memory, inhibition, cognitive flexibility) that are essential for behavioral regulation. Also of interest was how this collective practice might encourage the emergence of motor synchronization and the understanding of emotion that are crucial in the process of establishing interpersonal relationships.

Executive functions

It has been shown that music learning improves executive functions. Executive functions—a set of general-purpose control processes that regulate thoughts and behaviors—are constantly shaped during the lifespan and strongly affected by learning (Takacs & Kassai, 2019). Since learning to play a musical instrument can be challenging for children, it draws on three core executive function abilities: inhibition, working memory, and cognitive flexibility. First, inhibition filters out thoughts as well as non-pertinent information, and controls motor responses. Second, the ability to dynamically update working memory content based on new information allows for the storage and recall of the information needed to perform a task, such as all the notes that compose the melody. Third, cognitive flexibility allows individuals

Donald Glowinski, Cecile Levacher, Florian Buchheit, Chiara Malagoli, Benjamin Matuszewski, Simon Schaerlaeken, Chiara Noera, Katie Edwards, Carlo Chiorri, Frédéric Bevilacqua, and Didier Grandjean, *Emotional, cognitive, and motor development in youth orchestras* In: *Together in music*. Edited by: Renee Timmers, Freya Bailes, and Helena Daffern, Oxford University Press. © Oxford University Press 2022. DOI: 10.1093/oso/9780198860761.003.0031

to adapt to changing situations, and smooth transitions between tasks. Executive functions are also important to support self-regulation, both in terms of emotions and behaviors. Each of these functions continues to develop through adolescence (Diamond, 2013). Therefore, it is imperative that young people can access support from an "external regulator" during this developmental period, particularly with respect to emotion regulation. In this regard, *Demos* promotes musical exchanges and assistance, fostered through the benevolent support of professional musicians and social educators. Training executive functions can be achieved by promoting autonomy (e.g. setting up, independent practice), creating rituals that structure the practice session to allow children to focus on what is new or difficult, creating a favorable environment (e.g. calm, stimulating curiosity, performing every time in the same place), and organizing inter-instrumental meetings with the entire orchestra.

As most studies of executive functions and music concern individual music learning (e.g. Sachs et al., 2017), an additional focus of the current study is to explore the improvement in cognitive abilities and executive function associated with collective music learning, in addition to emotion and coordination skills. Emotions, as part of musical experience, include both the expressive intentions of the musician and the emotions perceived by the listener (Juslin, 2013). Therefore, participating in an ensemble requires an understanding of the emotions and expressive intentions of other musicians, as well as the ability to synchronize with other musicians with an acuity of less than 100 milliseconds (see Chapter 17).

Method and findings

This project introduced a number of specifically designed methods and interactive applications. These used common mobile technologies to enable the analysis of children's cognitive and emotional abilities, as well as the interactive dynamics between the participants of the music ensemble. Specifically, we adapted three psychological tests tailored to the age group of the participants (6 to 14 years old)—Mr Peanut (Case, 1985; Morra, 1994), Dots (Davidson et al., 2006), and the Test of Emotion Comprehension (TEC) (Cavioni et al., 2020)—to assess working memory, inhibition and cognitive flexibility, and understanding of emotions, respectively. Additionally, we developed methods to quantify the degree of motor synchronization between musicians as detailed below. We performed psychological tests in the field, over 20 different sites in France, mostly French education priority zones (ZEPs). The individual abilities were assessed yearly, while the synchronization abilities were assessed at six-monthly intervals during a school year, allowing us to assess progress. With this set of tools, a unique database was developed encompassing psychological response and physical movement data from all of the 255 children and 42 professional musicians and social educators participating in the two-year study.

Three orchestras were studied, each at a different stage of the three-year curriculum. During the first year of data collection, the three orchestras were, respectively, in the first, second, and third year of the curriculum. While the third-year (last year of the course) orchestra could be assessed only once, the first- and second-year orchestras were assessed again the following year (see Table 31.1).

Linear mixed models were used to assess the relationship between time participating in the program, changes in cognitive and emotional measures, and degree of motor synchrony, while controlling for background variables such as age, sex, and the played instrument.

Table 31.1 Distribution of children's age and sex for each orchestra evaluated in this study

Orchestra (year at the beginning of the study)	Numbers of participants	Sex distribution	Mean age at the beginning of the study	Age standard deviation
Orchestra 1 (first year)	118	♀ 72 | 46 ♂	8.16 [7–10]	0.92
Orchestra 2 (second year)	99	♀ 68 | 31 ♂	9.47 [7–13]	1.42
Orchestra 3 (third year)	38	♀ 29 | 9 ♂	10.55 [8–13]	1.20

First, the inter-individual differences in executive functions and understanding of emotions were assessed. To do this, three tests were implemented on digital tablets, as already mentioned: Mr Peanut, a game which requires visual working memory by asking children to remember the positions of stickers on a figure and then place them again on a blank figure; Dots, a game that requires inhibition and cognitive flexibility to handle competing concurrent information at the same time (the child has to shift between rules according to the stimulus presented), and the TEC, a questionnaire that asks children to associate a particular emotion with a presented scenario, from four possible choices.

A significant improvement was observed over the two-year period for the cognitive and emotional skills. First, working memory as assessed by the visual span was significantly increased in the Mr Peanut test; inhibition and cognitive flexibility as evaluated by the precision scores in the Dots test also increased, while reaction time significantly decreased. Emotional skills tested by the TEC allowed us to also observe significant improvements in emotion comprehension skills, particularly for complex emotions such as mixed emotions. The progression observed in executive functions over time was consistent with the literature (Takacs & Kassai, 2019), and showed significant improvement for orchestras 1 and 2 from year to year (respectively, from first to second year and from second to third year of the program). Behaviorally, these observations were confirmed by music teachers and social educators from the *Demos* staff, who reported, via semi-structured interviews, significant improvement in behavioral and perceived attentional abilities exhibited by children, as well as a progression in the ability to adapt their behavior to changing contexts.

A specific protocol and dedicated tools were developed to assess collective movement synchronization, coordination, and imitation (see Chapter 26). The protocol was designed to incorporate teachers, with the aim of using various exercises and games similar to the ones already used as part of the *Demos* pedagogy. More precisely, three types of exercise were developed: a collective movement exercise following a conductor, a dyadic movement imitation exercise, and a short collective improvisation game. For each exercise, students made use of an iPod attached to their hand, which played various sounds according to the movements made (making use of the embedded motion sensors). The screen was blank, and the iPod acted thus as a lightweight motion-based sonic interactive system. The iPod captured postural and movement parameters, thanks to embedded three-dimensional accelerometers and gyroscopes. A web-based system was implemented to control, synchronize, and record all the devices through dedicated WiFi. The efficiency of this inexpensive and simple system was confirmed to measure, with 20-millisecond accuracy, movement synchronization in groups (testing up to 15 members). The movement data collected allowed us to find significant improvement over six months for the orchestra of level 1. Specifically, we found that the students' hand movement was closer to the teacher's movement over a specific gesture sequence they learn. Interestingly, this proximity was associated with homogenization of the group performance for this task from the beginning of the class in October to April/May, which could be explained by collective musical practice. Overall, we found that our protocol and tools were able to follow and assess progress in collective motor synchronization in children. This setup thus opens new possibilities of investigation in this under-researched, although important-to-understand, area of ensemble music-making.

The main limitation of this study is the absence of a control group. Unfortunately, we were not allowed to involve cohorts of children from the same geographical areas in the research study who could not benefit from the *Demos* program. Thus, we could not formally test whether the differences in terms of the measured abilities, observed between both sessions and tests, were due to the practice of music or simply an effect of normal cognitive development, or a complex interaction of these factors. However, we controlled for the effect of age of the participants as a further predictor in the linear mixed models, allowing us to rule out the variance accounted for by age effects. Since the statistical improvements in measures remained significant, the results suggest that one year in *Demos* orchestra might be more efficient in improving the measured skills than one year of "normal development," although the effect of age was considered between, and not within, participants. We also compared sample test scores of executive function before and after the treatment with those of normative populations, in particular the results reported by Davidson et al. (2006) with regard to the inhibition and cognitive flexibility capacities, and by Morra (1994) with regard to the working memory capacity. We observed that the initial level of *Demos* children was often lower than these studies reported, but that the progression tended to be steeper in *Demos* children. This seems to support the indication that children participating in *Demos* may show a faster progression in terms of task performance than that registered in children of the same age in previous studies.

Conclusion

Children recruited to participate in the *Demos* project often initially have difficulties in attention, inhibition, or concentration. The first and main mission of the music teachers, and especially of the social educators, is to help students focus and share emotions to facilitate collective musical learning. Musicians and social educators reported significant improvements in those abilities, thanks to the *Demos* program. Our intervention's main goal, with the help of games and short questionnaires, was to contribute to the *Demos* educators a scientific investigation of their observations of progress in learning. This reflects a great development in executive functions and emotional skills. In addition, our study allowed *Demos* agents to specify some of their objectives using appropriate scientific terms. The project's participatory design allowed us to create a combination of research tools, integrating methods and adapting to the music teachers' needs. Collaboration between scientific and musical teams requires adaptation and flexibility from both sides, as well as active communication.

Our study of the *Demos* orchestra suggests that it provides children with opportunities to develop emotional understanding, executive functions, and motor imitation skills in a musical environment. While the absence of a control group represents a major limitation to the explanation and the generalization of our results, this study represents an important step in field research on collective music playing, considering the tools and specific methods we developed. Future studies should be able to further investigate the fascinating complexity of orchestral playing whereby musicians should use both their personal expressive skills as well as their ability to precisely synchronize and blend with the ensemble.

References

Case, R. (1985). *Intellectual development: Birth to adulthood*. New York Academic Press.

Cavioni, V., Grazzani, I., Ornaghi, V., Pepe, A., & Pons, F. (2020). Assessing the factor structure and measurement invariance of the test of emotion comprehension (TEC): A large cross-sectional study with children aged 3–10 years. *Journal of Cognition and Development*, *21*(3), 406–24.

Davidson, M. C., Amso, D., Anderson, L. C., & Diamond, A. (2006). Development of cognitive control and executive functions from 4 to 13 years: Evidence from manipulations of memory, inhibition, and task switching. *Neuropsychologia*, *44*(11), 2037–78.

Diamond, A. (2013). Executive functions. *Annual Review of Psychology*, *64*, 135–68.

Juslin, P. N. (2013). What does music express? Basic emotions and beyond. *Frontiers in Psychology*, *4*, 596. https://doi.org/10.3389/fpsyg.2013.00596

Morra, S. (1994). Issues in working memory measurement: Testing for M capacity. *International Journal of Behavioral Development*, *17*(1), 143–59.

Sachs, M., Kaplan, J., Der Sarkissian, A., & Habibi, A. (2017). Increased engagement of the cognitive control network associated with music training in children during an fMRI Stroop task. *PLoS One*, *12*, 1–29. https://doi.org/10.1371/journal.pone.0187254

Takacs, Z. K., & Kassai, R. (2019). The efficacy of different interventions to foster children's executive function skills: A series of meta-analyses. *Psychological Bulletin*, *145*(7), 653–97.

32

Enhanced learning through joint instrumental education

Andrea Schiavio

Introduction

This chapter examines the challenges and responsibilities of both educators and learners, offering some preliminary answers to questions, including: what is it like to learn music together with peers? What roles do educators and learners take in a collective instrumental lesson? What challenges emerge during the tuition? And what are the main benefits of collaborative music learning? Challenges and responsibilities of both educators and learners are given specific attention for the following reasons. First, they can highlight the different levels of interaction between students and teachers and between students and peers, in turn helping to discover any particular benefits of collaboration, as compared to individual tuition. Second, they can offer practical solutions to improve existing learning paradigms. For example, if a specific challenge is faced by both students and teachers, different aspects of the lesson can be modified to facilitate a collaborative solution. In what follows, these aspects are addressed through qualitative data collected with music teachers and students who participated in both individual and joint music classes. Having presented the quotes that best capture challenges and responsibilities in collective pedagogical settings, results are briefly discussed in light of previous work by Piaget and Vygotsky, and through the lens of embodied cognitive science.

Methods

This chapter brings together qualitative data reported in two previous studies. These explored the personal experience of individual and collaborative learning from the perspectives of music teachers (Schiavio et al., 2020) and music students (Schiavio et al., 2019). Ethical approval for data collection was granted by the University of Graz.

Participants

Thirty participants from Europe and North America who attended or taught in individual and collective (with various numbers of attendees) instrumental music classes took part in the study. Participants were music students (n = 19; mean age: 28.5 years old) and music teachers (n = 11; mean age: 43.3 years old) at private schools, academies, conservatoires, and universities.

Andrea Schiavio, *Enhanced learning through joint instrumental education* In: *Together in music.* Edited by: Renee Timmers, Freya Bailes, and Helena Daffern, Oxford University Press. © Oxford University Press 2022. DOI: 10.1093/oso/9780198860761.003.0032

Data collection

Data from most participants were collected by means of an open-ended questionnaire comprising 18 items.[1] The questionnaires were administered in English or Italian, and were based on deliberately general questions concerning various experiences associated with individual and collective pedagogical settings. These related to topics such as the corporeal sensations emerging during solo or joint learning, as well as challenges, emotional engagement, collaborative strategies, and preparation for class. The items were general enough so that the same questionnaire was administered to both student and teacher groups. Participants were instructed to reply freely—without word limit—and provide personal examples where possible. In addition to written questionnaires, a total of seven semi-structured interviews were conducted with participants from the students' group (n = 4) and from the teachers' group (n = 3). In the former case, the students were contacted after their questionnaire was received to elaborate on their written responses and clarify ambiguous passages. In the latter case, teachers were contacted after an initial set of data were collected from other teachers: this helped the interviewer develop new questions and sub-questions that addressed specific experiences which did not emerge in the first data set. As mentioned in this chapter, these data appear in published work but were reanalyzed for the present contribution.

Data analysis

For the present chapter, questionnaires and interview transcripts were (re)analyzed in light of two predefined categories chosen to explore the benefits of collaborative tuition from both a teaching and a learning perspective: these are *responsibilities* and *challenges*. The analysis involved two main steps: (1) categorization, in which quotes were assigned to a predefined category, and (2) interpretation where themes emerging from the quotes were briefly discussed.

Results

Learning music with peers involves novel challenges and forms of shared responsibility that make this pedagogical setting particularly valuable for musical and social development. In what follows, considerations relating to challenges and responsibilities are offered through examples of quotes that report personal teaching and learning experiences. To ensure anonymity of the participants, the following coding has been used: *Teachers* (T1—T11), *Students* (S1–S19).

Challenges

From a teacher's perspective, working with a group can be challenging for several reasons. One example involves the creation and maintenance of a learning space where students can feel engaged and protected. As one teacher reported:

---

[1] Among these, three students received an adapted version of the questionnaire comprising a total of 13 items.

I would like to make sure that everyone always feels safe. Occasionally some of the participants may overstep boundaries and disrespect one another. I would like to catch that even faster than I have. (T8)

Not only is a good learning environment defined by mutual respect and trust, but it is also determined by the sense of equality that a teacher can instill in the group. A student, for example, mentioned that:

it is difficult for the teacher to find a good balance between all the students. There are different levels of preparation, and expressiveness can be difficult to be learnt this way. Also, advanced students might be less motivated, and novices more stressed when put together in the same class. (S7)

It should be noted that fostering an effective learning environment is not only a teacher's job; as we will see later in more detail, students are equally responsible for its enactment. For now, consider the following quotes where two students describe the positive outcomes of such joint activity:

In my program there were ensemble classes that were focused on learning tunes and putting together performances, often in a matter of a few rehearsals. What I really enjoyed about those was the collaboration from all band members that was required in order to have efficient rehearsals that yielded a good final product. In many cases it was a matter of speed-arranging tunes, so everyone was able to contribute ideas for how to best arrange the material to optimize the final performance. (S3)

Chamber music lessons were great. Again, when you like your partner, it is great when you have the same musical intention and want to realize it when playing. (S6)

Reaching similar achievements, however, comes at a price. As a teacher reports, it entailed an important challenge for each student, namely:

Learning to reveal [the student's] artistic personality in front of others, is the main aim of the lesson. (T11)

The following quote by another teacher offers a concrete example of this:

In group class, one of the most important aspects is observing and listening to others while being engaged in music, or musical-related activities. (T1)

A safe learning setting might help students flourish musically and socially. In order to do so, however, students need to take a responsible role and be ready to open up to others as well as listen and learn from peers.

Responsibilities

Peer-learning offers an excellent opportunity for students to engage in collaborative action and shared forms of musicking, despite the issue illustrated by the following quote:

> There is shared responsibility in the collective lessons, and the teacher doesn't only focus on me, so I care much less about the quality of my work. (S8)

Such an observation expresses a potentially critical point: if students are not willing to take more responsibility for their own learning, there is a risk that the outcomes of the lesson will not be effective, or even that they will not be reached. Teachers were aware of this, and one insisted that "in a group you must become a positive leader, an example on both a personal and a musical level" (T9). Consider also the following quote from another teacher:

> Students have to take more responsibility for the role they play in the group and the effects their actions or inaction may have on the collective. In a large group, students can learn from each other as well as from the instructor. (T4)

Learners can develop novel skills by watching others and participating in the collective musicking in ways that can complement verbal instructions from the teacher:

> Just by watching other students play, you can get an idea of new fingering styles or expressive phrasing that may have not been discussed with your teacher. (S10)

And indeed, students did enjoy this group setting—where peers and instructors negotiated their roles, leaving more space for the autonomous action of the learners. These final two quotes from the students may help us better capture this point:

> I like the repertoire that you can play with others. I like responding to each other's impulses. (S12)

> I felt like I was actually "doing the thing" that we were all there to study. No textbooks, few requirements, just music-making with a professor to offer suggestions and to critique our playing. (S3)

Discussion

The reported quotes suggest that the creation of a safe learning environment is at the same time a challenge and a responsible behavior for a teacher: this facilitates musical interaction among students, and helps them develop responsible ways of learning, such as being more open to others, or listening to and learning from peers. These positive outcomes emerge from the interactive dynamics of joint music classes, and should therefore be addressed by educators and researchers interested in collaborative music-making and learning. Classic views on collaborative learning offered by Vygotsky and Piaget may provide a useful interpretative tool to understand such results. As described by Webb and Farivar (1999), Vygotsky argued that learners may internalize the skills practiced together with a peer, transforming social knowledge into individual potential. Piaget, conversely, proposed a process by which individual knowledge can be complemented by social action, giving rise to a re-examination and evaluation of existing skills, which may lead to novel valuable outcomes.

In both cases, however, the unit of analysis remains the individual: it is the single agent who uses social knowledge to optimize or create new abilities. This may downplay the interactive experiences reported by teachers and students, and the sense of collaborative effort that emerges from the analysis. The conceptual resources of embodied cognitive science (e.g. Gallagher, 2005) may offer novel tools to capture the complexity of peer-learning from a more interactive perspective. By posing a deep continuity between thought and bodily action, many advocates of this approach shift the unit of analysis from the individual to the collective (see De Jaegher & Di Paolo, 2007)—where bodily activity takes place. From this view, it might be argued that learning does not occur *after* internalizing or evaluating social interaction; instead, it occurs *through* interactive experience. In the context of this study, this suggests that peer-learning can enhance instrumental education because of its interactive features, rather than its impact on existing knowledge or individual agency.

Conclusion

Such insights may help educators and students involved in individual tuition (re-)examine their respective experiences more openly, and develop opportunities for distributed forms of musicking. For instance, consider how teachers could facilitate open discussions on the repertoire to be performed, and its cultural and personal significance for students, as well as its technical and expressive characteristics in solo and collective situations. By stimulating interest and curiosity, such a dialogue might inspire pupils to organize and participate in collective musical activities on their own, allowing them to approach instrumental learning from the perspective of their peers. This can disclose novel musical possibilities based on social experience, where the focus on imitation of the expert (i.e. the teacher) is traded for knowledge co-determination. As students are encouraged to actively seek challenges and responsibilities autonomously, educators can develop learning environments in which these challenges are addressed, and where responsibilities discovered through peer interaction can be adequately discussed and put into context. Future research may build on the results presented here, comparing the formation of shared responsibilities in formal and informal settings and exploring how the same musical challenges can be faced collectively or individually.

Acknowledgments

I am thankful to Dylan van der Schyff, Michele Biasutti, Nikki Moran, and Richard Parncutt, with whom the original studies were designed and conducted. This work was supported by a Lise Meitner Postdoctoral Fellowship granted by the Austrian Science Fund (FWF), project number M2148.

References

De Jaegher, H., & Di Paolo, E. A. (2007). Participatory sense-making: An enactive approach to social cognition. *Phenomenology and the Cognitive Sciences*, 6, 485–507.

Gallagher, S. (2005). *How the body shapes the mind*. Oxford University Press.

Schiavio, A., Biasutti, M., van der Schyff, D., & Parncutt, R. (2020). A matter of presence: A qualitative study on teaching individual and collective music classes. *Musicae Scientiae*, 24(3), 356–76.

Schiavio, A., van der Schyff, D., Biasutti, M., Moran, N., & Parncutt, R. (2019). Instrumental technique, expressivity, and communication. A qualitative study on learning music in individual and collective settings. *Frontiers in Psychology*, 10, 737. https://doi.org/10.3389/fpsyg.2019.00737

Webb, N. M., & Farivar, S. (1999). Developing productive group interaction in middle-school mathematics. In A. M. O'Donnell, & A. King (Eds.), *Cognitive perspectives on peer learning* (pp. 117–50). Lawrence Erlbaum Associates.

33

Collaborative composition and performance in arts and health workshops

How notating in groups enables creative interaction and communication for social wellbeing

James Williams

Introduction

This chapter presents a pilot study conducted by the author in June 2017 at Vic University, Catalonia, entitled "Collective Music-Making as Social Interaction" (CMSI). The study is a music-based therapeutic workshop, featuring as part of the University's *Art as a Tool for Social Transformation* (ARTOOL) program of practical research. Data were captured through ethnographically informed approaches, including reflective comments from a structured questionnaire on the creative process, and underpinned by videos, recordings, and photographs of the project. In this short write-up, the questionnaire feedback sits at the crux of the discussion, used exclusively to explore the impact of the workshop's practical elements on improving group communication. The workshop involved 20 participants comprising students and academics from arts and health backgrounds (including music, art, dance, and drama) and occupational therapy. Participation was available to all of the ARTOOL delegates, who were briefed on the workshop aims to improve wellbeing through social transformation. The core aim of the study was to explore the extent to which development of a collaborative, bespoke musical language could enable creativity and communication among participants. Because participants were from multiple institutions and from different national backgrounds (including UK, Spanish, and Dutch), it meant that not all participants shared a common spoken language. Furthermore, not all participants considered themselves musically orientated. Combined, these two factors encouraged alternative means of communication.

The project uncovers the therapeutic process of the design of musical notation in collaborative workshops, and how such compositional and performance processes can be of social benefit to the participants. Themes of sociocultural creativity and collaboration at the intersection(s) between people, music, and notation in therapeutic arts workshops arose from the project's questionnaire. Findings firstly reveal how a creative, collaborative process can demonstrate a group's capacity to learn new ways of socially interacting and communicating. Secondly, the study shows how the collective product (both score and ensemble performance) is representative of such social interaction. It is suggested that the collaborative design of musical notation in collective workshops can facilitate healthy engagement between individuals, proposing applications of the model for use with healthcare users in the wellbeing sector subscribing to arts on prescription and social prescribing schemes.

James Williams, *Collaborative composition and performance in arts and health workshops* In: *Together in music*. Edited by: Renee Timmers, Freya Bailes, and Helena Daffern, Oxford University Press. © Oxford University Press 2022. DOI: 10.1093/oso/9780198860761.003.0033

Design

The project comprised six sections across a full afternoon (around four hours):

1. Warm-up;
2. Workshop (in three parts):
   Part A: Expressivity with Instruments;
   Part B: Creativity with Drawing;
   Part C: Sounding Notation;
3. Discussion 1: Reflections on Workshop;
4. Group Composition Task;
5. Group Performance Task;
6. Discussion 2: Reflection on Tasks (including questions and answers).

The warm-up (of around 20 minutes) was broken down into four short music-based games, with the aim of having a preliminary set of exercises to engage participants. These drew on well-known games, for instance "jump in, jump out, jump left, jump right" exercises, and a separate game allowing participants to communicate through movement, gesture, and voice. Other musical games (for example, a rhythmic exercise with tapping, and the "pass the beat around the room" game) allowed individuals an initial opportunity to express and to communicate musically, under a warm-up setting.

The core three-part workshop was designed by the researcher/author to explore inclusion, trialing the efficiency of arts-based and music-based practices as a means of communication. This was the first instance running these activities.

In Part A (Expressivity with Instruments), instruments (mostly pitched and non-pitched percussion) were placed in the center of a group circle formed by participants who were then invited to choose an instrument and return to their seat on the floor. Participants were allowed a 30-second opportunity to explore their instrument of choice and to play with sound. They were then asked to pass their instrument to the right, and thus to receive a new instrument from the left, where they were given a further 30 seconds. This pattern was repeated until their instrument was returned to them. This session allowed participants an independent moment to express themselves with their instruments, but as part of a wider group, without others focusing on them. A short five minutes was then offered for reflection, allowing participants to discuss with the group the techniques they uncovered via play.

In Part B, the instruments were set aside, behind each individual and outside the group circle. This section focused on a visual arts activity, where participants were offered a range of materials (including pen, chalk, paints, pastels, oils, ink, markers, etc.) and asked to draw two distinct symbols on an A3 piece of paper using a single color (see Figure 33.1). The symbols could be as basic or as complex as desired. This offered a second opportunity for participants to be individual and independent, but as part of a group exercise. On completion, participants were encouraged to walk around the circle, looking at their peers' symbols, but not touching/altering them or questioning them.

In Part C, participants were invited to "perform" or to create "sound" for the symbols they had designed, using their instrument. They were allowed 30 seconds to turn each

Figure 33.1 Example of symbols transcribed from the workshop—designed to be used as musical notation.

symbol drawn into a sonic gesture, bridging the gap between what we see and what we hear. The drawings were passed around the group circle, enabling each individual the chance to create a sonic gesture from a visual cue. This was repeated until their notation was returned to them.

The workshop ended with participants discussing their symbols, showing some of their sonic gestures, and sharing their experiences of turning graphics into sound. A discussion on the role of *notation* as a means of communication was encouraged. Drawings were then collated into the center of the circle.

The practical component of the afternoon featured a composition task and a performance task, adopting material from the communication exercises in the prior workshop. Participants arranged themselves into groups of five, and were asked to negotiate and develop their own meaning of the symbols as a musical alphabet (or language), with the aim of creating a short composition (of around five minutes). A1 paper was provided for each group to encourage the creation of a score, allowing participants to layer, organize, order, and/or adjust the notational symbols creatively, based on in-group decisions and negotiations. The aim was for participants to interact and develop communication skills through group composition and symbolism.

This development of a shared musical graphic language was explored further in final group performances of the compositions. Other members of the workshop were asked not only to listen to the performances, but also to observe the performances alongside each group's "score." This allowed each group to perform their work and to have it listened to by their peers, and also allowed their peers to see their fellow groups' scores being performed, thus strengthening the correlation between a visual graphic notational cue and an audible sonic gesture as response to that cue.

Reflective discussion(s) followed, allowing participants to comment on anything from the day, including the design of notation, the creation of scored composition, and the musical performances. Individuals were later given a six-part feedback form/questionnaire to complete anonymously.

Findings and discussion

For the purpose of the current chapter, findings are discussed by extracting key themes from the questionnaire and exploring their claimed impact (via reflection) on group communication and the potential for improved social interaction.[1]

In general, the questionnaire responses, in the form of rich qualitative data, *do* support the hypothesis of improved social interaction. The design enabled participants to self-report/reflect on the extent to which the activities enabled group communication. Reflections were organized into thematic categories relating to creativity, group work, and communication (see footnote 1 to access table). Such analysis has enabled the following narratives to be identified.

Firstly, participants found that their capacity to express (*musically* through the instruments, and *artistically* through the drawing of symbols) improved within the group. One participant said:

> Sharing our symbols and images, and learning about others helped to bring the group closer together and better connected. It was enjoyable to communicate without language and just through playing the instruments as well, regardless of our primary language differences. (Participant A)

Similar reflections included themes such as unity, closeness, being better connected, communication without language, language differences, shared understanding(s), and engagement with group members.

Secondly, participants realized the potential of group-based notation for improved language-building, specifically with regard to communication around composing. One participant reflected:

> It opened up a lot of conversation about what we wanted our song to be like and why. It encouraged people to communicate through music, not just voice. Teamwork was definitely required to get a finished song in that time, which again opened up communication through speech, art and music. (Participant C)

Another stated:

> We created our own language in music and art, and we could communicate with our group and other groups with it. The period allowed us to develop this communication and language as a group. (Participant D)

Thirdly, participants found that the performance component to the workshop increased social confidence, self-esteem, and shared purpose (see Chapter 27). One participant commented: "the performance at the end gave us something to work towards, therefore a shared purpose in creating this language" (Participant B)—this emphasizes the communal nature of language. Another commented: "moreover, thanks to the performance, the question of belonging to the group comes into play, a certain idea of camaraderie and trust" (Participant G).

---

[1] The complete data set of questionnaire responses (including thematic annotations) can be downloaded from the following: http://dx.doi.org/10.13140/RG.2.2.27484.54408

Feedback from participants confirmed the hypothesis of this small project: collaboratively designing notation in groups enables creative interaction and communication through processes of both composition and performance. But *how* has this occurred? The varying backgrounds (educational, cultural, language) of participants in this study is an important consideration to make when evaluating this research. Difference in musical experience and difference in *communication* ability (spoken language, confidence, etc.) were likely to mean that some individuals would take the lead in these tasks, while others with limited musical or communication abilities might follow. Such power dynamics are inevitable in all group work. However, in this study, the *need* to negotiate the use of a *shared* language was integral to a successful outcome (a "prescriptive" score and/or group performance). Dialogue between participants was essential not only for *productive* group work, but also (and importantly) for *creative* group work. In this case study, creativity enabled communication, and communication enabled creativity. This was due to the development of a bespoke language within a group—*individually* designed, but *collectively* developed. Each participant having their own individual input into the alphabet enabled the formation of a collective language.

Conclusion

Involving participants without a communication and/or social wellbeing diagnosis allowed for the activities of this workshop to be piloted. It is important to note that these participants were likely to be cognizant of the way in which arts and health workshops function, especially when compared with a regular service-user, and as such, this should be recognized as a potential limitation when considering the wider applicability of the activities. Development of this study will now move towards working in a similar way with individuals with identified diagnoses. Specifically, the practical components of the study could be used in workshops for patients who have been referred to link-workers from family doctors for arts on prescription and social prescribing schemes. Findings from this project are most applicable to community musicians and arts and/in/for health practitioners who work with people with social interaction and communication difficulties. Recently, the nature of applied arts for wellbeing has become increasingly supported both politically and financially across the UK health and social care landscape, through a range of public-facing groups and organizations, notably: the Royal Society for Public Health (RSPH) Working Group on Arts, Health and Wellbeing (report published 2013); the All-Party Parliamentary Group (APPG) on Arts, Health and Wellbeing (*Creative Health* report published 2017); and most recently the World Health Organization (Fancourt & Finn, 2019). With the implementation of social prescribing schemes now in place in the UK (as recommended by the RSPH, the APPG, and the WHO), an increasing number of arts-led (music-led) studies designed to support individuals with social wellbeing difficulties are required to accommodate public health demands, as outlined in the National Health Service (NHS) long-term plan. Examples such as the study presented here demonstrate how specific aspects of music (such as creative notation design) can afford opportunities for individuals with social interaction difficulties to develop their communication skills through creative group work. Moreover, repetition of working with the material over a longer period of time (for example, across six weeks) could have potential to reinforce the use of language further. Music-based workshops aimed to help with social transformation are an important tool for arts and health practitioners responding to government-backed social prescribing schemes. The activities in this particular workshop acted as a platform for discovery, expression, perception, recognition, imagination, communication, cohesiveness, confidence, and self-esteem among the participants, and it is these features that have been shown to contribute towards increasingly engaged social interaction between peers.

References

All-Party Parliamentary Group on Arts, Health and Wellbeing. (2017). *All-party parliamentary group on arts, health and wellbeing inquiry report — Creative health: The arts for health and wellbeing.* https://www.culturehealthandwellbeing.org.uk/appg-inquiry/

Fancourt, D., & Finn, S. (2019). *What is the evidence on the role of the arts in improving health and well-being? A scoping review.* World Health Organization. https://apps.who.int/iris/bitstream/handle/10665/329834/9789289054553-eng.pdf

Royal Society for Public Health (2013). *Arts, health and wellbeing beyond the millennium: How far have we come and where do we want to go?* Royal Society for Public Health and the Philipp Family Foundation. https://www.rsph.org.uk/static/uploaded/6e174021-82a6-4083-85f5eca6b6fdd303.pdf

34

Encountering the singing body

Vocal physicality and interactivity

Daniel Galbreath and Gavin Thatcher

Introduction

Historically, much of Western philosophy has held that the mind and body are distinct entities. If this were so, where would this leave the voice? A dualist view relegates the body to the service of the mind: accordingly, the voice is trained to articulate the workings of the mind through the mechanism of the body. Consciousness and learning, however, happen *through* and *with* the body, not just *to* it (see, for example, Sheets-Johnstone, 2009, or Chapters 7, 13, and 26). In this vein, we developed a group of ensemble exercises (Thatcher & Galbreath, 2019), refined over several collaborative performance projects and our respective teaching activity, which seek to facilitate singers' awareness that the unified mind–body can be inhabited, explored, and understood through singing. In this case study, we step back and invite singers' reflections on this practice. During three workshops with classically trained singers from the vocal ensemble *Via Nova*, we investigated how encouraging singers to perceive their own and others' sounding bodies as something to be explored creatively, rather than disciplined, might benefit their wellbeing.

Background and methods

Our post-dualist view of vocal training borrows the idea of "physiovocality" from Konstantinos Thomaidis (2014). Physiovocality refers to the practice of the unified training of the voice and body: theatrical practices (such as Jerzy Grotowski's *Workcentre*) and vocal pedagogies (such as those of Kristen Linklater or Jo Estill) that treat body and voice as unified can be described as physiovocal. Through their use of set exercises and technical regiments, these processes necessarily prioritize the expertise and objectives of the teacher or creative leader. Our approach grew out of a desire to expand physiovocal practice by inviting singers to encounter their own vocal corporealities subjectively, in a non-mechanized way that suspends any specific aims or objectives. In so doing, we aim to create a shared, relational experience of voice–body interaction among the group of singers.

Over the course of three 45-minute workshops (August, 2019), we led members of the British vocal ensemble *Via Nova* through exercises that blend and expand physical theatre and vocal training practices, so that performers might discover their own and each other's

Daniel Galbreath and Gavin Thatcher, *Encountering the singing body* In: *Together in music*. Edited by: Renee Timmers, Freya Bailes, and Helena Daffern, Oxford University Press. © Oxford University Press 2022. DOI: 10.1093/oso/9780198860761.003.0034

embodied voices through improvisatory movement and sonic interaction. *Via Nova* is directed by Daniel Galbreath and had previously undertaken physiovocal improvisations and contributed to research. These singers offered rich responses, founded on informed complicity in the construction of an "insider" view of embodied vocal interaction. Workshop 1 served to pilot our practice and questionnaire, and included three participants and the researchers; workshops 2 and 3 included six singers from *Via Nova*, one guest conductor, and the researchers. Following each workshop, participants took approximately 15 minutes to complete a questionnaire. Ethical approval was gained from Brunel University London, and participants were made aware of how their responses would be used, and of the option to withdraw from the workshops or research at any point without negative consequences. Questionnaires were not anonymized; our long-standing relationships with the singers enabled candor in their responses, although likewise there may have been some attempts to write what they felt we wanted to see. To mitigate somewhat the effects of this methodological hazard, data were broken down into small segments and coded. These codes were then able to coalesce into themes, which were identified and developed using the grounded theory method (Charmaz, 2004).[1] The themes that emerged following the first two workshops dictated what questions we asked in the subsequent questionnaire, allowing us to refine our focus iteratively. The final group of categories is presented in Findings, in this chapter, allowing respondents to guide our conclusions rather than reinforcing our own preconceptions. Questionnaires focused on how singers' perceptions of their own bodies changed, how they felt about, or connected with, others in the space, and how the experience compared to their usual practice.

The exercises that were used have been detailed elsewhere (Thatcher & Galbreath, 2019); this summary is offered to contextualize our findings. In the first workshop, singers completed a warm-up sequence which progressed from lying down to standing, exploring the physical sensations of breathing and sustaining various sounds. Singers then undertook movement exercises, exploring their ranges of motion with loose guidance, while also "moving" their voice through free improvisations. In the second workshop, this warm-up was repeated, after which singers were invited into a kind of game, moving around the space and swapping improvised vocalizations upon making eye contact with a colleague. In the final workshop, singers walked to a shared pulse while singing free pitches. They stopped walking and singing upon making eye contact with a colleague; both singers were challenged to reinitiate movement and singing by breathing together in a non-verbal, shared impulse. This activity progressed into different types of shared-rhythm movement (walking, running, jumping on the spot) to various rhythms, improvising melodically while moving around the room and making physical contact while jumping. The singers were encouraged to respond to others' improvisations; this peripheral awareness was augmented when they attempted to reach out to someone for physical contact.

---

[1] The grounded theory method is much written about. Our approach draws primarily from Kathy Charmaz's constructivist approach (2004), which acknowledges that respondents construct their views of the experience in question, while the researcher also participates in that construction through the act of coding.

Findings

Reconceptualizing one's own embodied vocality

Participants recalled reconceptualizing their own embodied voices during workshops in various ways. Some experienced their voices through non-vocal physical activity; conversely, some felt they discovered the body via the voice: through vocalizing, they encountered their bodies in a new way. Sometimes this awareness began by mechanizing the body: one singer became "[m]ore conscious of [the] body as [an] instrument, and perhaps aspects of technique that I had been neglecting" (S6 WS2).[2] These mechanizing notions gave way to less disciplined, more holistic views: one singer progressed towards "focusing on what my body needed, rather than looking and wondering what others were doing" (S3 WS2); another stated, "[o]nce a full range of body motions are underway vocalizing is freer" (S1 WS2).

This broadening corporeal awareness was reflected on through lenses of enjoyment and pleasure. Comments frequently touched positively on feeling more energized, focused, and released. Many singers framed the release of physical and emotional tension as being one and the same. Part of this feeling included awareness, and relinquishing, of certain inhibitions. One singer felt exposed while making eye contact with colleagues (S7 WS2), but the group as a whole recalled becoming less self-conscious through (often good-humored) relation to one another as the workshops progressed. Perhaps most tellingly, the singer who felt exposed also observed that "[i]t feels so good not to be in control" (S7 WS2): this response suggests that interactive, de-inhibiting processes might shift focus away from the more dualistic notions of "control."

Crucially, reconceptualization did not occur immediately: singers were aware of the processual nature of this shift, and reflected on it positively.[3] One singer felt that an "extended warm-up session – unpressured by upcoming ensemble singing" afforded "revelations about my body in relation to [my] voice" (S2 WS1). Many responses touched on the benefits of undertaking physiovocal exploration over the course of an expanse of time, unencumbered by imposed objectives. This process even felt necessary for maintaining vocal health (S2 WS1). The frequency of responses commenting on time and process suggests that physiovocal freedom has multiple dimensions: relieving pressures of both time and objective is important for physiovocal self-discovery.

Contrasting with training and experience

Removing the constraints of a typical rehearsal or singing lesson was one of many ways in which these workshops' activities contrasted with singers' training. Many singers' responses suggested keen awareness of these differences, and generally framed them positively. Moreover, the singers expressed that it would be useful to incorporate exercises and approaches from these workshops into more traditional rehearsal situations. They felt able to explore their voices according to their *own* objectives, critically reflect on the process at hand,

---

[2] To reinforce the groundedness of our findings, specific comments and quotations are cited by referring to the random number the singer was assigned (i.e. singer 3 is S3), followed by the workshop in which that response was provided (i.e. the third workshop is WS3).

[3] An extended discussion of the importance of time for ensemble formation is dealt with in Chapter 1.

and re-examine their own training. One singer, for instance, relished "thinking about how body and voice connect instead of what we are generally taught" in classical Conservatoire settings (S4 WS1); another observed that other "stiff upper lip" training was "stifling" (S7 WS2). The process offered permission to "let go of any idea of what I should be doing and just feel free to experiment and notice how my body felt" (S7 WS2). This singer's phrasing— "should be doing"—recalls the inhibitions discussed in the section *Reconceptualizing one's own embodied vocality*, in this chapter, and suggests that these inhibitions are perpetuated through much of their training (see Chapter 25 which discusses how music-making often prioritizes sonic outcomes over physical wellbeing). Many expressed a need for "permission" to use their bodies and voices creatively. For one singer, the researchers' active participation in exercises revealed possibilities and boundaries (S2 WS1); it was necessary to be "told/advised not to necessarily move in an ordered or conventional way" (S2 WS1) (see also Chapter 8). This need for permission, present across several responses, has important implications. First, it is clear that physiovocal improvisation might be seen as something one must be given permission to do; by extension, these responses indicate that even in an exploratory process such as ours, it is important to remain conscious of this dynamic of discipline. The process might, in short, benefit from giving permission not to ask permission.

Relating to the space, and to each other

The final group of findings dealt with how the singers related to their surroundings, particularly each other. This relational dynamic was key to singers' positive experiences of their own physiovocality. Unsurprisingly, since ensemble awareness aspects were present in many exercises, several singers noticed, and enjoyed, "syncing" up and sharing rhythms. The activities, with their inbuilt permission to transgress, helped one singer to relate to others with whom they were less familiar, creating "rapport and sense of ensemble" (S6 WS3). In many cases, awareness of others shifted how they conceptualized themselves. One singer found themselves able to attend to their own breathing *despite* being surrounded by others (S3 WS2); another felt "lifted and relaxed" as a result of "the opportunity to engage with other singers" (S1 WS2). As exercises progressed, interacting with others often seemed to decrease self-consciousness (though it should be recalled that most of these singers had already worked together extensively in *Via Nova*).

Through creative, physiovocal exploration, singers also became more externally aware. As one singer summarized this experience:

> [It m]ade me aware how separate people are in their existence and how we enjoy our space. I felt uncomfortable to begin with but soon became more content to be in contact and singing while maintaining eye contact. (S5 WS3)

This singer commented on "becoming aware of the space aurally as well as physically with the room and those around it" (S5 WS2). For another singer, more deliberate exploration of space enabled the creation of "a more open sound" (S3 WS1). Another observed that their own vocal creativity depended on both the person with whom they interacted, as much as it did on that person's improvisations (S1 WS3). Both internal and external inhibitions were overcome together, enabling singers to engage creatively with their own and others' voices.

Conclusion

These responses suggest that interactive, improvisatory exploration might positively shift how singers conceptualize both their own physiovocality and that of the ensemble. In the case of our workshops, this reconceptualization occurred over the course of a collaborative process, during which singers felt greater autonomy to deviate from their own experiences of the mechanized, disciplining expectations placed upon their bodies. With the space—and often the permission—to deviate, singers experienced decreased inhibitions about the workings of their own bodies, and greater comfort in relating to others in a vocal-embodied way. This sense of physical freedom and decreased inhibitions, about both the self and others, has clear implications for the wellbeing of singers. Importantly, just as a sense of personal physical wellbeing provoked greater interactivity among the group, that interactivity in turn yielded greater comfort and freedom for each individual. Wellbeing can be cultivated through a cycle of relational physiovocality.

As hoped, these findings reveal certain limitations of our own physiovocal process and practice. The emphasis on receiving permission highlighted the importance of prompting singers to question boundaries rather than construct new ones. More significantly, the singers expressed a desire to enfold elements of ensemble interactivity into more traditional rehearsal settings, where conductors might understandably be reluctant to expend valuable time on relational explorations, and other singers may have limited experience of physiovocal practices. This challenge elicits the question: how might improvisatory, physiovocal exercises like our own be incorporated into traditional practices, in such a way as benefits the wellbeing of singers? Any such enquiry builds on the pivotal idea that singers with a less mechanizing, disciplined view of their own bodies might better relate to those of others. Not only are mind and body not discrete, but individual and group physiovocality are also profoundly interconnected. This notion might shift how ensemble singing is regarded more broadly, even short of the further explorations pointed to in this Conclusion: singing together might come to be less about disciplining bodies into unity, and more about individuals freeing each other.

References

Charmaz, K. (2004). *Constructing grounded theory* (2nd ed.). Sage.

Sheets-Johnstone, M. (2009). *The corporeal turn: An interdisciplinary reader*. Imprint Academic.

Thatcher, G., & Galbreath, D. (2019). Singing bodies: Reconsidering and retraining the corporeal voice. *Theatre, Dance and Performance Training, 10*(1), 349–64.

Thomaidis, K. (2014). Singing from stones: Physiovocality and Gardzienice's theatre of musicality. In D. Symonds, & M. Taylor (Eds.), *Gestures of music theatre: The performativity of song and dance* (pp. 242–58). Oxford University Press.

35

Ensemble singing for wellbeing and social inclusion of street children

Music-based social action research

Juliana Moonette Manrique and Angelina Gutiérrez

Introduction

Support for street youth remains a crucial task as the population of homeless individuals continues to rise globally. Among the 100 million homeless people across the world, the Philippines had an estimated 1.2 million street children in 2016 (UN Human Rights Commission, 2017). Manila, the nation's capital, is home to about 75,000 street children. Displaced by poverty, armed conflicts, and environmental calamities, these street children suffer malnutrition, health problems, violence, child trafficking, sexual exploitation, drugs, and various types of abuse in their daily struggle to survive.

Rationale of the study

Awareness and support for rough sleepers and street children remain a crucial social responsibility not only for socio-political institutions, but also for academics who believe that research, education, and public policy can transform society for the common good. In dealing with the issues of social inclusion and development, diverse international government ministries and agencies view music and arts as strategic channels through which the social needs of marginalized populations can be partially addressed. This chapter reports an investigation to explore the outcomes of ensemble singing on the wellbeing and social integration of street children in the Philippines. Drawing on studies from the global north (Bailey & Davidson, 2005; Clift & Morrison, 2010; Welch et al., 2014) that suggest engaging in music activity may impact individual health and social inclusion, this case study from South East Asia answered the following research questions:

1. What are the perceived effects of ensemble singing on the wellbeing and social inclusion of street children?
2. What are the challenges of ensemble singing as a type of intervention for health and social integration of marginalized groups?
3. What are the implications of this social action research for ensemble performance studies?

Juliana Moonette Manrique and Angelina Gutiérrez, *Ensemble singing for wellbeing and social inclusion of street children* In: *Together in music*. Edited by: Renee Timmers, Freya Bailes, and Helena Daffern, Oxford University Press. © Oxford University Press 2022.
DOI: 10.1093/oso/9780198860761.003.0035

Methods

The participants in the study were street children in Manila, the Philippines, who were members of a children's concert choir, aged 9 to 17 years, under the sponsorship of the Virlanie Foundation. This foundation is a French-based, nonprofit, charitable organization that provides shelter, food, and education to street children in the inner city of Manila. The research sample size (n = 30) consisted of 25 choristers (15 girls and ten boys) and five adult facilitators, namely the choir director, choir accompanist, and three officers of the Virlanie Foundation. The choristers are trained to perform classical European and indigenous choral repertoire for international and local concert performances. They perform annually in Western and Eastern Europe through invitations sponsored by the foundation's benefactors.

As exploratory research, the investigation used a mixed-method design comprising the following procedures: survey questionnaire, face-to-face interview, focus group discussion, and observations/use of field notes to find out the benefits and drawbacks of ensemble music-making from the experience of these young choristers coming from a marginalized population. Descriptive analysis of the questionnaire data calculated and compared the mean scale responses of the participants relating to the four variables of group singing, namely: physical, psychological, social, and spiritual dimensions. Qualitative data were analyzed by coding narrative data, tabulating and synthesizing themes, interpretive comparisons of the participants' responses to the survey questionnaire and the face-to-face interview that was conducted after the focus group discussion, and observations. To cross-check findings and analysis, triangulation of data sets was applied to discover fresh interpretations regarding ensemble performance as a potential music-based social action research methodology for documenting processes of belonging and connecting communities through participatory arts.

Findings and discussion

The authors designed the questionnaire to use a five-point Likert scale with the following response categories: 5 (*strongly agree*), 4 (*agree*), 3 (*not sure*), 2 (*disagree*), and 1 (*strongly disagree*). The questionnaire was answered by the young choristers to find out their level of agreement with the influence of choir singing on their wellbeing or health, and on their social inclusion, which includes their sense of identity and social integration with one another. The following findings from the questionnaire indicated the perceived benefits of ensemble singing.

The reported physical benefits of ensemble singing were: skeletal-muscular discipline through good posture ($M = 4.9$ or strongly agree (SA)); improvement in breathing or lung capacity ($M = 4.8$ SA); coordination and exercise of muscles involved in singing ($M = 4.75$ SA); improved listening skills ($M = 4.65$ SA); singing giving a sense of energy ($M = 4.75$ SA); and singing bringing relaxation ($M = 4.45$ A).

The psychological benefits of singing together were: bringing calmness and personal peace ($M = 4.9$ SA); improving creativity and imagination ($M = 4.9$ SA); giving them positive emotions such as feeling good and happy ($M = 4.8$ SA); improving alertness or focus ($M = 4.7$ SA); reducing their stress and worries ($M = 4.65$ SA); therapeutic healing of their negative feelings such as anger, sadness, depression, or memories of violence ($M = 4.6$ SA); a sense of achievement or satisfaction with their life ($M = 4.55$ SA); coordination of their body and mental faculties ($M = 4.5$ A); and improved cognitive abilities of concentration, memory, and learning music theory/skills ($M = 4.45$ A).

The social benefits of collective singing were: gaining supportive friendships ($M = 5$ SA); enjoying the shared activity or common hobby of singing with one another ($M = 4.95$ SA); giving them a sense of bonding or positive connection with others ($M = 4.85$ SA); learning teamwork in their social activities ($M = 4.75$ SA); cultivating their collaborative skills in performing with other choristers ($M = 4.7$ SA); developing their trust in working with others ($M = 4.65$ SA); and giving them a sense of social engagement that increased their focus or absorption ($M = 4.6$ SA).

The spiritual benefits of choir singing were described as: helping them to be optimistic or have positive attitudes toward life and others ($M = 4.8$ SA); teaching them appreciation of fine arts that inspire ($M = 4.8$ SA); improving the quality of their life because they enjoy the social activities ($M = 4.75$ SA); developing their self-discipline through practices/rehearsals ($M = 4.7$ SA); giving them a sense of beauty that uplifts or transcends themselves ($M = 4.7$ SA); initiating a sense of meaning and purpose in their lives ($M = 4.6$ SA); and giving them a sense of self-fulfillment in contributing to the community ($M = 4.15$ A).

The above quantitative data from the young choristers were compared with the responses of the adult facilitators, which generated the comparative summary of the perceptions of both groups regarding the positive effects of ensemble singing as a structured activity, listed in Table 35.1.

On average, the respondents rated the social benefits of singing the highest. These findings are in line with those of Welch et al. (2014), Clift and Morrison (2010), and Bailey and Davidson (2005), who highlighted benefits of group singing such as increased levels of social connectedness, increased sense of self and belonging, physical and emotional benefits, and reduced personal stress.

Capitalizing on the beneficial aspects of ensemble music-making among these street children, the study explored the challenges of choir singing that need to be overcome. A summary of the survey results from all the respondents disclosed their following struggles: singing is linked to muscle pain and physical fatigue; it was associated with mental and physical exhaustion; it led to feelings of competition or jealousy; they feel lazy or bored during routine or monotonous singing activities; and singing was linked to performance anxiety or stage fright. Overall, the choristers agreed ($M = 4.2$) on the difficulties of group singing, while the adult facilitators were less aware ($M = 2.84$) of these difficulties indicated by the young choristers.

While these descriptive results represented the perceived challenges of group singing in the physical and psychological domain, additional qualitative data from the face-to-face interview, focus group discussions, and field observations revealed other informative concerns.

Table 35.1 Mean response ratings per participant type

Positive outcomes	Choristers	Facilitators
Social benefits	4.78	4.77
Physical benefits	4.71	4.70
Psychological benefits	4.67	4.68
Spiritual benefits	4.64	4.51

Note: 5 = strongly agree; 4 = agree; 3 = not sure; 2 = disagree; and 1 = strongly disagree.

The challenges of choir singing expressed by the choristers were:

> It is hard to juggle our school schedules & choir rehearsals/performances. (Respondent/R3)
> We sometimes fight when a member is out of tune. (R8)
> We cannot focus always. (R20)
> There is lack of cooperation with one's peer who heads the choir section. (R10)
> Sometimes, disruptive behavior happens due to boredom and peer competition. (R15)
> Rehearsals for concert performances become physically and mentally tiring especially when certain music passages are constantly repeated. (R25).
> Performance anxiety or stage fright is not fun. (R9)

The difficulties of managing the children's concert choir, quoted by the adult facilitators were:

> It is not easy to manage their concert performance preparation such as enforcing the discipline to observe the house rules during performance trips, getting to bed early at night and waking up early, avoiding sweets, performance protocols, and other concerns. (R3)
> There is lack of stability in keeping young choristers who are adopted by families. (R1)
> Training new choir members is demanding. (R5)
> Dealing with the psychological scars of individual choristers can be tough. (R2)

The ensemble context

These findings still leave much room for further inquiry regarding ensemble singing as an intervention toward the wellbeing and social inclusion of disadvantaged groups such as street children. Data from the adult facilitators explored the implications of participating in this music-based social action research to understand the specific benefits of ensemble performance.

On ensemble performance and expression for wellbeing and social inclusion, the facilitators commented:

> Listening sensitively to oneself and to one another's pitch, rhythm, dynamics, and harmony during rehearsals and performances is essential in ensemble performance. (R4)
> Young choristers are directed by the conductor through bodily cues on how to emote or express the stylistic interpretation of repertoire. (R1)
> The kids learn to be responsible as they develop collaborative skills and become a community of musicians. (R3)
> Development of the children's musical skills for collaborative performance, expression and communication contributes to their positive self-image and social wellbeing. (R2)

On ensemble singing as participatory arts for social action, the respondents said:

> We have seen how ensemble singing has transformed these formerly at-risk street children to become productive and inspiring role models for their peers. (R5)

> For these young people, the music ensemble setting nurtured their sense of identity and belonging to a community. (R4)

Their musical training empowered them to develop wholesome personal and social values. (R3)

In their public performances, they experience the rewards of self-accomplishment and their contribution in bringing joy and inspiration to the communities. (R2)

These comments highlight the spectrum of the benefits and challenges of choir singing by giving voice to a marginalized group. Extant studies on community music by McPherson and McCormick (2006) have examined the role of music activities in building communities. The responses of the participants in this case study validate the potential of ensemble performance in empowering the members through meaning-making, especially for those who are stigmatized (see Chapter 28). This chapter suggests how group music-making can be a potent source for identity, connection, and empowerment (Gutiérrez & Manrique, 2013). As music-based social action research, drawing attention to these findings points to future approaches as to how group music activities could be a sustainable community project through which local and international social needs can be addressed.

Conclusion

In conclusion, this unprecedented investigation from the Philippines identified the potential and drawbacks of ensemble singing to suggest how it can be a transformative driver in advancing the wellbeing and social inclusion of marginalized populations. In linking collaborative music engagement activities with social action research, it underlined the potential of ensemble music-making as a social capital, which can be explored in research, educational practice, and public policy. While this study does not suggest that group singing is the only solution to social issues, it reinforces the positive contribution that ensemble music activities may have for the development of individuals and communities.

References

Bailey, B., & Davidson, J. (2005). Effects of group singing and performance for marginalized and middle-class singers. *Psychology of Music, 33*(3), 269–303.

Clift, S., & Morrison, I. (2010). Choral singing and psychological wellbeing: Quantitative and qualitative findings from English choirs in a cross-national survey. *Journal of Applied Arts & Health, 1*(1), 19–34.

Gutiérrez, A., & Manrique, J. (2013). *Empowering young women to engage in social change through popular music* [Paper presentation]. Conference on Music, Gender and Difference, University of Music & Performing Arts.

McPherson, G., & McCormick, J. (2006). Self efficacy and music performance. *Psychology of Music, 34*, 322–36.

Welch, G., Himonides, E., Saunders, J., Papageorgiand, I., & Sarazin, M. (2014). Singing and social inclusion. *Frontiers in Psychology: Cognitive Science, 5*(2). https://www.frontiersin.org/articles/10.3389/fpsyg.2014.00803/full

36

Together in music

Embodiment, multidimensionality, and musical–social interaction

Renee Timmers, Freya Bailes, and Helena Daffern

Introduction

Looking back at the review and case study chapters of this book, we are gratefully humbled by the richness of insights, ideas, findings, approaches, and techniques. It was indeed the aim of this volume to bring together different disciplines and perspectives to further our understanding of musical ensembles, and to inspire both research dialogue and synthesis. It is clear that this is an area of research that is quickly developing: finding and trying out new forms and shapes as it develops theories, frameworks, and methodologies. To contribute to the synthesis of ideas, we have identified and will discuss three main themes that run through the book. Several emergent directions for future research will also be discussed, including addressing the relatively limited focus of much work in this area on particular musical genres and contexts. Challenges for future research will be plenty, both technically and epistemologically, for example balancing sensitivity to specific contexts and situations with the quest for scale enlargement, standardization of methodologies, and generalizability. Let us first turn to the main themes.

Embodiment and emergence in ensemble performance

Embodiment and emergence are strong themes throughout the book: despite increased practices of separate recording of different parts in music studios, central to music-making is still real-time interaction, where multiple bodies interact through sound and movement (see, for example, Chapter 13). Contextually shaped and non-predetermined interaction is central to many practices of music therapy (see Chapter 29), where group formation and type of music-making (referred to as "assemblage") are adjusted to the therapeutic context and process. While therapeutic contexts may aim to optimize the facilitation of change and the trying out of different forms of interaction, Chapter 1 emphasizes the tension between change and stability in teamwork, including ensembles. As ensembles form, early interaction patterns become quickly established (see also Chapter 5). Change and input from a coach may be most effective midway in the rehearsal process, at moments of transition, while working towards stability may characterize later stages when approaching the goal of performance.

   A number of case studies have highlighted the deliberate use of emergence and embodied in-the-moment interaction as a creative and educational power. By adjusting rules or methods of interaction, and forms of musical material and performance instruction, open-ended,

Renee Timmers, Freya Bailes, and Helena Daffern, *Together in music* In: *Together in music*. Edited by: Renee Timmers, Freya Bailes, and Helena Daffern, Oxford University Press. © Oxford University Press 2022. DOI: 10.1093/oso/9780198860761.003.0036

distributed, and democratic forms of musical creation are realized and explored (see Chapters 7 and 18). This is documented as liberating and supportive of musical development (see Chapters 8 and 32), but it can (intentionally) disrupt the ensemble to such an extent that musical breakdown is narrowly avoided (see Chapter 18).

Embodiment and in-the-moment adjustment are considered central to the performance process and the communication between musicians. Micro-adjustments in timing, pitch, and intensity are continuously made to realize a coordinated performance (see Chapters 13, 16, and 17). While sound is key for close coordination to be realized, movements, gaze, gestures, and embodied metaphors support the communication of intention, motivation, and instruction (see Chapters 14, 21, and 23). This time-sensitive expression and communication offers a cognitive challenge identified as beneficial by older musicians (see Chapter 30), while physical interaction and expression are experienced as one of the main affordances and pleasures of music-making and can have a beneficial effect on wellbeing (see Chapter 34). Technology offers new forms of musical interaction, as increasingly used due to the Covid-19 pandemic. For this technology to be rewarding and effective, it will do well to afford in-the-moment, micro-level subliminal synchronization between bodies, sounds, and brains (see Chapter 17), as well as organic, creative exploration over larger timescales (see Chapter 20).

Relationships between the musical and the social in ensembles

Composer James Saunders illustrates in Chapter 2 how the social and the musical can integrate through the employment of various compositional strategies. Musicians are assigned roles and given behavioral instructions, and their dynamic interaction determines the development of the music (see also Chapter 18). These practices bring to the front the social dynamics of ensemble performance, indicating that while always present and intrinsic, they often remain implicit and unaddressed. Explicit addressing of social interaction is central to educational innovations documented in this book, where the roles of the musicians are equalized, including the lecturer's role (see Chapters 7 and 8), or instrumental learning is enhanced through joint music-making (see Chapter 32).

That music-making is a social endeavor does not require much explanation and is a recurring theme in musicians' verbal accounts in many of the qualitative studies included in this book (see Chapters 11 and 12). Indeed, key to an ensemble's success is the appropriate managing of the social. Ensembles may be more or less inclusive, more or less accommodating towards newcomers, and represent certain values and attitudes with which people may or may not identify (see Chapters 3, 6, 9, 10, and 28). Even in well-established traditions, such as the Anglican Church, feeling connected is not a given and may be influenced by local musical traditions (see Chapter 6). Some ensembles have inclusivity at their heart, and Wendy Moy (see Chapter 10) offers the example of the successful Seattle Men's Chorus that acts as an extended family for gay men who may have experienced rejection in other contexts, including their closest family. With over 300 choir members, it exemplifies the power of music to literally bring people together. Offering an accommodating social context that can also be a place for enjoyment, personal growth, and development is increasingly recognized as a potential music-based intervention to support vulnerable groups (see Chapter 33). Moonette Manrique and Gutiérrez (see Chapter 35) show this in the context of a choir for children without a regular home in the Philippines, while Helen English (see Chapter 28) goes back to Australian settlers to discuss the role of ensemble music-making for identity, care, and connection with the past and present for displaced individuals, families, or small communities.

How and why specifically music-making may be socially connecting and rewarding is part of a research strand that examines interrelationships between close interpersonal synchronization and feelings of social bonding and empathy (see Chapter 26). A growing body of evidence is available that shows that micro-level behavioral synchronization has a demonstrable role in achieving a sense of social connectedness (see Chapter 26). Nevertheless, a multi-dimensional interpretation seems most appropriate to enhance our understanding of music as beneficial (see also next theme). Indeed, social, organizational, and sonic/musical factors are crucial for the long-term enjoyment of music-making, including for professional musicians (see Chapters 11, 12, and 25).

Multi-dimensionality of musical participation

This book was organized with three analytical levels in mind—a micro-level of in-the-moment joint action and musical coordination through sounds, movements, glances, and gestures (Part 2), a meso-level of rehearsal and socio-musical organization (Part 1), and a macro-level of longer-term affordances and cognitive, social, and emotional outcomes of participatory music-making (Part 3). This organization is in line with research that tends to prioritize a particular analytical perspective above others, depending on the research objectives and associated methodology. Indeed, each of the levels offers rich insights into musical coordination (see Chapters 16, 17, and 22), organization (see Chapters 11, 12, and 18), and affordances (see Chapters 24, 27, and 29) and will benefit from further investment and investigation, specifically where it includes the examination of a broader range of music and contexts.

Nevertheless, it is clear from the many cross-connections between chapters from different parts of the book that this is an artificial separation and that meaningful music-making requires all three levels. Longitudinal studies such as reported by Glowinski and colleagues (see Chapter 31) highlight the relationship between micro-level interaction and macro-level developments (see also Chapter 30). Similarly, chapters on musical participation highlight the interconnectedness of levels, when pointing out the relevance for participatory enjoyment of finding the right degree of musical challenge, interest, and support, identifying with the musical and social values of an ensemble, feeling part of the ensemble in musical and social terms, and the ability to integrate the ensemble into one's life (see Chapters 3, 6, 10, and 27). The concept of agency offers an interesting example, as examined by Mak and colleagues (see Chapter 4): musicians may attribute agency to the composer and elements in the notated music, while taking agency in rehearsals and performance. Agency may influence and be acted out in gestures and communicative patterns (see Chapters 4 and 14), while care is taken to balance democratic and inclusive decision development with clarity of communication (see Chapters 8, 11, 12, and 21). A sense of empowerment may be fostered by joint music-making, including creating temporal continuity by connecting with musical traditions from one's past and adapting music as a way of projecting to the future (see Chapter 28). Ironically, the same shared and joint music-making processes may also lead to negative experiences of disempowerment and lack of agency (see Chapter 25), again illustrating the interconnectedness between levels. Techniques such as those developed by Seibert (see Chapter 19) may be useful to visualize the social dynamics at micro- and meso-level, which may interactively develop, depending on context and musical as well as social pressures.

Digital technology and future directions

Technology features consistently in the volume, providing insight into current and future possibilities presented by its rapid development. Chapter 15 provides a comprehensive review of technologies employed in relation to large ensembles, but the approaches described, from questionnaires to music information retrieval software and MoCap technology, also reflect the representation of technology utilized across the book, and in music performance research more generally. The potential to contribute to the landscape of music ensemble research through increasingly easy-to-use audio digital signal processing software is demonstrated in the context of reflecting on historical performance practices and concepts of ensemble in Chapter 22, and as a means to isolate specific acoustic features of ensemble singing (see Chapter 16). Innovations in hardware also present opportunities for new insights into physical performance processes as they take place, such as the measurement of gaze and its relationship to synchrony outcomes (see Chapter 23). Providing a different perspective on the utility of digital technology in ensemble performance, Chapters 14 and 20 explore existing machine musicianship approaches and collaborative live coding software, respectively, as the instrument and creative tool facilitating ensemble music-making rather than a tool to measure aspects of its process or product. There is an opportunity here to explore the possibilities of live coding and other digital music-making tools and experiences (such as virtual reality) within the frameworks of research on music ensembles for social, wellbeing, and therapeutic practice. In particular, it might be possible to exploit the available technology to address the mostly unexplored area of non-participation in music ensembles, to create new environments of musical participation (see Chapter 3), including those that are possible within a context of social distancing.

The diversity of methodological approaches explored across the volume, from lab-based experiments to ethnographic studies, highlights the importance of interdisciplinarity in the field of ensemble performance, and the potential for cross-fertilization of these perspectives. Valuable insights into micro-level performance processes and outcomes, such as those associated with the measurement of synchrony as described in Chapter 17, have been formed through experimental approaches which involve unusually constrained environments. Such studies provide foundations of understanding that inform and find meaning in relation to broader, macro-level theories, whether to support approaches to teaching and learning or, as in the case of Chapter 26, to consider the role of synchrony in social communication and wellbeing.

In terms of future directions and continuations of the research presented in this volume, we believe that technology will offer important pathways, as well as continued synergies between methodologies and disciplines. Technology has been at the heart of opening up research in performance science, and will be crucial in pushing this area forward, specifically when we are serious about connecting the analytical levels: what happens at micro- and meso-level and how do these interact with longer-term developments? Does temporal coordination have prioritized status in fostering social and emotional bonding or are other forms of creating unison in sound, harmony, and bodily entrainment equally powerful? What is the role of social interaction and implicit behavioral patterns during performance and rehearsal? Is it useful to visualize or modify these interactions as part of the development of expressive performance or therapeutic socio-emotional transformation?

One of the important challenges for further work is to broaden out the scope of empirical interdisciplinary research on ensemble performance to include a greater diversity of populations, cultures, and genres—not with the aim to demonstrate universality, but rather to celebrate nuances and diversities in music cognition and behavior. The chapters in this volume are strongly focused on, and have arisen from, the epistemology of Western classical, formal education music traditions. Even if research focuses on basic cognitive skills, these are nevertheless formed and shaped in specific sociocultural traditions that influence cognition, behavior, and expression (Hannon & Trehub, 2005; Jacoby & McDermott, 2017; Laukka et al., 2013; Mampe et al., 2009). In fact, music has played an important role in helping to demonstrate such malleability of the brain and behavior (e.g. Moreno et al., 2011; Strait et al., 2009). The danger is that this book represents and emphasizes a W.E.I.R.D. (Western, Educated, Industrialized, Rich, and Democratic) perspective that is taken as the norm (see Jacoby et al., 2020). We believe that the best we can do in the context of this volume is to signal caution in interpreting the results presented in the book, specifically in terms of generalization, and signpost the potential danger for the prioritization of perspectives from privileged groups. The inclusion of other perspectives, practices, and musical genres could be achieved using case studies that understand musical behavior with respect to its specific context and manifestation, being sensitive to, and in dialogue with, the relevant practitioners (Clayton et al., 2013). We are very much looking forward to the next generation of studies that have a greater diversity and inclusivity.

Conclusion

In the meantime, and in conclusion, let us not ignore the many useful and insightful learning points offered by this volume. These include the role of emergence and embodiment for creativity in ensemble music-making, the interrelationships between micro-, meso-, and macro-level behavior and cognition and their relevance for the multi-dimensional appreciation of musical participation, and the fundamental alignment between the musical, the social, and the emotional in music ensembles.

References

Clayton, M., Dueck, B., & Leante, L. (Eds.). (2013). *Experience and meaning in music performance*. Oxford University Press.

Hannon, E. E., & Trehub, S. E. (2005). Metrical categories in infancy and adulthood. *Psychological Science, 16*(1), 48–55.

Jacoby, N., & McDermott, J. H. (2017). Integer ratio priors on musical rhythm revealed cross-culturally by iterated reproduction. *Current Biology, 27*(3), 359–70.

Jacoby, N., Margulis, E. H., Clayton, M., Hannon, E., Honing, H., Iversen, J., Klein, T. R., Mehr, S. A., Pearson, L., Peretz, I., Perlman, M., Polak, R., Ravignani, A., Savage, P. E., Steingo, G.,

Stevens, C. J., Trehub, S., Veal, M., & Wald-Fuhrmann, M. (2020). Cross-cultural work in music cognition: Challenges, insights, and recommendations. *Music Perception*, *37*(3), 185–95.

Laukka, P., Eerola, T., Thingujam, N. S., Yamasaki, T., & Beller, G. (2013). Universal and culture-specific factors in the recognition and performance of musical affect expressions. *Emotion*, *13*(3), 434–49.

Mampe, B., Friederici, A. D., Christophe, A., & Wermke, K. (2009). Newborns' cry melody is shaped by their native language. *Current Biology*, *19*(23), 1994–7.

Moreno, S., Bialystok, E., Barac, R., Schellenberg, E. G., Cepeda, N. J., & Chau, T. (2011). Short-term music training enhances verbal intelligence and executive function. *Psychological Science*, *22*(11), 1425–33.

Strait, D. L., Kraus, N., Skoe, E., & Ashley, R. (2009). Musical experience and neural efficiency–effects of training on subcortical processing of vocal expressions of emotion. *European Journal of Neuroscience*, *29*(3), 661–8.

Index

For the benefit of digital users, indexed terms that span two pages (e.g., 52–53) may, on occasion, appear on only one of those pages.

Tables and figures are indicated by *t* and *f* following the page number